INSIGHT ● GUIDES

ECUADOR
& GALÁPAGOS

PLAN & BOOK
YOUR TAILOR-MADE TRIP

BRAZIL   CHILE   ECUADOR

TAILOR-MADE TRIPS & UNIQUE EXPERIENCES CREATED BY LOCAL TRAVEL EXPERTS AT INSIGHTGUIDES.COM/HOLIDAYS

Insight Guides has been inspiring travellers with high-quality travel content for over 45 years. As well as our popular guidebooks, we now offer the opportunity to book tailor-made private trips completely personalised to your needs and interests. By connecting with one of our local experts, you will directly benefit from their expertise and local know-how, helping you create memories that will last a lifetime.

HOW INSIGHTGUIDES.COM/HOLIDAYS WORKS

STEP 1

Pick your dream destination and submit an enquiry, or modify an existing itinerary if you prefer.

STEP 2

Fill in a short form, sharing details of your travel plans and preferences with a local expert.

STEP 3

Your local expert will create your personalised itinerary, which you can amend until you are completely satisfied.

STEP 4

Book securely online. Pack your bags and enjoy your holiday! Your local expert will be available to answer questions during your trip.

BENEFITS OF PLANNING & BOOKING AT
INSIGHTGUIDES.COM/HOLIDAYS

PLANNED BY LOCAL EXPERTS

The Insight Guides local experts are hand-picked, based on their experience in the travel industry and their impeccable standards of customer service.

SAVE TIME & MONEY

When a local expert plans your trip, you save time and money when you book, even during high season. You won't be charged for using a credit card either.

TAILOR-MADE TRIPS

Book with Insight Guides, and you will be in complete control of the planning process, from the initial selections to amending your final itinerary.

BOOK & TRAVEL STRESS-FREE

Enjoy stress-free travel when you use the Insight Guides secure online booking platform. All bookings come with a money-back guarantee.

WHAT OTHER TRAVELLERS THINK ABOUT TRIPS BOOKED AT
INSIGHTGUIDES.COM/HOLIDAYS

Trip to Portugal

Every step of the planning process and the trip itself was effortless and exceptional. Our special interests, preferences and requests were accommodated resulting in a trip that exceeded our expectations.

Corinne, USA ★★★★★

Trip to Vietnam

The organization was superb, the drivers professional, and accommodation quite comfortable. I was well taken care of! My thanks to your colleagues who helped make my trip to Vietnam such a great experience. My only regret is that I couldn't spend more time in the country.

Heather ★★★★★

DON'T MISS OUT
BOOK NOW AT
INSIGHTGUIDES.COM/HOLIDAYS

CONTENTS

Travel tips

TRANSPORTATION

A – Z

LANGUAGE

FURTHER READING

Maps

LEGEND
🔎 Insight on
📷 Photo story

6

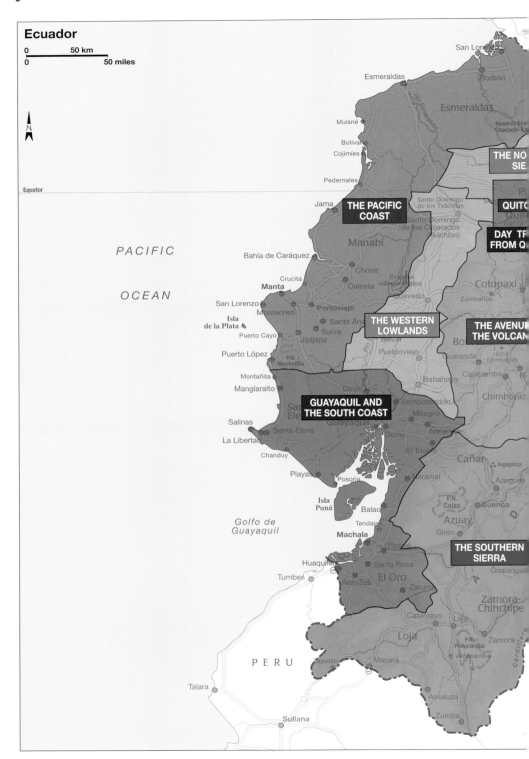

Ecuador

0   50 km

0   50 miles

N

San Lor...

Esmeraldas

Borbón

Esmeraldas

Muisné

Reserva Eco
Coacachi-Ca

Bolívar

THE NO
SIE

Cojimíes

Pedernales

PI

Equator

Santo Domingo
de los Tsáchilas

M

QUITO

Jama

**THE PACIFIC
COAST**

Santo Domingo
de los Colorados
(sáchilas)

San...

DAY TR
FROM Q

Manabí

PACIFIC

Bahía de Caráquez

Chone

Cotopaxi

Crucita

Calceta

Embalse
Daule-Peripa

Zumbahua

OCEAN

Manta

Quevedo

San Lorenzo

Portoviejo

Montecristi

Santa Ana

Isla
de la Plata

Sucre

**THE WESTERN
LOWLANDS**

Bo

6310
Chimborazo

**THE AVENU
THE VOLCAN**

Puerto Cayo

Jipijapa

Balzar

Guaranda

Puerto López

P.N.
Machalilla

Puebloviejo

Babahoyo

Cajabamba

Ri

Montañita

Daule

Chimboraz

Manglaralto

Samborondón

Sa
Ele

**GUAYAQUIL AND
THE SOUTH COAST**

Guayaquil

Milagro

Cañar

Ingapirca

Salinas

Santa Elena

Durán

Naran

Azogues

La Libertad

El Triunfo

Chanduy

Naranjal

P.N.
Cajas

Cuenca

Playas

Posoria

Azuay

Isla
Puná

Balao

Tendale

Girón

*Golfo de
Guayaquil*

Machala

Pasaje

**THE SOUTHERN
SIERRA**

Huaquilla

Santa Rosa

Gualaquiza

Tumbes

Arenillas

El Oro

Zaruma

Zamora-
Chinchipe

Catamayo

Loja

Loja

P.N.
Podocarpus

Zamora

PERU

Zapotillo

Macará

Vilcabamba

Talara

Amaluza

Cordillera

Sullana

Zumba

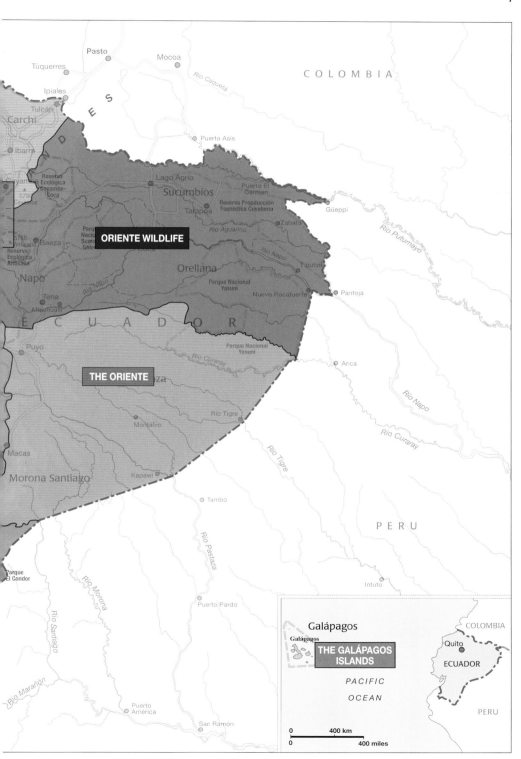

COLOMBIA

Pasto
Mocoa
Túquerres
Ipiales
Tulcán
Carchi
Ibarra
Puerto Asis
Rio Caquetá
Reserva
Ecológica
Cayambe-
Coca
Lago Agrio
Sucumbíos
Puerto El
Cermen
Reserva Propducción
Faunística Cuyabeno
Güeppi
Rio Putumayo
Tarapoa
Zabalo
ORIENTE WILDLIFE
Rio Aguarico
Baeza
Rio Napo
Reserva
Ecológica
Antisana
Coca
Orellana
Tiputini
Napo
Rio Napo
Parque Nacional
Yasuni
Nuevo Rocafuerte
Pantoja
Tena
Archidona
ECUADOR
Puyo
Rio Curaray
Parque Nacional
Yasuni
THE ORIENTE
Arica
Rio Napo
Montalvo
Rio Tigre
Rio Curaray
Macas
Morona Santiago
Kapawi
Rio Tigre
Tambo
PERU
Parque
El Condor
Rio Pastaza
Intuto
Rio Morona
Puerto Pardo
Rio Santiago
Rio Marañón
Puerto
América
San Ramón

Galápagos
Galápagos
**THE GALÁPAGOS
ISLANDS**
PACIFIC
OCEAN

COLOMBIA
Quito
ECUADOR
PERU

0   400 km
0   400 miles

THE BEST OF ECUADOR: TOP ATTRACTIONS

△ **Avenue of the Volcanoes.** These snow-capped peaks span Ecuador's Andean spine. Hike and climb at the top of the world, as measured from the earth's center. See page 165.

▽ **Baños.** Nestled in the Andes, this traveler magnet boasts thermal springs heated by the volcano above, and two little-visited national parks. See page 172.

△ **Otavalo.** Culture does not get more Andean than in Otavalo, with its vibrant indigenous culture and excellent textile market. Nearby lakes, haciendas, and the colonial architecture of Ibarra round off the experience. See page 155.

▽ **Cuenca.** Cupolas of the 19th-century Catedral Nueva blend in with the older buildings of Cuenca, a UNESCO World Heritage Site, and one of Latin America's best-preserved colonial Spanish cities. See page 185.

△ **Pacific coast beaches.** Offering leaping whales, water sports, and some of the oldest archeological remains in the Americas. See page 231.

△ **Quito.** The historic Old Town of Quito, one of the biggest in the Americas, is studded with historic churches, such as La Basílica del Voto. See page 127.

◁ **Galápagos Islands.** Marvels of isolated evolution, the Galápagos Islands boast unique wildlife, approachable like nowhere else on the planet. Swim with sea lions, and dive with sharks and marine iguanas. See page 273.

▽ **Ingapirca.** Possibly a temple for sun worship, fortress-like Ingapirca is Ecuador's best-preserved pre-Colonial monument, built by the Inca Tupac Yupanqui in the late 15th century in imperial Inca style. See page 194.

▽ **Amazon lodges.** Accessible by bus or plane plus a boat ride, Amazon lodges offer a doorway to the world's most diverse ecosystem. See page 204.

THE BEST OF ECUADOR: EDITOR'S CHOICE

View of El Panecillo from the Old Town, Quito.

BEST ART MUSEUMS

Capilla del Hombre. Guayasamín's masterpiece in the Bellavista district of Quito is perhaps the most stunning example of Modernist Latin American art on the continent. See page 143.

Centro Cultural Libertador Simón Bolívar. On Guayaquil's Malecón 2000, this modern museum has some of the best contemporary art in the country, along with a fascinating anthropological collection. See page 257.

Casa del Alabado. This superbly presented museum in Quito showcases around 500 pre-Columbian artifacts in stone, ceramic and gold, as well as providing many insights into these ancient civilizations. See page 141.

BEST WILDLIFE-WATCHING

The Galápagos Islands. The most famous wildlife reserve in the world and the place where Charles Darwin formed his theory of evolution. See page 273.

Parque Nacional Machalilla. Most visitors come for the whale-watching around Isla de la Plata, but you can also see frigate birds and blue-footed boobies on the island. See page 247.

Parque Nacional Yasuní. Ecuador's largest nature reserve is home to the elusive jaguar and the vocal howler monkey. See page 53.

Mashpi Biodiversity Reserve. A private 1,200-hectare (3,000-acre) cloud forest reserve only accessible if you're a guest at the lavish Mashpi Lodge (located here), where over 30 endemic bird species have been spotted in the surrounding area. See page 148.

Sculptures at La Capilla del Hombre.

Blue-footed boobies, Galápagos Islands.

BEST FOR FAMILIES

Balancing an egg along the equator line at the Museo Solar Intiñan.

Salinas. The most complete beach resort on Ecuador's coast. See page 263.

Teleférico. Quito's cable car whisks you to the top of a hill, beside an active volcano, for awe-inspiring views of the city. See page 131.

Museo Solar Intiñan. Located right on the equator, this small museum to the north of Quito has interactive exhibits that will keep kids of all ages amused. See page 147.

BEST CHURCHES

La Compañía de Jésus. With ornate gilded walls and ceilings, this church in Quito is one of the most impressive religious buildings in Latin America. See page 134.

El Sagrario and Catedral de la Inmaculada Concepción. Cuenca's "old" and "new" cathedrals dominate the main plaza. The first dates back to the mid-16th century, while the second was built in the late 19th century and contains a famous crowned image of the Virgin. See page 186.

White-water rafting in the Andes.

BEST ADVENTURES

Hiking the Inca Trail to Ingapirca. This three-day trek is not nearly as crowded as its Peruvian cousin, but it takes you to a magnificent Inca ruin just the same. See page 194.

Climbing Volcán Cotopaxi. Over ice and snow, the 5–8-hour ascent takes you to the top of one of the world's highest active volcanoes. See page 166.

Surfing in Montañita. Hang ten in this all-encompassing surfing resort on the Pacific coast. See page 248.

White-water rafting in the Andes. Take a multiple-day rafting trip down the Class III and IV rapids at the eastern edge of the Andes mountains right into the heart of the Amazon jungle. See page 208.

Riding the Nariz del Diablo train. Ecuador's great train journey is the mesmerising run from Alausí to Sibambe via the thrilling switchbacks of the Nariz del Diablo (Devil's Nose), a sheer bluff of rock somehow scaled by rails. See page 183.

Stunning decor at Quito's Iglesia de Santo Domingo.

Female white-necked jacobin hummingbird in flight.

SUSTAINABLE TRAVEL

From community-based tourism projects to shopping locally, there are many things visitors can do to help preserve Ecuador's culture and wildlife.

Ecuador's staggering biodiversity and diverse indigenous cultures are closely intertwined. Both are threatened by extractive activities such as oil drilling, mining, and logging – both legal and illegal – as well as climate change. Visitors can do their bit to help both the environment and indigenous rural communities, enabling the latter to improve their livelihoods where they are, rather than being forced to move to the city.

COMMUNITY-BASED TOURISM

Ecuador is rife with community-based tourism (CBT) projects. Booking a day or multi-day stay can be a rewarding intercultural experience, and can also supply vital income to communities, allowing them to live their lives on their own terms while improving their standard of living. In Imbabura, award-winning tour operator *Runa Tupari* (www.runatupari.com) – which means "encounter with local people" in Kichwa – works with various communities round Cotacachi, Otavalo and the Intag. They organize a range of activities, from conventional day tours hiking, riding, or cycling, to multi-day homestays, participating in everyday life, or volunteer work. All profits are ploughed back into the communities.

At Saraguro, in southern Ecuador, the community hostel *Achik Wasi* ("House of light" in Kichwa; www.sites.google.com/view/hotelachikwasi/inicio) is a good place to start, offering accommodation and traditional meals using locally sourced produce. The hostel can organise activities with surrounding communities, such as guided walks, visits to local fiestas, or in wool-shearing and carpentry workshops.

Around Riobamba, CBT (www.riobamba.com.ec/es-ec/search?q=turismo+comunitario) is thriving in the folds of the mighty Chimborazo volcano

Huaorani man, Yasuní National Park.

among Kichwa-Puruhá peoples. There are plenty of opportunities for hiking, learning about current and ancestral cultural practices, and sampling traditional food. Given the popularity of certain places with Ecuadorian tourist groups some visits can seem a little staged. The helpful ITur office in Riobamba has more information.

Pakiñaran, in Cuenca, is another network of CBT. Drop into their office (Sucre 14-96 and Coronel Tálbot) in Cuenca's Centro Histórico.

HELPING PRESERVE THE FORESTS

In the Oriente, there are many opportunities to help indigenous communities in their struggle to maintain their way of life while keeping resource extraction at bay. A stay with the indigenous Huaorani of the Oriente promises an unforgettable inter-cultural and wildlife-viewing experience, as you learn about medicinal plants and survival skills, ancestral tales, and accompany them hunting and fishing. Many inhabit their own reserve within the Yasuní National Park, arguably the most biologically diverse place on the planet. It is also Ecuador's largest national park, unfortunately sitting atop an estimated 1.7 billion barrels of crude oil. Oil has deeply divided the Huaorani nation; some have been lured away from their traditional way of life by the oil companies; others strive to hang on to their

Bird-watching tour, Yasuní National Park.

culture and their rainforest lifestyle. Community-based tourism provides a means of protecting their lifestyle and the rainforest and its inhabitants. Try the Huaorani-owned and -operated Bameno Tours (www.facebook.com/huaocommunitytours), rather than organising through an operator. For last-minute stays with Huaorani, Shuar, or Kichwa communities, rather than booking through a Quito tour operator, get in touch with the tourist office in Coca, which can facilitate a direct arrangement with a rainforest community.

COMMUNITY-RUN LUXURY LODGES

If you still prefer the comfort of a more conventional lodge-based stay, Napo Wildlife Center (www.napowildlifecenter.com) and sibling lodge the Napo Cultural Center (www.napoculturalcenter.com) offer superlative wildlife-watching and cultural experiences, respectively. Both lodges support the Kichwa Añangu people in education, health, and renewable energy projects. Even more remote Kapawi Lodge (www.kapawi.com), wholly owned and managed by the Achuar nation, down by the Peruvian border, provides crucial income for community development on their own terms and helps them to protect the rainforest, providing viable alternatives to working for oil companies.

BUYING *ARTESANÍA* AT SOURCE

Ecuador is renowned for its high-quality crafts including textiles, leatherwork, *shigra* bags, ceramics, Panama hats, and jewelry. By buying crafts in markets, or community tourism centers, rather than from boutique shops in Guayaquil and Cuenca, more money goes to the artisans – and you're also likely to get a better deal yourself.

STOCK UP AT MARKETS

If you're heading for the hills to go camping and mountaineering, stocking up at Ecuador's many local markets, rather than the local supermarket, will both save some money and help support struggling rural farmers.

GALÁPAGOS TIPS

It goes without saying that Galápagos is a fragile ecological environment reaching crisis point, which is why making decisions that will have a positive impact is so important. The most obvious point is to follow the rules, keeping the two-meter distance from the wildlife, and not touching any of the animals, even if they come up to you, as humans can unwittingly pass on diseases.

When it comes to sunscreen, choose a reef-friendly brand that is free of oxybenzone and octinoxate, especially if you're intending to snorkel. Minimize waste and avoid single-use plastics, since any recycling has to be transported back to the mainland. Taking a water bottle to refill is one way to help achieve this; several boats and accommodations have water points for you to refill. Alternatively, bring water-purification tablets. Choose to stay with locally owned establishments and choose restaurants and boats prioritizing locally produced food, rather than items that have to be flown in from the mainland, or even further away.

Waterfall near Pedro Vicente
Maldonado, northwest of Quito.

Climbers descending Cotopaxi.

Young women in their finery near Cotacachi.

ECUADOR

Small but spectacular, Ecuador is one of Latin America's most attractive destinations, with fabulous diversity in both culture and nature.

At Guamote's Thursday market.

In 1736 Charles-Marie de la Condamine and Pierre Bouguer headed a pioneering expedition mounted by the French Academy of Science to study the equatorial line at its highest points. Close to a century later, the founders of the Republic of Ecuador chose the invisible line in the Andes as its namesake, already well aware of the geographical diversity of its territories.

Among the world's most biodiverse countries – 1 hectare (2.5 acres) of Ecuadorian Amazon forest holds more tree species than all of North America, and one in three bird species is found in Ecuador – the country has drawn explorers and researchers for more than 300 years, from German explorer Alexander von Humboldt and Charles Darwin in the 19th century, to modern biologists who still record previously undescribed species. Although occupying an area only slightly larger than the US state of Colorado, Ecuador contains the snow-capped Andes, the wide, largely deserted beaches of the Pacific coast, and expanses of steamy Amazon jungle.

Butterfly in Parque Nacional Machalilla on the Pacific coast.

Historically one of Latin America's least stable countries, Ecuador has had around 100 presidents since full independence in 1830, officially recognised or otherwise, amid a succession of minor civil wars through the early 20th century, and numerous coups and defenestrations of leaders at the hands of the people or the military. Yet these events were short-lived, and for many years Ecuador almost entirely escaped the brutal violence that has haunted so many of its Latin American neighbors. However, pickpocketing and instances of armed robbery are on the increase in some tourist areas, and conflicts over natural resources are becoming increasingly violent. But for all that, Ecuador is still one of the safest Latin American countries to travel round.

Ecuador is not, and has never been, a prosperous country, but government spending in the early twenty-first century resulted in a substantial middle class. However, recent years of austerity have resulted in increasing poverty and inequality. The oil prospects deep within the jungle have dramatically increased government wealth, but jeopardise the natural resources on which indigenous and other local populations are reliant, and which make Ecuador such an appealing travel destination. Close to a dozen indigenous groups account for only around six percent of the total 17 million inhabitants. Many of these still speak Quichua and maintain traditions from Inca times and earlier.

The verdant hills of the Riobamba region.

COAST, SIERRA, AND JUNGLE

Sandy beaches, snowy volcanoes, Amazon rainforests, the Galápagos Islands... Ecuador's vivid diversity is one of its greatest attractions.

Straddling the Andes on the most westerly point of South America, Ecuador is half the size of France (271,000 sq km/103,000 sq miles), making it the smallest of the Andean countries. The Andean mountain chain divides the country into three distinct regions: the coastal plain, or Costa, the mountains themselves, or Sierra, and the Amazon jungle, or Oriente. A fourth region, the Galápagos Islands, is a volcanic archipelago in the Pacific Ocean some 1,000km (620 miles) west of the mainland.

Ecuador's population is about 19 million, two-thirds of whom live in cities. The capital, Quito, has just under 2.7 million inhabitants, but the commercial hub is Guayaquil, with a population of just over 2.7 million.

Young Indígena minding sheep near Guamote.

CONTRASTING ECOSYSTEMS

The gently rolling hills of the Costa lie between sea and mountains. Frequent seasonal flooding makes access to some low-lying areas difficult in the rainy season. Much of this area was virgin coastal rainforest at the turn of the 20th century, but now it is devoted primarily to agriculture. The shoreline offers long stretches of sandy palm-lined beaches, and the sea is warm all year round. The river estuaries harbor mangrove swamps, many of which are used for shrimp-ranching; inland there are plantations of bananas, sugarcane, cacao, and rice.

The Andes consist of an eastern and western range, joined at intervals by transverse foothills. Nestling between the ranges are valleys with highly productive volcanic soils that have been farmed for several thousand years. From the valley floors, a patchwork quilt of small fields climbs far up the mountainsides, using every available centimeter of land. The Quichua communities who own this land produce a variety of crops, including potatoes, corn, beans, wheat, barley, and carrots.

The northern half of the Ecuadorian Andes is dominated by 10 volcanoes that tower to over 5,000 meters (16,000ft). These peaks are covered by ice and snow that draw mountaineers from all over the world, while trekkers are enchanted by the surrounding sub-Alpine grasslands known locally as *páramo,* and host wildlife such as the Andean condor, Andean fox, and spectacled bear, as well as hundreds of wildflowers.

The Amazon rainforest of the Oriente begins in the foothills of the eastern Andes. River systems flowing from this rainy wilderness become tributaries of the Amazon, the longest being the Río Napo (885km/550 miles). Settlement, previously limited to the banks of these rivers, is rapidly being changed by an expanding road network begun by the oil industry in the early 1970s. Settlers and agricultural interests are converting once virgin rainforest into pastures and croplands, but for the moment, much of the original forest survives and offers both magnificent scenery and ideal terrain for adventure.

Clouds forming over the rainforest canopy, with the Río Napo in the background.

The Galápagos Islands, home to the famous giant tortoises, blue-footed boobies, and marine iguanas, consist of 13 islands (the biggest, Isabela, measures over 4,000 sq km/1,520 sq miles) and 40 to 50 islets. Since this archipelago was never directly connected to the mainland, the wildlife that exists here evolved in isolation, and many species are endemic. The area is biologically unique, and all of the islands are protected both by a national park and a marine reserve.

LAND OF SUN AND RAIN

Being right on the equator, Ecuador lacks the four seasons of the temperate zones. Every location in the country generally has a wet (winter)

and dry (summer) season, but it is difficult to predict the weather on a day-to-day basis, especially during an El Niño year, when much of the country gets drenched by heavy rains.

The rainy season for the Costa is between January and June. It rains most of the time in the Oriente, though December to February are usually drier. Both these regions are hot (above 25°C/80°F) all year round. The Galápagos Islands are hot and arid. Weather patterns in the Sierra are complex, and each region has its own microclimate. Generally, the central valleys

The term "Avenue of the Volcanoes" was coined by the German explorer Alexander von Humboldt in 1802. Just south of Quito lies Volcán Cotopaxi, the world's highest active volcano.

are rainy between February and May, while the rest of the year is drier, with a short wet season in October and November. The climate overall is mild, and Quiteños brag about their perpetual spring, where gardens bloom all year round.

A DYNAMIC LANDSCAPE

The forces of tectonic plates, volcanoes, and water have sculpted an exquisite array of landscapes, but have also caused devastating natural disasters like the earthquake which shook the province of Manabí in 2016, causing c.670 deaths and leaving thousands severely injured.

In 1660, a century after the colonial city of Quito was founded, the nearby volcano of Guagua Pichincha erupted catastrophically, dumping several feet of ash onto the city. It began erupting again in 1998, causing the evacuation of villages near the crater. However, Quito is safe from lava and pyroclastic flows: the crater opens to the west away from the city, and another lower, dormant crater, Rucu Pichincha, blocks any potential flows. Farther south, Tungurahua started spitting out ash and incandescent rocks soon after Guagua and is still restless. Volcán Cotopaxi awoke again in mid-2015 spewing fumes, steam, and ash, and prompting the government to declare a state of emergency and evacuate nearby villages. The volcano was reopened to climbers in 2017, but later closed with renewed eruptions, and is still volatile.

Curious sea lion.

La Cruz del Vado, Cuenca.

DECISIVE DATES

Pre-Columbian Manabí pottery.

PRE-CERAMIC PERIOD

30,000–6000 BC
Hunter-gatherers using stone axes inhabit the Andes.

FORMATIVE PERIOD

3500–500 BC
First permanent settlements and communities. Surviving pottery testifies to the sophistication of the society.

3500 BC
Earliest Valdivian site, called Loma Alta, is established.

1500 BC
Ceremonial temples are built in Real Alto.

REGIONAL CULTURES

6th century BC–16th century AD
Distinct cultural hubs develop along the coast (Manteño culture), the northern Andes (Quitu-Caras) and the central-southern Andes (Puruháes, Cañaris), with metallurgy, pottery, and textile production.

1460–1520
Inca conquest under Tupac Yupanqui amid fierce resistance (Quitu taken in 1492). Forced resettlement and construction of Ingapirca under Huayna Cápac.

1527–32
Civil war between Atahualpa, heir to the Kingdom of Quito, and his half-brother Huascar ends with Huascar's defeat.

SPANISH COLONY AND EARLY INDEPENDENCE

1526
First *conquistadores*, under Bartolomé Ruiz, land near Esmeraldas.

1530
Francisco Pizarro lands near Manabí.

1532
Atahualpa captured and killed.

1534
Pedro de Alvarado lands in Manta. An army led by Simón de Benalcázar defeats the Incas when thousands of members of the Inca army stage a mutiny. Benalcázar founds San Francisco de Quito on the ruins of the city burned by Inca leader Rumiñahui.

1535
Guayaquil is founded.

1549
The Spanish conquest is completed, but the *conquistadores* fight over gold until subdued by the Spanish crown in 1554.

1550s
The land is divided up among the Spaniards and worked under a form of oppressive serfdom on huge estates (*encomiendas*). *Obrajes* (textiles workshops) using forced labor are established in Otavalo.

1563
Quito becomes the seat of a *Real Audiencia* (royal court).

17th century
Seminaries and universities are established in Quito.

1720
Encomiendas are abolished, but indigenous peoples become serfs on large *haciendas* under the *wasipungo*, or debt peonage, system.

1736
Expedition by the French Academy of Sciences measures a degree of the meridian near the equator and determines the circumference of the earth.

1794
María Chinquinquirá, enslaved black activist brings a legal case against her former "owners" to demand freedom for her and her daughter.

1801–3
Alexander von Humboldt travels through Ecuador.

1809–22
Ecuadorian fight for independence from Spain culminates in the Battle of Pichincha on May 24, 1822: the forces of Antonio José de Sucre defeat the royalist army and liberate Quito.

1823
Simón Bolívar's Gran Colombia, incorporating

Ecuador, Venezuela, and Colombia, is formed, but lasts only seven years.

1830
General Juan José Flores announces the creation of the Republic of Ecuador. Sucre is assassinated, and Bolívar later dies in exile.

1835
Charles Darwin spends five weeks on the Galápagos Islands, where he makes many of the observations underpinning his theories of evolution.

1858–75
After years of instability, Gabriel García Moreno imposes an ultra-Catholic dictatorship, yet begins amid a boom in cocoa exports. He is assassinated in 1875.

MODERN TIMES
1895–1912
Liberal Revolution under Eloy Alfaro. Completion of railway, separation of Church and state.

1925–9
Instability amid decline in cocoa exports, introduction of habeas corpus and women's right to vote.

1933–72
José María Velasco Ibarra elected president five times, but fails to end a term in office.

1941
Border war with Peru ends with loss of almost half of Ecuador's claimed Amazon territory.

1950s
Crisis in the *hacienda* system triggers intermittent military dictatorships.

1964
Land reform gives *indígenas* titles to their plots of land.

1972–82
Oil becomes main export under military dictatorship.

1984–92
Conservative León Febres Cordero violently represses small guerrilla movement.

1987–8
Earthquake shuts down oil pipeline.

1995
Border war with Peru; border treaty signed in 1999.

1997
Ousting of Abdalá Bucaram starts decade of instability amid widespread allegations of corruption. All three presidents elected between 1997 and 2002 are toppled amid a deep crisis brought on by renewed El Niño flooding and the collapse of oil prices and the banking system.

2000
US dollar replaces sucre.

2006
Rafael Correa wins presidential elections, ushering in a period of stability.

2008–9
Correa allies rewrite the Constitution, approved by voters in a referendum. Correa wins early re-election, promising to accelerate his "Citizens' Revolution."

2013
Correa wins another four-year term. The National Assembly passes a Communications Law, dubbed the *Ley Mordaza* (Gag

A five-centavo Ecuadorean postage stamp issued in 1930.

Law) by its critics, giving the government greater power to regulate the media. Three army and police officers stand trial for alleged crimes against humanity committed in the 1980s.

2015
Cotopaxi volcano erupts again.

2016
Roughly 670 people are killed by a 7.8-magnitude earthquake in the northwest.

2018
Ecuadorians vote to maintain the cap on presidents sitting no more than two terms in office.

2022
A'i Cofan leaders Alex Lucitante and Alexandra Narvaez awarded Goldman Environmental prize after court battle cancelling 52 illegal gold mining operations in their ancestral lands.

2023
To avoid impeachment, President Lasso dissolves the National Assembly, prompting elections, marred by violence. Thirty-five-year-old Daniel Noboa becomes the country's youngest ever president.

Pre-Columbian ceramic figure,
Museo Nacional del Ecuador,
Quito.

LOST WORLDS

Ancient civilizations bequeathed a rich variety of cultural remains that continue to intrigue both archeologists and visitors.

The archeology of the Americas shines, in the public mind, with a few especially bright stars: the Incas of Peru, the Aztecs of central Mexico, and the Maya of southern Mexico and Guatemala. The many pre-Columbian cultures beyond those centers are still relatively unknown, in spite of some astonishing recent discoveries.

Ecuador comprises one of those *tierras incognitas*, even though it has a fabulously rich archeological heritage. Because of the close proximity between coast, Sierra, and Amazonia, experts are able to study the movements that shaped civilization on the entire continent. It is becoming clear that many key developments defining pre-Columbian South America took place in Ecuador. The oldest pottery in all of the Americas has been found here. Cultures have been discovered that worked in platinum, a metal unknown in Europe until the 1850s. Ancient trade links have been established between Ecuador, Mexico, and Amazonia. And it seems likely that pre-Columbian Ecuadorians sailed to and explored the Galápagos Islands.

THE REMOTE PAST

The first human beings who came to Ecuador were hunters and gatherers. The approximate period of their arrival is still debated, but it is certain that human beings have been in the Andes for 15,000 years, probably 30,000 years, and perhaps even for as long as 50,000 years. But the crucial question in Ecuador itself surrounds the gradual, all-important transformation from the hunting and gathering way of life to what archeologists call the "formative period."

While hunters and gatherers led a nomadic existence, formative cultures featured permanent settlements. This transformation in the

Necklaces at MAAC, Guayaquil.

Americas occurred over a 2,000- or 3,000-year period, beginning around 3000 BC in the most advanced areas. To the great surprise of many archeologists, the earliest pottery and other evidence of formative cultures in the whole of South America has been found on the coast of Ecuador, from a culture known as Valdivia.

The Valdivian culture stretched along the Ecuadorian coast of modern-day Manabí province, with its extensive, ecologically rich mangrove swamps, reaching inland to the drier hilly country. The earliest Valdivian site, dating back perhaps to 3500 BC, is called Loma Alta. A range of extraordinary pottery has been found at this site, decorated with different carved motifs and a variety of colored clays. The Valdivian potters also formed multicolored female figurines that turn up in late strata in the archeological sites.

In Real Alto, a large Valdivian town continuously inhabited for over 2,000 years, archeologists have found the remains of over 100 household structures, each of which may have housed 20 or more people. By 1500 BC, the Real Alto people had built ceremonial temples on the tops of hills in the center of their town, where complex rituals obviously took place.

For archeologists, the biggest puzzle surrounding the Valdivian culture, with highly

Pre-Columbian ceramic figurine at MAAC, Guayaquil.

⊘ THE JAPANESE IN ECUADOR?

The well-known Ecuadorian archeologist Emilio Estrada, at first working alone, and later with the collaboration of Smithsonian Institute archeologists Betty Meggers and Clifford Evans, postulated that Valdivia's origins were to be found on the Japanese island of Kyushu. In 1956, Estrada was the first archeologist to describe the Valdivia culture, noting that the Jomon culture, which existed on Kyushu around 3000 BC, produced pottery strikingly similar to that found at the Valdivian sites. However, this theory never caught on, as clear evidence of trans-Pacific trade at the time hadn't emerged, and now it has been virtually abandoned.

developed pottery, agricultural cultivation, and social organization firmly under its belt, is that it could not have appeared out of nowhere. There must have been a long series of precursors, of trial-and-error development that led up to these cultural achievements. Conclusive evidence to show that these developments occurred on the coast of Ecuador hasn't been found.

The daring and well-publicized voyages of Thor Heyerdahl, a Norwegian adventurer who sailed across the Pacific from South America to the Tumatou archipelago in French Polynesia in a raft he'd built himself in 1947, encouraged such archeologists as Emilio Estrada to link Valdivia to prehistoric Japan. Indeed, visitors to the Museo Nacional del Ecuador, Quito's most important archeological museum, may still encounter this theory as if it were a proven fact. Decorative motifs common to both Valdivia and Japan's Jomon cultures are, however, found all over the world, because the techniques that produced them are precisely those which potters choose almost automatically when they experiment with the results of applying a finger, a bone tool, a leaf, or a stone to the wet clay.

ORIGINS IN THE AMAZON

In the Oriente region of Ecuador, as elsewhere in Amazonia, the persistent presence of hunting and gathering peoples has led many observers to regard Amazonia as a historical backwater, incapable of supporting large populations and advanced civilizations. The first hint that this could not be the case came from agricultural scientists investigating the domestication of manioc, which they concluded had taken place in the Amazon basin at least 8,000 years ago.

Archeologists believe that large cities of more than 10,000 people, supported by manioc cultivation, grew up on the Amazon's fertile flood-plain as well as in the jungles on the eastern slope of the Ecuadorian and Peruvian Andes. The cultures of the Amazonian cities, which archeologists are now starting to find in Ecuador and Peru, may, according to some, have given pottery and manioc to South America. Manioc, along with corn (which came to Ecuador from Central America by way of trade), formed the agricultural foundation for a series of advanced coastal cultures, starting with Valdivia, according to some archeologists.

An important site near Cuenca, called Cerro Narrio, sits at the crossroads of a route following the drainages of the Pastaza and Paute rivers. From around 2000 BC, Cerro Narrio may have been a key trading center, where exchanges of technologies, products, and ideas from the coast, Amazonia, and the Sierra took place. Ceramics bearing unmistakably similar designs to those of coastal cultures have been found at Cerro Narrio, but archeologists are unable to determine whether these pots were imported from the coast or were made at Cerro Narrio by potters who had come from the coast to live in the Sierra.

networks, stretching from Mexico to Peru and from the Amazon to the coast, archeologists describe a period of "regional development" (500 BC–AD 500) followed by a period of "integration" (AD 500–1500). The final period culminated in the conquest of all of present-day Ecuador by the Inca Empire, which undertook an extensive program of city-building and artistic creativity, before being itself destroyed by the Spaniards. A grand flowering of cultural activity preceded the Inca conquest of Ecuador, and the abundance of distinctive phases, especially on the coast, is overwhelming.

Pre-Columbian figure playing the panpipe, Museo Centro Cultural Manta.

A number of important items were traded between coast, Sierra, and jungle. Coastal societies collected spondylus shells, which were processed into beads in the Sierra and traded in Amazonia, where the shell design appears on much of the pottery that has been discovered. The Sierran societies cultivated the potato – used for trade – as well as coca, crucially important in rituals and ceremonies in the area. Meanwhile, Amazonian societies were renowned for their ritual vessels, made for more than 3,000 years, and for their hallucinogenic potions.

FLOWERING OF COASTAL ACTIVITY

Following the establishment of formative cultures and of wide-ranging trade and exchange

⊙ FINDING NEW DIGS

Hundreds of new sites have been uncovered or revisited in recent decades, particularly in Moroni-Santiago, where the Santa Ana-La Florida site has turned up evidence of a complex Amazon society 4,500 years old. In Manabí, sites like Cerro de Hojas and the underwater remains of the city of the Caras are being investigated. Restoration projects are under way at the Cochasquí pyramids and Pambamarca fortresses north of Quito, and much of the Tulipe site of the Yumbo culture northwest of the city has been restored, as has Cuenca's Pumapungo Inca site. A large stone structure found in Parque Nacional Llanganates in 2012 is believed to be the mausoleum of the last Inca emperor, Atahualpa.

The extraordinary achievement of these coastal cultures is embodied in the goldwork and sculpture of the La Tolita and Manta civilizations.

LA TOLITA CIVILIZATION

The La Tolita culture reached its zenith around 300 BC, and its star shone for perhaps 700 years on the coast of northern Ecuador and southwestern Colombia. The key site is a small, swampy island in the coastal province of Esmeraldas. Now inhabited by Afro-Ecuadorian fisherfolk, La Tolita came to the attention of Westerners

Stone carving from the Manta culture c.200–500 AD.

in the 1920s, when several European explorers announced the discovery of unprecedented numbers of finely crafted gold objects.

The merciless pillage of these priceless objects went on for years, and was even industrialized by prospectors, who mechanized the milling of thousands of tons of sand, from which gold artifacts were extracted and then melted down into ingots. Despite this, many gold objects are still found on La Tolita, such as the magnificent mask of the Sun God, with its ornately detailed fan of sun rays, and the symbol of Ecuador's Banco Central. So much gold has been uncovered there that archeologists believe that the island was a sacred place, a pre-Columbian Mecca or Jerusalem, a city of goldsmiths, devoted to the production of

holy images. It may have been the destination of pilgrims from the coast, the Sierra, and possibly Amazonia, who went there to obtain the sacred symbols of an ancient cult that influenced most of what is now Ecuador.

The quality and beauty of La Tolita goldwork is matched by the sculpture found on the island. The free-standing, detailed figures in active poses make La Tolita sculpture unique in pre-Columbian art. The sculptures depict both deities and mortals, the latter displaying deformities and diseases, or experiencing emotions of joy, sadness, or surprise.

La Tolita artisans also excelled in a form of metalcraft unknown in Europe until the 1850s. Smiths on the island worked in platinum, creating intricate masks, pendants, pectorals, and nose-rings in a metal with a very high melting point. Archeologists have puzzled over how they were able to do this, with only rudimentary tools and technology. One theory is that by combining pure platinum with bits of gold, which melts at a much lower temperature, the smiths created an alloy with which they could work.

THE MANTA CULTURE

The Manta culture, in the modern province of Manabí, flourished during the period of integration, and also produced objects of outstanding beauty in gold, silver, cotton textiles, pottery, and stone. The great city of Manta housed more than 20,000 people, and by including the population of outlying villages, archeologists believe very high numbers of people lived during the Manta culture. There is evidence that the Manta people settled along extensive stretches of the coast and traded with the coastal peoples of western Mexico and central Peru.

There is an intriguing theory held by some archeologists that Manteño mariners, along with pre-Columbian Peruvian sailors, discovered the Galápagos Islands. A quantity of ceramic shards, almost certainly of pre-Columbian vintage, have been uncovered on three of the islands; the presence of cotton plants, cultivated on the continent, also indicates some sort of contact between the islands and the mainland. Whether the contacts were only occasional, whether the islands were used as a seasonal fishing outpost, as Thor Heyerdahl and others favor, or whether they were settled by groups of Manteños, as a few archeologists assert, has yet to be established.

A 19th-century illustration of the scientist Alexander von Humboldt watching the sky.

HUB OF TWO EMPIRES

Fought over and dominated by the Incas and the conquistadores,
Ecuador became a key center for both of their empires.

Within the space of a century, successive invaders – the Incas and the Spaniards – swept across the country in great waves of destruction, each seeking to remake it in their own image. Their impact is reflected in the varied ethnicity of the Ecuadorian people – 7 percent indigenous, 72 percent mestizos (mixed European-indigenous blood), 7 percent montubios (a distinctive coastal metizaje), 6 percent white (often of European heritage) and 7 percent Afro-Ecuadorians, the descendants of enslaved Africans. Their legacy of brutal exploitation constitutes an ongoing struggle for modern Ecuadorians.

SIERRA CULTURES

The land that is now Ecuador was first brought under one rule when the Incas of Peru invaded in the middle of the 15th century. By this time, the dazzling cultures of Manta and La Tolita on the Ecuadorian coast had flowered and faded, while an increasingly powerful series of agricultural societies had divided the region's highlands among themselves.

The greatest were the Cañaris, who inhabited the present-day towns of Cuenca, Chordaleg, Gualaceo, and Cañar. Theirs was a rigidly hierarchical society. Only the Cañari elite were allowed to wear the fine, elaborate gold and silver produced by their metalsmiths. Among the Cañari artifacts, figures of jaguars, caimans, and other jungle animals predominate, showing their strong links with Amazonian groups.

In the north, archeological evidence points to a more fragmented rule, though often still called "the Kingdom of Quito." Research has all but dispelled the existence of the legendary Shyri and Duchicela dynasties. Rather than a centralized state, local chieftains formed periodical military

Atahualpa's funeral.

alliances, possibly giving the attacking Incas the impression of centralized rule under the Quitu-Cara people based around Quitu, particularly in light of their fierce defense of their independence. The city was already an established commercial center on the site of present-day Quito.

Other peoples in the area included the Yumbos, traders between the Andes and the coast, Cochasquies, Cayambis, Otavaleños, and the Pasto on the present-day border with Colombia. The pre-Inca Cochasquí pyramids north of Quito are among Ecuador's most important archeological ruins. Locals were well aware of the equator as "the path of the sun." Their economy was based on spinning and weaving wool, and there was a traveling class of merchants who traded with groups in the

Amazon Oriente. Further south, the Puruháes, ferocious warriors based around Ambato, were more closely related to the Cañaris.

THE INCA INVASION

Into this landscape of distinctive identities marched the Incas – literally, "Children of the Sun" – who were to be the short-lived precursors of the Spaniards. Although established in the Peruvian Andes from the 11th century, it was not until about 1460 that they attacked the Cañaris, with the ultimate objective of subjugating the Kingdom of Quitu. Ecuador became brutally embroiled in imperial ambitions as armies dispatched from distant capitals turned the country into a battlefield.

The Cañaris fought valiantly against all odds for several years before being subdued by the Inca Tupac Yupanqui. His revenge severely depleted the indigenous male population: when the Spanish chronicler Cieza de León visited Cañari territory in 1547, he found 15 women to every man. Inca occupation was focused on the construction of a major city called Tomebamba on the site of present-day Cuenca. It was intended to rival the

Famous Inca masonry at the ruins of Ingapirca.

⊘ LEGENDARY DYNASTIES

According to local lore, the Caras – who, it is thought, arrived in the Andes by traveling upriver from the areas around Esmeraldas and Bahía de Caráquez on the coast – were under the rule of the Shyri ("lord") dynasty. They then conquered an area including Cayambe and Otavalo in the north down to Latacunga and Ambato in the south. The Puruháes, ruled by the Duchicela family, intermarried with the Shyri in the 14th century, so creating a "Kingdom of Quito," the core of a pre-Hispanic Ecuadorian nation. Belief in this realm is still widespread, though historians as early as the 19th century began to question its very existence.

Inca capital of Cuzco, from where stonemasons were summoned to build a massive temple of the sun and splendid palaces with walls of gold.

But by the time Cieza de León arrived, Tomebamba was already a ghost town. He found enormous warehouses stocked with grain, barracks for the imperial troops, and houses formerly occupied by "more than two hundred virgins, who were very beautiful, dedicated to the service of the sun." At nearby Ingapirca, the best-preserved pre-Hispanic site in Ecuador, the Incas built an imposing complex that also served as temple, storehouse, and observatory.

Inca conquest along the spine of the Andes continued inexorably. Quitu, which had fallen by 1492, became a garrison town on the empire's northern

The Incas made battle drums from the stomachs of their enemies. By 1492, they had conquered much of present-day Ecuador, ending with the epic battle that gave Yahuarcocha, or blood lake, near Ibarra its name.

frontier and, like Tomebamba, the focus of ostentatious construction. Battles continued to rage: for 17 years the Caras resisted the Inca onslaught before

beast of burden and an excellent source of wool. The chewing of coca, previously unknown in highland Ecuador, soon became a popular habit. The Imperial Highway (Qhapaq Ñan) was extended to Quitu, which – although 1,980km (1,230 miles) from Cuzco – could be reached by a team of relay runners in eight days. Inca colonization also brought large numbers of loyal Quechua subjects from southern Peru, and many Cañaris and Caras were in turn shipped to Peru as so-called *mitimaes*. Loyalty to the Inca, with his mandate from the sun, was exacted through the system

The capture of Huascar during the Incas' bitter civil war.

Huayna Cápac, Tupac's son, captured the Caras' capital, Caranqui, and massacred thousands.

The Incas at war were a fearsome sight. Dressed in quilted armor and cane or woolen helmets, and armed with spears, *champis* (headsplitters), slingshots, and shields, they attacked with blood-curdling cries. Prisoners taken in battle were led to a sun temple and slaughtered. The heads of enemy chieftains became ceremonial drinking cups, and their bodies were stuffed and paraded through the streets.

IMPOSING THE NEW ORDER

The Incas introduced their impressive irrigation methods and some new crops – sweet potatoes, coca, and peanuts – as well as the llama, a sturdy

of *mita* – imperial work or service – rather than taxation. As large areas came under centralized control for the first time, a nascent sense of unity stirred; but it was an alien and oppressive regime, attracting little genuine loyalty.

The indigenous Ecuadorians who suffered Inca domination were proud, handsome peoples. Cieza de León spoke of the Cañaris as "good-looking and well grown," and the native Quiteños as "more gentle and better disposed, and with fewer vices than all Indians of Peru." Tupac Yupanqui married a Cañari princess, and Huayna Cápac, in turn, the daughter of a Quitu aristocrat. This was to play a crucial part in the collapse of the empire, for Huayna Cápac, seeking to unite his domain through marriage, achieved just the opposite.

Huayna Cápac had been born and raised in Tomebamba; his favorite son, Atahualpa, was the offspring of the Quitu marriage and heir to the northern quarter of the empire. Atahualpa's half-brother Huascar was descended from Inca lineage on both sides, and thus the legitimate heir. In 1527, Huascar ascended the Cuzco throne, dividing the empire. Civil war soon broke out, and continued for five years before Atahualpa defeated and imprisoned Huascar after a major battle near Ambato.

Atahualpa, an able and intelligent leader, established the new capital of Cajamarca in

desperate owners of ruined lands – and the Church – and spawned dreams of other such empires in the so-called "New World".

The first conquistadors to set foot on Ecuadorian soil landed near Esmeraldas in September 1526. They had been dispatched from Colombia by Francisco Pizarro to explore lands to the south. The party, led by Bartolomé Ruiz, came upon several villages where people were wearing splendid objects of gold and silver, news of which prompted Pizarro himself, with just 13 men, to follow a year or so later. Near Tumbes,

A 19th-century illustration of conquistadores massacring the indigenous population.

northern Peru. But the war had severely weakened both the infrastructure and the will of the Incas, and by a remarkable historical coincidence, it was only a matter of months before their death-knell sounded.

THE BEARDED WHITE STRANGERS

Rarely have the pages of history been stalked by such a greedy, treacherous, bloodthirsty band of villains as the Spanish *conquistadores*. With their homeland ravaged by 700 years of war with the Moors, the Spanish believed they had paid a heavy price for saving Christian Europe from Muslim domination. When news reached Spain of the glittering Aztec treasury, snatched by Cortés in 1521, it fired the imaginations of

he found an indigenous settlement whose inhabitants were similarly adorned, and so planned a full-scale invasion. Late in 1530, having traveled to Spain to secure the patronage of King Carlos I (or Carlos V, Holy Roman Emperor) and the title of governor and captain-general of Peru, Pizarro – this time with 180 men and 27 horses – landed in the Bay of San Mateo near Manabí.

For two years the conquistadors battled against the local peoples and against the treacherous terrain of mosquito-infested swamps and jungles, and frozen, cloud-buffeted mountain passes. Arriving exhausted in Cajamarca in November 1532, they formulated a plan to trap the Inca Atahualpa. At a pre-arranged meeting, the Inca and several thousand followers – many

HUB OF TWO EMPIRES | 39

of them unarmed – entered the great square of Cajamarca. A Spanish priest outlined the tenets of Christianity to Atahualpa, calling upon him to embrace the faith and accept the sovereignty of Carlos I. Predictably, Atahualpa refused, flinging the priest's Bible to the ground; Pizarro and his men rushed out from the surrounding buildings and set upon the astonished Incas. Of the Spaniards, only Pizarro himself was wounded when he seized Atahualpa, while the Incas were cut down in their hundreds.

Atahualpa was imprisoned, and a ransom demanded: a roomful of gold and silver weighing 24 tons was amassed, but the Inca leader was not freed. He was held for nine months, during which time he learned Spanish and mastered the arts of writing, chess, and cards. His authority was never questioned: female attendants dressed him in robes of vampire-bat fur, fed him, and ceremoniously burned everything he used. The Spaniards melted down the finely wrought treasures, and accused Atahualpa of treason. Curiously, Pizarro baptized him "Francisco," and then garroted him with an iron collar.

TWO WORLDS COLLIDE

To the Incas, the Spanish conquest was an apocalyptic reversal of the natural order. In the eyes of a 16th-century local chronicler, Waman Puma, these strangers were "all enshrouded from head to foot, with their faces completely covered in wool... men who never sleep."

The Incas had no monetary system and no concept of private wealth: they believed the only possible explanation for the Spaniards' craving for gold was that they either ate precious metals, or suffered from a disease that could be cured only by gold. Their horses were "beasts who wear sandals of silver."

Conversely, the conquerors perceived the indigenous population as semi-naked barbarians who worshiped false gods and were good for nothing; Cieza de León's positive remarks (see page 37) only illustrate his unusual fair-mindedness.

While Pizarro continued southward toward Cuzco, his lieutenant, Sebastián de Benalcázar, was dispatched to Piura to ship the Inca booty to Panama. But rumors of these treasures had traveled north, and Pedro de Alvarado, another Spaniard in search of riches, set out from Guatemala to conquer Quitu. With 500 men and 120 horses, he landed at Manta in early 1534 and, during an epic trek, slaughtered all the coastal people who crossed his path.

Hearing of this, Benalcázar quickly mounted his own expedition to capture Quitu. Approaching Riobamba in May, he encountered a massive Quiteño army under the Inca general Quisquis. Fifty thousand, the largest Inca force ever assembled, were deployed, hopelessly outnumbering the Spaniards. But the indigenous population, owing no loyalty to the Incas, mutinied and dispersed, and the best opportunity to defeat the

Francisco Pizarro

◉ LAMENT FOR ATAHUALPA

An elegiac lament was composed by the Incas upon Atahualpa's death: "Hail is falling/Lightning strikes/The sun is sinking/It has become forever night." Atahualpa is still considered by many people to have been the first great Ecuadorian. Curiously, Pizarro baptized him with his own Christian name, Francisco, before garroting him with an iron collar.

There are indigenous people today, in the Saraguro region, who are said to wear their habitual somber black and indigo ponchos and dresses because they are still in mourning for the death of Atahualpa, nearly 500 years ago.

Spanish was lost. Alvarado was paid a handsome sum by Pizarro to abandon his Ecuadorian excursion and return quietly to Guatemala.

Benalcázar marched northward with thousands of Cañaris and Puruháes in his ranks, for both groups sought revenge on the brutal Incas. Arriving in Quitu in December, 1534, he found the city in ruins; Rumiñahui, the Inca general, had destroyed and evacuated it rather than lose it intact. Atop Cara and Inca rubble, with a mere 206 inhabitants, the Villa de San Francisco de Quito was founded on December 6, and Guayaquil the following year.

found the colonists in revolt. Gonzalo fought off the viceroy's forces in 1546, only to be deposed and executed by another official army two years later. During Gonzalo's governorship, an expedition was mounted to explore the lands east of Quito. The undertaking was a disaster (see page 41), but under the renegade leadership of Francisco de Orellana, the first transcontinental journey by Europeans was made in 1541.

When Cortés cried, "I don't want land; give me gold!" he spoke for all *conquistadores*. But the immediately available treasures were soon

The construction of San Francisco in Quito.

Rumiñahui launched a counter-attack a month later, but was captured, tortured, and executed.

By 1549, the conquest was complete: a mere 2,000 Spaniards had subjugated an estimated local population of 500,000. The number of casualties is impossible to ascertain, but tens of thousands died in this 15-year period, through starvation, disease, and suicide, as well as in battle.

THE SPANISH YOKE

With the local populations quieted, the *conquistadores* fought each other for the prizes: not until 1554 did the Spanish crown finally subdue them. In 1539, Pizarro appointed his brother Gonzalo governor of Quito, but when the first viceroy to Peru passed through shortly there-after, he

exhausted. The land and its inhabitants were divided among the *conquistadores*, and the first settlers soon followed. Of the Quito region, in contrast to the damp, ghostly barrenness of Lima, Cieza de León wrote: "The country is very pleasant, and particularly resembles Spain in its pastures and climate."

The Avenue of the Volcanoes, the strip of land 40 to 60km (25 to 40 miles) wide running the length of Ecuador between two towering rows of volcanoes, was ideal farmland. In addition, workshops were established to produce textiles, and enslaved Africans were shipped across the Atlantic to labor on the coastal cacao plantations. Ecuador escaped the grim excesses of mining that befell Peru and Bolivia, as the

INTO THE AMAZON

Once Quito had been settled, the *conquistadores* began to seek new lands and adventures.

Tales of El Dorado and Canelos (the Land of Cinnamon, supposedly to the east) filled the air. Francisco Pizarro appointed his brother Gonzalo to lead an expedition to find these magical destinations.

THE SEARCH FOR EL DORADO

On Christmas Day, 1539, Gonzalo Pizarro left Quito with 340 soldiers, 4,000 *indígenas*, 150 horses, a flock of llamas, 4,000 swine, 900 dogs, and plentiful supplies of food and water. Surviving an earthquake and an attack by local people who were determined to protect their lands, the expedition descended the Cordillera. At Sumaco on the Río Coca they were joined by Francisco de Orellana, who had been called from his governorship of Guayaquil to be Gonzalo's lieutenant.

Hacking their way through dense, swampy undergrowth, and hampered by incessant heavy rain, they were reduced to eating roots, berries, herbs, frogs, and snakes. The first indigenous people they met denied all knowledge of El Dorado, so Gonzalo had them burned alive and torn to pieces by dogs. They met another group who spoke of a city, supposedly rich in provisions and gold, just 10 days' march away at the junction of the Coca and Napo rivers.

A large raft was constructed, and 50 soldiers under Orellana's command were dispatched to find the city and return with food: already 2,000 indigenous people and scores of Spaniards had starved to death. Hearing nothing of the advance party after two months, Gonzalo trekked to the junction, but there was no city. The pragmatic local populations had very sensibly lied to save their skins. In early June, 1542, the 80 surviving Spaniards from Pizarro's group staggered into Quito, "naked and barefooted." By then, Orellana was far away. The brigantine's provisions were exhausted by the time the party reached the river junction: sailing back upstream was impossible, and blazing a jungle trail would have killed the weary men. Hearing the call of destiny and whispers of El Dorado across the wilderness, Orellana sailed on.

For nine months the expedition drifted on the current. Crude wooden crosses were erected as they progressed, purporting to claim the lands in the name of the Spanish king. They encountered many indigenous peoples: some gave them food and ornaments of gold and silver; others attacked them with spears and poisoned arrows, claiming many Spanish lives. On one occasion, a force of 10,000 indigenous warriors are said to have attacked the soldiers from the river banks and from canoes, but the Spaniards' arquebuses soon repelled them. They heard frequent reports of a group of fearsome women known as "Amazons", who lived in gold-plated houses. Near

Gonzalo Ximénes de Quesada searched (without success) for El Dorado.

Obidos, the "Amazons" attacked. They were "very tall, robust, fair, with long hair twisted over their heads, skins round their loins, and bows and arrows in their hands." From this report, the great South American river and jungle area took its name.

Finally, in a lowland area with many inhabited islands, Orellana noticed signs of the ebb of the tide and, in August 1541, sailed out into the open sea. For the first time, Europeans had traversed South America. Today, if you want to get a taste of this experience in style and comfort, you can take a cruise aboard the Manatee Amazon Explorer, a comfortable riverboat which operates on the Río Napo from the town of Francisco de Orellana, colloquially known as Coca.

Spanish, to their disappointment, found few precious metals here.

As well as horses, pigs and cattle were introduced, and Ecuador nurtured the first crops of bananas and wheat in South America. The Spaniards also imported diseases such as smallpox, influenza, measles, and cholera. But with much of the highlands and all of the Oriente so inaccessible, Spanish settlement was relatively light, so geography saved the local population from extermination, if not from subjugation and exploitation.

Eugenio Espejo.

Colonial administration was based on the twin pillars of the Church and the *encomienda* system, where *encomenderos* (land-owners) were given tracts of land and the right to unpaid labor, and in return were responsible for the religious conversion of their laborers. The indigenous people were obliged to bring tribute, in the form of animals, vegetables, and blankets, to their new masters, as they had to the Incas. It was a brutally efficient form of feudalism whereby the Spanish crown not only pacified the *conquistadores* with a life of luxury, but also gained an empire at no risk or expense. For centuries, the main landowner was the Church, as dying *encomenderos* donated their estates, in the hope of gaining salvation. Pragmatically, *indígenas* accepted the

new faith, embellishing it with their own beliefs and rituals. Days after Benalcázar founded Quito, the cornerstone of the first major place of Christian worship, the Church of San Francisco, was laid. Franciscans were followed by Jesuits and Dominicans, each group of missionaries enriching themselves at the local population's expense.

Methods of conversion could be brutal: children were separated from their families to receive the catechism; lapsing converts were imprisoned, flogged, and their heads were shaved. Some priests took indigenous women as mistresses, and their children contributed to the number of mestizos, people of mixed Spanish-native blood. Quito – seat of a Viceregal Court or *Audiencia* from 1563 – grew into a religious and intellectual center during the 17th century as seminaries, libraries, and universities were established. Art, particularly painting and sculpture, flourished in Quito and was exported to other parts of the Spanish Empire.

PUSH FOR INDEPENDENCE

In reaction to the Spaniards' oppressive socioeconomic actions there sprouted violent popular uprisings and nascent cries of "Liberty!" As early as 1592, the lower clergy supported merchants and workers in the Alcabalas Revolution, protesting against increased taxes on food and fabrics. The authorities put an end to the agitation by executing 24 conspirators and displaying their heads in iron cages.

During the 1700s, the ideas of the European Enlightenment crept slowly toward the University of Quito. The works of Voltaire, Leibnitz, Descartes, and Rousseau, and the revolutions in the United States and France, gave intellectual succor to colonial libertarians. The physician-journalist Eugenio Espejo, born in 1747 of an indigenous father and a mulatto (Afro-Hispanic) mother, emerged as the anti-imperialists' leader.

Espejo was a fearless humanist. He published satirical, bitterly combative books on Spanish colonialism; and as founding editor of the liberal newspaper *Primicias de la Cultura de Quito*, was probably the first American journalist. He was repeatedly jailed, exiled to Bogotá for four years, and finally died, aged 48, in a Quito dungeon. From his cell, he wrote to the President of the *Audiencia*: "I have produced writings for the happiness of the country, as yet a barbarian one."

VON HUMBOLDT: ECUADOR'S FIRST TRAVEL WRITER

Simón Bolívar described Alexander von Humboldt as "the true discoverer of America, because his work has produced more benefit to our people than all the conquistadors."

Praise indeed from the liberator of the Americas, although it's obvious that Humboldt no more "discovered" America, than did Columbus. But how did this wealthy Prussian mineralogist come to play such a vital role in the history of the continent?

Humboldt was born in Berlin in 1769. As a young man he studied botany, chemistry, astronomy, and mineralogy, and traveled with Georg Forster, who had accompanied Captain James Cook on his second world voyage. At the age of 27 he received a legacy large enough to finance a scientific expedition, and made such an impression on Carlos IV of Spain that he received special permission to travel to South America.

HUMBOLDT'S EXPEDITION

With his companion Aimé Bonpland, Humboldt set off for Caracas in November 1799. During their five-year expedition the two men covered some 9,600km (6,000 miles) on foot, horseback, and by canoe; suffered from malaria; and were reduced to a diet of ground cacao beans when damp and insects destroyed their supplies. Following the course of the Orinoco and Casiquiare rivers, they established that the Casiquiare channel linked the Orinoco and the Amazon. In 1802 they reached Quito, where Humboldt climbed Chimborazo, failing to attain the summit but setting a world record (unbroken for 30 years) by reaching almost 6,000 meters (19,500ft). He coined the name "Avenue of the Volcanoes" and, after suffering from altitude sickness, was the first westerner to realize its connection with a lack of oxygen – as many of the indigenous folk of the Andes may well have been already aware. Between ascents he studied the role of eruptive forces in the development of the earth's crust, establishing that Latin America was not, as had been believed, a geologically young country.

A MAN OF MANY INTERESTS

While in Ecuador, Humboldt began assembling notes for his *Essays on the Geography of Plants*, pioneering investigations into the relationship between a region's geography and its flora and fauna. He claimed another first by listing many of the indigenous, pre-conquest species; and he was responsible for the birth of the guano industry, after he sent samples of the substance back to Europe for analysis.

Humboldt's contributions seem endless: off the west coast he studied the oceanic current, which was named after him; his work on isotherms and isobars laid the foundation for the science of climatology; he

A color print after a drawing by Alexander von Humboldt from his expedition rafting on the Río Guayas.

invented the term "magnetic storms," and as a result of his interest the Royal Society in London promoted the establishment of observatories, which led to the correlation of such storms with sunspot activity.

He was also deeply interested in social and economic issues and was adamantly opposed to slavery, which he considered "the greatest evil that afflicts human nature." Goethe, a close friend, found him "exceedingly interesting and stimulating," a man who "overwhelms one with intellectual treasure"; while Charles Darwin had been inspired by Humboldt's earlier journey to Tenerife, in the Canary Islands, and his description of the volcanic Pico de Teide and the dragon tree. Darwin respectfully described him as "the parent of a grand progeny of scientific travellers."

INDEPENDENCE AND AFTER

From the battle for independence to recent oil exploitation in the Amazon, the history of modern Ecuador has been turbulent.

As the crown's grip on its colonies began to loosen, the ghost of the *conquistadores* stirred from its slumber. From the beginning of the Spanish era, money and muscle had meant power; laws, constitutions, and governments were subject to the greed of reckless individuals. Cortés and Orellana disobeyed orders and attained greatness, and Pizarro answered to no one.

The ethos they bequeathed to those who came after them was devoid of ideas and morality. Through the age of *caudillos* – warlords – in the 19th century, and of military dictators in the 20th, Ecuador was viewed as a treasure, like Inca gold, conveniently there for the taking.

THE ROAD TO FREEDOM

Ecuador's first step toward independence was also its first coup. In response to the fall of Spain to Napoleon in 1808, a new wave of repressive measures was enforced in the colonies, prompting members of the criollo oligarchy to seize power in Quito in August, 1809, and imprison the president of the *Audiencia*. Within a month, loyalist troops from Bogotá and Lima had displaced the usurpers, but the subsequent reprisals were so harsh that they prompted a second rebellion two years later. This time, a constitution for an independent state was formulated, but the uprising remained confined to Quito, and so was easily suppressed.

But the whole continent was moving inexorably toward liberation. With English support, Simón Bolívar – "El Libertador" – had taken on the Spanish loyalists in his native Venezuela, where he became dictator, and then in Colombia. In October, 1820, Guayaquil ousted the local authorities and established a revolutionary

A view of Quito in 1846.

junta; and following the Battle of Pichincha in May, 1822, when forces led by Antonio José de Sucre resoundingly defeated the royalist army, Quito was liberated.

A few weeks later, Bolívar arrived in Quito. He was the archetypal criollo – ambitious, paternalistic, impatient, never doubting his methods or goals. His brilliance sprang from the singular intensity of his vision, which brought liberation to a continent, but he failed to appreciate the dynamics of the new nations. His Argentine counterpart, José de San Martín, was stoic, taciturn, and self-effacing, Bolívar's ideal complement. But at their only meeting, in Guayaquil in July, 1822, to plot the future of a proposed Gran Colombia, they had a fundamental disagreement: Bolívar wanted a republic, while San Martín envisaged a monarchy. What happened at that meeting is not known, but Bolívar triumphed, and San Martín went into self-imposed exile in Europe.

Gran Colombia was formed in 1823, incorporating Ecuador, Colombia, and Venezuela. But the new, united nation lasted just seven years: in September, 1830, the military commander of Quito, General Juan José Flores – a Venezuelan who had married into the Quiteño aristocracy – announced the creation of the Republic of Ecuador. The new republic's population now stood at approximately 700,000 and its ill-defined borders were based on those of the colonial *Audiencia*.

That same year, Sucre – Bolívar's chosen successor – was assassinated en route from Bogotá to his home in Quito, prompting Bolívar to grieve, "They have slain Abel." On the northern shores of the continent that he had transformed, *El Libertador* died a broken man: overcome with frustration, he said of his life's work, "Those who serve the revolution plough the sea."

FALSE FREEDOM

The inequalities of the colonial social structure were preserved with ruthless duplicity by the new Ecuadorian elite. While cries of "Fatherland" and "Freedom" echoed across the country, the poor remained enslaved in workshops, on haciendas and plantations. National power was up for grabs, and the struggle between the Conservatives of Quito and the Liberals of Guayaquil began immediately. Flores made a deal with the opposition Liberal leader, Vicente Rocafuerte, to alternate the presidency, with Flores retaining military control, but in 1843 he refused to step down from his second term and was bribed into exile. Flores held power for two more years before being toppled by the Liberals.

In the subsequent period of chronic political disorder, the next 15 years saw 11 governments and three constitutions come and go, while the economy stagnated. This morass was tidied up by strongman Gabriel García Moreno, who had risen from humble origins to the rectorship of the University of Quito. During his decade in power, the nation became a theocracy where only practicing Catholics could vote. He frequently indulged in acts of self-humiliation:

Eloy Alfaro (1842–1912) completed the railway started by García Moreno but was his complete ideological adversary. Dubbed the "Old Fighter," he led a revolution that made Ecuador an early adopter of divorce and civil marriage.

photographs capture him carrying a heavy wooden cross through the streets, followed by his cabinet.

General Simón Bolívar, El Libertador.

Freedom of speech was non-existent, and political opponents were imprisoned or exiled. But there was progress too: hospitals, roads, and railways were constructed; schools were opened to the indigenous population and women; Guayaquil's port facilities were improved; and new crops enhanced agricultural productivity. Quiteño journalist and leading intellectual Juan Montalvo railed against the president's tyrannical clericalism. From his exile in Colombia, he rejoiced on hearing of the president's assassination in 1875, declaring: "My pen has killed him."

As the century turned, the Liberal President Eloy Alfaro managed to improve the lot of the indigenous peoples, modernize the legal code, and separate Church and state before an incensed pro-clerical mob tore him to pieces. His liberal reforms, however, mostly remained in place.

DEMOCRATIC LEADERS

Over the 20th century, nepotism, populism, and instability have characterized the political landscape. José María Velasco Ibarra, a populist firebrand who appealed to the poor and on one occasion cried, "Give me a balcony and I will be president," was elected to five presidential terms between 1934 and 1972. But he was toppled four times, last by the military that grabbed control of the new oil wealth.

The dictators were comparatively weak, however, and Ecuador in 1978 was the first Latin American country to restore democracy, soon after Spain. The center-left government of Jaime Roldós, elected the following year, launched massive literacy and housing programs. The government also increased workers' wages and encouraged the emergence of a politically articulate middle class, and of

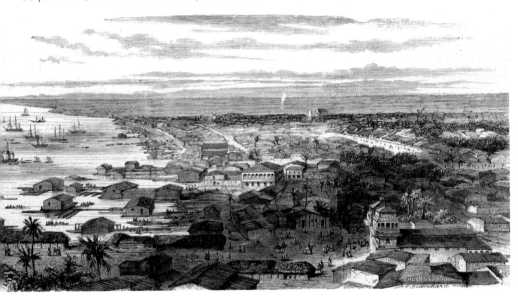

A bird's-eye view of Guayaquil port, 1868.

⊘ BOUNDARY CONFLICTS

Ecuador was originally more than double its present size, but Colombia and Peru have each taken generously from its territory over the years.

1822–29 Ecuador plays a central role in the border dispute between Peru and Gran Colombia. Conflict is eventually resolved by an 1829 treaty defining Ecuador's boundary along the pre-independence line between Quito and the Viceroyalty of Peru.

1941 Peru snatches almost half of Ecuador's territory in an invasion that is largely uncontested.

1942 Ecuador subsequently reneges on the Rio de Janeiro Protocol which imposes the new boundary, but has to accept that its Amazon territory includes only a small part of the river's headwaters. Several skirmishes break out over the following years.

1995 One of the most significant Ecuador–Peru border conflicts erupts, costing both sides hundreds of casualties and damaging Ecuador's economy. A ceasefire finally takes place, with Ecuador reluctantly accepting the border imposed in 1942.

1998 Leaders of Ecuador and Peru, both anxious for a real solution to border disputes, agree to submit their unresolved issues to arbitration by guarantor countries Brazil, Argentina, and Chile. The historic Acta de Brasília Peace Treaty is signed, the conflict zone demilitarized, and bi-national development plans put into place.

The Ecuadorian economy has expanded from its original bases of textiles, Panama hats, and cacao to include coffee, tourism, seafood and oil. Under the iron fist of the now defunct United Fruit Company, it also became one of the world's leading exporter of bananas.

mass-based organizations such as peasant co-operatives and labor unions. But an economic

human rights violations associated with the fight against the rebel movement. He overshadowed Ecuadorian politics until his death in 2008.

Elections in 1988 brought to power President Rodrigo Borja, a Social Democrat from Quito. He set an honest, competent political course: civil disturbances such as transport workers' strikes and student riots over price rises were handled leniently. Inflation fell, foreign debt was serviced regularly, and foreign investors continued to be attracted, both under Borja and under his successor, Sixto Durán Ballén

García Moreno, former president of Ecuador, is assassinated on the steps of the palace.

crisis eventually loomed as oil prices dropped and payments on foreign debt fell due, and for a while rumors of a military coup were rife.

In 1981, Roldós died in a plane crash. Vice-President Osvaldo Hurtado fulfilled his pledges to serve his full term, to continue Roldós's reforms, and to maintain civil liberties, despite the added difficulty of the great El Niño floods of late 1982, which ruined banana and rice crops and destroyed roads and railways. León Febres Cordero, a Conservative, won the 1984 elections. Febres Cordero oversaw sustained economic growth, but his rule was marred by charges of misuse of public funds, which he allegedly paid to an Israeli counter-insurgency adviser to help to dismantle a guerrilla movement, and

⊘ MORENO'S DE-CORREIZATION

President Lenín Moreno won the presidential election in 2017 with former President Rafael Correa's Alianza PAÍS party. The wheelchair-bound leader served as Correa's Vice President from 2007–13, before working for the UN. Once President, Moreno decided to roll back many of his predecessor's policies, effectively neutering Correa's lingering control. In a 2018 referendum, Ecuadoreans voted to approve restricting presidents to two terms in office and to establish a Council allowing President Moreno to hand-pick replacements for all judges and control authorities. This exacted a double blow by blocking Correa's future presidential bids and removing some of his allies.

of the Christian Social Party, who was elected in 1992. He was succeeded in 1996 by populist Abdalá Bucaram who set the stage for a decade of turmoil. Bucaram, a former mayor of Guayaquil nicknamed "El Loco" (the madman), introduced rigorous economic measures that caused steep price increases and those already living in poverty – the people he had promised to help – found themselves worse off. This, combined with his blatant corruption, caused a two-day strike in February 1997 which brought the country to a standstill. By the end of the second day, Congress conveniently found a clause in the constitution that enabled them to oust Bucaram

President Daniel Noboa at his inauguration in November 2023.

on grounds of mental incapacity. Confusion followed as both Vice-President Rosalia Arteaga and Fabián Alarcón, President of Congress, claimed the presidency. Finally, Congress officially voted in Alarcón as interim president.

Mismanagement and corruption continued, and reform was delayed until the new president, Jamil Mahuad, a Harvard-educated centrist, took office in August 1998. An economic slide was exacerbated by El Niño floods on the coast that destroyed crops of key agricultural exports.

With the price of oil collapsing, Mahuad's success in bringing about peace with Peru was overshadowed by his unpopular introduction of austere economic reforms to secure IMF loans and the collapse of the banking system still not completely resolved a decade later. At the end of 1999, Mahuad announced his plan to replace the sucre with the dollar. The aim was to curb the 60 percent inflation rate, bring down interest rates, and spur investment. Many sectors accepted the measure, but it incensed indigenous groups, who rallied together and marched to Quito in protest. On January 21, 2000, Mahuad was forced to flee to the US as thousands of indigenous protesters stormed the Congress Building with the help of junior military officers, including Colonel Lucio Gutiérrez. (In 2014 Mahuad was found guilty of embezzlement by the court in Ecuador and sentenced in absentia to 12 years in prison.) US threats of withdrawing financial aid pressured the military chief in command of the new junta to back down in a matter of hours.

Power passed to the vice-president, Gustavo Noboa, who faced the challenge of a radicalized and strong indigenous movement amid a general distrust of politicians, and the country's worst economic crisis in 70 years. He, however, presided over a transformation of Ecuador's economy, helped by declining inflation since dollarization and millions of dollars of foreign investment in oil exploration and production.

In late 2002, former coup leader Gutiérrez won the election, and soon secured IMF financing, but he lacked congressional support and became the third president in eight years to be toppled after inviting Bucaram home. He was

⊘ THE RECEDING PINK TIDE

Like much of Latin America once under the sway of the Pink Tide of Socialism, Ecuador's politics move increasingly to the right, incapable of sustaining socialist reforms under global financial duress. Only the Chavista government of Nicolás Maduro in Venezuela holds on, and with inflation running out of control there, it's hardly a good advertisement. In the summer of 2018, President Moreno withdrew Ecuador from ALBA, an intergovernmental trade bloc started by Cuba and Venezuela in 2004 and made up of a number of Latin and Caribbean nations. Moreno stated a desire to be independent of the specific views of certain nations.

In 2011 WikiLeaks published US documents questioning Correa's integrity, prompting both countries to expel each other's ambassadors. In 2012, tensions flared again as Ecuador granted immunity to WikiLeaks founder Julian Assange.

replaced by Alfredo Palacio, his vice-president, under whom relations with the US deteriorated, as he refused to go ahead with a free trade agreement with the US and expelled US oil company Occidental Petroleum. He was succeeded by Rafael Correa, whose political career began in a brief stint as Palacio's Finance Minister.

Correa won on a platform of radical constitutional reform and economic equality. A former economics lecturer, the popular leader aped the model of Hugo Chávez of Venezuela, with whom he shared many ideological ties. Correa won an unprecedented slew of elections as voters gave his party a majority in the constitutional assembly, approved a new charter giving the government greater control of the economy, and re-elected him to a second term in early elections in 2009. Attacks on the privileged were accompanied by harsh criticism, and indeed persecution, of the media and the breaking of diplomatic ties with Colombia in the wake of an unauthorized Colombian raid on a rebel camp inside Ecuador in March 2008.

Despite the political turmoil, Ecuador's economy experienced an annual average growth of 4.4 percent between 2006 and 2014 but fell thereafter due to declining global oil prices. Correa's agenda of massive government spending was credited with lifting more than 1 million people out of poverty, while spending on education increased eight-fold, health spending more than doubled and the minimum wage increased by 80 percent under his administration. Correa's program of reform, including the adoption of a new constitution in 2008, has not always been well received. The government's reforms of the water and land laws triggered indigenous protests in 2010, while 2015 saw widespread demonstrations against controversial new inheritance tax laws.

With the election of President Moreno in 2017 relations between the US and Ecuador initially

improved – in part by Moreno going back on his election promises and implementing neo-liberal policies – in the hope of stabilizing a fluctuating economy. Since then both Correa and Moreno have become enmired in corruption charges. Correa was accused of running a "criminal structure" and sentenced in absentia to eight years imprisonment in 2020, while Moreno is due to face charges of accepting bribes (alongside 37 others) for a contract on a hydro-electric plant. In the meantime, the center-right president Guillermo Lasso, elected in 2021, has

Bananas for sale in Guamote market.

struggled to make any progress, in part because political opponents were bent on removing him through impeachment, though with scant evidence. In response, he dissolved the national assembly in May 2023 and a snap general election was announced.

The run-up to the elections was marred by violence, including the assassination of one presidential candidate. In October, 35-year-old business heir Daniel Noboa became the country's youngest president. He has plenty to tackle: an ailing post-pandemic economy and cost of living crisis – which has prompted mass emigration – and rising crime, much of it drug-trafficking related. With elections due again in 2025, he has little time to make an impact.

Trans-Andean oil pipeline.

ECONOMY AND ENVIRONMENT

Ecuador has a difficult balancing act to perform if it is to conserve the environment while accelerating growth that has been fueled largely by the oil industry.

Agro-exporter Ecuador was transformed by the discovery of large petroleum reserves in the pristine Amazon rainforest of the Oriente by Texaco in 1968. The development of these oilfields spurred an economic boom in the 1970s – helped by a dramatic rise in world oil prices – but also resulted in profound damage to the rivers, rainforest, and the indigenous way of life. The government quadrupled its budget in three years, and public spending on social services was proportionally higher than in any other country in Latin America. Investments were made in education, health, and infrastructure that improved the lives of many Ecuadorians.

ORIENTE, THE OIL PROVINCE

While oil money was raked in in Quito, in the Amazon settlers, large oil corporations, and indigenous peoples competed for land and resources. Little thought was given to the potential impact on the environment, and the local population initially had no concept of ownership, allowing oil companies to build roads and drill in exchange for gifts.

Settlers were awarded plots of land if they were willing to "improve" it, which meant clearing it for agriculture or pasture. As their land was usurped by settlers, the indigenous peoples in the Lago Agrio area were forced to enter the new Ecuadorian capitalist society, often at the lowest social rung as laborers, domestic workers, or sex workers. Or they fled deeper into the rainforest, coming into conflict with other groups. Additionally, thousands of Colombian refugees entered from the north during wars with drug barons and rebel groups. Road construction continues, aiding the influx of settlers into remote regions and destroying the forest. However, settlers demand more roads as they provide access to basic healthcare and schools.

Shuar women protest against mining and oil concessions.

With the support of the environmental lobby in the 1980s, however, indigenous groups began to raise awareness in Ecuador and abroad through protests, putting pressure on the government to recognize their land rights, and for the oil companies to clean up their act. Initially, oil production was solely in the hands of US company Texaco, that dumped 16 billion gallons of highly poisonous wastewater in a swathe of the northeast Amazon from 1971 to 1992. In 2011 the US oil giant (now part of the Chevron Corporation) was fined over $8 billion by the Ecuadorian court for polluting the Amazon (see page 207). The sum was increased to $18.6 billion after the company refused to make a public apology.

OIL, AGRICULTURE, AND DEVELOPMENT

The oil industry provides crucial income but few of the steady jobs Ecuador so desperately needs. The boom years of the early 21st century provided some $30 billion in revenue, and before former president Rafael Correa refused to continue payments on a third of its foreign debt, Ecuador's debt levels were already among the lowest in Latin America. Oil accounted for more than 60 percent of Ecuador's exports at its peak price in July 2008, and it will remain a crucial source of foreign income in the foreseeable future.

Logging roads cut deep into the Chocó rainforest.

Pressured by some international shareholders, oil companies have begun to clean up their act. The development of rainforest is difficult to manage and the threat from companies who extract its resources for profit, illegally and legally, is almost constant. However, when done well, oil development is arguably less damaging than the rampant illegal logging, which governments have done little to stop. Exotic hardwoods are smuggled to Colombia, Peru, and the US. Wide tracts of rainforest on both sides of the Andes are being cleared at an annual rate among the highest in Latin America (around 300,000 hectares/750,000 acres each year). Both subsistence farmers trying to eke out a meager living, clearing land for grazing and planting, and large companies cutting down trees around Esmeraldas on the coast and in the Oriente to make way for a mono-culture of African palms, are primarily to blame. Agriculture accounts for 20 percent of foreign earnings, just behind petroleum in importance, and pesticides are used extensively to maximize production. The laws regulating pesticide use and residues on food are strict, but rarely enforced; most farmers have no training or protective equipment. The proper management of water is an important issue, too, and doubts about the country's reliability from a business perspective have slowed private foreign investment.

If managed well, eco-tourism has the potential to provide alternative incomes and can help protect the environment. Community-based tourism is also becoming more popular. High-quality lodges have sprung up in the Andean foothills northwest of Quito, all along the Andean chain, and in Oriente around places like Tena, and east of Coca and Lago Agrio. The most famous of these is Kapawi on the jungle border with Peru, which established milestones for co-operative management with local communities.

CLIMATE CHANGE

Since the early 1900s, annual rainfall has significantly decreased, and glaciers have retreated on average 300 meters (950ft). In 1995–6 electricity was rationed because the Paute hydroelectric plant that provides 65 percent of the country's electricity was dry due to lack of rain as well as deforestation, which causes soil to absorb water less efficiently. Recurring El Niño weather patterns, however, have caused periodic widespread flooding and destruction, driving up prices for the poor and saddling the government with infrastructure costs.

In an attempt to escape from the ridiculous amounts of money that used to be spent on importing subsidized diesel and gasoline, the Ecuadorian government decided to increase its reliance on hydropower. From only supplying about 40 percent of the country's electricity in 2013, hydro dams were producing 80 percent by 2021, and more constructions are planned. But beyond the obvious environmental damage of constructing dams, continuing reductions in rainfall means new investment is needed in other renewable forms of energy. Wind farms and solar farms are being planned for the southern Sierra.

NATIONAL PARKS

While protection on paper is better than nothing, much needs to be done to save Ecuador's hugely diverse ecology from destruction.

Ecuador's Ministry of the Environment currently manages and protects 71 protected areas that include 11 national parks. They cover 19 percent of the country, concentrated in the Galápagos, the northeast Oriente, and the eastern slopes of the Andes.

PRESERVING MANGROVE SWAMPS

The entrance fees to the most popular national parks (Galápagos, Cotopaxi, and Cotocachi-Cayapas) help subsidize some of the less visited and more threatened reserves. For instance, the Cayapas-Mataje and the Manglares-Churute reserves were created to protect a small portion of rapidly disappearing coastal mangroves. These provide vital breeding grounds for marine fish species, but have been destroyed for "shrimp-ranching."

THE VALUE OF UNTOUCHED FORESTS

Cloud forests were being cleared from the Andean central valley long before the Spanish conquered Ecuador in the first half of the 16th century, but the Andean eastern slope has never been cut because it is so wet, rugged, and inaccessible. However, as more roads encroach into the Oriente and colonists begin to fell the old-growth mahoganies and alders, protected areas such as Cayambe-Coca Ecological Reserve, Llanganates and Sangay national parks become important refuges for rare species such as the Andean spectacled bear, woolly mountain tapir, and Andean condor. The bi-national Parque Nacional Cordillera del Cóndor, which escaped deforestation and development because it was located along the disputed border with Peru, is also of cultural importance for the indigenous Shuar and Ashuar communities of Ecuador, and the Awajún and Wampis of Peru.

YASUNÍ NATIONAL PARK

Yasuní National Park in the Oriente is considered the most biologically diverse place in the world, where over 900 different species of trees have been identified in a single 2-hectare (5-acre) plot. Even with Unesco Biosphere Reserve status, however, the howler monkeys and jaguars of Yasuní still have to share their habitat with oil companies and aggressively colonizing groups. Conservationists are extremely wary of this experiment, since the nearby Cuyabeno Reserve lost its western half, and the area is now filled with colonists and oil wells. Encouragingly, a landmark national referendum in

Pelican in Parque Nacional Machalilla.

August 2023 resulted in 59 percent voting "to keep oil in the soil" and stop drilling in Yasuní, while 68 percent voted to stop mining in the Chocó Andino area.

ENVIRONMENTAL CHALLENGES

Mediating land-use conflicts presents a significant challenge to the environmental protection offices. Environmentally damaging activities such as timber harvesting, grazing, mining, and oil production are permitted by other government agencies in the protected areas, or are carried out illegally. Cynics often refer to Ecuadorian protected areas as "paper parks" since essential environmental policing is still lacking, but it is still commendable that a country with limited resources has had the foresight to sketch out so many natural areas that are worth saving for the future.

THE ECUADORIANS

The people of Ecuador inhabit a relatively small land, but they are as diverse as the landscape with many of mixed heritage.

Like other Andean countries, Ecuadorian society reflects divisions that can be traced back to the Spanish conquest of the early 16th century. But the people have been shaped as much by Ecuador's wild geography as its history: the racial make-up, accent, temperament, and outlook of Ecuadorians is radically different on the coast, in the Sierra, and in the jungle.

Until the discovery of oil in the early 1970s prompted an urban explosion, Ecuador was an almost completely rural society. To a large extent it still is: although more than two-thirds of the population live in towns or cities, how they behave and think is closely linked to their relationship with the land, and modern urban life conserves elements of traditional rural customs.

IMAGES FROM THE COUNTRYSIDE

The typical *campesino* (peasant) of the Sierra works hard to obtain a meager living from rocky, volcanic soil. Andean families live in a harsh environment, where bare mountains descend into shelving ravines and gentle valleys. The land is rarely flat, except on the valley bottom, which generally belongs to the rich landowners. The *campesino* must use ingenuity to terrace and cultivate the steep mountainsides on slopes with up to 60-degree angles, where the topsoil is easily washed away by rain.

In harmony with this environment, the typical *serrano* (mountain-dweller) tends to be tough, patient, frugal, and resigned to the difficulties of life. Yet *serranos* can be vivacious when their imaginations are fired. Andean music, with its plaintive tones, melodic pipes, and sorrowful lyrics, expresses the *serrano* temperament.

The agriculturalists of the Costa live in contact with the abundant nature of the green lowlands,

Herding alpacas near Chugchilán, Cotopaxi Province.

where the warm climate and fertile soil make daily living easier. Like their environment, the *costeños* (coast-dwellers) tend to be easygoing and exuberant, but also quick-tempered, and unconcerned about what tomorrow may bring.

The Oriente is a case apart; it represents scarcely 4 percent of the population. Indigenous peoples have lived there for centuries in relative isolation, and their ways of being are very different from those of the people of the Sierra, who have suffered long years of discrimination. Light-hearted and self-confident, they are accustomed to a generous natural environment and a relatively free lifestyle. This situation began to change with the incursion of timber and oil companies that are endangering their environment, as well as encroaching colonization, which has brought about an accelerated process of assimilation.

Natural differences between the regions have been accentuated by slow, hazardous transport and difficult communications. But within each region, society is characterized by diverse racial and ethnic groups.

TRADITIONAL ANDEAN SOCIETY

The rigid social order that reigned in the Sierra from colonial times until the land reform of 1964 is the basis on which modern society was built. Cut off by the difficult mountain passes and under the strong influence of the Catholic Church, Andean elite society engendered a world of traditional values centered around the family.

The nucleus of rural life was the hacienda, or estate. These large properties were the main pole of production. Their owners were descendants of the Spanish *conquistadores* and later immigrants who controlled the country's economy and politics. They allowed indigenous families a small plot of land for their own subsistence in exchange for

Indígenas, Guamote.

Tending the land near Quilotoa.

⊘ CONFLICTING VALUES

The typical Spanish settler in the Sierra considered the act of work to be degrading, whereas the indigenous population valued it and disapproved of laziness. This was a further element that exacerbated racial tension, since the Spaniard expected the local populace to work for him, but then despised him for doing so.

These perceptions – Spanish intolerance and indigenous incomprehension – still survive in diluted forms today, particularly within the realm of public service. It is this lack of mutual understanding that is largely to blame for the fundamental disunity which is so characteristic of Ecuadorian society.

labor. Mestizos (of indigenous and Hispanic origin) were employed as managers, stewards, or clerks. The power they wielded over those under their authority fueled racial animosity between indigenous and mestizo populations, generally.

The traditional social order of the Sierra began to disintegrate in the 1960s with the introduction of agrarian reform. In the face of rapid population growth and increasing unrest among the peasants, the authorities passed legislation to break up the larger estates and hand over uncultivated land to the peasants.

FRONTIER SETTLEMENTS

While the Sierra has mainly produced food for local consumption, the Costa has been developed over the past 100 years for exporting cash crops. Cocoa, bananas and, more recently, cultivated shrimp have each had their boom period.

Landless peasants from the Sierra traveled to the coast, either in search of work on the plantations there or on a piece of undeveloped land to till and develop for their own use. Thus, in the space of a century, the inhabitants of the Costa changed from being a small fraction to slightly more than half of the total population.

The owners of the coastal haciendas tended to be more business-minded and enterprising than

the same time, those peasants who had been unable to obtain land under the agrarian reform of 1964 had to leave the haciendas, and many of them sought work in the towns.

In just two decades, a quarter of Ecuador's population uprooted from a lifetime of rural living to the noise and pace of towns and cities, causing an urban explosion that the country was unable to support. Housing, and water and electricity supplies, could not possibly keep up with the huge increase in demand. Neither were there enough jobs – a situation, admittedly, exac-

Farmer and his family, Cañar Province.

Washing clothes in the street, Ambato.

their *serrano* counterparts, and generally did not mind dirtying their hands alongside their wage-earning farmhands. This helped to create a more liberal and egalitarian society, which was accelerated by greater contact with the outside world via the seaports. The ports in turn have allowed *costeños* to benefit more from international trade.

Today the Ecuadorian Costa has a Caribbean flavor, which has led to Guayaquil being called "the last port of the Caribbean."

THE URBAN EXPLOSION

In the 1970s, following the discovery of petroleum deposits in the Oriente, Ecuador began to export oil, which meant more jobs and the promise of new opportunities in the cities. At

erbated by the foreign debt crisis of the 1980s.

With unemployment rising, the new urban population had few places to turn, except to the streets to scrape together a living by their wits. Vendors of trinkets, clothes, or electrical goods of doubtful origin throng intersections, competing for the attention of passers-by. And on street corners, young kids sell newspapers, shine shoes, or urge you to buy chewing gum in the hope of earning their daily meal.

Today, under half the workforce has a steady full-time job; over two thirds are in the informal sector, including street vendors and self-employed craftspeople, and roughly one in twenty is unemployed. Over 2 million households are short of housing space and among the existing houses, around a third lack running water, electricity, or sewage facilities.

Meanwhile, the well-to-do find all the comforts of modern life in smart apartment blocks protected by armed guards. Shopping precincts display a broad variety of goods, and chauffeur-driven limos wait at the doors of luxury restaurants.

These contrasts are an expression of the erratic modernization of Ecuador, which has radically changed living and working conditions in scarcely three decades, without being able to answer the basic needs of many of its popula-

Fisherman's catch in Puerto López.

tion. The most flagrant social contradictions are to be found in Guayaquil, center of the nation's wealth, which is surrounded by vast slum areas, the scene of abject poverty and high crime.

CHRONIC POVERTY

It is ironic that in Ecuador, a country rich in natural resources with its fertile valleys, abundant marine life, extensive forests, and reserves of oil and gold, most people face a daily struggle to scrape together the bare necessities. Since the US dollar replaced the sucre as Ecuador's currency in 2000, poverty rates have declined and are currently around 23–25 percent, but numbers remain substantially higher in rural areas than in the cities, especially among indigenous

communities, and single female-headed households. However, the combined effects of the fallout from the Covid-19 pandemic, climate change, and Russia's invasion of Ukraine – which impacted global food prices – have resulted in rising costs, while wages have stagnated and more people are being employed for fewer hours. As Ecuador produces most of its own food, relatively few families are unable to get a square meal each day, and though most do have a roof of some kind over their heads, increasing numbers of households are struggling to cover other basic needs, including healthcare.

Hardship is not reserved to the towns. In rural areas, those who became small landowners cannot keep up with production costs, which rise faster than the price they receive for their crops. Small farmers also struggle to get cheap credit or adequate technical help. And once the paternalistic relations of the hacienda disappeared, the lack of social services became acute.

Successive governments have implemented social welfare programs in healthcare, aid to small farmers, food distribution, cash transfers, cheap housing, childcare, employment, and other support, but there are never enough resources.

INDIGENOUS GROUPS

The visitor to Ecuador is readily seduced by the colorful costumes and skillful handicrafts of the indigenous population: the women's embroidered blouses, the ponchos, the woven belts. But these are just the outward embodiment of a whole culture, an identity and a long history of resistance to assimilation by colonial society.

In the most recent census in 2022, about 7 percent of the population self-identified as indigenous. There are 13 different indigenous groups in Ecuador, each of which considers itself a distinct nationality, with its own language and culture. The most numerous are the Quichua, who live mainly in the Sierra and are related to the Quechuas of Peru and Bolivia.

Language is an essential component of identity, and indigenous languages are losing ground in part through modern schooling. Although the country has a thriving Intercultural Bilingual Education system at primary level, once students move to secondary school, Spanish tends to take over.

However, ethnicity in Ecuador is, to some degree, fluid. To an extent, over a generation or two, people can change their ethnic identity. An indigenous family can move to Quito, send their children to school dressed in Western-style clothes, and the children may self-identify as mestizo. But these same children can return to their parents' community and identify themselves as *indígenas* should they so choose.

Some Ecuadorian indigenous groups have been residents of the land for centuries, while others are descendants of people (called *mitmakuna*) who were moved around the Andes by the Incas: loyal Inca Quichua-speakers who

Many *indígenas* have defied attempts to integrate them into mestizo society, manifesting a tacit resistance to the ill-treatment and discrimination practiced against them. The survival of indigenous culture and identity despite the odds is witness to their endurance.

The Quichuas and the indigenous Amazonians in the Oriente have retained their own identities more than most. They lived for centuries in almost complete isolation from the rest of the world, apart from a few missions that were established there. But when oil companies began

Tsáchila man from the Western Lowlands.

Modern footwear meets traditional embroidery.

were sent to recently conquered areas to serve as a teaching and garrison population, and people who were moved far from their homelands as a punishment for resistance to Inca rule.

Racism is deeply ingrained in Ecuadorian society, despite changing laws and policies from the 2010s, which academics have identified as a "turn towards anti-racism" across Latin America. Indigenous people who become "white" by leaving aside their traditional dress, language, and identity are often those who show the most virulently racist attitudes. "Stupid Indian" or "dirty Indian" are typical epithets used about people who for years were excluded from public education, while their cultural heritage and language were treated with disdain.

⊙ LEGACY OF SLAVERY

The origin of Ecuador's black population goes back to the slave trade. Historians believe that a Spanish frigate loaded with enslaved Africans was shipwrecked off the northern coast of Ecuador around the middle of the 17th century, and that the Africans who survived the wreck spread gradually across the province of Esmeraldas, living practically in isolation there for many years. The black population of the Chota Valley, on the other hand, are the descendants of people who were brought to Ecuador to work on the sugarcane plantations at the height of the slave trade, and who were given their freedom when slavery was finally abolished in the region in 1851.

to dig pipelines and build roads into the region, settlers soon followed, and many of the indigenous people with whom they came into contact were rapidly assimilated into modern society.

Recently, with international campaigning for protection of the Amazonian forest, indigenous groups who are still seeking to preserve their environment and lifestyle have found a worldwide audience for their claims, which gives them greater leverage with governments. In the late 1990s CONAIE (Confederación de Nacionalidades Indígenas del Ecuador) gathered steam in its

Afro-Ecuadorian from Bahía de Caráquez on the Pacific coast.

fight for economic reform and has become the most cohesive and influential indigenous organization in South America. The storming of the Congressional Building by thousands of indigenous protestors in January 2000 and the subsequent overthrow of President Jamil Mahuad and widespread protests in 2012 and 2015 demonstrated the growing influence that these groups are finally having on national politics. With their land often in remote resource-rich areas liable to becoming primary targets for development, indigenous groups are increasingly at the forefront of Ecuadorian domestic policy. At the same time, however, their leaders are also increasingly targets of violence by both illegal settlers, and state-sanctioned mining and petroleum industries. Two indigenous leaders – Shuar leader José Tendetza and Cofan leader Eduardo Mendúa – were assassinated in 2022 and 2023 respectively, for standing up for their people's land rights.

AFRO-ECUADORIANS

Afro-Ecuadorians make up around 7 percent of the population. Many coastal people are descended from enslaved Africans, yet it took until 1998 for Afro-Ecuadorians to be recognised as a distinctive ethnic group. In two areas of the country, the warm Chota Valley in the mountainous province of Imbabura, and the northwestern province of Esmeraldas, the population is predominantly black. In both areas there is a strong African cultural heritage, which has mixed with indigenous culture. The people of the Chota Valley, for example, play the plaintive local music of the Sierra on African-type instruments, while the Awa from north of Esmeraldas have adopted the marimba, which is of West African origin.

There are also significant black populations in Guayaquil and Ibarra. Like many minority populations, Afro-Ecuadorians have faced discrimination but have formed strong organisations. The Confederación Nacional Afroecuatoriana (CNA) and the National Coordinator of Black Women (CONAMUNE) have been particularly active. In 2019 Dra Diana Salazar became the first black female Attorney General in Ecuador, and has won international praise for her fight against corruption.

IMMIGRANT GROUPS

Early sizeable migrant groups included the Lebanese, who came to Ecuador at the beginning of the 20th century and have accumulated considerable economic and political power. After 2000, an influx of Colombians arrived from the north, fleeing the escalation of armed conflict. Haitians and Cubans arrived during 2008 and 2016, encouraged by Correa's free movement policy. Since 2017, immigration has been characterized by increasing numbers of Venezuelans – over 500,000 according to 2022 figures.

RELIGIOUS FERVOR

Since the arrival of the early missionaries, Ecuador has been under the strong influence of the Catholic Church. The word of the local priest or bishop still holds great weight, especially in the rural Sierra. However, since the end of the 19th century, when the anticlerical liberal movement of the Costa took power, state and Church have been separated. In state schools, the curriculum does not include religion.

Since the election of Pope Francis in particular, the Catholic Church in Latin America has reaffirmed its intention to work on behalf of the poor. Some Catholic groups have taken this attitude further and are promoting political organization among the rural and urban slum populations as a means of seeking solutions to their grave problems.

Meanwhile, Protestant groups are engaged in active evangelization, particularly among the indigenous population. Their success is due partly to the funding they provide for development projects and infrastructure, but also to the Protestant work ethic, which has been favorably received in many communities, as it has much in common with the indigenous belief in the dignity of labor. For several Protestant sects, however, the priority is to counteract the work of progressive sectors of the Catholic Church.

COMMUNITY LIFE

Indigenous peoples advocate communal ownership of land, a concept that often comes into conflict with Ecuadorian tenancy laws. Another facet of the community spirit is the *minga* – a collective work effort inherited from Inca times via the hacienda system (see page 68).

Ecuadorians are generally glad to share whatever they have with family and friends, whether there is abundance or scarcity. The kind of individualism typical in northern countries, such as wanting to live alone, is considered a strange and antisocial aberration. But this sense of community operates only within the immediate group of family and acquaintances; in the cement jungle of the cities, the rule is everyone for themselves.

THE FAMILY UNIT

Many middle-class families in Ecuador are typical of Latin countries: they value strong family ties and the close supervision of womenfolk, while men tend to take their sexual freedom for granted, priding themselves on their gallantry and their *machismo*. Among the poorer urban classes, especially those in the Costa, family relations are often far more informal, and it is not unusual for a man to have several families with different women, with whom he lives in turn, rarely contributing much to their upkeep. Young indigenous couples often have a "trial marriage" before formalizing their relationship with wedding vows.

THE STATUS OF WOMEN

Although Ecuador was the first country in South America to grant women the right to vote, it has

Holy Week (Semana Santa) Passion Play, Otavalo.

been one of the slowest to embrace the principle of equality of the sexes in the workplace and at home. However, attitudes are beginning to shift. In 1989 a law prohibiting all forms of discrimination against women was introduced, and in 1995 an inter-American law against violence to women was written.

Another legal breakthrough has been the provision of free legal assistance to women when proceeding with charges of violence against them and the adoption of the amended Penal Code in 2014 which clearly stipulates types of

Teenagers in Puyo.

punishable violence against women and family members. However, domestic violence continues to occur at an alarming rate. In 2021, emergency services received around 290 calls daily from women reporting domestic violence, totalling well over 100,000 calls nationally over the twelve-month period, with Guayas province recording the highest numbers.

The number of women's organizations working toward making the laws effective in practice is increasing. Notably, there has been active participation of indigenous women in promoting such issues in the Sierra. The migration of more men than women from the Sierra to urban areas has led to indigenous women taking on new responsibilities in their communities.

Organizations are focusing on providing education and healthcare for women. In 2018 the government passed a new law to prevent and eradicate gender violence, based on this citizen participation.

While more and more women are economically active, they tend to work longer hours and receive less pay than their male counterparts – as elsewhere in the world – while still shouldering most of the domestic burden. They have entered most fields, although you are unlikely to see a female bus driver or welder. In 2021 women made up 12 percent of the police force. Although numbers are relatively low, slightly more women than men study at university level, though more women tend to drop out.

Despite ingrained attitudes about traditional gender roles in Ecuadorian society, women are making inroads into national politics. The first female vice-president of Ecuador, Rosalia Arteaga, was elected in 1996. In a decisively pro-woman stance, President Moreno named eight women to his first cabinet, including María Alejandra Vicuña as Vice President. Indigenous women are also gaining a political voice, both within and outside the indigenous movement. Tránsito Amaguaña, who died at the grand age of 99 in 2009, pioneered resistance and organization of agricultural workers in the Sierra.

URBAN YOUTH

Lifestyles in urban Ecuador are rapidly modernizing and changing the face of Ecuadorian culture. A middle-class teenager from Quito or Guayaquil probably identifies more with peers from the US than with those in an isolated mountain village. These young people have access to cable TV, internet, and MP3s. Western rock and pop are often more popular than traditional Latin music. Shopping malls are popular meeting places for teenagers before a night out at one of the modern multi-screen cinemas.

The best jobs for young professionals are often with foreign companies. As a result, night schools are as full as the *discotecas*, with students studying English and computer programming. As Ecuadorian yuppies enjoy their symbols of success – cell phones, credit cards, espresso coffees, and copies of *Newsweek* – they are worlds away from the rural *campesino* who still earns about $100 a week.

Stallholder at the Plaza de Ponchos in Otavalo market.

THE BRIGHT COLORS OF EVERYDAY WEAR

The distinctive clothes of Ecuador's indigenous peoples are not just worn on holy days and holidays, but can be seen in any market or village street.

The diversity of indigenous dress in Ecuador is witness to the strong sense of identity which the various groups have retained throughout the centuries. Some of the clothes that the *indígenas* wear so proudly today are in fact adaptations of the 16th-century Spanish-style costumes that were once a kind of uniform, indicating which hacienda they belonged to.

INCA INSPIRATION

Some items go back much further: it is said that the indigo and black clothing of the Saraguro people is worn as a sign of perpetual mourning for the Inca Atahualpa, killed in 1533 at the beginning of the Spanish conquest. Hats, too, date back to before the colonial period. Even the Panama is an adaptation of the headgear worn by the Manabí people at the time of the conquest. Fragments of *ikat* tie-dyed textiles from the pre-Hispanic period have also been found.

Traveling around the many markets in Ecuador, you are bound to notice the wide variety of colors and styles of shawls, ponchos, and *macanas*, the ubiquitous carrying cloths which are used to carry various items from kindling to babies.

A Cañari woman wearing a blue-trimmed white bowler hat.

The multi-colored clothing of women in Alausí, Chimborazo province, waiting for their turn with the bank teller.

Otavalo women traditionally bind their long hair with brightly colored ribbons called cintas.

The women of Otavalo wear intricately embroidered cotton blouses, hand-spun shirts, and shoulder-wraps, with gold beaded necklaces. Their teeth are often capped with gold.

Colors to dye for

The rich, vibrant colors of the ponchos, shawls, and scarves are the most striking thing about the dress of indigenous Ecuadorians.

Many of the shades come from natural dyes: the deep indigo blue worn by the Saraguro comes from the Indigofera, a tropical bean-producing plant; and the rich red of the scarves and wraps worn by *indígenas* of Salasaca is produced from cochineal, which is extracted from the crushed bodies of female insects *(Dactylopius coccus)* which live on the Opuntia cactus. *Ikat* textiles – made into ponchos, shawls, and belts – are also richly colored. They are created by a process of tying and dyeing before the garment is woven.

The indigo-dyed cotton shawls are called *paños*, or macanas, which are made in towns like Gualaceo, and are the best known of the *ikat* products. These shawls have macramé fringes which are an art form in themselves, as they can take many months to make. The process of making *ikat* textiles is so complicated that the number of practitioners of the craft dwindled almost into non-existence, but is today experiencing a slight revival.

Preparing dyes for fabrics.

Musician in traditional dress at Christmas celebrations in Cuenca.

Woman selling shigra bags at Guamote market. Shigras are brightly colored bags made of agave fiber, which are made by hand and only found in the central Sierra region and nowhere else in the Andes.

Shepherdess and her flock, Saquisilí market.

LIFE AND LORE IN THE SIERRA

Ancient values, traditional healers, and Christian festivals are all part of life in the Sierra, an area that has seen little change for hundreds of years.

Every valley of the Ecuadorian highlands is populated by distinct indigenous groups, some descendants of original Ecuadorian groups, others descendants of the Incas or of people imported by the Incas from other areas of the country.

Europeans and Ecuadorian *indígenas* have been in contact for nearly 500 years, with the former influencing the lives of the latter in profound ways. Language, clothing, food, housing, and religion all have a European imprint. The influence has also worked the other way round: for example, more than half the food crops consumed in the world today were domesticated in the Americas before the arrival of Europeans. Most significant are maize and potatoes, which were the economic foundation of the Inca Empire.

DISTINCTIVE SUBCULTURES

Indigenous people still retain a number of customs of pre-Hispanic origin. Although the various groups have distinctive subcultures, they share a number of traits. Some might argue that a poor, evangelical Protestant family in Chimborazo that ekes out a living on half an acre of bad land has nothing in common with a wealthy Catholic weaving family in Otavalo that has just finished the construction of a four-story apartment building in town. Yet both families consider themselves *indígenas*, both wear a distinctive dress that identifies them as members of a particular ethnic group, and both families may speak Quichua inside their homes.

Quichua or Runa Shimi (The People's Tongue) is part of the Quechua language family. There are several Quechua languages spoken today in Peru, and two or three different Quichua dialects spoken in Ecuador. This means that *indígenas* from different regions of Ecuador do not necessarily

Quilotoa woman.

understand each other. The origins of Quechua are unknown, but we do know that the Chinchay, a trading group on the coast of Peru, spoke it around the time of Christ. The Incas adopted Quechua from the Chinchay and spread it throughout the Andes as they expanded their empire in the 14th and 15th centuries. Then the church employed Quichua as a lingua franca to help them Christianize the *indígenas*, who resisted Spanish.

The Quechua language family is growing; more people speak it now than in Inca times, including in Ecuador. Organisations like Tinkunakuy (www.facebook.com/tinkunakuy), in Quito, have been teaching Quechua languages, culture and cosmology since 2004. Today most *indígenas* are bilingual in Quichua and Spanish, but some older people, especially in remote communities, speak Quichua only.

Despite efforts, no standard version of Quichua or Quechua spelling has yet been set. Various alphabets have been devised over the centuries, and this accounts for inconsistencies in spelling. The Quichua word for baby, for example, can be spelled *wawa*, *guagua*, or *huahua*.

COOPERATIVE VALUES

If there is a core value in indigenous society it is reciprocity, and naturally there are Quichua

Shaman ritual near Cotacachi.

words that express this. One such word is *minga*, a collective work effort, which operates in various ways. In community *minga* the leaders organize an effort to repair the roads, or clean the irrigation channels, and every family must furnish several workers. If they fail to show up, some communities levy a fine.

Then there is a private *minga*. If a family needs to roof a house, for example, they invite the neighbors to a roofing *minga*, supplying copious quantities of food and *chicha* (a local beer made from corn and manioc or *yuca*) for the workers, and people come willingly because they know they will need help themselves one day.

In the same way, *compadres* (two couples who are ritual kin because they are godparents to one another's children) also know they can call upon each other for help, anything from a loan of money to working in the kitchen at a fiesta.

Before the Spanish conquest, money did not exist in indigenous societies. Items were bartered or labor was traded. Under the Incas, people paid their taxes in the form of labor (*mita*) or goods, and in return were taken care of with food from central storehouses in times of famine. In many places, reciprocity still means the exchange of goods or services rather than money. It is useful, as a tourist, to bear this in mind: for example, giving people photographs is much better than paying them to let you take their picture. However, this is not always applicable in public places such as markets, where you're likely to draw a huge crowd. Sharing food or gifts of food is culturally appropriate in most situations.

SACRED MOUNTAINS

Indígenas throughout the Andes have worshiped mountains for millennia. In Ecuador, mountains are seen as male or female individuals, inhabited by powerful spirits. Mountains are also believed to control the rain and therefore the fertility and well-being of the entire region. The highest peak in any area was considered to be a *waka* (*huaca*) or sacred spot by the Incas. The Spanish decided to construct Catholic shrines over Inca sacred places, which is why you will see so many isolated chapels on hilltops.

Chimborazo, in the western cordillera of central Ecuador, is the highest mountain in the country, an enormous snow-cap that looms over the province like a giant ice cream. It is known as Taita (Father)

Chimborazo, while slightly to the north and in the eastern cordillera is Mama Tungurahua. Lesser peaks in the region are also seen as male and female pairs. Offerings such as guinea pigs, *trago* (a fierce sugarcane liquor), or plants are sometimes made to the mountains to propitiate them.

In Imbabura province, Mama Cotacachi reigns to the west of Otavalo while Taita Imbabura dominates the east. When Cotacachi's peak is snow-capped the *indígenas* say it is because Taita Imbabura visited her during the night. Needless to say, this encounter resulted in a

were the chosen ones. The ritual was considered a great honor.

SHAMANISM AND HEALING

Virtually every Ecuadorian community has a man or woman who knows the healing properties of various plants, or who can diagnose and cure by correcting spiritual imbalances or undoing spells. Healers are known by various Spanish names: *curanderos* (curers), *brujos* (witches), or *hechiceros* (sorcerers, witches). In Quichua, traditional healers are called *yachaj mamas* or *yachaj*

Tilling the earth, Chimborazo Province.

baby, Urcu (Mountain) Mojanda, which lies just to the south of Otavalo. The connection of mountains with fertility is obvious here, and many *indígenas* carry it even further. When, for example, people who live on the flanks of Imbabura plant crops they first ask Taita Imbabura to give them an abundant harvest. And when it rains in the region people say that Taita Imbabura is peeing on the valley below. If the mountains send the rain, Mother Earth (Allpa Mama or Pacha Mama) feeds the people by producing crops. It is customary to throw the last few drops of an alcoholic drink on the ground as an offering to her.

It was not uncommon for the Incas to sacrifice humans on the mountain tops, most often teenage girls who were told from a young age they

taitas (knowledgeable mothers or fathers). There are also midwives, who are known as *parteras*. The details of healing vary among the different ethnic groups, but in the Sierra people might go to a local healer for a number of reasons: because they have intestinal parasites, or because they believe an envious neighbor has cast a spell on them (*envidia*), or because they are looking for success in love or business. In addition, many people in the highlands have combined the Quichua belief in an inner and outer body, which must be kept in balance, with the medieval European belief in humoral medicine. This ancient tradition held that the body was composed of four humors: yellow bile, black bile, phlegm, and blood, whose relationships determined a person's disposition and health.

Today people believe that such illnesses as infant diarrhea occur because the baby has had a fright, which caused the inner and outer bodies to become unbalanced. If the inner body actually flees, then death can result, so the healer performs a ceremony known as "calling the soul" to bring back the baby's inner body. Bodies can also become diseased because of bad air (wayrashka in Quichua), known as mal aire in Spanish. Mal aire gave us our word malaria, because people initially believed that the disease came

used in healing and religious rituals throughout the Americas.

While most communities have their own healers, several areas are famous for their curanderos. People in the Sierra believe that the Shuar people have special healing powers, as do the Tsáchila of Santo Domingo de los Tsáchilas (colloquially known as colorados because men dye their hair red) west of the Andes. The healers of Ilumán, outside Otavalo, are also famous, and people come from all over the highlands to be treated by them.

These healers rely on centuries of knowledge

Tsáchila man with dyed red hair.

Corpus Christi parade in Pujilí.

from swamp vapors rather than from the bites of mosquitoes that lived in the swamps.

Calling the soul involves a cleansing, in which the patient's body is rubbed with a raw egg. The egg is shaken, and the sounds it makes indicate that the bad air is being absorbed. After the cleansing a child is sent to hide the eggs in the fields nearby. Calling the soul also includes prayers in Quichua to God the Father, Son, and Holy Spirit, the Virgin Mary and the saints. The healer tells the patient's heart to rise up (that is, to come back), passes alcohol to all present, and smokes cigarettes, blowing the smoke on the patient. Tobacco has long been used by indigenous groups for healing. There are many early Spanish accounts of its use among the Maya, and it is still

passed down from their ancestors. In ayahuasca rituals, a psychotropic plant is given to the patient, allowing the shaman to enter the sick person's body, find the illness, and cure it. These medicine men are well-respected members of their communities – the Cofan are renowned practitioners – and are given credit for saving many indigenous communities from death. The practice is making a comeback as Ecuadorians and international tourists frustrated with modern medicines look for alternative methods of treating disease and mental anguish.

A CALENDAR FULL OF FIESTAS

Latin America's reputation for partying and festivities has a long history. In pre-Hispanic times community fiestas were organized around the agricultural and solar cycle. After the Spanish conquest, the Church cleverly turned many traditional indigenous religious celebrations into Catholic feast days on the grounds that people were going to celebrate anyway, so they might as well observe a Christian occasion. Heavy drinking of *chicha* (local beer made from maize or other cereals) is associated with nearly all Andean festivals, despite the Catholic Church's efforts to phase it out.

While a number of civic festivals are observed throughout the year in Ecuador, the most inter-

back with a water balloon or to have a bucket of water dumped on your head in a chilly mountain village. Ambato, however, was the first to outlaw water-throwing – Quito and other places have attempted to stop the practice more recently – and has a fiesta of fruit and flowers that includes street dances and folkloric events. Hotels fill up early, but Ambato is easily reachable from Baños by bus, so it's possible to make a day trip out of it.

Holy Week (Semana Santa, the week before Easter) begins with Palm Sunday (Domingo de

Celebrating Holy Week (Semana Santa) in Quito.

esting fiestas by far are the traditional celebrations in the country. These mainly occur in the spring and summer, especially after the harvest and during the dry season. Every community has its own ritual calendar, so you might at any time of the year wander into a town in the middle of a fiesta in honor of its patron saint. However, here are a few of the major Sierra fiestas that are well worth catching:

Carnival (February or March) is held during the week before Lent begins on Ash Wednesday. *Carnaval* is a transplant from Europe, and represents a last fling before the austerity of Lent. Carnival in Ecuador is not like the one in Rio. In the Sierra the main activity is throwing water, and it is definitely not fun to be hit in the

Ramos). Throughout Ecuador people buy palm fronds in the market, weave them into different shapes and take them to church. Four days later, on Maundy Thursday, families visit the cemetery and bring food and drink for the dead in an observance similar to that of the Day of the Dead (see page 74).

In Quito on Good Friday there is an enormous, spectacular procession through the streets of the city, complete with flagellants, men dragging huge wooden crosses, and penitents dressed in what look rather like purple Ku Klux Klan outfits. There are also impressive Good Friday processions, with costumed penitents in such Chimborazo towns as Yaruquíes, Tixán, Chambo, and Chunchi.

Corpus Christi, in honor of the Eucharist, is a movable feast, held on the Thursday after Trinity Sunday, usually late May or early June. It is a major fiesta in the central Sierra, especially in Cotopaxi and Tungurahua provinces, but it is celebrated in many places, including some communities in Chimborazo province, in Cuenca, and in Saraguro, Loja province. Dancers with ornate headdresses and spectacularly embroidered costumes are now found only in such communities as Pujilí, Cotopaxi, and San Antonio de Píllaro, Tungurahua. In Salasaca, the *indígenas* wear plaster masks, bright ribbons and feathers on their hats, and dance from Salasaca to the nearby town of Pelileo. In Cuenca, celebrations include tiny paper hot-air balloons, fireworks, and special sweets.

The winter solstice, Inti Raymi, celebrated on June 21, was once a major event in the Inca festival calendar. In the Cuzco area, south of the equator, the winter solstice is the shortest day and longest night of the year. Closer to the equator, the differences in the length of the day and night are less dramatic, but astute indig-

Marching band, Plaza San Blas, Cuenca.

⊘ RITUAL BATTLES

Also connected with the festival of San Juan is a ritual battle that involves rock-throwing, and takes place at the chapel of San Juan. The chapel is located on the west side of the Pan-American Highway, away from the town proper. Until the 1960s people were sometimes killed during these fights, and there are still some nasty injuries sustained. The point of spilling blood seems to be a payment or sacrifice to Mother Earth (Pacha Mama), in gratitude for the corn harvest.

Similar ritual battles (called *tinku*), fought with rocks and fists, still occur in the highlands of Peru and Bolivia, with corresponding casualties.

enous astronomers still recognized them.

Today, **Saint John the Baptist** (San Juan Bautista, June 24) is the major fiesta in the Otavalo Valley and probably replaced an ancient, pre-Inca solstice festival.

Among the Otavaleños, San Juan is a male fiesta lasting the better part of a week. On the night of the 23rd, the male vespers (la víspera) dress up in costumes. The dancing begins after dark both in Otavalo and in the outlying towns.

The variety and ingenuity of the costumes is a sight to see, from Batman, Kalimán, and Native Americans with feathered headdresses, to Mexicans with giant sombreros, women, and soldiers. Some *indígenas* even parody gringos by wearing blond wigs, down jackets, jeans and

Commonly used for transportation in tropical areas, open-sided buses called chivas play a big role in Quito's fiesta, where they parade through the city day and night, with bands playing on the roof.

running shoes, and carrying backpacks. The dancing goes on each night for a week, with groups of musicians and dancers moving from house to house and dancing (actually stomping) in a circle, with sudden reversals of direction which may represent the movement of the sun.

Saints Peter and Paul (San Pedro y San Pablo, June 29) is a major fiesta that takes place in Imbabura province, and in many towns and villages the San Juan and San Pedro y Pablo festivities run together.

On the night of June 28 bonfires are lit in the streets throughout the province. This seems to be a combination of indigenous and Spanish customs. Young women who want to have a child are supposed to leap over the fires. San Pedro is especially important in Cotacachi, where there are also ritual fights, and in Cayambe. While San Juan is important to the Otavaleños, San Pedro is the big event for the other main ethnic group in Imbabura, the people who live on the east side of the mountain in the communities of Zuleta, Rinconada, La Esperanza, and Angochagua.

Because San Pedro is the patron saint of the canton of Cayambe, hundreds of *indígenas* come into town and parade under the banners of their communities. The groups dance down the streets, around the main plaza, and past a reviewing stand, where local officials award prizes to the best groups. Among the dancers are men and women carrying roosters in wooden cages or tied to poles for a ceremony called the *entrega de gallos* (delivery of roosters). In the days of *wasipungo* (serfdom) the indigenous people on the haciendas had to show their loyalty to the landowner by making a ceremonial gift of roosters at this time. Today the ceremony is most often performed for the indigenous sponsor (called the *prioste*) of local fiestas.

The feast of the **Virgin of Carmen** (La Virgen del Carmen, July 16) is a notably larger celebration in the southern provinces than in the north.

There is a fair *(feria)* in front of the church of that name in downtown Cuenca. In Chimborazo this fiesta is celebrated in Pumallacta and in Chambo.

Chambo, located just outside Riobamba, is the site of a miraculous shrine and fountain, one of those instances where a Catholic church was built on a mountain over what was undoubtedly a pre-conquest holy site. The shrine is dedicated to the Virgen de la Fuente del Carmelo de Catequilla. *Indígenas* from throughout Chimborazo, in their finest traditional dress, visit the shrine

Traditional dancing is a vital part of many Andean festivals.

and chapel on July 16. There is also a small fair at the base of the springs where food, drink, candles, and holy items are sold.

Saint James (Santiago, July 25) is the patron saint of Spain, and his image (on horseback with a raised sword) was carried into battle by the Spanish. The Spanish had firearms, which were unknown to *indígenas*, who associated Santiago with the powerful Inca god of thunder and lightning (Illapa). Today Santiago is the patron of many communities, and there are many fiestas in his honor.

The feast of the **Virgin of Mercy** (La Virgen de la Merced, September 24) is a major two-day fiesta in Latacunga (Cotopaxi province), where a local dark-skinned statue of the Virgin is known as La Mamá Negra, the black mother. This is one of the country's most visually-striking festivals, a pooling of cultural traditions from the Ayamara to the African, with the highlight being the parading of La Mama Negra (the black mother, an intriguing combination of the Virgin mixed with African deities) through streets on horseback. La Merced is also celebrated in Columbe (Chimborazo province).

All Saints' Day and the Day of the Dead (Todos Santos and Día de Difuntos, November 1 and 2). These two Catholic feast days are another example of the blending of Andean and European traditions. In pre-conquest burials, food and drink were placed in graves to feed the dead in the next life. Some people believe that the spirits of the dead return to earth for 24 hours and will be unhappy if they aren't remembered.

If you are in Quito in early December you will get swept along in the festivities that celebrate **The Founding of Quito** (December 6). There are parades, bullfights, dancing in the street, and general merriment.

Finally, there are many beautiful **Christmas** (Navidad, December 25) pageants and celebrations throughout Ecuador; it's a wonderful time of

Open-sided chiva bus en route to Guamote market.

⊘ SPIRITUAL FOOD

All over Ecuador, little human and animal figures are baked from bread dough and taken to the cemeteries on November 2, where they are placed on graves along with paper wreaths and other offerings of food and drink. It sounds as if it would be a very sad occasion, but in fact it is often quite cheerful and festive.

In a nice local variation on the theme of "waste not, want not," poor people often come to the cemeteries and offer prayers at each grave site in return for some of the food. It's a sensible idea, as they need the food more than the departed, and, of course, a few extra prayers never go amiss.

year to be traveling there. Christmas is the main religious holiday, though as commercial here as anywhere else, with stores setting up Christmas displays as early as September. Among the local Christmas customs is the Pase del Niño (Presentation of the Christ Child). Families who own statues of the baby Jesus carry them in a street procession to the church, accompanied by musicians and by children dressed as Mary, Joseph, and other Nativity figures. The baby Jesus statues are blessed during a special Mass and then taken back to the household cribs.

The most famous Pase del Niño occurs in Cuenca, on the morning of December 24. It begins at the churches of San Sebastián and Corazón de Jesús and converges on the cathedral on the

Plaza de Armas. Families from around the region bring their children, some dressed as *indígenas* and mounted on horseback, their horses decked with gifts of food, liquor, sweets, and fruits. Other children are on foot, dressed as Nativity figures or as gypsies, gauchos, or Moors, each group carrying its own statue of Jesus. Inside the cathedral the children are given *chicha* and bread, then the participants wind their way through the streets to celebrate Christmas at home. The Pase has grown so large, however, that its quality has declined over the years.

FIESTA ETIQUETTE

There are appropriate and inappropriate ways to behave at fiestas, and everyone will have a better time if you know how to act. If you want to take photographs, for example, you will be less conspicuous and find it much easier at the larger and more public events. If you are the only outsider at a small village event, then circumspection is the word. Put your camera away, watch the festivities, talk to people, and then ask if you can photograph them. *Indígenas* have been pushed around by people for nearly 500 years, and they are pushing

Pase del Niño Viajero Christmas Parade in Cuenca.

In Saraguro, Loja province, each indigenous community owns a statue of the Christ Child which is carried in a procession on Christmas Day from the main church to the home of the Christ Child's "godparents," the *marcan taita* and *marcan mama*. The procession is led by violinists and drummers and accompanied by costumed dancers. At the *marcan taita*'s house the statue is placed on a decorated altar, and the entire community assembles for a huge meal and an afternoon of music and dancing.

Other Christmas observances include the fiesta of the Holy Innocents (Santos Inocentes) on December 28 (in Quito), and the feast of Epiphany or Three Kings (Tres Reyes or Reyes Magos), on January 6.

back. They resent the arrogance of some outsiders who assume they can photograph anything, anywhere without asking permission. Remember, you're a guest here, not Sebastián de Benalcázar.

Ritual drinking is customary at all fiestas, and by late in the day many participants are hopelessly intoxicated. It is insulting if you refuse to drink when the *trago* bottle is passed around, so join the revelers in a drink or two and throw the dregs on the ground as an offering to Pacha Mama. One of the best ways to enjoy a fiesta without causing or taking offense is to arrive fairly early in the morning and leave by about 2pm, before things get seriously out of hand and before you've shared so many drinks that you can't find your way back to the bus stop.

A shaman conducting an
Ayahuasca ceremony.

PEOPLES OF THE AMAZON

The Amazonian people preserve many of the old ways, but are learning how to live with changes, both good and bad, that the modern world has introduced.

When Westerners think of indigenous Amazonian peoples, they conjure up strings of age-old stereotypes. The popular image is of naked men and women slipping through the jungle with Stone Age tools, isolated until recently from history and the outside world. According to this school of thought, they have always hunted for their food rather than grown it, and often engaged in brutal wars, shrinking their enemies' heads and occasionally eating their flesh. Conversely, they are held to be ecological saints, protecting their delicate environment at all costs.

Not surprisingly, the image has little to do with reality, as anthropologists in the Ecuadorian Oriente are rapidly finding out.

COPING WITH CHANGE

Far from being unchanging, undeveloping societies – and therefore "idyllic" – all Amazonian peoples have their own histories, and very dynamic histories at that.

Because Amazonians did not possess writing systems and, even more importantly, because their rainforest home is particularly unconducive to preserving the remains of past civilizations, there is little data with which to reconstruct Amazonian history. However, archeologists can now show that human beings have lived in the Amazon since at least 10,000 BC, and that major technological breakthroughs occurred in the Amazon basin.

Amazonians domesticated manioc around 8000 BC, and probably invented clay pottery around 4000 BC, before any other indigenous cultures in South America. Migrations, new languages, and vast cultural and religious transformations characterize the history of the Amazon basin. Archeologists believe that cultural advances moved out of Amazonia into the Andes, not the reverse.

Quichua man wearing a headdress made from bird feathers and a necklace made from seeds.

After the arrival of the *conquistadores*, Amazonian societies changed tremendously, whether they had direct contact with the invaders or not. Plagues of diseases to which indigenous peoples had no resistance moved in waves from the coast, over the Andes, into the rainforest, drastically reducing the population. Migrations of peoples away from regions conquered and colonized by the Spanish and Portuguese provoked chain reactions of indigenous peoples being forced off their original lands into unfamiliar territories.

New technologies reached the Amazon as well, again brought by intermediaries, so that no direct contact occurred with Europeans. Steel tools and new foods (especially the banana, plantain, and papaya, which originated in South-east Asia) were traded from one people to the next throughout the jungle, transforming the ways of life throughout the Amazon. In this way, the pressures created by the Spanish conquest of Ecuador and Peru transformed Amazonia, and the pre-conquest jungle lifestyle will forever remain a mystery to people today.

A RANGE OF JUNGLE GROUPS

The Ecuadorian Amazon is small compared with the vast jungles of Brazil, but it is nevertheless an important, even crucial, part of the region. It is inhabited by six major ethnic groups. The largest grouping is the Quichua people (60,000), followed by the Shuar (40,000), Achuar (5,000), Huaorani (4,000), Siona-Secoya (700), and the Cofan (600).

The Huaorani people remain the most nomadic of Ecuador's indigenous Amazonians, and the least interested in cultivation, but during the 20th century they too partially adopted horticulture. Because they customarily went about naked, and relied so much on hunting and gathering wild foods, the Huaorani were originally

A local man traverses Laguna Grande, in Cuyabeno National Park, by canoe.

⊙ MYTH AND REALITY

Although the popular Western image persists of Amazonians surviving by hunting wild game and gathering fruits, the truth is that most indigenous peoples are no longer true hunter-gatherers. They are either horticulturists, which means that they establish moderate-sized, temporary gardens; or agriculturalists, planting crops on a permanent basis and on a much larger scale. The only partial exception to this is the Huaorani, the most nomadic of Ecuadorian Amazonian peoples. Whilst some of the 4,000-strong population hold university degrees and work in fields like politics, others spend time hunting and gathering just like their ancestors.

called "Aucas," which means "savages" in the Quichua language. The Huaorani understandably rejected the derogatory term.

It appears almost certain that the Huaorani, who are composed of a number of discrete groups (Guequetairi, Pijemoiri, Baihuairi, Huepeiri, etc) are an amalgamation of survivors from many different groups diminished by disease, war, and migrations. For this reason, anthropologists view the sparse material culture of the Huaorani, not as evidence of "backwardness," but as the basic survival mechanisms of those forest cultures that endured the most intensive stresses.

The Amazonian Quichuas are closely related to the people of the same name who dominate the Andean highlands of Ecuador. Anthropologists surmise that Quichua-speakers migrated down into the rainforests after the Spanish conquered the highlands in the early 1500s. The most numerous of the indigenous Amazonians, the Quichuas are composed of two distinct ethnic groups, the Canelos and the Quijos. These peoples brought the knowledge of well-developed agricultural systems from the Andes to the jungle, although they had to learn how to grow very different crops in their new territory. Living in dispersed, permanent settlements on individually owned plots of land, the Quichua men clear

Survival International (tel: 0044 207-687 8700, www.survivalinternational.org) is a charity working with many communities across the Amazon rainforest, and a great resource of information on Amazon indigenous peoples.

consecutive years and then must be abandoned to replenish their fertility. The Siona-Secoya usually leave big trees standing, especially those

Cofan shaman performs a healing ritual.

land and plant crops, while the women maintain, weed, and harvest them. They use a rotation system, resting the plot for three years after approximately five years of cultivation.

IN THE NORTHERN ORIENTE

The small ethnic groups that live in the northern region of the Ecuadorian Amazon are the Cofan (who call themselves the A'I) and the Siona-Secoya, a combination of two once separate groups with very similar customs that unified when their numbers dwindled drastically in the 20th century. These peoples practice what anthropologists call "slash and burn," a technique of creating small clearings in the forest which produces food for two or three

that produce fruits, and they do not always burn off the vegetation they have cut, but sometimes allow it to rot and mulch the exposed earth.

These peoples are semi-nomadic, which is to say that they move about within defined territories, abandoning old plots for new ones located in richer hunting grounds. They most frequently locate their gardens close to their houses, but sometimes plant smaller, less complex gardens at some distance from home. Siona-Secoya and Cofan farmers are women, and the profundity of their knowledge about soils and maintaining their fertility, about weather patterns, plant behavior and diseases, and crop combinations (beans and corn, or corn and manioc, for example) is truly astounding.

The Shuar people of the southern region of Ecuadorian Amazonia, and their closely related cousins the Achuar, practice a horticultural system heavily dependent upon one crop plant; sweet manioc. Women harvest the tuber a year or more after planting it, and, as they harvest, they re-sow small tuber cuttings. When manioc is mature, it can be left in the ground to continue growing without any risk of spoilage, which has obvious advantages in tropical Amazonia. The Shuar and Achuar may perhaps be described as semi-settled, rather than semi-nomadic.

In recent years, Shuar and Achuar men have started raising cattle in increasing numbers, converting jungle to pasture. This income-earning strategy is probably not sustainable considering the fragile soil and subsoil ecology of the jungle, yet the Shuar and Achuar are finding increasingly sophisticated methods of planning their survival in the rainforest.

MOVEMENTS THROUGH THE FOREST

It is still true that hunting, gathering, and fishing determine the movements and rhythms of

Traditional bamboo hut, near Misahuallí.

⊘ BENEFICIAL TABOOS

The Shuar and Achuar people believe that deer, owls, and rabbits are the temporarily visible embodiments of the "true soul" of dead human beings, and therefore they do not hunt these animals.

The Siona-Secoya will never eat deer for similar reasons, and they prohibit the hunting of tree-sloths, black monkeys, opossums, and weasels. They also revere and fear the pink river dolphins, and never harm them.

The Quichua honor the jungle puma, a very rare feline, and would never shoot one. It is thanks to these beliefs that many of these creatures still flourish in Ecuador's jungles.

life for many indigenous peoples. Anthropologists once assumed that hunting was the most important of these activities, but the gathering of wild fruits, honey, nuts, roots, grubs, and insects – a task performed exclusively by indigenous women – actually provides the largest part of the diet. The origin of the "hunting" myth was probably due to the fact that the mostly male Western anthropologists talked almost exclusively to indigenous men, who would have discussed their own activities, and not those of their womenfolk.

Another, more recent, myth held about indigenous Amazonians is that they never kill more than they need in the rainforest, that they revere the jungle's animals, and are attuned to the natural balances of their environment. There is some validity to this view, but much of it stems from the industrialized nations' recent awareness of how they themselves have abused the planet's ecology, coupled with an all-too romantic view of Amazonian life. In fact, it is fairly obvious that the indigenous people of the Oriente kill animals for food until those animals become scarce. Then they move on.

Yet the nomadic and semi-nomadic lifestyles of most indigenous Amazonians have prevented and continue to prevent the extermination of

wore wrap-around kilts, tied in place by bark string, and the women fastened their dresses over their right shoulders, using a belt around their waists. The Siona-Secoya and Cofan men wove ultra-lightweight knee-length cotton smocks, called *cushmas*, which they dyed blue or red. The Quichuas adapted the forms of clothing their highland cousins wore. All of these peoples now usually wear trousers, shirts, and blouses, dresses, skirts, and shorts that are indistinguishable from those of other Ecuadorians.

Huaorani mother and child in Yasuní National Park.

game animals upon which indigenous peoples depend. The horticultural groups have always placed an overwhelming social emphasis upon having small families with no more than two children. Population stability unlocks the door to ecological stability. Amazonian belief systems also encompass a number of iron-clad taboos against hunting and killing certain animals.

CRAFTS OF THE ORIENTE

For all groups except the Huaorani (who wore nothing, though men would use string to tie their penises up by the foreskin), a major craft was clothes-making. Shuar men and Achuar women spun homegrown cotton, wove it into cloth and dyed it with vegetable dyes. The men

Basket-weaving, a male craft, has survived a lot better than the production of clothes. Plastics simply do not perform as well as baskets made of natural materials in the tropics because they are much heavier, induce food to rot, and are not nearly so versatile. The normal carrying basket of the Amazon is a plaited, openwork cylinder, no more than a meter high, tightly woven and very sturdy. The finest baskets are woven by the Shuar, for holding personal ornaments and other finery; they are lined with smooth banana leaves, and have an attached cover.

The tourist market has almost completely transformed another craft, pottery, which has always been the domain of women. Quichua women make clay vessels for household use, as well as sacred vessels with ritual character. These vessels are meticulously executed, elaborate, and eggshell-thin, with geometric and zoomorphic shapes and motifs. Shuar women lavish intricate geometrical adornments on the jars used to boil and serve the hallucinogenic beverage *ayahuasca* (see page 83). Tourist demand for Amazonian pottery has transformed its production into something resembling an assembly line, where duplicates are produced with patterns that have no significance. The income derived from the sale of ceramics is, relative to the overall monetary most colorful, and usually the most endangered, birds at an accelerated rate.

AMAZONIAN SHAMANS

It was in the realm of spiritual and mythical creativity that indigenous Amazonians made their greatest strides and their most momentous discoveries. Because the Amazonian storehouse of knowledge and wisdom has always been transmitted orally, a great deal of the complexity has been lost. Indigenous spirituality has been mercilessly attacked by missionaries ever since

Cofan woman cooking maitos, Sucumbíos Province.

income of indigenous Amazonians, quite considerable, and has given women a degree of power over their lives in the midst of ongoing cultural transition.

Most fantastic of all Amazonian arts are the feather and beadwork crowns, necklaces, earrings, and other ornaments, which rely upon the plumage of magnificent birds like toucans, parrots, and hummingbirds. These stunningly beautiful works of art have always possessed enormous ritual and spiritual significance for Amazonian peoples, directly linked to their use in the *ayahuasca* ceremony. Today, tourist demand for such ornaments as souvenirs is encouraging indigenous Amazonians to kill the

⊘ DON'T EVEN THINK ABOUT IT

Don't buy anything made from the plumage of Amazonian birds.

Because the importation of products which cause the death of any endangered species is prohibited by the United States, Australia, and all of Western Europe, tourists who are irresponsible enough to attempt to take their "trinkets" home will inevitably have to surrender them at the customs office. This makes the death of these magnificent birds, and the devaluation of the traditions of Amazonian peoples, a tragic exercise in futility. The lower the demand for such souvenirs, the fewer birds will be killed.

the Spanish conquest. In recent years Protestant groups have worked to blot out the legacy of thousands of years, preventing the transmission of traditions from the old to the young. Nevertheless, the enduring center of that legacy, shamanism, survives among the six principal peoples, albeit by ever more slender threads.

Shamans are the individuals who preserve the oral histories, myths, legends, and other belief systems of their peoples. Among the Siona-Secoya, Quichua, and Cofan groups shamans are usually men, but female shamans are not unknown in the Shuar and Achuar cultures. Many shamans devote their time to curing diseases through elaborate rituals. There are shamans who bewitch others, causing disease and misfortune to their enemies, or to the enemies of those who pay them to do so. Shamans enact the ceremonies of initiation, the rites of passage of young men and women into adulthood; and they train others to take on the role, passing on the knowledge and the rituals.

The tools they use vary. Quichua shamans own magical stones, which act as their familiars. The Shuar and Achuar shamans utilize magical darts called *tsentsak*, to bring about both healing and harm. But the most important tools they all employ are hallucinogenic substances extracted from jungle plants. The vine known as *ayahuasca*, Quichua for "vine of the soul," is the hallucinogen par excellence.

Using drum rhythms and other musical patterns, vocal incantations, the light of fires, and the colors provided by feather ornaments and body paint, the shamans guide those who have drunk potions derived from *ayahuasca* to see visions based on the symbolism and mythology of their cultures. The jaguar, anaconda, and harpy eagle recur over and over again in such visions. This communion with their ancestral past and the supernatural is a continuous source of social and cultural cohesion for indigenous Amazonians, and has nothing in common with the often self-destructive use of drugs encountered in Western cultures.

THE POWER OF THE FAMILY UNIT

In indigenous Amazonian society the most important organizational unit is the extended family. The rules of kinship define the individuals' rights of inheritance, whom they should marry, and where they should live.

The Huaorani, a society pared down to essentials in its struggle to survive, have very loosely defined kinship rules that do not even insist on the authority of older people over younger. Cofan and Siona-Secoya men may only marry women allowed to them by a patrilineal system: couples live with the family of the man's father, or in a house built close to the father's home, and they inherit property and privileges from the man's father.

Shuar men initially live close to their wives' families, before moving to their own houses, but

Achiote seeds are used as food coloring and also hair dye.

inherit through their fathers' line. Achuar men permanently reside near their wives' families, inherit through their mothers' lines, and marry women according to matrilineal relationships. The Quichua people possess a patrilineal system, but one which is broader and more complex, defining a kinship group called the *ayllu*, several of which compose a community.

Amazonian cultures traditionally have no single leader or chief. Instead, leadership has always been provided in crises by shamans and military men. While Quichua farmers did not wage wars or carry out raids as much as they suffered from them, the lives of all the other groups were defined by feuds, raids, and war. The Siona-Secoya, Cofan, and Huaorani raided to capture women and to avenge raids against them, but never for territory. For the Shuar and Achuar, warfare symbolized the spiritual quest for power: by killing a designated enemy a man could gain the visionary magical soul called *arutam*, and possess the power to lead others.

The practice of severing an enemy's head, removing the skull, and shrinking the skin is a source of great notoriety for the Shuar and Achuar. As gruesome as this practice may seem and as perverse as it became in the early 1900s due to Westerners' fascination with it, the rituals

Protest against oil and mineral extraction outside the CONAIE building in Quito.

associated with shrinking heads were an integral part of the shaman-leader complex that defined war and peace among these peoples. Today, far from shrinking heads, the Shuar and the Achuar have organized the most successful ethnic federation in the Amazon basin, a model for groups in Ecuador and other nations.

21ST-CENTURY POLITICS

Oil development over the past 40 years has changed the rainforest environment forever. The indigenous Amazonians have no choice but to adapt and develop different strategies in order to survive. The Federation of Shuar Centers fights for land rights and is involved in the

protection of the environment in the southern region of the Ecuadorian Amazon. It has also published scores of books about Shuar and Achuar oral traditions, which will make them more accessible to future generations; and shamans now use their powers for health and community issues.

For the Quichuas, organizational models are available from their highland cousins, who have become intensely political. The Quichua regional federations have helped to link indigenous Amazonians and the peoples of the highlands; as a result, an Amazonian and highlander confederation, CONAIE, was formed at national level in 1986.

The Siona-Secoya community on the edge of the Cuyabeno Fauna Reserve has resisted oil development in its territory and worked with the Ministry of Environment in putting together a sustainable development plan for the reserve and buffer zones. These people are committed to maintaining its close relationship with and dependence on the rainforest.

Faced with the multinational oil companies and the subsequent influx of outsiders, a small number of the Cofan people, the tiniest of the groups, are developing their own survival mechanisms in the village of Zabalo. Meanwhile, working through CONAIE, the Huaorani have struggled to gain title to about 600,000 hectares (1.5 million acres) of their former territory; theoretically, enough land to sustain a way of life that retains some elements of hunting and gathering. Although the Ecuadorian government maintains the right to exploit deposits of oil under some of these lands, much of the area near the Peruvian border was declared "untouchable" by an act of congress in 1999. The creation of an 809,000-hectare (2-million-acre) zone to the south of Yasuní National Park in 2007, goes some way to making up for the lack of protection from oil exploration. Sadly, the ambitious Yasuní-ITT initiative aimed at keeping oil in the ground in return for international donations foundered in 2013 after a government commission concluded that the economic benefits were insufficient. In 2014 the Ecuadorian government issued permits for oil drilling, and green-lit a second phase of drilling, deeper in the Yasuní National Park, in 2018, though this has now been halted thanks to the 2023 national referendum that determined that drilling in the park should stop.

THE LAST HIDDEN PEOPLES

Despite legislative protection, the outlook for Ecuador's few isolated Amazon communities is bleak, due to the onslaught of the modern world.

At most, there are just 400 groups of Isolated Indigenous Peoples (IIPs) believed to be living in Ecuador's northeast Amazon refusing contact with mainstream civilization. Most of the evidence known of these rainforest warriors still clinging to their ancient way of life stems from violent encounters. In 1987, as oil companies encroached on land inhabited by the Tagaeri – a group of Huaorani – Coca's Spanish-born bishop Alejandro Labaka sought to contact them in a last-ditch pitch for their survival. He and Inés Arango, a Colombian nun, gave their lives in the attempt as they were found dead. The ensuing media exposure, however, kept the oil industry at bay, as Labaka had hoped.

Nevertheless, conflicts continue. Many Huaorani today work for oil companies or in tourism; some also work with the loggers. In 2008, poachers of rare rainforest woods were found dead, fatally wounded by the Huaorani's heavy spears. Encouraged by loggers and poachers, in 2013 a group of Huaorani sought to avenge a Tagaeri "kidnapping" by killing up to 30 forest dwellers, including women and children, who were burned to death inside a large dwelling. However, the dead turned out to be members of the previously unknown Taromenani who had moved into a jungle building abandoned by the Tagaeri. Judicial authorities did almost nothing to investigate the Taromenani massacre.

PROTECTIVE MEASURES

While remaining members of the Taromenani and Tagaeri are few, they are widely dispersed amid the vast tracts of jungle. Nevertheless, pressure on their land in the 21st century continues to increase, both from inside Ecuador and from across the border in Peru. Aware of the race against the clock to save the two groups, the Correa government set up half a dozen control posts staffed with police and scientists to stop access to the "intangible zone" established for their protection in and around the southern part of the Yasuní National Park. Under President Moreno, the government insists it is doing more to control the boom of hardwood smuggling to the US and Colombia. More usefully, a ruling by the Constitutional Court in 2022 mandated that all 14 indigenous peoples in the Amazon have veto rights to any project in the territories.

Most oil companies demand proof of vaccination and special permits from visitors in an attempt to protect the people from the common diseases that eradicated so many other indigenous people since

Aerial view of an isolated Amazon village.

the arrival of the first Europeans. Contact with anyone, from tourists to other indigenous communities, could wipe them out in one devastating epidemic. To the exasperation of the government, however, the "intangible zone" means nothing to the Tagaeri and Taromenani as they roam to hunt, and live in such proximity to outposts of mainstream society that they occasionally steal machetes and axes from nearby tourist lodges.

Environmentalists say that current steps to protect them are too little too late. Some advocate a more aggressive, pre-emptive attempt to vaccinate them against disease before a plague can break out. Such is the pressure from a greedy outside world that their traditional way of life will almost certainly end in the foreseeable future, even if they survive.

A stallholder and her display of colorful rugs and wall hangings, Otavalo market.

ARTESANÍAS

The ancient crafts traditions of the indigenous peoples of Ecuador have become much sought after by Western visitors.

There are no words in the indigenous languages of Ecuador for "art", nor is there a distinction between fine arts and crafts. Seduced by their beauty, Westerners have included many traditional Ecuadorian *artesanías* in their own category of fine art, particularly textiles, ceramics, and jewelry. If you have the time, there's something particularly satisfying about buying from the artisans themselves or shopping in the market, but products from throughout the country make their way into Quito and to the famous market in Otavalo.

WOVEN TEXTILES

Four or five thousand years ago, some genius in the northern Andes invented the stick loom, which is still in use and generally called the backstrap loom (local names include *awana*, *macana*, and *telar*). This loom, sophisticated in concept and simple in form, is made of sticks and poles, with one end fastened to a stationary object and the other to the weaver's back.

When the Incas made a census of their empire they counted humans first, cameloids (llamas and alpacas) second, and textiles third, before precious metals, gemstones, ceramics, or food. The Spanish were amazed by their superb hand-woven cloth made of cotton, and cameloid wool.

Ecuador's damper climate has not been as conducive as Peru's to the preservation of organic materials, but the few pre-Hispanic textile fragments that exist suggest a tradition as venerable and as exquisite as that of Peru. The Spanish introduced the treadle loom, spinning wheel, sheep, and silk; much later came electric looms and synthetic fibers. But an amazing number of weavers still use

Stallholder in Otavalo market.

the stick loom. Even in Otavalo, where most weaving is done on the treadle loom, some ponchos and virtually all belts are made on the backstrap loom. In Saraguro, blankets (*cobijas*), grain sacks (*costales*), and most items of traditional dress are hand-spun on simple spindles of the kind you see throughout the Sierra, and hand-woven on the stick loom. These pieces are difficult to come by, but some are sold in Quito stores. In Ecuador, the majority of weavers are men, although many women also weave.

Azuay is famous for its *ikat* textiles. *Ikat* (*amarrado* or *watado*) is a dyeing rather than weaving technique, where the warp threads are tied and dyed *before* the piece is woven. Pre-Hispanic *ikat* fragments have been found. The best-known *ikat* textiles are *paños*, indigo-dyed cotton shawls with elaborate macramé fringes; a newer style is black and red with a macraméd, embroidered fringe. It takes only hours to wrap the design, dye and weave the shawl, but up to three months to knot the fringe. *Paños* were traditionally worn by indigenous women, but young women no longer wear them, so fine ones are becoming rare. If you want to see the older women in their finery, proud as queens, visit the Sunday market at Gualaceo.

Making a Panama hat in Montecristi.

The skilled dyers and weavers now make *ikat* woolen belts, scarves, and shawls without fringes, usually dyed black or brown over red, blue, green or purple. Some of these shawls are made into high-fashion clothing, available in Quito.

Ikat carrying-cloths called *macanas* are made around Salcedo and in Chimborazo province. The Salcedo *macanas* are of deep indigo like the Cuenca *paños*, but the designs are coarser and they have a short fringe. *Macanas* are used throughout the Sierra as carrying-cloths, to haul everything from a baby to a load of firewood.

Ikat ponchos are made and worn in the Sierra from Cañar to Natabuela, north of Otavalo. The poncho is a post-conquest garment, an adaptation of the Inca tunic. Various kinds of plain ponchos are woven for daily wear, while the *ikat* ones are reserved for weddings and fiestas. Especially beautiful *ikat* ponchos are made in Cañar, Chordeleg, Cacha Obraje (outside Riobamba), and Paniquindra. Like ponchos, *ikat* blankets are made in every highland province, but these are for daily (or nightly) use. A good one of hand-spun wool, woven in two sections and sewn together, weighs 4.5kg (10lb).

Belts *(chumbis)* are woven on the backstrap loom. Double-faced belts with motifs ranging from Inca pots to farm animals are woven from hand-spun wool or commercial cotton thread in Cañar. These are among the finest belts made in Ecuador, rivaled only by those of Salasaca.

Salasaca belts are still made of hand-spun wool, and many are dyed with cochineal, a natural dye made from crushed female insects which live on the Opuntia cactus. Running a close race are a number of double- and single-faced belts with woven motifs made in Chimborazo and Bolívar provinces, followed by belts made in Otavalo and nearby Paniquindra.

TAPESTRIES

In the late 1950s the Andean Mission embarked on a craft project that was a resounding success. Weavers from Salasaca and Otavalo were taught how to make tapestries *(tapices)* on the treadle loom. This technique, in which the weft threads interlock, gives tapestries a painterly quality. Today the stores around the main plaza in Salasaca and half the Otavalo market are filled with tapestries, including wall hangings, handbags *(bolsas)*, and cushion covers *(cojines)*.

HAND-KNIT CLOTHING

While Ecuadorian women have been knitting since the colonial era, a Peace Corps project in the 1960s gave the modern industry extra impetus. Today sweaters *(chompas)*, vests *(chalecos)*, and hats *(gorros)* of hand-spun wool are made in Cuenca and in the northern towns of Ibarra, Mira, San Gabriel, San Isidro, and Atuntaqui. The highest-quality ones are usually sold in Quito or abroad, although you can find some fine quality knitwear in some of the smarter boutiques in Otavalo. Wherever you buy a sweater, try it on. The knitter's idea of size may not necessarily be the same as yours.

When the Incas conducted a census they rated textiles more highly than food, precious metals, or gemstones. To measure inventories, their accounting system used multi-colored and knotted wool strings, or quipus.

EMBROIDERY

If you look carefully in the Otavalo market you will see women from an ethnic group other than the Otavaleños, wearing pleated skirts and blouses with extremely fine, intricate embroidery on the bodice and sleeves. The women come from communities on the south and eastern sides of Imbabura Mountain, such as Zuleta, La Esperanza, San Isidro de Cajas, and Rinconada. You can buy these blouses in the Otavalo and Ibarra markets. In addition, the women embroider a range of more commercial items, such as dresses, napkins, towels, and tablecloths.

HATS, BASKETS, AND BAGS

Contrary to popular belief, Panama hats aren't made in Panama; they're made in southern Ecuador in and around Cuenca and in Montecristi on the coast, where they're called *sombreros de paja toquilla* after the palm fiber from which they are woven (see page 244). They have been made here for more than a century, with the industry going through cycles of boom and bust. In the 1960s the Peace Corps introduced other items such as Nativity sets and Christmas tree ornaments to help tide the *paja* weavers over hard times in the hat industry.

Shigra means sack in Quichua. *Shigras* are made of *cabuya* (agave) fiber in the central Sierra provinces of Cotopaxi, Tungurahua, and Chimborazo. These bags, made by hand with a buttonhole stitch, are found nowhere else in the Andes although many Amazonian indigenous groups make similar kinds of bag with other plant fibres. Tied over the shoulders, *shigras* serve as a carry-all for *indígena* men and women. While originally meant for local use, *shigras* found ready acceptance in the tourist and ethnic arts markets, and the best of them are true collectors' items. Baskets (*canastas*) made from various plants including cane and *totora* reeds are

made throughout Ecuador and found in every market. Giant ones with lids come from Cuenca, smaller ones from around Latacunga, and fine two-color baskets from the Oriente.

LEATHERWORK

Cotacachi is the main center for wallets, purses, knapsacks, and clothes made from leather (*cuero*). The main street of the town is lined with shops, and there's a Sunday morning craft market. Leather items can also be found in the Otavalo market and in many Quito shops.

Otavaleña embroidering by machine.

The leatherwork is usually good, but be sure to check the quality of zippers and clasps before you make a purchase.

JEWELRY

Ancient Ecuadorians were also master metalworkers. In indigenous communities jewelers make silver, nickel, and brass shawl pins (*tupus*), with the finest coming from Saraguro. Contemporary gold and silver filigree jewelry is a specialty of Chordeleg, where jewelry stores (*joyerías*) line the road into town and the main plaza. The workmanship is excellent and the prices are reasonable. In pre-Hispanic times the Ecuadorian coastline was the source of the prized, coral-colored spondylus shell, traded throughout the Andes. Beads are still an essential part of women's traditional dress. The preference for red or coral-colored beads goes back to the days when spondylus was queen. In the Amazon region, the vivid red-and-black *huayruro* seeds are believed to bring good luck and are frequently used to make attractive jewelry.

CERAMICS

The most beautiful ceramics in Ecuador – perhaps in the entire upper Amazon – are made by the Canelos Quichua *indígenas*, or Sacha Runa (jungle

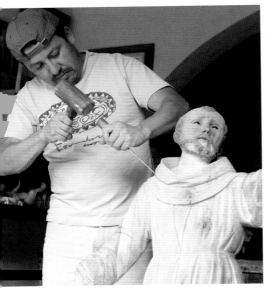
Carving a religious statue, San Antonio.

people), who live between the Napo and Pastaza rivers in the Oriente. Women make the bowls and pots for household and ceremonial use, by hand-coiling. The finest pieces are eggshell-thin, with painted designs representing various aspects of their life and mythology. Some beautiful ceramics are now also made for the indigenous arts market.

Several ceramic factories have showrooms in Cuenca. The Cuenca *barrio* of Corazón de Jesús, and the towns of San Miguel and Chordeleg, are traditional producers of pottery, which is sold at the Cuenca market. These potters use the imported wheel, and in San Miguel and Chordeleg you can see their wares drying in the shade outside their houses. The Sierra around Latacunga and Saquisilí is another pottery

Balsa trees thrive in the tropical Andean foothills. In Ecuador, Canelos Quichua craftsmen in the Oriente developed a carving industry producing brightly painted balsawood sculptures of tropical birds, fish, and other animals.

center, where enormous Inca-style amphoras (*tinajas* or *ollas*) for making *chicha* are produced in the town of Tejar. Pujilí, noted for its Corpus Christi celebration, also has potters who make figurines of birds, animals, and fiesta scenes.

WOODCARVING

There are two main centers of woodcarving: the Canelos Quichua region in the Amazon and San Antonio de Ibarra north of Otavalo. The former's woodcarvings of tropical birds and animals are designed expressly for the indigenous arts market. Most of the carvings are made from balsawood, painted, and lacquered.

Woodcarvings in San Antonio de Ibarra run the gamut from elaborate furniture to Nativity sets, boxes, wall plaques, and statues of the Virgin, saints, and beggars. Some are kitsch, but there are some treasures, and you can watch the carvers at work in the rear of their shops.

BREAD FIGURES

The productions of brightly dyed dough figures of humans and animals for sale and for export is a main industry in the community of Calderón at the northeast end of Quito. They are placed on graves as offerings to the dead on the feasts of Todos Santos (All Saints Day) and the *Día de Difuntos* (Day of the Dead) on November 1 and 2 respectively.

TAGUA NUTS

Tagua (also known as vegetable ivory) is very much in demand (again) in the Western world. This beautifully-textured, rounded nut with an aesthetically-pleasing grain heralds from a palm (Phytelephas aequatorialis) that grows mainly in the coastal areas of Manabí. The nuts are dyed and sold either as beads on jewelry or as buttons for various items of upmarket clothing (indeed, several leading fashion brands have been known to feature them), or carved into small animals as ornaments.

Artisan weavers at a workshop in Otavalo.

A NATION OF PAINTERS

Quito has a thriving artistic scene that may yet rival the accomplishments of its 16th-century precursor, though today, the subject matter is often Ecuador's indigenous population rather than Christian motifs.

Until early in the 20th century, art in Ecuador was mainly associated with the colonial Escuela de Quito (or Quito School in English)(see page 145), but the first three decades of the 1900s saw the rise of a school called *indigenismo* (indigenism).

As Ecuadorian artists have not been isolated from currents in the international art world and many of them have studied or traveled in Europe and North America, the unifying factor of the indigenist school does not refer to the style of painting, which ranges from Realist to Impressionist, Cubist, and Surrealist, but the subject matter; Ecuador's exploited indigenous population.

INSPIRED BY A SIERRA LIFE

Eduardo Kingman is perhaps the prototypical indigenist. From the 1930s until his death in 1998 he painted murals and canvases, and illustrated books exploring social themes and the use of color. *Juguetería* (Toy Store), an oil painted in 1985, shows the back of a barefoot *indígena* girl peering into the window of a brightly lit toy shop. The toys are rendered in cheerful primary colors, while the girl outside in the shadows, the picture of longing, is painted in somber burgundy, black, and blue.

Such paintings as *Mujeres con Santo* (Women with Saint), *El Maizal* (The Maize-Grower) and *La Sed* (Thirst) are characteristic of Kingman's work: the indigenist subject matter and highly

Camilo Egas went through a Dalíesque period before he went on to become the most indigenist of the Ecuadorian painters.

An Oswaldo Guayasamín mural at Madrid–Barajas Airport.

stylized, semi-abstract human figures with heavy facial features and huge, distorted hands. These paintings convey powerful images of oppression, sorrow, and suffering.

Camilo Egas, who died in 1961, lived in France for long periods of time and moved through a range of styles, from Surrealist to Realist, and abstract Expressionist. In *Indios* (Indians), painted in the 1950s, three longhaired men lean diagonally into the picture, using ropes to haul an unseen burden. The painting is executed in a few bright, clear colors: blue sky, black hair, brown skin, red, white, and yellow clothing. Neither the bodies nor the features of the men are abstract or distorted, and the impression conveyed is one of dignity and strength rather than misery. He also produced *El Indio Mariano*, a beautiful profile portrait in the same idiom.

Manuel Rendón was a prolific painter who produced a remarkably diverse body of work. Rendón spent his youth in Paris, where his father was the Ecuadorian ambassador, and he was greatly influenced by the modern art movement in France. Rendón is considered an indigenist artist, but he is equally well known for his Cubist-style paintings of men and women in the 1920s and for a series on the *Sagrada Familia* (Holy Family) in the 1940s. He also painted poin-

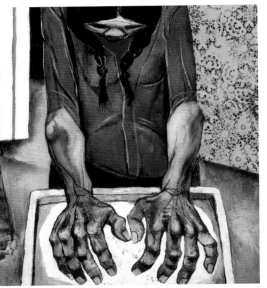

An example of the indigenist painting style, by Eduardo Kingman.

tillistic figurative and abstract works, and did many sketches in pencil and pen and ink.

ECUADORIAN MAESTRO

Oswaldo Guayasamín, who died in 1999, is the best known of the generation of artists who came of age in the 1930s and 1940s. His father was an *indígena*, and Guayasamín consistently and proudly emphasized his indigenous heritage. Few people are neutral about Guayasamín's work, with its message of social protest. His admirers see him as a gifted artistic visionary and social critic, while his detractors see him as a third-rate Picasso imitator whose innumerable paintings of *indígenas* with coarse features and gnarled hands have

become parodies of the genre. Make up your own mind by visiting the Museo Guayasamín in Quito.

Anyone familiar with the graphic paintings and statues of Christ, agonized and bleeding, in Spanish colonial churches can trace this theme of suffering in Guayasamín's work, although his figures are secular rather than religious.

One of his early works, the 1942 painting *Los Trabajadores* (The Workers) is realistic in a manner similar to that of the Mexican muralist José Clemente Orozco. The similarity is more than coincidental, as Guayasamín worked with Orozco in Mexico. Guayasamín went on to develop a style influenced by Cubism, with its chopped-up and oddly reassembled images, notably in his series of monumental paintings *La Edad de la Ira* (The Age of Anger), *Los Torturados* (The Tortured), and *Cabezas* (Heads).

In 1988 Guayasamín continued to make visual political statements with his enormous mural in the meeting hall of the Ecuadorian Congress in Quito, in which 23 panels convey episodes from Ecuador's history; Guayasamín produced anything but a romanticized picture. Nineteen of the panels are in color, four are in black and white. The latter depict the first Ecuadorian president to enslave the *indígenas*, Ecuador's civilian and military dictators, and a skeletal face wearing a Nazi helmet emblazoned with the letters "CIA."

While Ecuadorians took the mural in their stride, the United States was outraged. The US ambassador called for the letters to be painted out and various US congressmen discussed cutting off economic aid to Ecuador. Guayasamín regarded this as exactly the kind of bullying that he was protesting against, and the panel has remained unchanged.

Perhaps what will become his most famous work was only finished after his death at the insistence of his family. *La Capilla del Hombre*, in the Bellavista neighborhood of Quito, is rapidly becoming known as his masterpiece. The stone temple resembles an ancient pre-Columbian one on the outside, but inside it is very modern, with fine woodwork and architectural design. A mural depicts the Latin American man from pre-Columbian times to the present. An eternal flame marks the altar on the lower level, which burns for peace and human rights. The minimalist chapel shows the dreams, fears, anguish, inspirations, and love of this great artist.

AN ARTISTIC IMMIGRANT

Olga Fisch arrived in the country more than half a century ago as a refugee fleeing from Hitler, bringing with her a background in the visual arts. Fisch was among the first to recognize the value of Ecuadorian *artesanías* as art, and the design potential of traditional motifs. A talented painter, Fisch, who died in 1991, is best known for her work in textile design, especially rugs and tapestries, based on her interpretations of pottery, embroidery and weaving motifs. She also designed clothing and jewelry, avail-

brushstrokes. They lean against storefronts in what looks like a seedy downtown neighborhood, and the use of yellows and reds contributes to a carnival-like atmosphere. Jácome's 1990 oil *A la Cola* (To the End of the Line) depicts a slashing rainstorm in which three bright-yellow taxis outlined in black divide the canvas diagonally. Recent years have seen the emergence of several influential art centers, including Galería No Lugar (http://nolugar.org) in Quito which presents works of contemporary artists from Ecuador and other Latin American countries.

Oswaldo Guayasamín's mural, entitled El Descubrimiento del Amazonas, in the Presidential Palace.

able at her stores in Quito and Guayaquil, and in Santa Cruz in the Galápagos Islands (www.olgafisch.com).

MODERN-DAY ARTISTS

The younger generation of painters has moved away from *indigenismo* to more personal, idiosyncratic themes and subject matter. In the 1970s Ramiro Jácome was part of the neo-Figurative movement, a return to works with recognizable figures. In the early 1980s he changed his style, painting a series of abstract oils, characterized by deep, rich colors. Later in the 1980s he returned to figurative works. In *Barrio* (Neighborhood), painted in 1989, three semi-abstract people are delineated by swift, black

⊙ WHERE TO SEE MODERN ART

The Casa de la Cultura on 6 de Diciembre and Patria in Quito has some examples of modern art, with 20th-century sculptures on the lawn outside. The Museo y Taller Guayasamín, at Mariano Calvache E18-94 and Lorenzo Chávez, is devoted solely to Guayasamín's work. *La Capilla del Hombre* is nearby at Lorenzo Chávez EA18-143 and Mariano Calvache. The Centro Cultural Metropolitano, at García Moreno and Espejo, and the Museo de Arte Contemporánea, at Luis Dávila y Venezuela in the San Juan neighborhood, have exhibitions. Ecuador's largest international art exposition is the Cuenca Bienal (https://fundacion.bienaldecuenca.org), held in odd-numbered years.

Making a bamboo panpipe.

SOUNDS OF THE ANDES

Ecuador's diversity extends to its musical traditions: Andean pipes happily coexist with brass bands and salsa clubs. And then there are the weekend marimba parties...

At fiestas in Ecuador, two kinds of music are usually played: traditional, indigenous music and Spanish (or more generally European) music. But after almost 500 years there has been much blending of the two.

You can hear traditional music groups (*grupos* or *conjuntos*) at many indigenous fiestas and in folk music clubs (*peñas*). There are also local and national traditional music competitions, which are usually free to the public, with an amazing variety of talent (or lack thereof).

ANCIENT INSTRUMENTS

Pre-Hispanic vocal and instrumental music was based on a pentatonic (five-note) scale which, in contrast to the heptatonic (seven-note) scale, gives Andean music its distinctive haunting, melancholic sound. Pre-Hispanic instruments consisted of flutes, panpipes, conch shells, drums, and rattles and bells. Flute-like instruments used today include the seven-hole bamboo *quena*, a notched bamboo with six finger holes and a thumb hole, and a smaller flute, the *pingullu*, which has three or four holes. The pre-Hispanic flutes are always held vertically; flutes (*flautas*) held horizontally are modeled on the European instrument.

The panpipe (*rondador*) goes back at least 2,000 years, and is typically made of varying lengths and widths of cane or bamboo tied together in one long row, the different lengths and diameters producing distinct tones. Many Ecuadorian musicians now use *zampoñas*, the panpipes typical of Peru and Bolivia, which are tuned differently from the *rondador* and usually have two rows of pipes lashed together, which musicians say make it easier to play.

Musican playing a traditional Ecuadorian panpipe and charango.

The frequent use of Peruvian and Bolivian instruments by Ecuadorian musicians is indicative of the cross-fertilization that occurs as Ecuadorians travel in Peru and Bolivia, and southern Andean musicians (or their tape cassettes, CDs, and online recordings) come north.

Percussion instruments include drums (*bombos*) and gourd rattles (*maracas*). Bells (*campanas*) are still used, especially by dancers. In Imbabura province, for example, 10 or 12 cowbells are attached to a piece of cowhide and are worn over the shoulder by dancers at the fiestas of San Juan and San Pedro (June 24 and June 29).

SPANISH INFLUENCES

Stringed instruments were introduced by the Spanish and were soon incorporated into the traditional repertoire. These instruments include the guitar (*guitarra*), violin (*violín*), mandolin (*bandolín*), charango, and Andean harp (*arpa criolla*). The *charango* originated in Bolivia and looks like a ukulele, but has five pairs of strings and eight frets. The body is sometimes made of wood, but more often from an armadillo shell. The Andean harp is a homemade version of the European harp, beautiful to listen to but

Street musician playing the Andean harp.

difficult to make and transport, which is why few musicians use them.

After the Spanish introduced cattle into Ecuador, the indigenous peoples made a unique instrument from cow horns, called a *coroneta* or *bocina*. The tone of the *coroneta* depends on the number of horns used. The accordion (*acordeón*) and harmonica (*rondín*) were introduced in the 19th century. The most recent addition is the portable Yamaha organ.

Brass instruments are another European introduction, and it is traditional for brass bands to play at small-town fiestas and civic events, during which volume and enthusiasm often surpass musicianship. Another venerable musical tradition is the weekend concert

in the park. Many towns have municipal bands which assemble on Sunday mornings and rouse the populace from their Saturday-night torpor. It's not exactly indigenous music: you are quite likely to get a rendition of the theme tune from the latest hit television series.

In traditional music groups, men usually play musical instruments and sing, while women are only vocalists. Some types of music, including the *wayñu* (or *wayno*) and the *yaraví*, were probably introduced by the Incas and are almost always sung in Quichua. But the most common is the *sanjuanito*, which qualifies as Ecuador's national dance music. *Sanjuanitos* can be both instrumental and vocal and are played by folk-music groups and modern bands at most fiestas.

At a *peña* a typical group will be composed of young men playing the guitar, mandolin, *charango*, violin, drum, *quena*, *pingullu*, *zampoña*, and *rondador*, and they will alternate purely instrumental music with songs with musical accompaniment. Many of the songs will be in Quichua. Some you will hear all over the country, others are specific to certain provinces.

FESTIVAL MUSIC

To foreign ears, much traditional fiesta music sounds like an obsession with one theme. The same refrain is repeated over and over, endlessly hypnotic and great to dance to. During San Juan, the musical groups literally dance all night (to *sanjuanitos* naturally), moving from house to house throughout the village.

⊘ QUITO'S BIG PARTY

The anniversary of the founding of Quito (December 6) is celebrated in the capital with an abundance of music, parades, dancing, and drinking. Although bullfighting is prevalent across Ecuador – provided no harm comes to the bull – the bullfights that used to kickstart the Fiestas de Quito were outlawed in 2021.

Now the two-week celebrations which lead up to the big day rely on a host of musical concerts ranging from traditional folk music to rock and reggaeton. These are supplemented with street parades and the inevitable beauty pageant to elect the Reina de Quito.

Increasingly, traditional groups are being replaced by ones that use amplified instruments, especially for such occasions as weddings and other large parties. Into the house come the musicians in traditional dress, but instead of guitars and *quenas* they carry an electric sound system that will prevent any sleep in the *barrio* for days. The musicians will tune up and launch into "La Rasca Bonita," a *sanjuanito* with a catchy tune and upbeat tempo that qualifies as the national party melody. The band alternates *sanjuanitos* with *cumbias*, music of Afro-Caribbean origin from the coasts of Colombia and Ecuador. Everyone from grandparents to toddlers dances at these parties.

MARIMBA AND SALSA

In the Esmeraldas region, which is dominated by Afro-Ecuadorians, marimba is still very much alive. The marimba instrument itself, the *chonta*, is similar to a xylophone and is made of local hardwood. It is accompanied by *bombos* (drums), *cununeros* (small tambourines), and *guasos* or bamboo stalks filled with seeds.

In the villages near Borbón, every single house has its own marimba. At weekends and important holidays people head out to marimba parties. The local firewater *(aguardiente)* is often thrown on the instrument itself, to signify the beginning of the marimba. Each song tells a story, moralizing, instructing, illustrating daily life, or recognizing death. The haunting, passionate music goes on until dawn and sometimes for several days.

Salsa, merengue, and cumbia, essentially dance music from Caribbean countries, is particularly big on the coast. In shopping malls it is easy to find good recordings of salsa on CD. Music stores have rows of salsa compilations; however, many legitimate stores have been driven out of business by the plethora of stores and shacks selling illegally copied MP3 CDs, and, more recently, by online streaming.

RAP, REGGAE, AND ANDEAN CHILL

In larger cities popular Latin music is more likely to be played, along with foreign and local rock and pop. Reggaeton, a derivative of reggae blending Jamaican reggae rhythms with more conventional Latin American ones like salsa, is big in Ecuador, and a blend of rap and Latin pop

music is what you are most likely to hear in a *discoteca*.

Andean chill – a fusion of traditional songs, tunes, and instruments with electronica – is one of the more respected genres to have emerged in the Andes in recent years, and Miki González is one of the genre's premier artists with hits such as *Dímelo, Dímelo* and *Akundún*.

Quito's annual Verano de las Artes Quito music festival showcases local DJs and bands from various genres, from rock and punk to ambient and electronic.

Marimba players in Esmeraldas province.

⊘ ECUADORIAN RHYTHM

Segundo Quintero and Carmen González are two of the better-known marimba artists, but recordings of marimba are hard to find. The Centro Cultural Afro-Ecuatoriano, Tamayo 985 and Lizardo García, Quito, tel: 02-252 4429, has videos of some of these frantic dances and information about the bigger festivals.

Salsa is another popular rhythm in Ecuador, which you can hear on many a long bus ride. If you have time, there are plenty of schools in Quito where you can learn to dance to the tropical rhythms of salsa and merengue, in individual or group lessons.

Hiking to the summit of Rucu
Pichincha.

Descending Volcán Cotopaxi.

OUTDOOR ADVENTURES

Climbing, trekking, rafting, or biking; the astonishing variety of terrain in Ecuador is a big attraction for many sports enthusiasts.

Outdoor enthusiasts have discovered that Ecuador's diverse topography provides an ideal environment for "adventure travel." The country's small size makes getting around easy: nothing is too far away from anything else, and there are roads to almost everywhere.

Yet, for its size, Ecuador has an amazing assortment of terrain, while the climate is favorable for almost year-round excursions. Except for February and March, when it seems to be raining everywhere, good weather can be found in one region or another throughout the year.

TREKKING IN THE SIERRA

Trekking is one of the most popular adventure activities. A number of national parks offer uninhabited areas for days of wandering, while the populated highlands of the Sierra are dotted with small villages whose inhabitants usually offer a welcome to backpacking foreigners.

One of the most popular treks in Ecuador is the easy three-day hike to the ruins of Ingapirca, the finest example of Inca stonework in the country. The hike begins in the charming village of Achupallas, north of Cuenca, 15km (9 miles) off the Pan-American Highway, where you can engage a local guide if desired. A dirt track eventually gives way to a cobbled footpath leading to a pass. You have to squeeze through a small cave to get to the other side. After a brief descent, the trail starts to climb again and traverses a mountain slope above the green valley of the Río Cadrul. An excellent site for the first night's camp is beside the sparkling waters of the high mountain lake Laguna Las Tres Cruces (Lake of the Three Crosses).

After about a half-day walk on the second day – crossing rocky ridges and skirting boggy

Climbing a ladder over an ice wall on Cotopaxi.

valleys – the trail drops below the peak of Quilloloma. The remains of the old Inca road appear in the valley below. There is an excellent place to camp near Laguna Culebrillas and some minor Inca ruins, aptly named Paredones ("ruined walls") because of the surviving crude stonework. A final three- to four-hour hike on the third day follows the grassy Inca road to the ruins of Ingapirca (see page 194).

NATIONAL PARKS

Several national parks within the highland region of Ecuador are especially popular with trekkers because of the ease of accessibility, established trail systems, and marvelous scenery. In most cases, day hikes supplant longer treks for those who prefer to see the sights with a lighter load. Parks can be visited at any time of year, but facilities within them are at a minimum, if they exist at all. A small park entrance fee is usually charged.

Cotopaxi National Park not only attracts climbers who come to scale the Cotopaxi volcano, but also its wide open *páramo*, which is ideal for cross-country treks. The lower slopes (called the Arenal – a word that comes from the Spanish *arena* meaning sand) are an interesting landscape of volcanic sand and boulders

Cloud forest in Pichincha Province.

⊘ YOU GET WHAT YOU PAY FOR

Mountain guides are available for inexperienced climbers, but caution in selecting the proper guide is strongly recommended. There are people who claim to be guides when they do not have the appropriate experience, and the result is potentially dangerous. A decent guide charges a decent price, and it is not something that you should economize on.

It is best to go with an adventure outfitter or agency which specializes in mountain excursions, or you could hire one of the ASEGUIM (www.aseguim.org) certified guides listed on their website. Alternatively see page see page 106 for suggestions.

from an eruption and associated mud flows in the late 19th century. The Ruta del Cóndor is a three- to four-day hike from the village of Papallacta to the base of Cotopaxi. It passes several mountain lakes harboring Andean teal, Andean lapwing, *caricari*, and wild horses. The glaciers off Antisana loom over the *páramo*, and condors can sometimes be seen soaring around Sincholagua.

Parque Nacional El Cajas lies about 32km (20 miles) west of Cuenca. Within its 30,000 hectares (74,000 acres) there is a huge variety of landscapes, ranging from granite rock outcrops to barely penetrable cloud forests, where mountain toucans and tropical woodpeckers make their home. With the exception of day-hike trails around the ranger station, most of the area is totally without marked trails, yet a cross-country trek of several days is quite feasible. The region is dotted with some 250 lakes of various sizes and colors, and fishing for trout is encouraged.

Parque Nacional Podocarpus, south of Loja, is very popular with hikers. The area is largely cloud forest and is home to the reticent spectacled bear, the flamboyant Andean cock-of-the-rock, and the mountain tanager. A trail system includes several day hikes from the park headquarters, and there are various options for overnight camping.

MOUNTAINEERING

The Andean mountain range in Ecuador comprises one of the largest concentrations of volcanoes in the world. It is possible to gain valuable high-altitude experience on moderate routes that do not require technical ice-climbing skill. With proper acclimatization, most peaks can be conquered over a weekend. Huts, or *refugios*, have been constructed on many of the higher and more popular climbs. Some of the huts are equipped with bunks (bring a sleeping bag), a communal kitchen with gas stove – though the Cotopaxi refuge also sells food – and the services of a hut guardian who knows the present conditions and route descriptions. Bringing your own stove during peak climbing periods is a good idea, as the huts can get crowded and the communal kitchen overused. Water is available at the *refugios*, but must be treated with purification tablets or boiled before drinking.

Chewing coca leaves is not connected with cocaine. Purchasable at markets, these leaves, when masticated, combat altitude sickness: the best method is not to chew but place each leaf in your cheek, sucking out the nutrients.

Good climbing weather is possible almost year-round, but normally the best months are June through September and during a short dry spell in December and January. Being a tropical mountain range at the equator, the Ecuadorian Andes generate unusual weather conditions. One part of the cordillera may be inundated with rain, while the next section will have clear skies and perfect conditions. This, at least, makes for plenty of options.

Proper equipment is essential for safe climbing, regardless of how straightforward most routes may appear. Any climbs which involve ice or glacier travel are considered to be technical and require special equipment and knowledge of its use. Crampons, an ice axe, and rope are necessary, along with the warm clothing demanded by high-altitude mountain conditions.

A rucksack with plenty of water, food, and extra-warm clothing is vital for a summit attempt. Flag markers, or wands, are used during the ascent for route-finding, as cloudy conditions will often obscure the descent. In addition, a good headlamp with spare batteries is essential, since all climbing begins in the early hours of the morning. All mountaineering gear can be hired in Quito, and also Riobamba, and but, as with the trekking equipment, quality can vary.

Many climbs are so short that the need for proper acclimatization is often underestimated, but with major peaks above 5,700 meters (18,000ft), it should not be overlooked. The best way to accustom your system to altitude is to stay in a relatively high city or town, and take a few day hikes to higher elevations. Quito is a good choice, and there are several strenuous hikes that can help the climber get in shape. Pasachoa makes an ideal warm-up hike as far as the rock face at 4,100 meters (13,400ft), and on a clear day gives you fabulous views over the Valley of the Volcanoes.

EASIER CLIMBS

Climbers recently arrived have several options for warm-up peaks. The most popular is Tungurahua, which reopened in 2016, after 17 years of periodic eruptions. Iliniza Norte, Corazón, Atacazo, and Imbabura are other summits for climbers to get acclimatized. Iliniza Norte is a rocky 5,126-meter (6,800ft) peak about 55km (34 miles) southwest of Quito, which can be scaled in two days, and the climb is straightforward when the going is dry. A truck can be hired in Machachi or El Chaupi to get up to the parking

A hiker at high altitude.

area called La Virgen, named after a blue statue of the Virgin Mary. There is a three- to four-hour hike to the refuge, which is basic, but has a stove and bunks.

The next morning, around sunrise, climbers head up the rocky ridge to a cliff. There is a traverse named Paso de la Muerte (Death Pass), which is as difficult as it sounds, and a final scramble on loose rock to the summit.

MOUNTAIN HIGHS

For climbers with greater technical experience, the volcanoes of Cayambe, at 5,790 meters (almost 19,000ft), and Chimborazo (6,310 meters/20,700ft), or Antisana 5,755 meters (18,881 ft), are the main attractions. At

ADVENTURE TOURS FROM QUITO

With the abundance of tours available in Quito finding the right tour can be challenging. However, the real difficulty is deciding what activities to prioritize.

VOLCANO HIKES

Mountaineers tend to make a beeline for Cotopaxi from Quito, as well as the Ilinizas Sur and Norte. Iliniza Sur is one for the more experienced climbers.

A sea of cloud engulfs Cotopaxi.

Cotopaxi is a popular hike, but it is also an active volcano and was closed from 2015-7, and then again in 2023 (for two years) due to increased activity. Check online for the latest updates before planning a trip there. The climb is challenging for beginners, with some glacier hiking, but as the most climbed mountain in Ecuador, the route is well established and provided you are in decent shape, the main hurdle will be the altitude and the weather.

Good information about routes, and the various popular mountains in Ecuador for hikers, can be found on the website of **Ecuador Climbing** (www.ecuador-climbing.info). They run a range of tours, but particularly multi-day trips. Check their site for last minute offers.

Imagine Ecuador (www.imagineecuador.com), based in Baños, is one of the most popular tour providers in the region, running climbs of Cotopaxi and the Ilinizas, among others. They also offer kayaking and white-water rafting.

RAFTING

While Baños is a popular choice for rafting trips, there are also two rivers that are a great fit for experienced rafters near Quito: the Toachi, and Quijos rivers. The latter has hosted the World Rafting Championship in the past. Many tour operators run rafting trips down these torrents of foaming water, as well as multi-day tours to spots that are further afield.

Rios Ecuador (www.riosecuador.com) are a specialist rafting tour operator running trips from Quito for a range of abilities.

River People (www.riverpeopleecuador.com) offer their own lodging in the small town of Tena, and take people to tackle a range of rivers from Class I (which requires no specific skills), all the way up to Class IV+ (where there may be a significant risk of injury resulting from a mistake).

PARAGLIDING

If you'd prefer to get a great bird's eye view with minimal effort, paragliding might be the best way to go. There are a couple of reputable tour operators in Quito, but it is worth doing your own research and making sure that the safety record is still up to scratch before taking to the skies.

Quito Paragliding (http://quitoparagliding.com) offer paragliding courses for beginners, as well as tandem flights for those who simply wish to have the experience, but not the training.

BIKING

It might seem as though cycling is a little redundant in the country around Quito, especially given the tumultuous topography. But there are some great tours that drive you up to a high point then lead you down to the city, with gravity doing a lot of the hard work. A road runs up the side of Cotopaxi to about the 4,500-meter (14,800ft) mark.

Biking Dutchman (www.bikingdutchman.com) runs regular day tours down the side of Cotopaxi and longer ones further afield. This involves off-roading across lava fields.

weekends during the peak season, the *refugios* are packed with climbers preparing for the rigors of the climb ahead.

Start the climb at around midnight for a round trip of about 10 hours. Often large numbers of climbers set out at the same time, and the flickering light from their headlamps is all that is visible as they ascend through the darkness.

Antisana is the most difficult of the three peaks, but beautiful, with its rugged glacial terrain and views of other volcanoes. Cayambe,

as measured from the center of the planet. After several hours of negotiating one steep slope after another, the process becomes something of a slog, and one begins to wonder if the summit will ever appear. In the end, the persistent achieve their goal, and the final summit views are well worth the effort.

WHITE-WATER RAFTING

The attraction of running untamed rivers draws world-class rafters and kayakers to Ecuador. Those with little or no experience can also safely

White-water rafting on the Río Zamora in southeast Ecuador.

which affords fabulous views across the Oriente, is also a technical climb.

Cotopaxi (5,900 meters/19,340ft), though the country's second highest peak, is not a technical climb so accessible to climbers with no previous ice-climbing experience. It has gentle, curving snow slopes and the massive rock wall of Yanasacha just below the summit. It's a pleasurable ascent as the dawn rays of the sun set the whole glacier sparkling. The summit crater, which has periodically been spewing out ash in recent years, seems perfectly formed against the deep blue Andean sky.

Chimborazo holds the attraction of being Ecuador's highest peak, and, because of the equatorial bulge, it is the highest spot on earth,

enjoy the thrill of white water with the growing number of travel adventure companies operating out of Quito, Tena, and Baños.

Many of Ecuador's rivers can be run year-round, while some of the more technically difficult ones are possible only during certain seasons. The most accessible and commonly run ones are the Río Toachi and the Río Blanco, both two to three hours from Quito. These rivers traverse the Western Cordillera, passing through forested canyons interspersed with small farming villages. The best time to go is from February to May.

A popular Class III rafting trip, suitable for both beginners and experienced rafters, is along the upper Río Napo. It starts near Tena and is a fun trip through tropical rainforest descending the upper slopes of the Amazon basin and passing several indigenous Quichua communities. The trip is possible all year round, but the best months to do it are between March and October.

For the experienced rafter and kayaker Ecuador has many challenging Class IV and V rivers. One of the most exciting is the Río Misahuallí, organised from Tena. But beware of the Casanova Falls; the river can be run safely only from October to March in the low-water season when,

Bungee-jumping in Baños.

after a set of Class IV rapids, rafters must be able to stop themselves before the falls.

It is a beautiful trip through virgin rainforest; parrots, oropendulas, and other tropical birds abound. The combination of spectacular natural scenery and a strong feeling of isolation makes the adventure all the more exciting.

HORSEBACK RIDING

Horseback riding across the lush valleys and hills of the Sierra has become a popular leisure activity throughout Ecuador. Several agencies offer organized trips out of Otavalo, Baños, and Cuenca. Ride Andes (www.rideandes.com) offers a wide range of trips, including one-day rides around Quito as well as hacienda tours, cattle

Baños is the place to go for extreme sports. Try rafting, canyoning, or even puenting – bungee-jumping from bridges. There are six sets of hot pools to soak tired muscles, as well as some luxury spas.

round-ups, and volcano treks. Longer trips can be arranged into the Podocarpus Reserve in the very south of Ecuador from the village of Vilcabamba. Make sure the agency knows what your experience is, particularly if you are a beginner.

MOUNTAIN BIKING

The best way to get off the beaten track is on a mountain bike exploring the extensive dirt and cobbled roads that pass through villages rarely visited by tourists. The high elevation, hilly terrain, and poor road conditions are challenging, but the views and the local communities make cycling well worth the effort.

If you stay off the main paved roads such as the Pan-American Highway – the Ecuadorians are known for their unsafe driving – the unpaved routes selected from a good topographical map will usually offer solitude and pleasant surprises.

A good place to get acclimatized to the elevation is the market town of Otavalo, from where day trips can be made to the surrounding small villages known for their *artesanías*. Several outfitters in town will rent you bikes for the day and give advice about some good routes to follow. A more ambitious ride takes you 600 meters (2,000ft) up a paved road to Cuicocha, a spectacular collapsed volcanic caldera now filled with water. A labyrinth of unpaved roads leads back to Otavalo.

A popular day trip is a mostly downhill ride from Baños, where bikes of dubious quality can be rented, to the jungle town of Puyo. You follow the cliff-hugging road along the gorge of the Río Pastaza, passing several waterfalls. In Río Verde town, bikes may be left with a local shopkeeper while you visit local waterfalls. Buses pass at half-hourly intervals: put your bike on top of the bus and avoid the long climb back to Baños.

A popular three- to five-day ride takes you past the volcanic crater lake of Quilotoa. A long climb (or bus ride) from the Pan-American Highway to the indigenous village of Zumbahua is rewarded by views of a volcanic landscape decorated by wheat fields. A dirt track leads to the lake. The next day, after a cold night on the crater rim, you wind along the edge of a deeply eroded pumice plain to the town of Siglos, where a bus can be taken back to Quito.

PARAGLIDING

The topography of Ecuador is well suited for paragliding. One popular launch site is at the refuge (4,200 meters/13,800ft) on Cotopaxi, where you can ride thermals to the top of the highest volcano in the world. The best time of year to fly is December. Equally exciting is a flight from La Crucita on the coast, catching winds off the ocean, and following a ridgeline nearly 10km (6 miles) long, staying airborne for three to five hours. Some enthusiasts take off from the slopes of Volcán Pichincha and soar over the city of Quito. The best times to fly are during August and September. There is also a paragliding school called Fly Ecuador in Ibarra offering lessons (www.flyecuador.com.ec).

SURFING

Ecuador has much to offer as a surfing destination thanks to the Pacific storms which send waves directly towards its coast. In 2004, the country hosted the World Surfing Championships, in which more than 27 countries participated, and it has subsequently hosted other world league events. Kite-surfing has also become established.

Montañita, in Guayas province, is Ecuador's surfing hotspot and a popular backpacker hangout. In the north, Mompiche (Esmeraldas province) is renowned for its north break and 300-meter (985ft) ride. South breaks can be caught from June to October, while the north-facing breaks are better from December to April.

Buy topographical maps at the Military Geographical Institute (IGM) in Quito (see page 311). Its website (www.igm.gob.ec) has many maps, although their quality is inferior to those on paper.

The Galápagos Islands are another well-known surf spot. On San Cristóbal the waves are best from November to March, while Santa Cruz is best between April and August.

SCUBA-DIVING

Ecuador is home to some of the world's best diving sites. In the Parque Nacional Machalilla, the coral is in good condition and attracts porcupinefish, parrotfish, and broomtail groupers, as well as eels, rays, starfish, sea cucumbers, and green turtles. The waters of the park are best

Catching the waves at Montañita.

explored from June to September, as the drop in water temperature allows for greater visibility. Humpback whales can be seen around the Isla de la Plata at this time when they come to mate and give birth.

Diving in the Galápagos Islands is an unforgettable experience, although there are areas with strong currents. The reefs around Wolf and Darwin islands are home to dolphins, marine turtles, hammerhead and whale sharks, and moray eels, while schools of tropical fish can be seen at the Devil's Crown on Floreana. At Estrada Point on Santa Cruz, it is possible to see marine iguanas, sea lions, white-fin reef sharks, and at the nearby Caamaño islet pods of friendly sea lions.

Ceviche can be made from a variety of seafood.

FOOD

There's no escaping bananas. But Ecuador's topography has led to the development of some very distinctive dishes in different regions.

There is no single Ecuadorian cuisine, but several ones that correspond to Ecuador's geographical regions: Costa, Sierra, and Oriente. And what you will find in good restaurants is quite different from what most people eat in rural areas and what you will find in market booths and small cafés throughout the country.

Bananas, however, are everywhere. Several varieties are grown on the coast and in the Oriente, from tiny finger bananas (oritas) to large, green cooking plantains (plátanos or verdes). The yellow bananas of the kind Westerners are accustomed to are called guineos in Ecuador. Short, fat red bananas called maqueños are also good to eat raw. Bananas and plantains are trucked up to every highland town and market, so you'll have no trouble finding them.

STAPLE FOODS

Rice (arroz) is not an indigenous food, but it is ubiquitous, although potatoes (papas) are more of a highland staple. You can count on one or the other to come with every meal. And sometimes, for a complete carbohydrate overload, noodles (fideos), potatoes, rice, yuca (a white starchy tuber), and plátanos will be served, and that's the meal. This is poor people's food, and a partial explanation of why many Ecuadorians are short in stature: besides a genetic component, they do not consume much protein.

Ecuador was the original banana republic. For many years bananas were its principal export, and the country is still among the world's largest exporters.

Canelazo, a mix of hot spiced orange juice and aguardiente, for sale on La Ronda.

Ecuador is overflowing with fruit, from enormous papayas to more exotic treats like passion fruit (ayatacso, maracuyá, and granadilla are just a few varieties), sweet custard apples (chirimoyas) and tart tamarinds (tamarindos). The naranjilla, a tiny fruit that looks like a fuzzy, orangey-greenish crab apple, makes a strange-colored but tasty drink that is often served instead of orange juice. If you are uncertain about how to eat a fruit, try it as a juice (jugo). You can ask for juice without water (sin agua) and without sugar (sin azúcar).

Visit a market as soon as possible after your arrival. Do not be intimidated by the strange-looking array. Instead, buy every fruit you've never seen before, then go back to your hotel or *hostal* and ask the owner to share them with you and tell you the names of the different varieties. You'll discover some delicious fruits, which you can then enjoy for the rest of your trip.

PACIFIC FLAVORS

Many of the coastal dishes are typical of the entire Pacific coast from Chile to Mexico. They include ceviche, which is fish *(pescados)* or various types of seafood *(mariscos)* marinated in lemon or lime juice, onions, and chili peppers.

Some of the ingredients for making ceviche.

⊘ ANDEAN FESTIVAL DISHES

Andean festivals are a great place to try local foods. *Fanesca* is an incredibly rich soup served only during Holy Week (the week before Easter). You name it and *fanesca* has it: fish, eggs *(huevos)*, cheese *(queso)*, corn, and every imaginable grain and vegetable, but no meat. *Cuy*, or guinea pig, is often eaten on special occasions, and you can almost always find it in some form during Andean festivals. Whether it's fried, roasted with potatoes, or in a spicy sauce, *cuy* is a delicacy. Yahuarlocro is a hearty potato soup made with sheep's innards seasoned with oregano and peanuts and served with avocado, chopped red onion, and tomato.

The dish has been around since Inca times, when they marinated raw fish in *chicha*. Ecuadorian ceviche is quite soupy, uses oil and tomatoes, and is served with popcorn, or thinly sliced fried plantain *(chifles)* on the side.

Ecuador's superb sea bass *(corvina)* is served a number of ways, including fried *(frito)*, breaded and fried *(apanado)*, and filleted and grilled *(a la plancha)*. Try any seafood cooked in *agua de coco* (coconut milk), including clams *(almejas* or *conchas)*, grouper *(cherna)*, mackerel *(sierra)*, marlin *(picudo)*, snapper *(pargo)*, tuna *(atún)*, and squid *(calamares)*. The *dorado*, or dolphinfish, which is not a mammal like the true dolphin, is also popular and not to be missed.

A thoughtful Ecuadorian custom for regulating the spiciness of food is to serve hot sauce *(salsa picante)* made from chili peppers *(ají)* in a little side dish so that you can add as much or as little as you like.

TASTES OF THE ORIENTE

Coastal and Oriente foods are similar because of the two regions' low elevation and tropical climate, although there is more game-hunting in the jungle (everything from monkeys to tapir and *paca*, a large rodent) and freshwater fish instead of seafood. In both places you'll find lots of *plátanos*, *yuca*, rice, and fried fish. There are several dishes served exclusively in the Oriente, however. One is piranha, although it surprises many visitors that the notorious carnivorous fish is itself good for eating. The Oriente rivers also have lots of catfish *(challua* or *bagre)*, which people make into a stew with plantains, chili peppers, and *cilantro* (leaf coriander).

For a jungle salad, try *palmitos* (palm hearts) or chonta palm fruits *(frutas de chonta)*, both considered delicacies. *Chucula* is a tasty drink made with boiled and mashed plantains, which resembles a banana milkshake.

SERRANO CUISINE

As we climb to the highlands, a word about the tuber, that traditional mainstay of indigenous Andean life. There are a lot of tubers in the Andes, beginning with dozens of varieties of potatoes. The potato was cultivated around Lake Titicaca, the region that still has the most varieties, some of which are so specialized they grow only at altitudes above 2,400 meters (8,000ft).

Potatoes are served with almost every meal in the highlands, usually boiled, but sometimes cut up and added to thick soups. If you don't like potatoes you're in trouble in Ecuador. They are the food of the common people, and, as in Inca times, everyone plants and eats them. The great Inca terraces, however, used to be reserved for another crop, corn, which was much revered and usually made into *chicha*.

Besides regular white potatoes in many sizes and varieties, you will come across the sweet potato *(camote)* as well as the *oca*, which looks like a long, skinny, lumpy potato. One Ecuadorian potato specialty is *llapingachos*, potato pancakes made with potatoes, cheese, and onions and eaten with fried eggs and spicy sausage. A better lunch cannot be had.

Soups are the essence of meals in the Sierra. Before the Spanish conquest *indígenas* did not have ovens for baking, which meant that most food was boiled, a custom that survives today. Soup is called *caldo*, *sopa*, *chupe*, or *locra*.

Generally, a *sopa* or a *caldo* is a thin soup with potatoes and various unidentified floating objects of the faunal variety. A *locro* or *chupe* is a thick, creamy soup. *Sopa seca* or just plain *seco* (which means dry) is more of a stew than a soup, with meat and vegetables added according to the budget and whim of the cook. One of the most common *locros* is called *yaguar locro* (blood soup) that contains the heart, liver, and other internal organs (which is to say tripe, or *mondongo*) of a cow (*vaca*

or *res*), pig *(chancho)*, or sheep *(borrego)*; the soup is sprinkled with blood sausage or the animal's dried blood.

Mazamorra is a thick soup made with a ground corn base and cabbage, potatoes, onions, and spices. *Sancocho* is a stew made with *plátanos* and corn. Most soups and stews are liberally seasoned with *cilantro* and many are given a yellow or orange color by the addition of *achiote* seeds.

Corn (*maíz* or *sara*) is another staple, especially in the Sierra. Unlike in Mexico and Central

Chilis and limes for sale in Cuenca.

☉ SWEET SUCCESS

Ecuador produces one of the world's best cacaos due to its unique floral, fruity, and spicy notes. Nowadays it has regained its reputation as the big name in gourmet chocolate, being the number one exporter of top-quality chocolate (defined as containing over 70 percent cacao), but for a long time, the country's chocolate industry looked like fizzling out altogether.

To discuss cacao in Ecuador is to discuss Ecuadorian history itself. Indigenous cultures in Latin America had been using cacao well before the Spanish set foot on these shores in the 16th century; it was the Spanish who began exporting beans as early as 1630. It was initially a clandestine trade, but was booming by the late 19th century, when

Ecuador led the world in the cacao business. Unfortunately, in the early 1900s an unknown disease devastated most of the crops and plunged the country into crisis. However, the sector has now revived and today over 500,000 farmers make a living from this crop. Whilst heavy emphasis has been placed on exportation, chocolate's value as a consumable product and tourist draw within Ecuador has been realized. In Guayaquil, an area producing the renowned arriba cacao, you can take a tour on request, including cacao plantations, chocolate factories, and chocolate-themed meals, with Chchukululu (tel: 099-975 0023; www.facebook.com/Chchukululu). There are also plenty of interactive chocolate tours in Mindo.

America, corn in the Andes is not ground and made into tortillas. In northern Ecuador corn is most commonly served on the cob (choclo). Ecuadorian corn has enormous, sweet kernels arranged irregularly, and it's the best corn-on-the-cob imaginable. In the north, corn is also eaten as parched kernels (kamcha) or as popcorn (canguil). In southern Ecuador it is commonly served as boiled kernels (muti or mote). Humitas are corn tamales: cornmeal seasoned and steamed in the leaf. Don't eat the leaf – unwrap it

The Quichua language has contributed one word to English: "jerky," derived from charqui, meaning dried meat. Made from any form of meat, it is normally sun-dried and often "rehydrated" for use in empanadas.

and eat what's inside. *Tostadas de maíz* are corn pancakes that make a good breakfast or snack.

MIRACLE GRAIN

Other grains grown locally include *quinoa*, wheat (*trigo*), and barley (*cebada*). *Quinoa* is native to the Andes. This tiny, round grain is an amazingly nutritious food, consisting of 15 percent complete protein, 55 percent carbohydrate, and only 4 percent fat. The Incas regarded *quinoa* as sacred, and it was their second-most important food crop. *Quinoa* is usually served in soup, but it can also be eaten as a side dish, in the same way as rice. The grain has become a staple in Novo Andina, New Andean food which blends traditional Andean recipes with contemporary cooking methods. *Quinoa* is often served as a risotto or used to encrust a fish or meat.

Most barley is ground up and used in soup, but wheat flour is used to make a variety of good breads and rolls (*pan* and *panecitos*) and *empanadas*, which are baked pastries filled with cheese or meat. Around Latacunga you'll hear women at street stalls calling *allullas, allullas* (pronounced "azhúzhas"). These are homemade rolls, good when hot and fresh, but hard when they get cold.

Broad beans are called *habas*. These beans, which are much larger than you may have seen at home, are boiled and served hot, dipped in salty *campo* cheese, or cold in a salad dressed with butter and lemon juice.

Spit-roast pig is popular street food in Ecuador.

⊘ FROM PET TO POT

If you'll settle for something smaller than a sirloin, try guinea pig (*cuy*). Until the arrival of the Europeans, cuy was the main source of meat in the Andes. Every family had guinea pigs running around the kitchen, and some still do.

Cuy is eaten only on special occasions, when one is scooped up, killed, gutted, cleaned, rubbed with lard and spices, put on a spit, and roasted in the fire or baked in the oven. If you can bring yourself to try *cuy*, you will find that there's not much meat, but what there is is delicious, and, as the Ecuadorians put it, what else are guinea pigs good for?

IN SEARCH OF MEAT DISHES

You should ask for *lomo* or *bifstec*, or *chuleta* if you want a chop. *Parrilladas* are steakhouses or grills, where the meat is sometimes charcoal-grilled at your table. *A la parrilla* means grilled, and *churrasco* or *lomo montado* is meat (usually beef) topped with fried eggs. You can also order veal (*ternera*), lamb (*cordero*), or pork (*puerco* or *chanco*; *kuchi* in Quichua). *Lechón* is suckling pig.

Salchicha means sausage, while *chorizo* refers to pork sausage. Bacon is called *tocino*, ham is *jamón*.

Asado, which means roasted, always refers to whole roasted pig in Ecuador, unless otherwise modified. *Fritada* (fried pork) is cooked in large copper and brass *pailas* (wok-like pans) and *chicharrón* is fried pork skin, crispy and delicious.

Other sources of dietary protein include chicken *(pollo)* or hen *(gallina)*, and eggs served in the usual ways, as well as pasteurized cow's milk *(leche)*, which is sold in unwieldy liter-sized plastic bags, and excellent cheese *(queso)*, the quality of which has soared in recent years with the arrival of Swiss and Italian immigrants who have introduced European varieties. As for fish, in the Sierra many streams and lakes have been stocked with tasty, if rather bony, trout *(trucha)*.

SLAKING YOUR THIRST

Bebidas is the term for beverages in general, alcoholic or otherwise. Ecuadorian wine *(vino)* is unlikely to win any international awards, although occasionally bottles can be quite good. Argentinian and Chilean wines are often excellent, but expensive. You're better off sticking to soft drinks *(gaseosas)*, mineral water *(agua mineral)*, among which Güitig (pronounced wee-tig) is the most common brand, or beer *(cerveza)*. There are a number of locally brewed beers, the most common of which is Pilsener.

There is also tea *(té)*, herb tea *(agua aromática)*, hot chocolate (*chocolate caliente* or *cocóa*), and coffee *(café)*. This last is usually boiled until it becomes a sludge, then set on the table in a small carafe. Known as *esencia* (essence), it looks just like soy sauce and causes some interesting confusion in Chinese restaurants *(chifas)*. The *esencia* is poured in your cup and hot water or milk is added; its taste is similar to instant coffee. Black coffee is *tinto*, coffee with milk is *café con leche*, and coffee with hot water and milk is *pintado* ("painted"). *Api* is a thick, hot drink made from ground corn; *chicha morada* is a sweet, non-alcoholic drink made from purple corn.

When it comes to liquor, what you get is the most potent intoxicant with the highest imaginable octane rating: a distilled sugarcane liquor known as *trago* or *puntas*, which burns with a clear blue flame. Local brands include Cristal and Sinchi Shungu ("strong heart"); there are several nameless varieties that are produced without sanitary regulation in the countryside.

Hervidas are hot drinks served at every fiesta, intended to ward off the Andean chill, consisting of *trago* mixed with honey and *naranjilla* or blackberry juice; *guayusa* is *trago* mixed with sugar and hot *guayusa* tea, while *canelazo* is *trago* spiced with cinnamon, sugar, and lime.

As they say in Ecuador: *¡Buen provecho!*

Cooking cuy (guinea pig) in Baños.

⊙ A VERY SPECIAL SPECIALTY

One jungle specialty is *chicha* (or *aswa*), a fermented beer made from *yuca*, which is also known as *manioc* *(mucuna)*. In order to make the *chicha* ferment, women chew the *manioc*, spit it into a large jar, and add water – the enzymes in the saliva cause the fermentation. In the highlands, however, *chicha* is not made by mastication; instead yeast and sugar are added to make it ferment.

Generally, the drink will only be offered to you in people's homes, so if you find the thought of it unpalatable you needn't worry about encountering *chicha* in the course of ordinary travel, unless your tour includes remote rainforest homes.

Fishing boats at Playas.

Cuenca's centro histórico.

Colorful buildings in Guayaquil.

INTRODUCTION

A detailed guide to the entire country, with principal sights cross-referenced by number to the maps.

Market in Salasaca.

Ecuador is the smallest of South America's Andean republics and without doubt the easiest to explore. The capital city, Quito, is the perfect base for travelers; situated 24km (15 miles) south of the equator at an altitude of 2,800 meters (9,180ft), it has a pleasant, spring-like climate all year round. Despite its expanding population, its elegant colonial heart preserves the streets and buildings of the 18th century, while the modern "New Town" offers every comfort of the 21st.

The classic excursion from Quito, and one of the country's most famous attractions, is the short hop north for the Saturday craft market in Otavalo.

Volcán Cotopaxi.

Then, stretching south of the city, is the lush mountain valley that the German scientist Alexander von Humboldt dubbed "the Avenue of the Volcanoes." The city of Cuenca, considered Ecuador's most beautiful colonial treasure, marks the beginning of the Southern Sierra, a remote and strongly traditional region that has some of the country's most distinctive *indígena* (indigenous) communities and its most important Inca ruins.

But Ecuador offers much more than *serrano* (highland) cultures and the spectacle of ice on the equator. Just 20 minutes west of Quito by air is the Pacific coast. Moving to a more languid rhythm of life than the highlands, the coast is dotted with comfortable resorts and washed by warm sea currents from the northern Pacific. Travelers often head to the coast directly rather than passing through tropical Guayaquil, Ecuador's largest city and its often chaotic commercial heart.

Twenty minutes by air east of Quito is the Oriente region within the Amazon basin. Comfortable jungle lodges abound, and boat or canoe trips can take you to the farthest reaches of this threatened region, which is fast becoming one of the continent's greatest travel attractions.

Finally, the Galápagos archipelago is in a class of its own. Easily visited on a tour or independently, this naturalists' paradise alone can justify a visit to Ecuador. A journey here is an expensive treat, but it remains one of the world's unforgettable travel experiences.

122

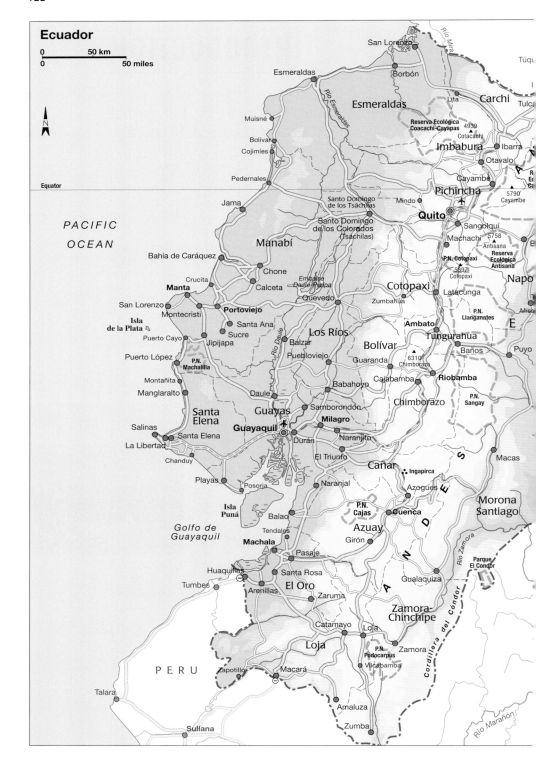

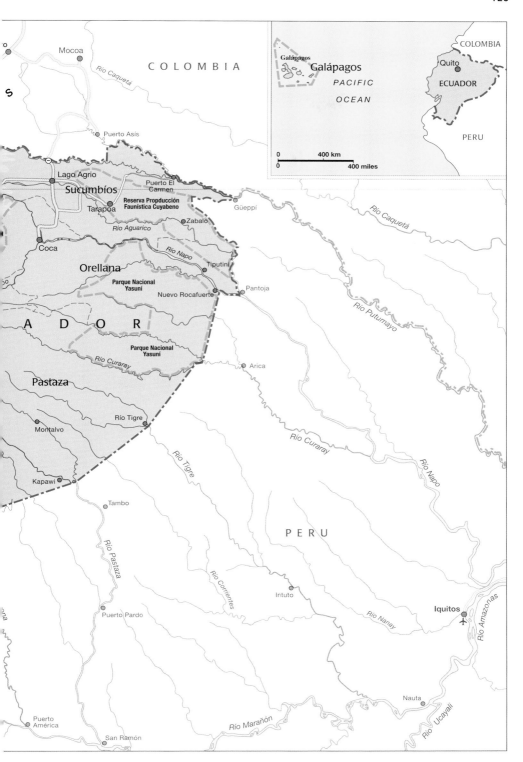

COLOMBIA

Mocoa

Río Caquetá

Puerto Asís

Galápagos

Galápagos

PACIFIC

OCEAN

COLOMBIA

Quito

ECUADOR

PERU

0   400 km
0   400 miles

Lago Agrio

Sucumbíos

Puerto El
Carmen

Tarapoa

Reserva Propducción
Faunística Cuyabeno

Güeppí

Río Caquetá

Zabalo

Río Aguarico

Coca

Río Napo

Tiputini

Orellana

Parque Nacional
Yasuní

Nuevo Rocafuerte

Pantoja

Río Putumayo

A   D   O   R

Parque Nacional
Yasuní

Río Curaray

Arica

Pastaza

Río Curaray

Montalvo

Río Tigre

Río Napo

Kapawi

Tambo

PERU

Río Tigre

Río Pastaza

Río Corrientes

Intuto

Río Nanay

Iquitos

Río Amazonas

Puerto Pardo

Puerto
América

San Ramón

Nauta

Río Ucayali

Río Marañón

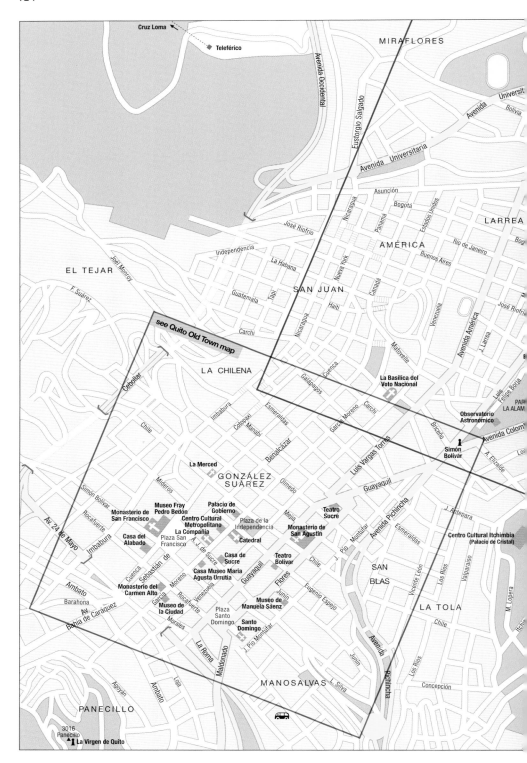

Cruz Loma

Teleférico

MIRAFLORES

Avenida Occidental

Eustorgio Salgado

Universit

Avenida

Bolivia

Avenida Universitaria

Asunción

Bogotá

LARREA

Estados Unidos

Panama

Río de Janeiro

Bog

José Riofrío

AMÉRICA

Buenos Aires

Nicaragua

Independencia

La Habana

Nueva York

Canadá

José Riofrío

EL TEJAR

José Monroy

Guatemala

Tapi

SAN JUAN

Haití

Venezuela

Avenida América

F. Suárez

Carchi

J. Larrea

see Quito Old Town map

LA CHILENA

Cuenca

Galápagos

La Basílica del
Voto Nacional

Luis Felipe Borja

PAR
LA ALAM

Cebollar

Imbabura

Cotopaxi

Esmeraldas

García Moreno

Carchi

Observatorio
Astronómico

Avenida Colom

Chile

Manabí

Benalcázar

Briceño

A. Elizalde

Los

Simón
Bolívar

La Merced

Mideros

GONZÁLEZ
SUÁREZ

Olmedo

Luis Vargas Torres

Guayaquil

Simón Bolívar

Museo Fray
Pedro Bedón

Palacio de
Gobierno

Mejía

Teatro
Sucre

J. Antepara

Rocafuerte

Monasterio de
San Francisco

Centro Cultural
Metropolitano

Plaza de la
Independencia

Avenida Pichincha

Esmeraldas

Casa del
Alabado

La Compañía

Plaza San
Francisco

A. J. de Sucre

Catedral

Monasterio de
San Agustín

J. Pío Montúfar

Centro Cultural Itchimbia
(Palacio de Cristal)

Av. 24 de Mayo

Imbabura

Cuenca

Sebastián de

Moreno

Casa de
Sucre

Teatro
Bolívar

Chile

SAN

Vicente León

Los Ríos

Ambato

Casa Museo María
Agusta Urrutia

Guayaquil

Flores

Eugenio Espejo

BLAS

Valparaíso

M. Lopera

Barahona

Monasterio del
Carmen Alto

García

Rocafuerte

Venezuela

Junín

LA TOLA

Itch

Av.
Bahía de Caráquez

Museo de
la Ciudad

Plaza
Santo
Domingo

Morales

Santo
Domingo

Museo de
Manuela Sáenz

Junín

Chile

Los Ríos

La Roma

Maldonado

J. Pío Montúfar

Agoyán

Ambato

Loja

MANOSALVAS

L. Silva

Avenida

Pichincha

Concepción

PANECILLO

3016
Panecillo

La Virgen de Quito

Parque Carolina, Jardín Botánico, Vivarium, Museo de la Biodiversidad

Museo de Artesanías Mindalae **25**

Museo Guaysamín **28**

COLÓN

Avenida Cristóbal Colón

Avenida Cristóbal Colón

MARISCAL SUCRE

Avenida 6 de Diciembre

Avenida 12 de Octubre

Hotel Hilton Colón

PARQUE EL EJIDO

LA FLORESTA

EL BELÉN

Museo de Jacinto Jijón y Caamaño

Museo Nacional/ Casa de la Cultura Ecuatoriana

Avenida 12 de Octubre

Palacio Legislativo

Diego Ladrón

de Guevara

de Guevara

Coliseo General Rumiñahui

Diego Ladrón

VICENTINA

EUGENIO ESPEJO

Instituto Geográfico Militar

La Condamine

Manuel Cajías

M. Albán

CHIMBÍA

Río Machángara

see Quito New Town map

PARQUE ITCHIMBIA

Quito

0 ___ 400 m

0 ___ 400 yds

La Virgen de Quito.

QUITO

Latin America's most beautiful church is here, along with splendid colonial buildings set against a dramatic mountainous backdrop. A grid system makes it easy to find your way around.

Surrounded by snow-capped volcanoes but only 24km (15 miles) from the equator, Quito is a strange and beautiful city with a year-round spring-like climate. Although an important city in Inca and pre-Inca times, its original buildings have been erased, and today the city center is divided between the colonial architecture and sculptures of its Spanish conquest days and the clean lines of its modern section. This combination of superb, well-preserved colonial churches and convents, shining glass, and sleek contemporary architecture against a mountainous backdrop, makes Quito a fascinating place to explore.

Nestled at the foot of 4,696-meter (15,402ft) high Rucu Pichincha volcano, Ecuador's capital owes its name to the Quitua people. When the Inca Empire spread as far as Ecuador under the leadership of Huayna Capac, the indigenous inhabitants living in what is now Quito put up impressive resistance to the invaders from Cuzco (in modern-day Peru). But, in the end, Huayna Capac not only added the area to the empire but married Paccha Duchicela, a princess from the conquered people, and set up the Incas' northern capital in Quito. A road was built to link Cuzco with Quito, from which Huayna Capac preferred to rule.

His decision to divide the Inca kingdom into northern and southern

Street in the colonial Old Town.

regions – and his fathering of sons in both – were key factors in the downfall of the empire. When Huayna Capac died, his legitimate heir in Cuzco, Huascar, claimed the throne at the same time as the leader's illegitimate (but some say favorite) son, Atahualpa, declared himself Inca in Quito. The rights to the throne were clouded, too, by the Inca line of succession – which was not based solely on birth order. In many instances, the first son of an Inca was passed over for younger siblings who showed greater leadership skills,

Main attractions

El Panecillo
Teleférico
La Compañía de Jesús
La Ronda
Teatro Bolívar
La Basílica del Voto
Museo Guayasamín
Capilla del Hombre

Maps on pages 128, 140

wisdom, and courage. And, in the case of Huascar and Atahualpa, their subjects at each end of the kingdom supported the local son.

A RAZED CITY

A year after Francisco Pizarro had Atahualpa executed on the main plaza of Cajamarca, now in northern Peru, Sebastián de Benalcázar, accompanied by *conquistador* Diego de Almagro, arrived to claim Quito for the Spanish crown. They skirmished with Atahualpa's general, Rumiñahui (Face of Stone), and when it became clear he would be overcome, he angrily set the Inca palace on fire. The flames spread and the city the Spanish finally claimed was razed. (Rumiñahui, meanwhile, was captured

and executed.) For that reason, Quito has no Inca structures; all that remained of those magnificent buildings perched on the city's beautiful high plain were massive rock foundations. On those bases, the Spanish conquerors built churches, convents, and palaces in the exuberant style of the Latin American Baroque.

By the end of the 16th century, the new colonial city's population reached 1,500 and it was declared the seat of the royal *Audiencia*, a legal subdivision of the so-called "New World" colony. The proliferation of churches, convents, and monasteries won Quito the nickname "The Cloister of America" and, in 1978, the same colonial buildings prompted the United Nations to declare the city a UNESCO World Heritage Site.

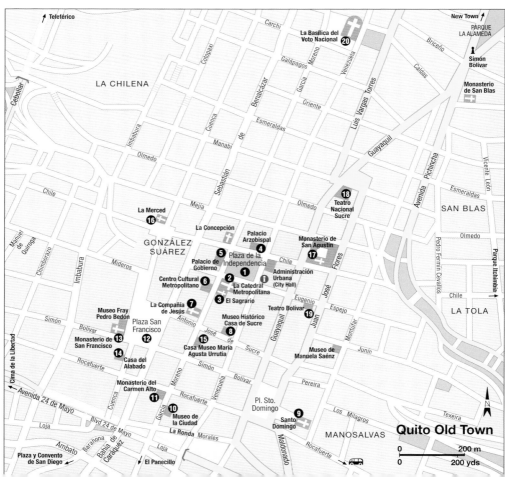

Quito Old Town

In early colonial Quito, changes came slowly but steadily as wheat farming was introduced; the indigenous population had Christianity forced upon them; and colonial rule and laws suppressed indigenous cultures. In the centuries that followed, Quito became a center for art and sculpture in the colonised continent, with the Quito School (see page 145) producing an art form characterized by Christian themes, yet which were infused with both Catholic and indigenous imagery and symbolism. Paintings used rich dark colors and gold brushwork, in a style similar to the work of the Cuzco School in Peru.

The growth and development of Quito was not problem-free. There was a bloody rebellion against a royal sales tax in 1592 and another in 1765, when a rumor spread that government-dispensed rum had been poisoned to eliminate the poorer classes. But things remained relatively peaceful until full-scale insurrection occurred when the winds of independence spreading across the continent reached this city. In August of 1809 the first sparks of revolution ignited in Quito and, on May 24, 1822, the city fell into the hands of the independence troops, led by Marshal Sucre, after a bloody battle in the foothills of Pichincha that overshadow the city. May 24 is now a national holiday. For eight years Ecuador was part of La Gran Colombia – modern-day Colombia, Venezuela, parts of southern Central America, and Ecuador, united under a single government. But, in 1830, Ecuador seceded from the union, to become independent under the presidency of former general Juan José Flores.

MODERN CITY, MODERN PROBLEMS

While the Old Town – the Centro Histórico – with its churches, convents, and whitewashed houses with red-tile roofs, has not changed much physically since colonial times, in contrast, northern Quito now boasts huge high rises, business centers, banks on every corner, shopping arcades, embassies, and smart government buildings. This part of Quito is where upper-class residential areas are concentrated. Quito's

> **⊘ Fact**
>
> The four corners of the Plaza de la Independencia are planted with flora from different parts of the word: tropical palm trees, European fruit trees that blossom in spring, an Australian eucalypt, and even an araucaria from southern Chile. It's a marvel how this diverse international collection can survive at an altitude of 2,800 meters (9,240ft), and almost on the equator.

View of El Panecillo from the Old Town.

⊘ QUITO'S IMPROVING TRANSPORTATION

Flying into Quito's international airport used to be an adventure: you plunged out of the clouds and appeared to be headed straight for a mountainside before the pilot miraculously alighted the plane on a modest runway hemmed in by apartment blocks and busy suburban life. That changed when Mariscal Sucre airport opened in 2013, some 20km (12 miles) east of the city on the Tababela Plateau. Set at a lower altitude of 2,400 meters (7,872ft), away from urban development, and with a longer runway, the facility is able to handle the largest planes.

In December 2022, Quito inaugurated the city's first underground railway line, Quito Metro, linking 15 stations from north to south. The new system – which had to close in 2023 after teething problems – should be fully functioning by 2024, and will complement the current (and ailing) "Metrobus Q", an integrated trolley-bus and articulated bus network. The metro line runs between El Labrador, in the northeast, close to the bus link to the Aeropuerto Internacional Mariscal Sucre, down to Quitumbe in Quito's southern suburbs, which handles transportation to southern and eastern Ecuador. Terminal Carcelén, is the main terminal north of Quito, for northern destinations such as Otavalo and Ibarra. Several smaller bus terminals exist, notably La Ofélia, also in northern Quito, where buses depart for Mindo and Mitad del Mundo.

La Ronda at dusk.

Quito's teleférico.

poorest areas are largely on the city's south side, together with the factories and heavy industry that stretches along the Pan-American Highway, known simply as the *Panamericana*.

Quito today extends far beyond the Old Town's borders, even spreading up the slopes of Pichincha on the west side. The city has grown to a length of over 40km (25 miles), with a width of just 3–5km (2–3 miles). On the eastern side of the city is the **Los Chillos** valley, a well-connected commuter area with over 300,000 habitants, which has experienced considerable urban development in recent years.

Despite its growing population of over two million, the city has fewer sprawling squatter settlements common to many other large cities on the South American continent. However, there are plenty of areas where the housing is at best basic and electricity and water supply erratic; and street crime has become a problem even in the smartest areas of Quito. Traffic jams on ancient cobbled streets never designed to carry cars and choking pollution from vehicles also contribute to Quito's problems.

QUITO FROM ABOVE

To get an idea of the city's layout before you start exploring, it's a good idea to head for somewhere that offers a fine panoramic view of Quito and the surrounding volcanoes. **El Panecillo (literally "the small breadloaf")** is a good place to start. Known as Shungoloma in Quechua, this domed hill dominating the Old Town is topped by a statue of the Virgen de Quito (among other names) and an observation deck, where you can survey the basin in which Quito sits. A series of steps and paths from streets García Moreno and Ambato enables you to walk up the hill but muggings are frequent and visitors are strongly advised to visit El Panecillo by taxi.

The hill marks an Inca site known as Yavirac, where a temple of the sun was once located. An even more splendid view is available from the **Cima de la Libertad**. Founded on the site of the 1822 Battle of Pichincha, this spot has a **museum** dedicated to

⊘ THE EFFECTS OF INEQUALITY

Like many Latin American cities, Quito is a mix of extremes. There are still colonial mansions, staffed by servants, that house luxury cars in their garages, boasting manicured gardens and equally manicured owners. The well off in Quito enjoy a comparatively luxurious lifestyle, and there is a growing middle class.

For the majority of the city's population, however, life is hard. Some of the poorest Quiteños migrated from the countryside in search of work. The few jobs available to them are basic and poorly paid and most families struggle to make ends meet in a city that is becoming increasingly expensive. More recent immigrants from Venezuela have added to the numbers of people desperately seeking employment. The economic fallout from the Covid-19 pandemic has also hit the city hard.

The result is a large wealth discrepancy between the haves and have-nots; a gap that has led to a rise in street crime in recent years. Quiteños are quite aware of it, and visitors need to be circumspect too: take common-sense precautions like carrying minimal cash in an internal pocket and only carrying your credit cards or passport when you need them. Take care, particularly after dark, in the Mariscal Sucre area, late at night in the Old Town, and watch your belongings if you travel on public transport. The larger bus terminals are notorious hotspots for theft.

the independence era in Quito. The museum exhibits flags, weapons, a model of this pivotal battle, and a sarcophagus containing the remains of its heroes. Dramatically, their tomb is guarded by an eternally burning flame.

On the east side of Quito's Centro Histórico, **Parque Itchimbia** at 2,910 meters (9,544ft) is another stellar viewpoint, affording excellent panoramas of the volcanoes on clear days. There are occasional art exhibitions in the beautiful **Palacio de Cristal** cultural center (https://quitocultura.com/team-member/centro-cultura-itchimbia), children's playgrounds, and plenty of green space with a network of walking trails. The best views over the Old Town from here are at dusk, when you can watch the city's lights come on. Some of the restaurants at the base of the park have balconies that hang spectacularly right over the city: a prime spot for an evening drink on your first night in Quito.

Quito's loftiest attraction, the **Teleférico** (Tue–Thu 9am–8pm, Fri–Mon 8am–8pm), starts at the base of Volcán Pichincha and transports visitors by cable car to the top of Cruz Loma at an altitude of 4,270 meters (14,000ft). The views over Quito and of the surrounding mountains are breathtaking, as is the altitude itself. From Cruz Loma, you can hike to the summit of Rucu Pichincha and back in five to six hours. Be prepared for the cold, and take things slowly in the thin air: the oxygen bar at Cruz Loma is not just for fun. Back at the cable car's base, the slightly tacky Vulqano Park has a number of fast food outlets, gift shops, and an amusement park (www.vulqanopark.com) that is popular with families with children. The line to get on the cable cars tends to grow as the day goes on, so try to get there early.

OLD TOWN

Quito's Old Town (often referred to as the Centro Histórico) was made a UNESCO World Heritage Site in 1978 and, thanks to a large-scale restoration project, it is now one of the most attractive colonial centers in Latin America. Much of the area's former grandeur has been restored, and it is dotted with boutique hotels, restaurants, museums and galleries.

Walking around the hilly, narrow streets is the best way to see Old Quito, and perhaps the best introduction to the Old Town is to take one of the guided walks of the historic center (for tours and hours see www.quito.com.ec) offered by the El Quinde Visitors' Center (Mon–Sat 8.30am–5pm). The walks follow various routes and leave from the visitor information center on the main plaza (Plaza de la Independencia) outside the Palacio Arzobispal (see page 132).

PLAZA DE LA INDEPENDENCIA

The heart of the historic center is the **Plaza de la Independencia ❶**. Also known locally as the Plaza Grande, this garden-graced square is dominated by **La Catedral Metropolitana ❷** (Metropolitan Cathedral https://visitquito.ec/lugar/catedral-metropolitana-de-quito/;

Cima de la Libertad.

Mon–Sat 9am–5pm, Sun 10am–2pm). At the center of the plaza is a bronze and marble monument celebrating Ecuador's first declaration of independence against its Spanish conquerors, in 1809.

Quito's cathedral is believed to have existed first as a wood and adobe structure before the official church was built on the site in 1565. Earthquake damage has forced restoration on three occasions. The cathedral is filled with paintings by some of Ecuador's finest early artists from what became known as the Quito School of Quito (see page 145). Outstanding amongst the cathedral's artworks is the sculpture known as the *Descent from the Cross*, by indigenous artist Caspicara. Like many churches built in Quito (and Cuenca) during the 16th and 17th centuries, the cathedral shows Moorish influences: its wooden ceiling is distinctive of the geometric-patterned *Mudéjar* style.

One of the side altars contains the remains of Venezuelan-born Marshal Antonio José de Sucre, leader of the liberation army. Left of the main altar is a statue of Ecuador's first president, Juan José Flores, and behind the altar is a plaque showing where President Gabriel García Moreno died on August 6, 1875, from gunshot wounds he received while returning to the Presidential Palace after Mass. He was carried back across the street to the church, but attempts to save his life proved futile.

Around the corner from the cathedral on pedestrianised Calle García Moreno is **El Sagrario ❸**, built between 1657 and 1706 as the cathedral's main chapel but now used as a separate church. In the cupola are some restored frescoes painted by Francisco de Albán.

Back in the Plaza Grande, on the east side of the square, is the Edificio de la Administración Urbana (**City Hall**) which was built in 1978. It is worth a visit to see the huge brightly colored naïf murals of Quito life by one of Ecuador's great artists of the 20th century, Eduardo Kingman (see page 93).

The north side of the plaza is taken up by the **Palacio Arzobispal ❹**. With its striking colonnaded facade, this was

Guards outside the Palacio de Gobierno.

the traditional residence of the archbishop from 1700: one of several buildings constructed around the cathedral to house men of the church. It's now a row of shops, but it's worth stepping inside the shopping centre to see the attractive interior courtyard that hosts several restaurants.

ROLLER-COASTER POLITICS

On the northwest side of the plaza is the **Palacio de Gobierno ⑤** (Government Palace), also known as the **Palacio de Carondelet**. The entrance is flanked by guards in red, blue, and gold 19th-century-style uniforms, which seem somewhat anachronistic in contrast with the automatic rifles they carry, and which were used during the attempted coup in 1976. This building has seen a great deal of activity, especially in the early days of the republic. From 1901 to 1948 alone, Ecuador had 39 governments and four constitutions, and at one point there were four presidents in a span of 26 days.

On guided tours of the palace (Tue–Sun 9am–4pm; ID must be produced and reservations must be made a week in advance either by phone on 02 3827000, Ext 7090, or e-mail at ucultural@presidencia.gob.ec), visitors are shown the interior patios, ornate with fountains, iron balconies and columns, and some of the halls of government if they are not in use. Correa turned the presidential residence into the Museum of the Presidency during his time in office. One of the palace's treasures is Oswaldo Guayasamín's famous mosaic mural depicting explorer Francisco de Orellana's voyage to the Amazon. Nearly 400 years old, the palace is an unusual mix of formal and informal, and must be one of the world's few presidential offices where the street-level floor has been converted into small shops that sell souvenirs.

Half a block from the plaza, at Eugenio Espejo 1147, is the **Centro Cultural Metropolitano ⑥** (https://quitocultura.com/team-member/centro-cultural-metropolitano), which includes the renovated Biblioteca Federico González Suárez and the Museo Alberto Mena Caamaño (https://quitocultura.com/team-member/

Taking it easy in the Plaza de la Independencia.

La Compañía's gilded altar and ceiling.

museo-alberto-mena-caamano/; Tue–Sat 9am–4pm). This museum is set in an early Jesuit house that later served as barracks for the royal Spanish troops in Quito and was the old headquarters of the Royal Audencia. The stone column in the patio was the pillory, and underneath it is the dungeon where 36 revolutionaries of the 1809 uprising were imprisoned for nine months before being executed. Wax figures in the museum graphically illustrate their deaths. The museum contains ecclesiastical art from the 16th and 17th centuries, as well as works from the 1900s.

LATIN AMERICA'S MOST BEAUTIFUL CHURCH

Almost next door to the museum is the impressive 16th-century church of **La Compañía de Jesús** ⑦ (http://fundacioniglesiadelacompania.org.ec; Mon–Fri 9.30am–6pm, Sat until 4pm, Sun 12.30–4pm). This Jesuit church took 163 years to finish and is the most ornate in the country. It was severely damaged by the 1987 earthquake, but an extensive restoration was completed in 2002.

Praying outside Iglesia de Santo Domingo.

Richly intricate both inside and out, it is a masterpiece of Baroque and Quiteño Colonial art: its altars are covered in gold leaf and the fine paintings on its vaulted ceiling have earned it the nickname "Quito's Sistine Chapel." The walls are covered with murals by the Quito School. The designs on the columns inside the church clearly show a Moorish influence, and the columns themselves are said to be copies of those by Bernini in the Vatican; they are reproduced in the main altar. However, the church's most precious treasures, including an emerald- and gold-laden painting of the *Virgen Dolorosa* (Our Lady of Sorrow), are kept in the country's Central Bank vaults and taken out only for special religious festivals. And the church's original holdings were far, far richer than what remains now. In 1767, when a decree banned the Jesuits from Spanish domains, the treasures in La Compañía were put into 36 boxes and shipped to Spain to pay war debts. What remained – mostly silver – was put up for sale but the devout Quiteños refused to buy it, saying that the items in question belonged to God.

At the foot of the altar in La Compañía are the remains of Saint Mariana de Jesús. In 1645, a combination of measles and diphtheria epidemics and an earthquake killed 14,000 people in Quito, prompting a frantic attempt to break the city's streak of bad luck. It was then that 26-year-old Mariana de Jesús stepped in. The orphaned daughter of an aristocratic family, she had already given all her wealth to the poor and was said to have miraculously healed the sick. Now she made a bargain with God, offering him her own life if the rest of the city's population could be saved. As the story goes, she fell ill immediately and, with her death, the plagues on the city ended. Just before she died, doctors bled her – as was the custom – and threw the blood into the garden of her home. It was said that a lily grew where the blood touched the earth and, for that reason, when the Pope canonized Mariana, he called her the "Lily of Quito."

When you come out of La Compañía, turn right, then immediately left down Avenida de Mariscal Sucre and between the streets of García Moreno and Venezuela you will find the **Museo Histórico Casa de Sucre** ❽ (https://museosdequito.wordpress.com/museo-casa-de-sucre/; Tue–Sun 9am–4pm, 3pm last tour), once the home of Marshal Antonio José de Sucre. The museum houses a collection of weapons, clothing, furniture, and documents both belonging to Sucre and from the independence era. A statue of Sucre, pointing in the direction of Pichincha where he led independence troops to victory in 1822, is two blocks away at Bolívar and Guayaquil on the busy little Plaza Santo Domingo. Also in this square is the **Iglesia de Santo Domingo** ❾ (Mon–Fri 9am–5pm, Sat 9am–2pm), a church that is especially attractive in the evening when its domes are illuminated against the sky. Inside the church is the beautiful wooden *Mudéjar* coffered ceiling. Santo Domingo has fine religious sculptures, especially those of the Virgen del Rosario, donated by the Spanish king Carlos I.

The Dominican **Museo Fray Pedro Bedón** (Mon–Sat 9am–1.30pm, 2.30–5pm, Sun 9am–2.30pm), attached to the church, also has an impressive collection of art (the friar himself was a painter). The museum is home to the astonishing silver throne used to carry the Virgen del Rosario during religious processions.

ROAMING LA RONDA

From Plaza Santo Domingo, turn down Guayaquil to Calle Juan de Dios Morales. This street is more commonly known as **La Ronda**, and is the most romantic slice of colonial Quito, with its bright white houses trimmed with ornate balconies and geraniums, and brightly painted window frames and doors opening out onto the narrow, cobbled street. Over the last decade La Ronda has become a mix of old-time artisans selling items such as ornate church candles and Panama hats and popular cafés and restaurants with a bohemian feel. La Ronda's

Detail from a door in the Monasterio de San Francisco.

Ornate Solomonic columns of La Compañía de Jesús.

name comes from the guitar serenades (rondas) that drew crowds here during colonial days. Quiet during the day, the place comes alive at weekends from around dusk. Take care here at night, when only the guard-patrolled street of La Ronda itself is safe.

From La Ronda it is only three blocks to the Plaza San Francisco, but en route you will pass Calle García Moreno and the engaging **Museo de la Ciudad** (tel: 02-381 3340; https://quitocultura.com/team-member/museo-de-la-ciudad; Wed–Sun 8.30am–5.30pm, last entry at 4.30pm), which is located at Rocafuerte 572 and García Moreno. The building, with two large courtyards, functioned as the San Juan de Dios Hospital from 1565 until 1973 and has since been beautifully restored. Exhibits show the stages of Quito's development and daily life from the pre-Hispanic era to the present day.

On the same block, at the corner of Calle Rocafuerte and García Moreno, the former home of Santa Mariana de Jesús (commemorated in La Compañía) houses the nuns of the **Monasterio del Carmen Alto** ⓫. This is a closed order: nuns who join never leave the building until they depart this world. The nuns are industrious, however, and make a range of products including shampoos, hand creams, natural remedies, honey, and biscuits, which can be bought by means of a revolving hatch to preserve the nuns' isolation. A small museum, the **Museo del Carmen Alto** (www.museocarmenalto.gob.ec; Wed–Sun 9.30am–5.30pm, last entry at 4.30pm), contains an interesting array of local religious art and tells the story of the order and its most prominent member, Santa Mariana de Jesús.

IN AND AROUND PLAZA SAN FRANCISCO

The expansive **Plaza San Francisco** ⓬ is named for its monastery church, **El Monasterio de San Francisco** ⓭, honoring Quito's patron saint. The Flemish missionary Fray Jodocko Ricke directed construction of the church and monastery on the site of an Inca palace only 50 days after the city's 1534 founding, making this the American continent's oldest church.

Santo Domingo's beautiful Mudéjar ceiling.

The San Francisco religious complex is the largest structure in colonial Quito, with a sumptuous Spanish Baroque interior. The indigenous heritage of Quito is also represented in this Christian enclave; the church ceiling is decorated with images of the sun, the Inca divinity. The church's main altar is spectacularly carved and the side aisles are banked with paintings by the Quito School masters, including the *Virgen Inmaculada de Quito* by Bernardo de Legarda. This is reportedly the only winged image of the Virgin Mary to be found in either Europe or the Americas. The complex's finest artwork, including paintings, sculptures, and furniture from the 16th and 17th centuries, can be viewed in the interesting **Museo Fray Pedro Gocial** (www.museofraypedrogocial.com; Mon–Sat 9am–5.30pm, Sun 9am–1pm; free guided tours – tipping is appreciated) to the right of the church's main entrance.

The museum is housed in a building that was originally established by Fray Ricke as a school of art and religious instruction for indigenous children. Note the details of the intricately wrought furniture: some pieces have thousands of mother-of-pearl mosaics in their construction. To one side of the San Francisco atrium is the **Cantuña Chapel**, built by the indigenous Cantuña, a Christian convert, and financed by treasures from the Inca Empire. Cantuña's remains lie in the church. The chapel has a magnificent carved altar – the work of Bernardo de Legarda – and its walls display finely carved wood. The guided tour also takes you up the belltowers and allows a peek into the adjacent church's otherwise closed choir.

Just off Plaza Francisco on Cuenca is the superbly presented **Casa del Alabado** ⑭ (http://alabado.org; Wed–Sun 9am–5pm; free guided tours), showcasing artifacts from Ecuador's ancient cultures, from the coastal Valvidia people to the Amazon-based Napo communities, all in a 17th-century building.

A block and a half away from Plaza San Francisco on Calle García Moreno is **Casa Museo María Augusta Urrutia** ⑮ (tel: 02-258 0103; Tue–Sat 9am–5pm). This beautiful 19th-century mansion became a museum in 1987 after the death of the former owner, Doña Urrutia. It offers a wonderful glimpse of high-society Quito of the Republican era, with its European furniture, sewing rooms, sophisticated drawing rooms, graceful courtyards, and salons.

Not far away is another of Quito's glorious churches – there are more than 80 in all. This one is **La Merced** ⑯ (Mon–Fri 6.30–11.30am and 3–6pm, Sat–Sun mass), located at the corner of calles Cuenca and Chile. Its monastery contains the city's oldest clock, built in 1817, and a striking statue of Neptune, which sits on the fountain in the cloister's main patio. The castle-like La Merced – constructed from 1700 to 1734 – was one of the last churches built during Quito's colonial

One of the courtyards at the Museo de la Ciudad.

View down colonial La Ronda.

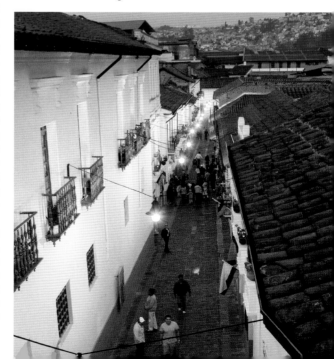

The extraordinary main altar of the Monasterio de San Francisco.

Flowers for the altar.

period, and it has the Old Town's tallest tower (47 meters/154ft) and its largest bell. The walls are decorated with pink and white reliefs displaying more than three dozen gilt-framed Quito School paintings, among them several with unusual scenes of erupting volcanoes and an ash-covered city. Bernardo de Legarda carved the main altarpiece in this serenely beautiful church. In front of the convent is the **Museo de Arte Colonial** (tel:02-228 2297; Tue–Sat 9.30am–5pm), part of the Casa de la Cultura Ecuatoriana (see page 141), dedicated to the art of the viceroyalty period. The beautiful 16th-century house alone is worth a visit.

QUITO'S LAVISH CONVENT

Turn down Calle Mejía when you leave the museum, and at the corner of calles Mejía and Flores you will find the **Monasterio de San Agustín** ⑰ (Mon–Fri 7am–12.30pm and 2–5pm), where Ecuador's first (short-lived) Act of Independence was signed in August 1809. Inside its flower-filled patio, robed monks pray against a backdrop of oil paintings by Miguel de Santiago, who spent most of his life in the monastery illustrating the life of St Augustine. The room where the independence document was signed is called the Sala Capitular and contains a portable altar in 18th-century Baroque style attributed to the indigenous artist Pampite. The remains of the leaders of the 1809 uprising are interred in San Agustín's catacombs.

Northeast along Calle Flores (toward the New Town) is the **Teatro Nacional Sucre** ⑱ (www.teatrosucre.com), the city's most beautiful theater, where concerts and plays are staged. This is the home of the National Symphony Orchestra.

Also on Calle Flores, four blocks back toward the Old Town is the **Teatro Bolívar** ⑲. This gorgeous Art Deco theater was inaugurated in 1933, and soon became the setting for the very best operas, ballets, concerts, and theater pieces seen in Ecuador, as well as a meeting place for high society. The theatre suffered a disastrous fire in 1999, but a painstaking restoration returned it to its former glory and it is once again home to the best of Ecuadorian performing arts. Guided visits (tel: 02-257 1911; www.teatrobolivar.org) reveal the plush, red main auditorium as well as taking fascinating peeks behind the scenes.

From Teatro Bolívar, Calle Guayaquil, with its 19th-century buildings, leads toward the area where the past is left behind. The **Monasterio de San Blas** is one of the last colonial complexes before you come to modern Quito lying ahead at the point where the two parts of the city meet. Before entering the New Town, however, make a slight detour two blocks west to view what is yet another of the city's magnificent churches. **La Basílica del Voto Nacional** ⑳ (https://visitquito.ec/lugar/basilica-del-voto-nacional/; basilica: daily 7am–7pm; towers: Mon–Fri 9am–5pm, Sat & Sun until 6pm) took over 100 years to build and was not completed

until the mid-20th century. This largest neo-Gothic basilica in Latin America is intricately decorated with gargoyles inspired by Ecuadorian fauna, and has a soaring 114-meter (376ft) spire that you can climb (for an additional cost) for expansive views over both Old and New towns. Every second Friday evening, you can climb the towers for stunning illuminated views across the Centro Histórico and beyond.

NEW TOWN

Heading for the New Town, wander through triangular **Parque La Alameda**, with its impressive monument of the liberation leader Simón Bolívar. The park contains a number of other busts and statues in honor of famous Latin Americans, among them Manuelita Sáenz, the Quito-born woman who was Bolívar's companion throughout the revolution.

It was in 1598 that Spanish officials in Quito obtained permission to build the Alameda, an area for recreation, brightened by well-tended gardens, flowers, and shade trees. The natural lagoon here is nowadays used for boating: the rowing boats for hire are a popular attraction on weekends. At the center of the park is South America's oldest observatory, the **Observatorio Astronómico** 🔵 (tel: 02-258 3451; http://oaq.epn.edu.ec; Mon–Fri 9am–5pm, late observation Tue–Thu 7–8.30pm, June–Aug clear nights only), begun in 1864 and still used by meteorologists and astronomers today.

The small church of **El Belén** 🔵 (daily) on the park's north side is a favorite subject of Quito's artists. It marks the site where the first Mass in Quito was said after the city was taken over by the Spanish. Simple and graceful, this church's lone nave contains a magnificent Christ believed to be the work of indigenous artist Caspicara.

One block up Avenida 6 de Diciembre and right on Calle Pedrahita is the **Palacio Legislativo** 🔵 (tel: 02-399 1488; www.asambleanacional.gob.ec; guided tours Mon–Fri 9am–4pm). The National Assembly's building has the history of Ecuador immortalized in carved stone along its north side. If you take Avenida

La Basílica del Voto, Latin America's largest neo-Gothic church.

Religious art at the Museo Nacional.

Gran Colombia from here to Avenida Paz and Calle Miño, you can see the hill-top home of the **Instituto Geográfico Militar** (Geographical Military Institute; www.igm.gob.ec). There is a combined entry for the museum and planetarium. The planetarium – distinguishable by its white dome – hosts shows at fixed times (Mon–Fri 9am, 11am and 3pm; Sat & Sun 11am and 3pm) and you can tour the museum, an hour in advance of the showing. If you turn right, however, from the Palacio Legislativo, and continue up Calle 6 de Diciembre, you will come to the **Parque El Ejido** (Communal Park). This park, the largest in central Quito, is a favorite spot – especially at weekends – for picnickers, soccer players, couples out for a stroll, energetic children, and street vendors seeking the park's shady trees as respite from the warm sun. Women carry huge trays of food balanced on their heads, offering for sale *fritada, papas, y mote* (grilled meat, potatoes, and corn). On weekends arts, crafts, music and all-round family entertainment often take place, put on by the municipality.

AROUND PARQUE EJIDO AND LA MARISCAL

At the north end of El Ejido, from Avenida Patria to Colón, lies Quito's modern tourist and business area with hotels, offices, banks, and restaurants. The main artery is **Avenida Amazonas, whose** southern end is home to travel agencies, money exchanges, the odd café, and some shops. While this top end of Amazonas, and the parallel Juan Leon Mera are good streets to find high-quality handicrafts – alongside the bargain Mercado Artesanal Mariscal.

However, care needs to be taken, since the once lively area of Mariscal Sucre – better known as La Mariscal – full of trendy cafés, restaurants, nightclubs, and bars is now rather run-down. La Mariscal was already suffering from economic decline before Covid hit, but the pandemic was the final nail in the coffin. It resulted in many places closing down, and the area generally has been taken over by undesirables. It's now a prime place for pickpocketing and robbery, so until the government's proposed regeneration plan takes effect, it's not a

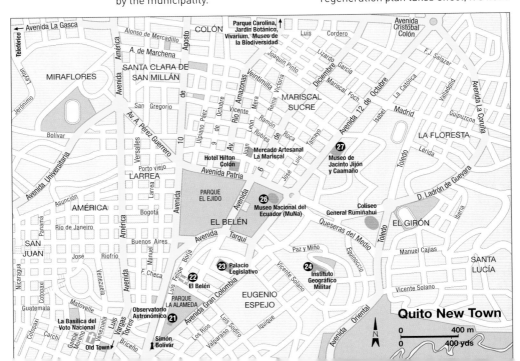

Quito New Town

place to linger. That said, a couple of the established tour operators and reputable restaurants are hanging in there. So too is the magnificent Galería Latina (www.galerialatina.com), which sells some of the country's most exquisite craftwork and knitwear, as well as items from Peru and Panama, at suitably elevated prices. Small but worth a visit is the **Museo de Artesanías Mindalae** ㉕ (www.mindalae. com.ec; Mon–Sat 9am–5pm), located on Calle La Niña, just off Avenida Reina Victoria in the north of La Mariscal. The museum gives an insight into the cultural and historical background to Ecuador's astounding range of handicrafts, and strives to preserve these art forms. Come here for a fascinating education in Ecuadorian folk art before you buy your souvenirs. There's also a good fair trade shop that sells top-quality handicrafts from all over the country.

Head east from Parque Elejido, along Avenida Patria, to the **Casa de la Cultura Ecuatoriana** (www.casadelacultura.gob.ec), a large organization that includes several modern cultural institutions such as the Cinemateca (film library), the Biblioteca Nacional (National Library), and the Teatro Nacional (National Theater). It also houses two museums (Tue–Sat 9am–1pm, 2–4pm): the Museo de Arte Moderno, and the Museo de Instrumentos Musicales Pedro Pablo Traversari that displays instruments from all over the world, many of them several centuries old. The large circular glass building also houses the **Museo Nacional del Ecuador (MuNa)** ㉖ (Wed–Sun 9am–5pm, Sat–Sun 10am–4pm). Unfortunately, what was once the city's premier museum, presenting Ecuadorian history in five connected salons, devoted respectively to archeology, gold, colonial art, republican art, and modern art, is now a mere shadow of its former self. After being closed for three years for renovations (2015–2018), the museum reopened with only a small proportion of its original exhibits on display. Although there are a few splendid pre-Columbian artefacts and figurines, and some interesting colonial, republican and modern art, much is still missing. Sadly lacking is the

Climbing sphere in Parque El Arbolito near the Casa de la Cultura.

spectacular gold room, containing the fabulous ceremonial gold-and-silver mask. Although there is now signage in Quechua, there is none in English. Visitors are warned on arrival that the museum is still under construction, but it is unclear when, and if, any more of Ecuador's priceless artistic heritage will make it back into the public domain. That said, visitors should persevere to the end of this limited collection to see the fascinating black-and-white film footage from the 1920s showing schooling for fair-skinned Ecuadorians, which aimed to produce disciplined girls and boys.

An upstairs salon is reserved for presentations of works that are rotated every month; it's certainly worth checking what is on while you are in the city.

Just two blocks away, another fine art, archeology, and ethnographic museum is run by the Póntifica Universidad Católica on Avenida 12 de Octubre. The **Museo de Jacinto Jijón y Caamaño ㉗** (www.puce.edu.ec; Mon–Fri 8am–4.30pm), located on the first floor of the library, contains the private collection donated by the family of the aristocratic archeologist after his death. It was the work of Jijón y Caamaño that provided the basis for the modern-day theories on how pre-Hispanic peoples lived in Ecuador; his books on the subject are valuable rarities.

The museum's collection includes *aribalos*, the graceful fluted-mouthed jars with pointed bottoms that are synonymous with pre-Inca cultures throughout the Andes, as well as a wide assortment of religious idols, masks, weapons, and shell and bone works. The museum also houses a small collection of colonial art.

PARKS, ART, AND ARTIFACTS

The **Museo Guayasamín ㉘** (www.guayasamin.org; Mon–Sat 9.30am–5pm), at Calle Bosmediano 543 in the Bellavista district, is located in one of the city's most beautiful modern houses, perched on a hillside overlooking Quito. The museum contains perhaps the most intriguing colonial art collection in the city. Set up by artist Oswaldo Guayasamín, the complex

Jardín Botánico in Parque Carolina.

is divided into three parts: a colonial art gallery (housing Guayasamín's own collection); the artist's gallery, where he displayed and sold his artworks, and a studio used by himself and his students. Provocative and political, Guayasamín's art made him the country's best-known artist, and the gallery of his works is considered a national treasure. Guayasamín was born of an indigenous father and mestizo mother, and much of his work represents the struggles and sufferings of indigenous people (see page 94). A fine collection of sculpture is displayed on the flower-splashed tile roof.

The artist began what would later be considered his masterpiece in 1995, and it was finished after his death in 1999 at the insistence of his heirs. The **Capilla del Hombre** (Pasaje Lorenzo Chávez and Mariano Calvache; Mon–Sat 9.30am–5pm) is located a few blocks away and is one of the most exciting contributions to Latin American art in recent years. There is a large collection of the artist's work including paintings, sculptures, and an eternal flame set in the center in defense of peace and human rights. The museum, modeled on an Inca temple, is dedicated to the values of the pre-Columbian man (the woman doesn't feature) and his struggle against colonization. Set in picturesque gardens, the chapel overlooks the city. If you plan to visit the Museo Guayasamín as well, it is best to take a taxi here first and then walk the five blocks to the museum. After your visit to the museum, take a stroll through the fragrant eucalyptus forests in the **Parque Ganguiltagua**, which affords splendid views of Quito and the nearby volcanic peaks of Cotopaxi and Cayambe, when clear.

To see what Quiteños do in their spare time, wander back down Bosmediano to the large **Parque Carolina**, located just off Avenida Eloy Alfaro. The green spaces here are crowded with soccer and volleyball players, runners, and groups of picnickers on weekends. There's even a boating lake, and every Sunday in August, outdoor concerts are held here. The **Museo de la Biodiversidad** (formerly the Museo de Ciencias Naturales; http://inabio.biodiversidad.gob.ec/museo-exhibicion/; Mon–Fri 8am–5pm) is on the south side of the park, at the corner of Rumipamba and Los Shyris. It has a good collection of endemic fauna and is worth a visit before you go to see the flora and fauna in the wild.

Also in the park, Quito's wonderful **Vivarium** (www.vivarium.org.ec; Tue–Sun 9.30am–1pm and 1.30–4.30pm) houses a large live collection of reptiles and amphibians, and explains some of the threats that face this aspect of Ecuador's spectacular wildlife. At the park's **Jardín Botánico** (Botanical Garden; www.jardinbotanicoquito.com; Mon–Fri 10am–3.30pm, Sat–Sun until 4pm; guided tours are available), some of Ecuador's amazing plant life is on display: a stroll through the gardens gives a glimpse of the mind-boggling variety that makes this country one of the world's biodiversity hotspots.

Pre-Columbian figure, Museo Nacional del Ecuador.

📷 COLONIAL ARCHITECTURE

Catholic concepts, indigenous motifs, and inspiration blend with North African influences to create the colonial style that has been carefully preserved in Quito and Cuenca.

When the Spanish conquered Ecuador they brought with them priests from different monastic orders: Franciscans, Augustinians, and Dominicans, and later the Jesuits. Within 50 days of the foundation of Quito in 1534, the Franciscan monks had begun constructing their own church. This was the first classic example of colonial architecture.

Each religious order was assigned land by the Spanish crown and each competed against the others in the construction of churches, convents, and plazas. Brother Jodocko Ricke, a Flemish Franciscan, set up an informal school for indigenous children to teach them religion and art. It was the first school of fine arts in South America.

The Franciscans discovered the creative skills of the indigenous people and also brought over talented converted Muslims. Sun motifs (the Sun being the principal Inca god) are commonly found alongside Madonna and Child representations, and ceilings often show Mudéjar influence. This blend of European and indigenous ideas created the Quiteño school of art and architecture.

The Jesuits strengthened the arts movement when they arrived in 1586. In the following 250 years ornate churches with richly adorned sacristies, carved choirs, and fine paintings flourished. Workshops and guilds were established and by the middle of the 18th century: 30 guilds in Quito controlled all artistic production.

A view of El Panecillo from Quito's Old Town.

A Baroque polychrome head of an angel from the Quito School displayed in Quito's Museo de la Ciudad.

El Monasterio de San Francisco is the largest structure in colonial Quito.

A detail of La Compañía de Jesús's intricate exterior.

The Quito School

The niches of early colonial altarpieces were first decorated with paintings, but polychrome statues became dominant later additions. When the first colonial buildings were constructed, statues were shipped over to Ecuador from Andalucía in Spain. However, by the 18th century a distinct style of Quiteño art had emerged.

Baroque, Rococo, and neoclassical styles from Europe reached Quito and were interpreted in a new way. Artists used different mediums: stone, ivory, tagua, clay, porcelain, and metal, but polychrome statues made from wood were the most popular.

Native cedarwood and sometimes alder from the hills surrounding Quito were used. Smaller figurines were usually made from balsawood. Trees were cut only at the full moon so that the sap would have risen to the highest level possible, making the wood stronger for carving. First the artists primed the statues and then painted directly on them with bright primary colors. They developed attention to detail and realism, reddening the cheeks, using false eyelashes and nails, and glass eyes. The figures were sometimes dressed from head to toe in sumptuous fabrics with floral designs.

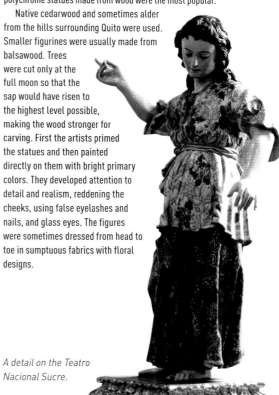

A detail on the Teatro Nacional Sucre.

The ornate Baroque facade of the Jesuit church La Compañía in Quito, best seen in early morning light. UNESCO considers it one of the world's 100 most exceptional buildings.

An example of an altar statue from the Quito School.

Folk dancers in Mitad del Mundo.

DAY TRIPS FROM QUITO

Mountains, forests, thermal springs, and wildlife sanctuaries are all within easy reach of the capital, and the Virgen de El Quinche is renowned for her miracles.

There are many day-long excursions from **Quito ❶** into the surrounding Andean Sierra. By renting a car, taking a tour, or using public transportation or taxis, you can discover a region crowded with mountains, waterfalls, thermal baths, and peaceful villages.

Buses to the Equatorial Line Monument, **La Mitad del Mundo ❷**, run about every half-hour on Avenida América, near the junction with Avenida Colón in the New Town, or from La Ofélia bus terminal. The monument is about a half-hour trip (22km/14 miles) to the north of Quito, located on latitude 0°, and provides an irresistible opportunity to straddle both hemispheres. It is a very popular spot, particularly at the equinoxes (March 21 and September 21), when the sun is directly overhead and neither monument nor visitors cast a shadow. The monument forms the focal point of a park and leisure area – some of it rather tacky – including gift shops and restaurants, and there is a good museum inside (https://mitaddelmundo.gob. ec; Mon–Fri 9am–5pm, Sat & Sun until 6pm). An elevator leads to the top for fine views. Close by is the quirky **Museo de Solar Intiñan ❸** (www.facebook.com/museo intinan?locale=es_LA; daily 9.30am–5pm), which claims to mark the true spot of the equator as measured by GPS. Fun, interactive exhibits include demonstrations of how water drains in different directions

on either side of the Equator, as well as sun clocks, ethnographic displays, and some incredible 150-year-old shrunken heads: ask the administration to show you if they are not on display.

About 4km (2 miles) farther on, toward the village of Calacalí, is the **Reserva Geobotánica Pululahua ❹**, centered on what is reputedly the biggest volcanic crater in South America. A rough path leads down from the rim, and the interior of the crater has its own microclimate, with rich vegetation and diverse birdlife. Nearby is the

◉ Main attractions

La Mitad del Mundo
Museo de Sitio Intiñan
Museo de Sitio Tulipe
Bosque Mindo-Nambillo
Parque Arqueológico
  Rumipamba

Map on page 148

The eccentric Museo de Solar Intiñan.

The Mitad del Mundo monument.

excellent El Crater restaurant and art gallery (www.elcrater.com), with fantastic views. Also to the north of Quito is the **Reserva Maquipucuna 5** (contact the Quito office at Baquerizo 238 and Tamayo; tel: 02-250 7200; www.maquipucuna.org): take the coast road through Calacalí to Nanegalito (61km/35 miles) and at the village follow the signposts for 19km (12 miles). The reserve consists of steeply sloping cloud forest, with a great diversity of fauna and flora.

Farther along the Calacalí–La Independencia road is the **Museo de Sitio Tulipe 6** (tel: 02-362 9605; Wed–Sun 9am–5pm), which is situated between Nanegalito and Gualea. The site has some 2,000 pyramids and mounds, constructed by the pre-Inca Yumbo people who inhabited the valleys north of Quito c.AD 800–1660. The ruins are thought to have been the Yumbos' main ceremonial site, with water being of great importance to rituals here, as shown by the remains of several channels and pools.

Further west, the **Bosque Mindo-Nambillo 7**, near Mindo, is a protected reserve that is home to birds, orchids, and bromeliads. The 20,000-hectare (49,400-acre) forest covers land of varying altitudes, which makes for a very diverse ecosystem, supporting some 325 species of bird. Tour operators in Quito offer all sorts of day excursions and longer trips to the forest, and there are several good lodges here which make Mindo a popular break from the city for nature-spotting and relaxation.

A further 60km (37 miles) on again along this road is the turning for the **Mashpi Biodiversity Reserve 8**, a pocket of privately-owned cloud forest 2.5 hours' drive from Quito where you will find the architecturally stunning Mashpi Lodge (US tel: 1-844 5895; www.mashpilodge.com), with floor-to-ceiling glass walls for optimum wildlife observation. There are phenomenal bird-watching opportunities here but the reserve is only accessible to guests.

Back closer to Quito, the **Parque Arqueológico Rumipamba 9** (Wed–Sun 8.30am–4.30pm) is making a stir. Located on the western edge of the city, the site was uncovered by

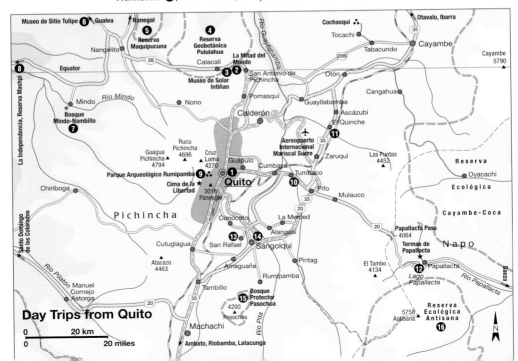

Day Trips from Quito

0 — 20 km
0 — 20 miles

excavators preparing to build a new housing project. The digging revealed Inca walls and thousands of artifacts from the Yumbo civilization. It is now all protected in this 32-hectare (79-acre) site, with an excellent museum in a restored hacienda as its centerpiece.

On Quito's eastern fringes, lies the tiny village of **Guápulo** with its 400-year-old church containing works by the country's best-known 17th-century artists: this was the founding spot of the Quito School (see page 145). This church and former convent has a pulpit carved by indigenous sculptor Juan Menacho that is unquestionably the loveliest in Quito. From here, you pass through the district of Cumbayá, into the valley of Los Chillos, and through the countryside along the winding Río San Pedro. **Tumbaco** ⑩ is a green oasis close to the city with good restaurants and a famous bungee-jump from the bridge at Chice.

MIRACLES AND HOT SPRINGS

The road through the Tumbaco valley passes through the sanctuary of **El Quinche** ⑪, which attracts pilgrims from all over the northern Sierra. The Virgen de El Quinche is renowned for her miracles, and is a favorite among drivers and transport workers. Many make the yearly pilgrimage to Oyacachi, where the Virgin Mary statue originated. This small isolated community has some hot springs set in a lush valley at 3,200 meters (10,500ft) in the Cayambe Coca Reserve. It is connected to Cayambe and Quito via Cangahua.

Descend the main road from El Quinche to the south. The view is wonderful, and snow and subtropical forests lie close together. At Km 59, the small **Lago Papallacta** ⑫ is renowned for trout fishing. At Km 60, a road branches off to the springs of Huanonumpa, commonly known as the thermal springs of Papallacta and the most attractively developed hot springs in Ecuador. Stay overnight in the Termas de Papallacta hotel and enjoy a dip in its private pools.

The **Valle de los Chillos**, another area of thermal springs, lies some 30 minutes' drive east of Quito. There is a fine descent into the valley on the Vía Oriental and the Autopista de Los Chillos. The highway crosses the valley's main road in **San Rafael** ⑬ (12km/8 miles). Stop here to visit **La Casa de Kingman Museo** (Mon–Sat 10am–5pm, Sun until 3pm), the former home of the artist Eduardo Kingman (see page 93). It now displays his works alongside other notable colonial and modern art. Ahead lies the village of **Sangolquí** ⑭, known for its Sunday market. Nearby, at La Merced and El Tingo, are some more thermal springs (turn left at San Rafael).

To the south of Sangolquí is the village of **Amaguaña**, which can be reached by bus from Quito. A few kilometers from Amaguaña, set around an extinct volcano, is the **Bosque Protector Pasochoa** ⑮, a sanctuary for birds and native plants. The road to **Volcán Antisana** goes through Pintag. The volcano, which is protected in the **Reserva Ecológica Antisana** ⑯, has four snowy peaks, which are very difficult to climb.

Relaxing at the Papallacta hot springs.

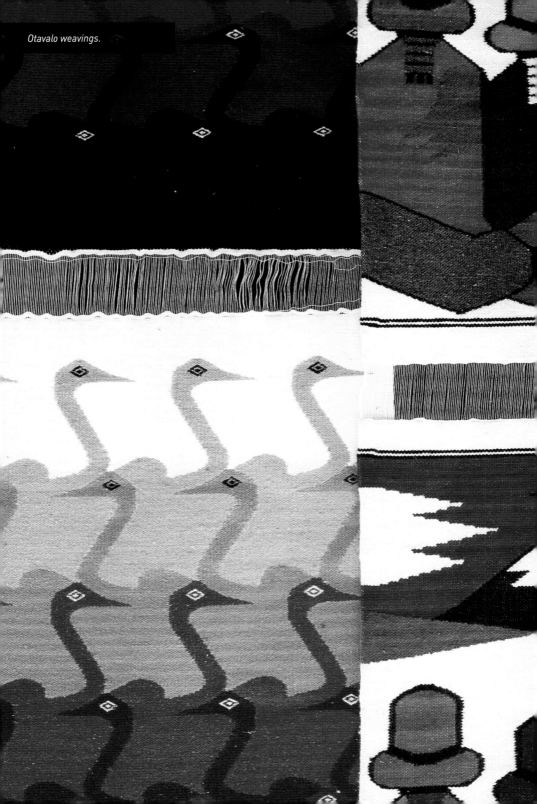

Otavalo weavings.

Selling woven cloth.

NORTHERN SIERRA

From Otavalo, home to South America's greatest market, to the surrounding lakes and artisans' villages and up to the Colombian border.

The province of **Imbabura**, just a short step north of Quito, is one of Ecuador's most popular destinations. Its numerous volcanoes, lakes, valleys, and forests combine to create a landscape of extraordinary beauty, while the variety of local indigenous groups makes the northern Sierra one of Ecuador's most culturally vibrant regions. Even more beguiling for many travelers is that Imbabura province is a rich source of handicrafts: it is home to the woodcarvers of San Antonio, the leatherworkers of Cotacachi, and, most famously, the weavers of Otavalo.

BEYOND THE CAPITAL

Leaving **Quito ❶** behind, most visitors take the shortest route to Imbabura, some 100km (60 miles) along the paved Pan-American Highway. For those who have time to explore, there are a number of ways of reaching the province and several places worth visiting en route. There are buses from Quito to Otavalo, Ibarra, San Gabriel, and Tulcán. Getting to some of the villages takes a little more ingenuity if you do not have your own transport, but many are walkable from the nearest town or village, and round-trip taxi journeys are not expensive.

The main road passes through the **Guayllabamba** Valley, which is warm and fertile, and famous for its orchards

and local fruit, such as the *chirimoya* (custard apple) and the local variety of avocado, which is small, roundish, and black-skinned. Visitors are pressed to buy the produce, and local women compete by offering a *yapa* (one extra for the same price). A local specialty is the tasty *locro de cueros* (potato soup with pork rind) with avocados on the side.

Guayllabamba is home to the **Zoológico de Quito** (tel: 02-359 1142; www.quitozoo.org; Tue–Sun 9am–4pm), which has over 50 species of native fauna representing all the diverse

Main attractions
Quito Zoo
Otavalo Market
Parque Condor
Cuicocha
Indigenous homestay with Runa Tupari
Hacienda Zuleta
Reserva Ecológica El Ángel

Maps on pages 154, 159

The road to Ilumán near Otavalo.

Colorful wools for sale. at Otavalo market.

ecological regions of Ecuador. Here, you can get close to rarely seen wildlife such as jaguars, moor wolves, Andean spectacled bears, ocelots, and sloths, along with a kaleidoscope of birds, monkeys, and squirrels. The zoo has a strong conservation ethos and many of its animals have been rescued from the illegal pet and fur trade.

Two roads lead out of Guayllabamba toward Cayambe: the left-hand one, via **Tabacundo**, follows a deep ravine, with curious rock formations. After crossing the Río Guayllabamba it is possible to make a detour along the riverside, known as the "Ruta Escondida" (the Hidden Way), down to the tranquil villages of **Puellaro** and **Perucho**, where fruit trees flourish and little seems to have changed for decades.

Another option is a visit to the archeological site of **Cochasquí**, on the southern slopes of **Mount Mojanda**, a short distance from Tabacundo. Some 15 flat-topped pyramids and 30 mounds are believed to have been built by the Caranqui around the 13th century, although some date from as

Otavaleña stallholder.

early as AD 900. Take a guided tour from the resident guardian, and learn about religious and funeral practices, living styles, and even the astronomical discoveries made in that era.

The small town of **Cayambe**, under the perpetual vigilance of the extinct volcano of the same name, is worth a stopover to try its famous local cheese, especially *queso de hoja*, and the *biscochos*, a savory shortbread.

A few kilometers south of Cayambe is the well-known **Hostería Guachalá** (tel: 02-361 0912; www.guachala.com), **one of** the oldest haciendas in Ecuador, dating from 1580. Set in pleasant grounds with a swimming pool and opportunities nearby for horseback riding, it is an attractive place where it is easy to conjure up the rich history that its owner, and former mayor of Cayambe, Diego Bonifaz, is more than willing to reveal to you.

Going north from Cayambe, a turn in the main road unexpectedly brings into view Lago San Pablo and, towering behind it, **Volcán Imbabura**, with its concave slopes covered in tiny

Northern Sierra

fields. Opposite is its sibling mountain, **Cotacachi**, and on the flat valley floor between the two, known as the "Valle del Amanecer" (the Valley of Dawn), lies Otavalo.

SOUTH AMERICA'S GREATEST MARKET

At dawn on Saturday mornings, the market square (called the Plaza de Ponchos) in **Otavalo** ❷ gets busy as the stallholders set up their displays. Handicraft workers from the outlying districts come to negotiate their wares with traders before the tourists arrive. By 9am the square is a feast of colors and textures: bolts of cloth; thick blankets; tapestry wall hangings; embroidered blouses and dresses; chunky hand-knitted sweaters; long patterned belts (fajas) that indigenous women wind round their waists; and cintas or tapes, with which they bind their long hair. The square is a maze of stands and narrow alleys with just enough room to pass.

Tourists making day trips from Quito arrive by bus at around 10am, and the haggling begins. The indígenas are experienced in business, can size up their customer, and know just how far to lower their price: several speak English.

Despite the crowds, the atmosphere is calm and relaxed; muffled, perhaps, by the walls of cloth. Most of the handicrafts are tailored to (assumed) foreign tastes, although some of the designs are reworkings of traditional motifs. There is plenty to choose from: Otavaleño work is usually well made, at prices that seem a dream to most foreigners, although naturally dyed cloth is harder to find these days. The very finest knitwear, though, is either sold in the boutiques of Quito or exported.

Saturday is also market day for the local population. At the north end of the Plaza de Ponchos, behind the tourist office, you will find hot prepared food in a patio de comidas. The streets radiating out from the main square also overflow with informal vendors selling an array of fruit, vegetables and grains.

The town's animal markets have been moved to the village of

La Plaza de Ponchos, the heart of Otavalo's market.

Quinchuqui, a ten-minute drive away, for reasons of health and safety. The main animal market also takes place on a Saturday morning, whereas smaller animals such as *cuyes* (guinea pigs) and rabbits are bought and sold on a Friday morning.

In parts of Plaza de Ponchos and along Calle Jaramillo, vendors sell every item of Otavaleño traditional dress, including the intricate hand embroidery of the indigenous women's blouses, as well as fleece, yarn, loom parts, aniline dyes, and carders. Although Saturday is the largest and busiest market day in Otavalo – when prices tend to be higher – its popularity has led to there being some sort of tourist market every day of the week.

Calle Jaramillo runs south into the new Plaza Cívica, an expansive public cultural space. It was inaugurated in 2022 but has yet to really come alive. The surrounding historical buildings have been restored and the plaza now contains sculptures by celebrated Ecuadorian sculptor Jesús Cobo; several represent the phases of the moon

while a tall monolith represents an Inti Watana (solar calendar) properly aligned with Volcán Imbabura. The two "blades" on one side represent the leaves of maize, and the seven holes in between symbolise the seven types of maize used to make the chicha del Yamor, so revered by Otavaleños and celebrated during the Fiesta de Yamor every September.

HACIENDA COUNTRY

While day tours to Otavalo from Quito are popular, many independent travelers arrive on the Friday night before the market and stay for the weekend to explore the attractive surrounding countryside. The area around Otavalo is hacienda country: there are several historic estates which now provide luxurious accommodation for visitors and staying at one of these is an unforgettable experience.

Closest to Otavalo – just 10 minutes by taxi north of town – the elegantly restored **Hacienda Pinsaquí** (tel: 06-294 6116; www.haciendapinsaqui.com) dates from 1790. Once dedicated to

Mouth-watering fruit for sale in Otavalo.

textile manufacturing, Pinsaquí had workshops that employed 1,000 local people. Now, this beautiful stately home set in graceful gardens welcomes guests to its polished halls. Dinners are set under chandeliers in rooms elegantly furnished with French and Spanish antiques, and are served by hotel staff in traditional Otavaleño dress. Out on the estate there is excellent horseback riding to be had on one of the hacienda's beautiful steeds.

Also restored to its former splendor is the 17th-century **Hacienda Cusín** (tel: 06-291 8013; www.haciendacusin. com) near the picturesque – but very cold – Laguna San Pablo. The rooms are crowded with antique religious paintings, wooden armchairs, and candelabras, while outside are elegant gardens, with ponds and banks of glorious flowers. All sorts of activities and excursions are offered, including riding and volcano climbing. One of the best is surely a visit to **Parque Cóndor** (www. parquecondor.com; Wed–Sun 9.30am–5pm) located, amidst panoramic views, at 2,800 meters (9,184ft) on top of a hill

called Pucara de Curilloma near the hacienda and not far from Otavalo. This excellent park displays rescued birds of prey, which are rehabilitated for release back into the wild. They include magnificent eagles, vultures and owls as well as slightly sad-looking condors. The center highlights the birds' importance in the ecosystem but the climax of a visit here is to watch the birds soaring high in one of the free flight demonstrations, which are given at 11.30am and 3.30pm.

For more fabulous mountain scenery, head for the beautiful **Lagunas de Mojanda** and the peak of **Fuya Fuya**, about 18km (11 miles) south of Otavalo. A dirt road leads to the lakes, divided by hills inhabited by wild rabbits. Go in a group, as robberies have become a problem near the lake.

OTAVALO'S SURROUNDINGS

The villages close to Otavalo provide a chance to see another aspect of the handicraft trade: the craftspeople themselves at work. In nearby **Carabuela Ⓐ**, they make scarves, woolen

Ñanda Mañachi workshop in Peguche, where traditional instruments are made.

The crater lake of Cuicocha, near Cotacachi.

Adding the finishing touches in San Antonio, a village of expert woodcarvers.

gloves, ponchos, and belts, some still using the pre-Hispanic loom. Other artisans here specialize in making Andean harps. The village of **Peguche** **B**, too, has its weavers, and is well worth a stop. Peguche is about 3km (2 miles) northeast of Otavalo, and is the home of several indigenous musical groups. The Taller Ñanda Mañachi, just north of the plaza produces many high-quality *rondadores* (Ecuadorian panpipes) and Andean flutes, among other instruments.

About 3km (2 miles) east of Peguche, **Agato** **C** is worth a visit if you are interested in textiles. The Tahuantin-suyo Workshop (https://miguelandrango. weebly.com) uses traditional looms and natural dyes, and makes some lovely items, which are often for sale at the Hacienda Cusín (www.haciendacusin.com). You can reach Agato by bus or taxi from Otavalo.

Another nearby village of artisans is **Ilumán** **D** (there are occasional buses, or it's a short taxi ride from Otavalo). The craftspeople make double-sided ponchos, felt hats, and tapestries.

Making helados de paila at an ice-cream parlor in Ibarra.

Ilumán is also famous for its traditional healers or *curanderos*, who use guinea pigs, candles, and ritual stones, as well as herbs and alcohol, to diagnose sicknesses and chase away evil spirits or negative energy.

EXPERT LEATHERWORKERS

About 15km (10 miles) north of Otavalo is the village of **Cotacachi** **E**, Ecuador's leatherwork center. Predominantly made of tough cowhide, the goods are mostly top-quality, and there is an excellent choice, including jackets, skirts, boots, briefcases, bags, riding equipment, and wallets. In addition to the shops that line the main commercial street, 10 de Agosto, you can pick up bargains at the Sunday morning craft market, which is sometimes accompanied by folk music and dancing.

While visiting, try Cotacachi's traditional *carne colorada*, made of sundried and fried pork or beef, colored with *achiote* (a red seed and natural dye), and served with avocados, jacket potatoes, a cheese, onion, egg sauce, and corn.

A community-based tourism operator called **Runa Tupari** (meaning "meeting the local people" in Quichua; tel: 0996337720; www.runatupari.com) has built simple guest accommodation in several indigenous communities around Cotacachi. Visitors can stay and experience the daily life of families: helping out in the fields or kitchen, learning weaving and handicraft production, taking meals with the family, and perhaps even visiting the village shaman. Indigenous guides also take guests on explorations of nearby lakes and volcanoes, or on horseback rides. This is a fantastic way to deepen your understanding of indigenous life in Ecuador: the families are welcoming, the guest cabins cozy, and the whole experience unforgettable.

West of Cotacachi lies **Cuicocha**, a sparkling blue crater lake situated at the southern end of the Reserva Ecológica Cotacachi-Cayapas. A well-marked hiking trail circles the lake; it takes 4–5 hours to complete the circuit. Take a taxi here from Otavalo and arrange pickup later in the day. It is advisable to visit the lake in groups, however, as robberies have occurred in the area.

FURTHER NORTH

The highway northward from Otavalo curves around Volcán Imbabura and descends toward Ibarra, passing through **Atuntaqui**, which reputedly serves the best *fritada* (deep-fried pork) in the region. Just before Ibarra, a right-hand turn leads into **San Antonio**, home to expert woodcarvers. You can watch the craftsmen at work and buy the finished articles.

A shorter, much slower, but very attractive route to Ibarra is along the old Pan-American Highway from Cayambe, heading around the far side of Volcán Imbabura via the villages of **Olmedo** and **Zuleta**. This narrow road winds through several of the region's oldest haciendas.

At Zuleta, you will find the incredibly beautiful **Hacienda Zuleta** (tel: 06-2662 182; www.zuleta.com), completed in 1691, and steeped in four centuries of colonial history. This 2,000-hectare

Otavalo and Surroundings

THE WEAVERS OF OTOVALO

Demand by Ecuadorians for good-quality fabrics has safeguarded the livelihoods of many households in the Otavalo region.

Ecuadorians have kept their traditional dress, but some can now afford more luxurious fabrics. The weaving families of Otavalo have transformed this demand into an impressive business.

For as far back as anyone knows, the people of the high, green Otavalo Valley have been spinners, weavers, and textile merchants. Because Ecuador lacks the mineral wealth of Peru and Bolivia, the Spanish were quick to exploit the country's human resources, and this included their textile skills. Under the *encomienda* system the colonizers were given the right to use forced indigenous labor in return for christening the workers, and by mid-1550s an *obraje* (textile workshop) using forced indigenous labor was established in Otavalo.

Between 1690 and 1720 the *encomiendas* were abolished by the Spanish crown, but native land fell into white hands, and many *indígenas* entered into a system of debt peonage *(wasipungo)* whereby they were virtual serfs on large haciendas, many of which continued to operate weaving workshops. In 1964 the Agrarian

An Otavalo embroiderer.

Reform Law outlawed debt peonage and granted *wasipungeros* title to their plots of land, leaving *indígenas* free to weave at home or to hire out their labor. Many of the most prosperous contemporary weaving families are descendants of the *wasipungeros*.

The Agrarian Reform Law coincided with an increase in tourism to the region. In 1966 there was one crafts store in Otavalo; by 1990 there were about 80, most of them *indígena*-owned and operated. It's a mistake, however, to think that the textile industry is mainly dependent on tourism; most Ecuadorians own something from Otavalo, and most textiles are sold to other South Americans. There is also a substantial export business to North America, Europe, and Japan, which brings several million dollars a year into the region.

A CREATIVE MAJORITY

About 85 percent of the estimated 90,000 Otavaleños in the valley are involved in the textile industry either full or part time. Almost all families have at least one spinning wheel or loom in the house. Involvement ranges from women who spin 2kg (5lb) of yarn a week, to families weaving a few ponchos a month on a backstrap loom, to the companies, which produce up to 300 ponchos a day on electric looms.

Increased prosperity has not meant the abandonment of traditional dress, but the use of more luxurious fabrics. The women's skirt wraps *(anakus)* and shoulder wraps *(fachalinas)* were traditionally made of handspun wool or cotton; today wealthy women wear velvet. The women's dress, incidentally, is one of the closest in form to the costume of Inca women worn anywhere in the Andes today. The men's dress is less conservative, being a mixture of colonial and modern elements, although the custom of wearing long hair and the use of *alpargatas* (espadrilles) are pre-Hispanic.

Although some older *indígenas* and residents of remote communities only speak Quichua, most *indígenas* are bilingual in Quichua and Spanish, and a few will surprise you by speaking fluent English, French, German, or Portuguese at the market *(feria)*. The famous market is the high point of the week, not only for visitors, but for the thousands of *indígenas* who come to buy, sell, and socialize, and maintain the great tradition of the Otavalo weavers.

(4,000-acre) working farm belongs to one of Ecuador's most illustrious families. Two presidents of the republic have come from here: Leónidas Plaza (1901–5) and Galo Plaza Lasso (1948–52). Today the presidents' descendants welcome guests to their 15 beautiful guestrooms in the exquisitely maintained colonial homestead. Meals are usually served family style round a large table, and out on the aesthetically gorgeous estate there are well-groomed horses to ride, condors to view, and long walks to take.

IBARRA, "THE WHITE CITY"

The provincial town of **Ibarra ❸**, about 22km (13 miles) north of Otavalo, has a population of about 158,000, and enjoys one of the best climates of the Sierra due to its moderate altitude of 2,225 meters (around 7,000ft). Despite severe damage in at least two earthquakes, Ibarra's city centre has retained a colonial style, with impressive leafy central squares lined with grand buildings, and streets lined with white-painted walls, which has earned Ibarra the nickname

of "the white city." The population is a cultural mix of *indígenas* and people of mixed heritage. Traditional dishes made in the area include *arrope de mora* (blackberry syrup) and *nogadas* (a sweet made with walnuts). Ice cream parlors abound, and the city's speciality is h*elados de paila* (fruit sorbets). These are made by continuously beating fruit juice in a copper *paila* or round-bottomed pan, while it sits on a pile of ice. The best place to sample some truly mouth-watering flavours is Momalia, on Calle Bolívar, north of Parque Pedro Moncayo – it's a gorgeous converted colonial mansion owned by the fifth generation of sorbet makers from the family of Rosalía Suárez.

Close to Ibarra is **Yaguarcocha**. Its name means "blood lake" in Quichua, because in the 15th century the tough inhabitants of this region held out against the Inca invaders for some 16 years, until they were finally defeated and massacred on the shore. Today the lake is sometimes used for sailing, but is mainly known for the

Parque Pedro Moncayo, Ibarra.

Colonial architecture in Ibarra.

A couple walk along one of Ibarra's old streets.

motor-racing track that surrounds it. Car races take place on this circuit during the September festival celebrations.

SUGARCANE VALLEY

On the other side of the mountain lies the warm **Chota Valley**, the lowest point in the northern Sierra, where sugarcane, vines, and tropical fruits grow. There are several thermal springs in this valley, such as **Chachimbiro**, which can be reached by bus from Ibarra.

The Chota Valley is the only zone of the Sierra that has a predominantly black population. Today they are farmers, but the older inhabitants tell tales of their ancestors who fought against slavery on the plantations of Colombia. In the village of **Chota** (about an hour's drive from Ibarra), a concert hall regularly presents the *bomba negra* music of the local black population, which is a mixture of the sounds of the Sierra with African-style instruments and rhythms. Drums feature prominently and one of the traditional "instruments"

is played by blowing tunes on a leaf held between the hands.

ON THE COLOMBIAN BORDER

The highway north from the Chota Valley climbs steeply with twists and turns into the province of **Carchi**, over the high pass of **El Ángel**, and down to the frontier town of Tulcán. The **Reserva Ecológica El Ángel**, 15km (9 miles) north of El Ángel, preserves over 15,000 hectares (37,000 acres) of this region, encompassing a remarkably varied ecosystem where foxes, deer, armadillos, hummingbirds, and condors can often be seen. In some sheltered pockets of this well-watered *páramo* environment, montane forest supplants grasses, and there are dense thickets of polylepis trees draped ethereally with mosses, orchids, and bromeliads. Arguably the star attraction is the otherworldly frailejones (*espeletia*) – thick trunks topped with crowns of hairy succulent leaves. The reserve's crystal-clear lakes are also popular with anglers. Access is by taxi from El Ángel, or you can stay in the rustic stone cottages at **Polylepis Lodge** (tel: 06-263 1819; www.polylepis.com), 1km (0.6 miles) from the entry checkpoint.

About 40km (25 miles) before the border with Colombia is Carchi's sanctuary, **La Gruta de La Paz**, near the village of **San Gabriel ❹**, where pilgrims visit the statue of the Virgin sheltered in a natural cave. There are two splendid waterfalls just outside the village. In the border town of **Tulcán ❺**, the main attraction is the topiary garden in the cemetery, where huge cypress hedges are clipped into the shapes of animals, houses, and pre-Columbian figures. It is sensible to take extra care when visiting Tulcán as the proximity to the border means there are both guerrillas and drug-trafficking in town. While daytime wandering is fine, it is best not to be on the streets after 10pm, and always carry your passport as there are frequent police checks.

Colorful wools for sale at Otavalo Market.

A chiva bus driving through the Avenue of the Volcanoes near Quilotoa

THE AVENUE OF THE VOLCANOES

The "spine" of Ecuador has hot springs and markets as well as a long line of breathtaking snow-capped mountains.

The **Andes** are often thought of as the spine of Ecuador, but a ladder is a better analogy. Think of the Eastern and Western cordilleras as the sides of the ladder, with the lower east–west connecting mountains (called *nudos* or knots) as the rungs. Between each rung is an intermontane valley at about 2,300 to 3,000 meters (7,000 to 9,000ft) in elevation, with fertile-volcanic soil.

The valleys are heavily settled and farmed today and were the territory of different ethnic groups in pre-Inca times. Both the **Pan-American Highway** and the railroad run north–south between the cordilleras, bobbing up and down over the *nudos* past fields, farms, and startled cows beneath a range of dormant and active volcanoes, some of which have snow all year round.

In 1802 the German explorer **Alexander von Humboldt** named this route the "Avenue of the Volcanoes." Ecuador's position on the equator means that you can travel through the avenue past orchids and palm trees, but with tundra vegetation, glaciers, and snow visible in the mountains above. By leaving the valley and hiking or climbing upwards, you can pass through all the earth's ecological zones from subtropical to Alpine.

A splendid way of traveling down the "avenue" is by rail, but only a couple of sections of track are active these

Cotopaxi, Ecuador's highest active volcano.

days. Check at a tourist office in Quito. If open, the railroad does allow you to get an intimate look at life along the tracks, traveling through people's back yards, so to speak, rather than down the main road. The route suggested in this chapter, however, takes the Pan-American Highway (*Panamericana*), with detours and side roads to places of interest on the way.

THE ROAD SOUTH

Leaving **Quito ❶** by car or bus for the south can seem to take forever, as the

◉ Main attractions
Parque Nacional Cotopaxi
Hacienda el Porvenir
Thermal waters at Baños
Volcán Chimborazo
Alausí

◉ Map on page 166

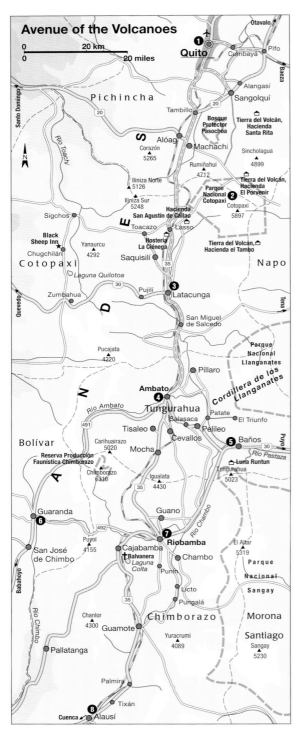

Avenue of the Volcanoes

0 — 20 km
0 — 20 miles

Otavalo
Quito ❶
Pifo
Cumbayá
Baeza

Santo Domingo

Pichincha

Alangasí
Sangolquí

Tambillo

Río Toachi

Bosque
Protector
Pasochoa

Tierra del Volcán,
Hacienda
Santa Rita

Aláag
Corazón
5265

Machachi

Sincholagua
4899

Rumiñahui
4712

Iliniza Norte
5126

Tierra del Volcán,
Hacienda
El Porvenir ❷

Parque
Nacional
Cotopaxi

Iliniza Sur
5248

Sigchos

Hacienda
San Agustín de Callao

Cotopaxi
5897

Toacazo
Lasso

Black
Sheep Inn
Chugchilán

Yanaurcu
4292

Hostería
La Ciénega

Tierra del Volcán,
Hacienda el Tambo

Cotopaxi

Saquisilí

Napo

Laguna Quilotoa

Zumbahua

Pujilí

Latacunga ❸

Tena

San Miguel
de Salcedo

Parque
Nacional
Llanganates

Pucajata
4220

Píllaro

Quevedo

Ambato ❹
Tungurahua

Río Ambato

Patate
Salasaca

Cordillera de los
Llanganates

El Triunfo

Tisaleo
Pelileo

Cevallos

Baños ❺

Puyo

Carihuairazo
5020

Mocha

Luna Runtun
Río Pastaza

Bolívar

Reserva Producción
Faunística Chimborazo

Tungurahua
5023

Chimborazo
6310

Igualata
4430

Guaranda ❻

Guano

Río Chambo

Puyol
4155

Riobamba ❼

El Altar
5319

San José
de Chimbo

Cajabamba
Balvanera
Laguna
Colta

Chambo

Parque

Nacional

Sangay

Babahoyo

Punín

Licto

Pungalá

Chanlor
4300

Guamote

Chimborazo

Morona

Río Chimbo

Yuracrumi
4089

Santiago
Sangay
5230

Pallatanga

Palmira

Tixán

Cuenca
Alausí ❽

streets leading to the Pan-American Highway are usually jammed. However, there is a bypass, the Nuevo Oriental, which connects with the Pan-American Highway on the outskirts of south Quito, and makes driving much less stressful. The road goes through the **Valle de los Chillos** and connects with the main highway about 8km (5 miles) farther south. The traffic eases a bit as you wind down off the Quito Plateau and into the first intermontane valley. Way off to the east the snowy peak of **Volcán Antisana** (5,750 meters/18,720ft) can be seen.

Looming over the region is **Volcán Cotopaxi** (5,897 meters/19,347ft), Ecuador's second-highest peak and one of the world's highest active volcanoes. On a clear day you can see its symmetrical, snow-capped cone from Quito. In the Western Cordillera, almost directly across from Cotopaxi, is **Volcán Illiniza** (5,265 meters/17,280ft), or the Illinizas as they are called, for there are actually two peaks. The lower, northern peak is a satisfying climb for non-technical climbers and hikers, while the southern one, Illiniza Sur, is only for those with experience.

Some 32km (20 miles) beyond Machachi, just over the first pass, is the entrance to the magnificent **Parque Nacional Cotopaxi** ❷.

Both sides of the highway are covered by a forest of Monterey pines, many of them unfortunately dying from a fungal disease. The pines are not native; they were introduced from California for a forestry project and are a textbook example of the dangers of monoculture: the pines have crowded out the indigenous vegetation and the fungus has spread rapidly from tree to tree.

The national park centers on Cotopaxi, of course, but there are several other peaks that attract rock climbers, including **Rumiñahui** (4,712 meters/15,430ft), and there is also a great variety of wildlife, ranging from falcons and highland hummingbirds to tiny deer and the endangered, and rarely seen, Andean puma.

HACIENDAS AND MARKETS

As elsewhere in Latin America, the prime agricultural land in the valley was taken from the indigenous population soon after the Spanish conquest and turned into large Spanish-owned haciendas (estates), on which the indigenous population were forced to labor. Many of these still exist and include vast landholdings, despite the Agrarian Reform of 1964.

Several haciendas are also found in the less productive, windswept high *páramo*. Of these, the closest to Cotopaxi is **Hacienda el Porvenir** (tel: 02-204 0208; www.tierradelvolcan. com). This is the perfect base for some high-altitude acclimatization: there are wonderful walks and bike rides on the property, as well as adventurous horseback riding into the national park. Guided ascents of the volcano can also be arranged. The same company

also owns remote, rustic **Hacienda El Tambo**, on the far side of Cotopaxi, and Hacienda Santa Maria, where there is a complex of aerial zip lines to take you flying over forest and river.

Very close by, just south of Machachi, is possibly one of Ecuador's most distinctive haciendas, **San Agustín de Callao** (tel: 03-271 9160; www.incahacienda. com). San Agustín is built on the site of an Inca palace, one of the two most important Inca constructions in Ecuador, and its dining room and chapel are built entirely within the original Inca stonework. Stay here amongst the antiques, murals, and whispering masonry walls, and you will feel deeply immersed in history. There's also a whole program of activities, including hikes to the top of Cotopaxi, visits to some secret angling spots, or horseback rides across the *páramo* on one of the hacienda's beautiful steeds.

Further south, towards Latacunga is the small town of **Lasso**. Turn off west here for **Hacienda La Ciénega** (tel: 03-271 9093; www.haciendalacienega. com). Now a hotel and restaurant, its

⊙ Fact

The origin of the Quichua name Cotopaxi is not clear, and has had several different interpretations. Some translate it as the combination of two Quichua words: kotto, meaning peak or mountain, and paksi, denoting shining. Another interpretation comes from the words cutu, meaning neck, and pachi, broken – which sees Cotopaxi as a headless neck with a white poncho of snow. Yet another translation denotes it, rather evocatively, as the "neck of the moon."

Parading through the streets of Latacunga during the Mamá Negra festival.

Sheep for sale in Saquisilí market.

Shepherd tending his flock near Quilotoa.

main house – a stone mansion with huge windows, stone-cobbled patios and Moorish-style fountains – was built in the mid-1600s for the Marquis de Maenza and was occupied by his family for more than 300 years. The stone chapel has a bell, still rung on Sunday mornings, which was installed in 1768 in thanksgiving when Cotopaxi ended 20 years of devastating eruptions. Von Humboldt stayed here in 1802 when he surveyed Cotopaxi, and the de Maenza-Lasso family plotted Ecuador's independence from Spain on this site in the 1800s. The comfortable rooms are beautifully furnished with antiques and chandeliers. Besides opportunities for excellent bird-watching in the gardens, you can ride horseback from here and make day trips to the **Parque Nacional Cotopaxi**.

The little towns in the valley, and the larger city of **Latacunga ❸** (pop. 98,000), are interesting primarily for their fiestas and market days. Some 90km (54 miles) from Quito, Latacunga is somnolent and pleasant, with a number of buildings constructed from local gray volcanic rock. It was founded in 1534 on the site of an Inca urban center and fortress. There are busy Saturday and Tuesday markets, where crafts are sold, especially *shigras* (bags made from woven natural fibres), baskets, and ponchos.

Latacunga's *municipio* (town hall) and cathedral are on the main plaza, the Parque Vicente León, which has topiary and a well-maintained garden. Behind the cathedral is a colonial building housing an arcade with shops, offices, and an art gallery. Five blocks west down Calle Maldonado at Calle Vela is the **Casa de la Cultura de Cotopaxi** (tel: 593 3-281-3247; Mon–Fri 8am–5pm), built on the remains of a Jesuit monastery and the old Montserrat watermill. The museum houses pre-Columbian ceramics and weavings, and a library, theater, and gallery. Some 10km (6 miles) west of Latacunga is **Pujilí**, which has a lively market on Sunday, and colorful Corpus Christi festivities in June.

A wild and scenic loop west of Latacunga takes you through the market

⊙ LA MAMÁ NEGRA

Latacunga's festival of the Virgin of the Mercedes, commonly known as the Fiesta de la Mamá Negra (the Festival of the Black Mother) takes place twice a year: on September 23 and 24, and again in November to coincide with the anniversary of the city's founding. It's a lively event with obvious indigenous influences, despite its Christian name and outward trappings, which pay homage to the figure of the black-faced Virgin Mary. Controversially, at least to Western eyes, she is always played by a "black-faced" mestizo man of standing in the community. There are street parades with allegorical figures; masquerades; local bands; noisy firework displays; and dancing and drinking late into the night. There is also a solemn Midnight Mass (*misa del gallo*) although some of the celebrants are a little less than solemn.

towns of Zumbagua, Chugchilán, Sigchos, and Saquisilí, then back to Latacunga. Zumbagua's market on Saturday is stocked with a kaleidoscopic array of fresh produce. Half an hour's drive farther on is **Lake Quilotoa**, an azure, water-filled volcanic crater, still considered active. Indigenous people from the Tigua Valley nearby sell naïve, brightly colored enamel paintings on sheepskin at the crater rim. On the way north from here to the village of Chugchilán is the Black Sheep Inn (tel: 03-270 8077; www.blacksheepinn.com), an ecological farm with delicious home cooking and great views over the sierra. The whole loop back takes several hours along mainly dirt roads, so a stop here is a welcome break. It's also a popular overnight sojourn for the few hardy travelers who are hiking or mountain biking the loop. **Saquisilí** only comes out of its torpor on Thursday market day. The market is an economic hub for the surrounding region, with *indígenas* buying and selling everything from cattle to cotton. The market is

decidedly a local, rather than tourist, affair and a favorite with many travelers for that reason.

Another 10km (6 miles) farther south **down the** Panamerican Highway you cross the provincial boundary and enter **Tungurahua province**, named after the area's dominant volcano. The region is known for its relatively mild climate and production of vegetables, grain, and fruit, including peaches, apricots, apples, pears, and strawberries, and you will encounter roadside vendors along the highway on both sides of Ambato.

AMBATO

Some 128km (80 miles) from Quito, **Ambato** ❹ is the capital of Tungurahua province. Arriving in the city brings you abruptly face to face with the 21st century. Ambato was almost totally destroyed by an earthquake in 1949 and then rebuilt, so virtually nothing of the colonial town remains. With a population of about 180,000, the city is the fourth-largest in Ecuador. Industries include some textiles (especially

Colorful woven bags in Guamote's Thursday market.

The statue of Nuestra Señora del Agua Santa, housed in her own basilica in Baños.

Traditional woven rugs for sale in Salasaca.

rug-weaving), leather goods, food-processing, and distilling, but the most interesting aspect of Ambato is its enormous Monday market, the largest in Ecuador. Thousands of *indígenas* and country people come into town for different activities, which take place in various parts of the city. Several plazas contain nothing but produce vendors, while the streets are lined with kiosks selling goods of all kinds. To reach the textiles, dyes, and crafts (ponchos, *ikat* blankets and shawls, *shigras* bags, belts, beads, hats, and embroidered blouses), follow Calle Bolívar or Cevallos about 10 blocks north from the center of town to the area around Calle Abdón Calderón.

Ambato's attractive central plaza is **Parque Montalvo**, named after the writer Juan Montalvo (1833–99) and bearing a statue of the same. Montalvo's house, at calles Bolívar and Montalvo nearby, is open to the public. Ambato, in fact, is often known as "La Tierra de los Tres Juanes" (Land of the Three Juans) because Juan Leon Mera (who wrote Ecuador's national anthem) and the renowned teacher Juan Benigno also heralded from here. On the north side of the plaza is Ambato's modern **cathedral**, and opposite is the post office. The **Parque Cevallos**, a few blocks to the northwest, is green and tree-lined, and is the site of the **Museo de Ciencias Naturales** (Natural Science Museum; tel: 02 282 7395; Mon–Fri 9am–12.30pm and 2.30–6.30pm), packed with stuffed animals and birds of the region. The Río Ambato flows through a gorge to the west of the town center. Also roughly in that direction are the attractive **botanical gardens**. A paved road leads out of Ambato to the east, past Volcán Tungurahua and down into the Oriente, forming one of the main east–west links between the jungle and Sierra.

From Ambato, catch a bus 20km (12 miles) northeast to the small town of **Píllaro**. This is the way to get to the **Parque Nacional Llanganates**, which is perpetually wrapped in fog and covered with virtually impenetrable cloud-forest vegetation. These remote

mountains appeal to the Indiana Jones in all of us because of various accounts of General Rumiñahui hiding Quito's gold here, before Benalcázar and the *conquistadores* could get to it.

THE PEOPLE OF SALASACA

About 14km (9 miles) east of Ambato on the road to Baños is **Salasaca**, the home of a small, beleaguered indigenous group, thought to be of Bolivian origin, which is struggling to hold on to its land and maintain its customs in the face of enormous pressure from criollos in the surrounding communities. This group is thought to be *mitmakuna*, living here as a result of the Incas' policy of forcibly moving whole ethnic groups of people from their homelands to distant foreign territories as punishment for uprising, or the threat of it.

Salasaca men wear black and white ponchos and handmade white felt hats with broad, upturned brims at the front and back. Unique to Salasaca are the men's purple or deep-red scarves dyed with cochineal, a natural dye that

comes from the female insects that live on the Opuntia (prickly pear) cactus. Salasaca women wear the same hats as the men, brown or black *anakus*, cochineal-dyed shoulder wraps, handwoven belts with motifs, and necklaces of red, Venetian glass beads.

A few kilometers past Salasaca is **Pelileo**, a little town where you would not want to invest in property: it has been leveled by earthquakes four times in the past 300 years. As the last quake was in 1949, the present Pelileo is an entirely modern town. There is a small Saturday market, which is attended by many *indígenas* from Salasaca. It is also Ecuador's major production center for blue jeans.

Salasaca market traders.

SUBTROPICAL CLIMATE

Beyond Pelileo the highway drops 850 meters (2,780ft) to Baños in only 24km (15 miles), following various tributaries and then the Río Pastaza itself in its headlong rush to the Amazon basin. The region produces sugarcane for distilled alcohol, and many kinds of fruits and vegetables.

Quilotoa crater lake.

Baños ❺ has always been famous for its thermal hot springs bubbling out of the side of the wild and unruly **Volcán Tungurahua** (5,023 meters/17,154ft). In 1999 the volcano started erupting again, and the 25,000 townsfolk were evacuated. Residents fought their way back in at the beginning of 2000 at their own risk, even with the volcano spewing hot rocks and ash only 7km (4 miles) away. Another major eruption took place in August 2006, accompanied by a 10km (6.5-mile) -high ash cloud and pyroclastic flows resulting in seven deaths and destroying hamlets and roads on the western and northwestern slopes of Tungurahua. Since then, volcanic activity has continued, most recently in 2014 when it once again spewed a column of ash 10km (6.5 miles) high; geologists are still keeping a close watch on the peak and will evacuate the town again if activity increases. In the meantime, however, its summit has reopened to hardy hikers. Check online to see if there has been any recent volcanic activity before you go.

The town of Baños attracts both Ecuadorian visitors and foreign travelers.

Baños is something of an adventure hub for backpackers. Streets full of tour operators tout four-wheel drive buggy tours, mountain biking, bungee-jumping, rafting, canyoning, and discount jungle visits. One of the classic routes in this area (for bicycle, scooter, or by 4WD bike) is to head along the road between Baños and Puyo skirting the deep canyon of the Río Pastaza, surrounded on all sides by cloud-forest-cloaked mountains, and waterfalls. Take care not to enter the many unlit road tunnels, though: there is an unpaved detour round each of them which is safer for pedestrians and cyclists. Some of the waterfalls along this route are spectacular, especially the plume-like **Pailón del Diablo** and **Manto de la Novia**, about 20km (12 miles) from Baños, which should not be missed.

The gentle, subtropical climate of Baños (altitude 1,800 meters/5,904ft) is another draw, and it makes the region a hiker's paradise. There are short trails in the hills directly above the town, and nearby, there are the little-explored

national parks of **Los Llanganates** and **Sangay**, two of the most biologically diverse areas in the world. With luck and patience, four kinds of monkey, spectacled bears, mountain tapirs, and birds such as the cock-of-the-rock and black and chestnut eagle can be seen in the forests here. The area is also home to an exceptionally high diversity of plants, many still unknown to modern science. A study of just one genus of orchid turned up 14 new species.

While foreign travelers come to Baños for the hot springs, hiking, and adventure activities, many Ecuadorians come here to pay homage to the Virgen de Baños, known as **Nuestra Señora del Agua Santa** (Our Lady of the Holy Water), whose statue is housed in the basilica in the center of town. The Virgin is credited with many miracles, including delivering people from certain death in a fire in Guayaquil, and saving the lives of travelers when a bridge over the Río Pastaza collapsed. The walls of the basilica are hung with paintings depicting these events. The basilica grounds have a small museum with moldering stuffed tropical birds and the Virgin's changes of clothing.

VOLCÁN CHIMBORAZO

From Baños, return to Ambato (buses are frequent and the journey takes about an hour) and make a trip to the west. A paved road circles around **Volcán Carihuairazo** (5,020 meters/16,470ft) and **Volcán Chimborazo** (6,310 meters/20,571ft) and heads for Guaranda and the coast. Chimborazo is the highest peak in Ecuador, and it looms over the provinces of Chimborazo, Bolívar, and southern Tungurahua like a giant ice cream, dominating the landscape. The **Reserva Faunística Chimborazo** (Chimborazo Fauna Reserve), which surrounds the mountain, is the place to visit for views, high-altitude hiking, and to see some of the way of life of the remote, chilly indigenous villages in the area. The reserve covers a vast 56,560 hectares (139,703 acres) between 3,800 meters (12,540ft) above sea level to the summit of Chimborazo, and is home to vicuña, llama, and alpaca; the last are

> **◉ Tip**
>
> One of the great experiences in this region is to soar down the side of Chimborazo from its Carrel Refuge (4,800 meters/15,744ft) on a mountain bike. Several companies offer this thrilling 55km (33-mile) descent, but the best is Riobamba bike tour operator Pro Bici (tel: 03-295 1760; www.probici.com).

Street stalls in front of the Basílica de Nuestra Señora del Agua Santa, Baños.

◉ THE TREES AT THE TOP OF THE WORLD

The amazing polylepis tree is found growing in sparse patches in the high Andes; indeed, it has the unique distinction of being the tree that grows at the highest elevations in the world. Stands of this ancient, gnarled, slow-growing tree with its bark as flaky as paper (hence the Greek name, meaning "many scales") are found between 3,800 and 4,600 meters (12,000–15,000ft) above sea level. This is remarkable because the natural treeline of the Andes (above which other trees cannot grow) is much lower: 3,200–3,500 meters (10,000–11,000ft) above sea level.

Polylepis trees usually grow in sheltered, inaccessible gullies in high-altitude grasslands such as the Ecuadorian *páramo*, but researchers believe they may once have covered much more extensive swathes of the Andean range, and that existing forests are just the remnants that remain after millennia of being used for fuel and construction material. Many polylepis species (there are thought to be 28) are now protected.

Ecuador's ancient forests are also an important habitat for other endangered plant, bird, and animal species. Furthermore, they help to prevent erosion on steep mountainsides and are the source of many medicinal plants.

18th-century architecture in Riobamba, with Chimborazo in the background.

Mural in the Parque 21 de Abril depicting the 1822 Battle of Riobamba.

also prized livestock for local people. Foxes and deer are also seen here; condors often soar overhead; and this is one of the few places to see the giant hummingbird (*Patagona gigas*), which due to its cold-temperature habitat, hibernates at night and wakes up with the sun. High-altitude polylepis forests are also a fascinating feature of the park, as are the pre-Inca sites of worship on the mountain's flanks, where local villagers still make ritual offerings.

The Western Cordillera outside Ambato is the land of emerald mountains. Every inch of the hillsides is farmed by the Chibuleo *indígenas*, turning the land into a patchwork quilt of every shade of green. Every so often, either Carihuairazo or Chimborazo pokes its snowy head out above the clouds. The road climbs to the *páramo* above 4,000 meters (13,000ft), with some superb views of Chimborazo, then drops again to Guaranda, which is 85km (53 miles) from Ambato. Midway through the journey you enter Bolívar province.

GUARANDA AND THE CHIMBO VALLEY

About 90km (55 miles) from Ambato, the capital of Bolívar province, **Guaranda** ⑥ (2,670 meters/8,725ft) is a small, sleepy town of 30,000 people that comes alive on Saturday with the weekly market. The town is set among seven hills, one of which, Cruz Loma (Cross Ridge), has a giant statue of an indigenous chief, **El Indio de Guarango**, a *mirador* (lookout), and a small, circular museum with pre-Hispanic and colonial artifacts. There are three other small museums in the town with mixed collections, including colonial art and ethnographic material: the **Museo Municipal**, the **Museo de la Casa de la Cultura Ecuatoriana**, and the **Museo del Colegio Pedro Carbo**. Opening hours are variable: check on arrival at the tourist information office located on García Moreno (Mon–Fri 8am–noon and 2–6pm). The **Parque Central** has a monument to Simón Bolívar, which was a gift from the government of Venezuela. There are several historical buildings close to the

park including the Catedral San Pedro, the palacio municipal, and the Casona Universitaria.

Guaranda is the market center for the **Valle de Chimbo** , a rich agricultural region that produces wheat *(trigo)* and corn *(maíz)*. A 16km (10-mile) ride through the valley south from Guaranda takes you to **San José de Chimbo**, an ancient town with colonial architecture and two thriving craft centers. The *barrio* (neighborhood) of Ayurco specializes in fine guitars, handmade from high-quality wood grown in the province. Tambán *barrio* produces hunting guns and fireworks, but these are not just any old fireworks. Bamboo frames *(castillos,* or castles) are fabricated in the shape of giant birds, huge towers, or enormous animals, with fireworks attached. They are set off to striking effect at fiestas throughout the country. It is not uncommon for the *castillo* to fall over, shooting sky rockets directly into the crowd. Gringos generally jump for cover behind the plaza fountain, but the Ecuadorians love it.

CHIMBORAZO PROVINCE

Chimborazo province was the pre-Inca territory of the Puruhá people. Modern towns such as Guano, Chambo, Pungalá, Licto, Punin, Yaruquíes, Alausí, Chunchi, and Chimbo were all originally Puruhá settlements. But, as elsewhere, the Incas forcibly moved people around: they settled *indígenas* from Cajamarca and Huamachuco, Peru, in the Chimbo region and moved many Puruhá people to the south.

Today, Chimborazo has an amazing mixture of people who wear different kinds of traditional dress, although there aren't necessarily special names for all these groups. Chimborazo was the site of many *obrajes* (textile sweatshops) in colonial times and after independence. The indigenous population became increasingly impoverished and marginalized through succeeding centuries as they were pushed by new settlers into the mountains or became attached to the country haciendas as *wasipungeros* (serfs).

The Chimborazo *indígenas* did not take mistreatment and injustice

Riobamba's cathedral.

Streamers hanging from a dancer's white felt hat at a fiesta in Riobamba.

lying down. There have been many revolts over the centuries, including an uprising of 8,000 *indígenas* around Riobamba in 1764, a revolt in Guano in 1778, and a rebellion in Columbe and Guamote in 1803. Land shortages are still a problem, and men from many communities frequently migrate temporarily to the larger cities in search of work. Chimborazo has also seen intensive Protestant evangelical activity, which has often exacerbated tensions.

The most obvious ethnic marker in Chimborazo is hats. While *indígenas* are increasingly wearing dark, commercially made fedoras, a large number still wear the handmade white felt hats, especially for fiestas and other special occasions. In the Guamote market you can spot as many as 15 different kinds of white, handmade hat being worn. Such variations as the size and shape of the brim and crown and the color and length of the streamers, tassels, or other decorations all indicate the wearer's community or ethnic group.

Landscape near Alausí in Chimborazo province.

RIOBAMBA

Riobamba ⑦ is the capital of Chimborazo province. A fossilized human skull found outside the town has been dated to 4750 BC, providing evidence of the area's pre-Colombian history as it is assumed to be from one of the indigenous groups that inhabited the area before the Incas took over. The Spanish chronicler Pedro de Cieza de León arrived in central Ecuador around 1534 heading for Riobamba. "Leaving Mocha," he wrote, "one comes to the lodgings of Riobamba, which are no less impressive than those of Mocha. They are situated in the province of the Puruhás in beautiful fair fields, whose climate, vegetation, flowers, and other features resemble those of Spain." Chimborazo is still primarily an agricultural province, growing crops such as wheat, barley, potatoes, and carrots, with some grazing land for small herds of sheep, llama, and cattle.

Although at 2,750 meters (8,993ft) Riobamba is only 180 meters (589ft) higher than Ambato, it feels much

colder, perhaps because of the wind sweeping down off the glaciers of Chimborazo. The original Riobamba was founded by the Spanish on the site of a major Inca settlement 21km (13 miles) away, where the modern town of Cajabamba stands, but the old town was flattened by an earthquake in 1797 and a new location was chosen. The new Riobamba (pop. 230,000) retains much of its 18th-century architecture and is a relatively sleepy town, except on Saturday, which is market day

Two areas of the Riobamba market are of particular interest to visitors. Traditional indigenous garments, including such items as hats, belts, ponchos, *ikat* shawls and blankets, fabric, *shigras*, and old jewelry (beautiful beads, earrings, and shawl pins) are sold in the **Plaza de la Concepción** on Orozco and 5 de Junio, along with baskets. In one corner of this plaza people set up their treadle sewing machines and mend clothes or sew the collars on ponchos, while other vendors sell aniline (synthetic) dyes. Just south of

this plaza on Calle Orozco is a small cooperative store selling crafts made by the *indígenas* of Cacha.

Another important craft of the Riobamba region is *tagua* nut carving. The egg-sized seeds of the lowland *tagua* palm are soft when first exposed to air but then harden to an ivory-like consistency. *Tagua* is carved into jewelry, chess sets, buttons, rings, busts, and tiny kitchen utensils. Stores selling *tagua* crafts are found opposite the train station on Avenida Primera Constituyente (Avenue of the First Constitution). The street acquired its name because, after winning independence from Spain, Ecuador's first constitution was written and signed in Riobamba on August 14, 1830.

About eight blocks northeast of the *artesanías* plaza is the **Plaza Dávalos**, where cabuya fiber (made from the *Agave americana* cactus, the century plant) and products are sold. *Cabuya* crafts have been an important local industry in the region since colonial times. *Indígena* women spin the fiber into cordage, used for the

Sewing the collar on a poncho in the Plaza de la Concepción, Riobamba.

Ornate ironwork, Riobamba.

Guamote's Thursday market draws indígenas from all over the region.

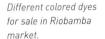

Different colored dyes for sale in Riobamba market.

soles of espadrilles, rope, sacks, and saddlebags.

After the market has finished, the town empties rapidly and lapses into somnolence for another week. This is your opportunity to visit the **Museo de Arte Religioso** (tel: 03-296 5212; Tue–Sat 9am–12.30pm and 3–5.30pm), housed in the Convento de la Concepción on Calle Argentinos. Among the items on display are statues, vestments and some splendid carved chests. Unfortunately, the star attraction, a fabulous gold monstrance encrusted with diamonds and pearls, was stolen in 2007, while the museum guard was allegedly distracted watching Ecuador's national football team on TV.

There is also the museum in the **Colegio Nacional Pedro Vicente Maldonado** (Mon–Fri 7am–7pm) at Avenida Primera Constituyente 2412, with natural history exhibits; the **Museo de la Casa de la Cultura** (www.culturaenecuador.org; Tue–Fri 8am–1pm and 3–5pm, Sat & Sun 10am–4pm) focuses on archeology; and the regional branch of

the **Museo Nacional** (tel: 03-296 5501; Mon–Fri 8.30am–5pm, Sat 10am–4pm) located in the bank building downtown, has ethnographic and modern art exhibitions. The **Museo de la Ciudad** (tel: 03-294 4420; Mon–Sat 8am–12.30pm and 2.30–6pm) has temporary and permanent exhibits. Opening times for all these museums can be erratic, so it is worth checking at the tourist information office on Avenida Daniel León Borja (www.riobamba.com.ec), which is not far from the train station. Riobamba also has some majestic old churches, including the **Catedral de San Pedro** on 5 de Junio and Veloz, and the circular **basilica** (the only one in Ecuador) on Veloz and Alvarado in the Parque La Libertad.

Climb to the top of the **Parque 21 de Abril** (located on Calle Argentinos north of the center of town) for views of Chimborazo, Carihuairazo, Tungurahua, and **El Altar** (5,319 meters/17,457ft). This brooding hulk to the south of the city in the Eastern Cordillera is known in Quichua as Capac Urcu (Great or Powerful Mountain). It is

better not to visit the viewpoint at sunset, however, as muggings can occur in the vicinity at that time.

EXPLORING THE REGION

Riobamba is a good base for excursions to the rest of Chimborazo province. For a day trip to buy rugs and visit the artisans at work, catch a bus or cab 12km (7 miles) north on a subsidiary road, not the Pan-American Highway, to **Guano**. The town is known for its cottage-industry production of fine rugs, hand-knotted on huge vertical-frame looms. Most shops have a workshop attached where you can watch the weavers at work. Just a kilometer or two beyond Guano (there is a bus service) is the small town of **Santa Teresita**, which specializes in the production of carrot or potato sacks woven from *cabuya* fiber. Many of the weavers have enormous warping frames in their yards, with hundreds of meters of *cabuya* on them, and you may also see the woven yardage stretched out along the road. At the edge of town is the

Parque Acuático Los Elenes, with several open-air pools (including one with artificial waves) and one covered pool – all fed by natural springs. There are also volleyball courts, saunas, slides, and a restaurant.

Most of Chimborazo province lies south of Riobamba, and it's a part of Ecuador worth exploring. The road to Licto climbs above Riobamba and offers views of the city and the volcanoes.

A quiet but extremely traditional Sunday market, drawing *indígenas* from the Laguna Colta area and the usual assortment of vendors, is held in **Cajabamba**, 13km (8 miles) south of Riobamba on the Pan-American Highway. This was the site of the old Riobamba, which was originally a Puruhá community, and then the Inca settlement of Liripamba when it had fine, mortarless stonework, including a temple of the sun, a house of the chosen women, and a royal *tambo* (lodge).

The stones from the Inca buildings were then incorporated into

Riobamba lies in the shadow of Volcán Chimborazo.

the Spanish town, which in turn was destroyed in the 1797 earthquake and subsequent landslide. The only building surviving from the 18th century is the chapel.

About 2km (1.2 miles) beyond Cajabamba is the tiny town of **Balvanera** (also spelled Balbanera), on the shores of **Laguna Colta**. Colta *indígenas* graze their cattle and sheep along the marshy shores of the lake, and use the lake's totora reeds to make *esteras* (mats) and *canastas* (baskets). Locals claim that the town's little church, with its image of the Virgen de Balvanera, is the oldest in Ecuador, constructed by the conquistador Sebastián de Benalcázar and his troops after a victory over the Inca forces, but there is no documentary evidence to support this.

In **Guamote** (51km/32 miles south of Riobamba), the Thursday market is the major weekly fair for the southern part of the province. *Indígenas* on horseback or leading llamas laden with produce arrive from communities where no road reaches. At the animal market much of the bargaining takes place in

Quichua, but at the food and clothing markets more vendors speak Spanish. You will see more *indígenas* in different kinds of traditional dress here than at any other market in Ecuador.

SWITCHBACK RAILROAD

From here, the highway drops down past Tixan and into **Alausí** ❽ (2,356 meters/7,704ft). Alausí was once used as a resort to escape from the heat of Guayaquil, and has a charming feel, with impressive mountain views, and a quiet way of life except for market day on Sunday. Alausí is most famous for the legendary **Nariz del Diablo** (Devil's Nose) railroad that switchbacks between here and Sibambe, dropping precipitously. The railroad used to run all the way to Guayaquil, but many switchbacks were washed away in the El Niño storms of 1982–3. Only the part between Riobamba and Sibambe has been repaired, though most travelers prefer to start the journey in Alausí. On a clear day, the exhilarating ride offers fabulous vistas down towards the lowlands.

Guamote's Thursday market.

PREFECTO

Guinea pigs for sale.

📷 RAILWAY JOURNEYS

In their heyday, Ecuador's railways were its life-blood. Today, road travel is the main means of transportation, and much of the country's train tracks and rolling stock have fallen into disrepair.

Former president Rafael Correa, a self-proclaimed rail enthusiast, declared a "Railway Emergency" in 2007, announcing $283 million spending on the network's rehabilitation, to return it to the glory days of rail of the early–mid-1900s, when the coast and the Andes were united by steam trains transporting goods and passengers. During Correa's ten years in office, nearly all sections were restored, including the original Quito–Durán (or "Train of Wonders", close to Guayaquil) line. Rather than a means to get from A to B, routes were developed as tourist excursions, both for Ecuadorians and international visitors, with passengers often taking a return trip to a destination, where they could enjoy traditional dancing and other cultural activities before tucking into some local cuisine. In this way, the revival of the railway also provided small communities along the routes with much needed tourist revenue. But once Correa left office, the network began to falter once more, and when the Covid-19 pandemic hit and all rail travel was suspended, the state railway company was finally closed down.

But the good news is that some sections of the track are reopening: first, the famous hair-raising Nariz del Diablo (Devil's Nose), from Alausí to Sibambe; then probably, the Tren del Hielo (ice train), from Riobamba round the flanks of Volcán Chimborazo; and the impressive Ibarra to Salinas Tren de Libertad. Check the tourist offices for the latest information..

Railway lines run through the colonial streets of Alausí.

Sibambe train station at the base of the Nariz del Diablo being restored and is set to host passengers again.

The attractive railway town of Alausí clings to a steep hillside above the Nariz del Diablo, surrounded by highland landscapes.

The Nariz del Diablo offers dazzling views.

Getting up the Devil's Nose

Train travel in Ecuador began in 1908, when the first train chugged its way into the Ecuadorian capital from the second city, Guayaquil. The opening of the Quito–Guayaquil line was a momentous achievement that had taken 30 years, huge financial investment, and had cost many lives. The route was immediately acclaimed as one of the "great railway journeys of the world," reducing to two days a former nine-day trek along a mule path often impassable due to rain.

The most technically challenging part of this route – and the most thrilling part of the section that still operates today – is the rightfully world-famous Nariz del Diablo (the Devil's Nose) between Alausí and Sibambe. This daredevil piece of engineering takes the train or *autoferro* plunging down the steep switchbacks of a precipitous descent crossing spindly bridges over heart-stoppingly deep ravines. There are stops for passengers to get out and marvel at the spectacular views as well as the engineering. There are several points where the train has to reverse to negotiate a radical switchback. Clouds of diesel smoke add to the atmosphere.

Conductors play a vital role on the autoferros, talking the driver around steep bends and waving back road traffic.

...toferros arrive in Alausí station with a loud blow of the ...rn. The smell of grease and diesel, the calls of the ...nductor, and the screeching of the rolling stock add to ...e atmosphere.

...e Nariz del Diablo train rounds a corner on a ...vitchback.

The 19th-century Catedral Nueva dominates colonial Cuenca's skyline.

THE SOUTHERN SIERRA

Beautiful colonial Cuenca, the Inca ruins of Ingapirca, and the valley of Vilcabamba are just three of many reasons for visiting Cañar, Azuay, and Loja provinces.

The **southern Sierra**, consisting of Cañar, Azuay, and Loja provinces, was until recently the least visited part of the highlands, mainly for reasons of accessibility rather than for lack of attractions. Once a very isolated region, it is now a major stop on the backpacker trail from Ecuador to Peru due to improved roads and an expanding tourist infrastructure. The Andes broaden and flatten out somewhat here, with none of the dramatic snow-caps of the central and northern highlands, but there are plenty of stunning green vistas and mountain roads guaranteed to give you an adrenaline rush.

HUB OF THE SOUTH

The jumping-off point for most trips in the south is **Cuenca ❶**, capital of Azuay province, with a population of around 600,000, making it Ecuador's third-largest city. For many years, Cuenca was isolated from the rest of Ecuador by the lack of good roads, but now it is connected to both Guayaquil and the northern Sierra by paved highways, as well as by daily flights to Quito and Guayaquil.

The Cuenca basin is a major center for *artesanías*, producing ceramics, *paja toquilla* (Panama) hats, baskets, and Christmas ornaments, gold and silver jewelry, and *ikat* shawls, ponchos, and

blankets. Other industries include furniture making, and automobile tires. The city is the economic and intellectual center of the southern Sierra, with a state university and a long history as the birthplace of artists, writers, poets, and philosophers. The city regularly ranks first in the country for the lowest levels of unemployment and poverty.

Cuenca is considered to be Ecuador's most beautiful city, and in 1999 the city center was listed as a UNESCO World Heritage Site. Cuenca means river basin or bowl in Spanish, and the

◎ Main attractions
Cuenca
Museo y Parque
  Archeológico
  Pumapungo
Parque Nacional Cajas
Ingapirca
Vilcabamba

◉ Maps on pages
186, 190

Flower seller outside El Carmen de la Asunción church.

city is situated at 2,549 meters (8,335ft) on the banks of the **Río Tomebamba**. The center has retained its colonial architecture and feel, with new construction in a neo-colonial style that is compatible with existing structures. The blue domes of the Catedral Nueva dominate the skyline. Thanks to its cobblestone streets, interior patios, public plazas overflowing with flowers and greenery, and whitewashed buildings with huge wooden doors and ironwork balconies, central Cuenca is a walker's delight.

Originally, Cuenca was a major Cañari settlement named Guapondelig. After the Inca conquest, it became an important city called Tumipampa, the Plain of the Knife (Hispanicized as Tomebamba), intended to be the Cuzco of the north. Very little of that Inca city remains. If you follow Calle Larga southeast as it goes downhill along the Tomebamba River (near the junction of Calle Tomás Ordóñez with Calle Larga) you will come to the ruins of **Todos Santos**. This small site includes four perfect Inca trapezoidal, mortarless stonework niches, and the remains of the colonial mill of Todos Santos, which was constructed with stones taken from Inca buildings. There are also remains of Inca walls on the hillside above the mill, where ceramics and other evidence of Inca occupation were excavated, and a small museum (Mon–Fri 9.30am–1pm and 3–6pm) documenting the three civilisations (Cañari, Inca and Spanish).

COLONIAL CULTURE

In 1532 the Inca armies retreated north before the advancing forces of Sebastián de Benalcázar. Cuenca was founded on this site in 1557, and named Santa Ana de los Cuatro Ríos de Cuenca. As soon as the Spanish arrived in an area they built a church, and Cuenca was no exception. The **Catedral Vieja** (Old Cathedral) or **El Sagrario A** on the east side of the main plaza, the Parque Abdón Calderón, was begun the year the city was founded. But the city outgrew this simple old church and construction on the **Catedral Nueva** (New Cathedral) or

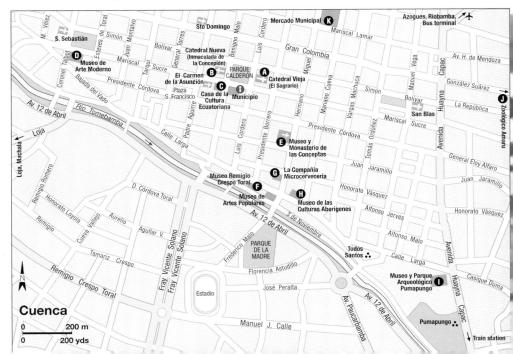

Cuenca

0   200 m
0   200 yds

Catedral de la Inmaculada Concepción **B** started in 1880. This new church was built to hold 10,000 celebrants during religious events and is located opposite the Catedral Vieja on the Parque Calderón, which now houses an interesting religious art museum (Mon–Fri 9am–1pm, 2–4pm, Sat 9am–1pm). The neo-Gothic Catedral Nueva was intended to be 42.5 meters (141ft) wide and 105 meters (351ft) tall, which would have made it the largest church in South America, but the architect miscalculated and designed bell towers too heavy for the structure to support, so work on the towers was halted before completion. It is constructed from alabaster and local marble with floors of pink marble imported from Carrara in Italy.

The **Parque Abdón Calderón** is Cuenca's main square, with the *municipio* (city hall) on the south side. The plaza is busy during the day with locals who come to relax on the many park benches amid the tall conifers, orchids, and other plant life. Just off the southwest corner of the square, on Calle Sucre, is the **Casa de la Cultura Ecuatoriana** **C** (tel: 07-284 2586; Mon–Fri 8am–4.30pm, plus occasional evening events). This small colonial-style building frequently has good exhibitions of local art. On the same block is the **Monasterio del Carmen de la Asunción**, founded in 1682. The church has a fine carved stone facade and the pulpit is gilded and embellished with mirrors. Theoretically open to the public (Mon–Sat 6.45–11am), the building is often closed. A daily flower market is held in the tiny plaza in front of the church, and for a few coins you can brighten your hotel room considerably. Also on Calle Sucre (between Benigno Malo and Luís Cordero) is the tourist information office (tel: 07-282 1035; www.cuencaecuador.com.ec; Mon–Fri 8am–8pm, Sat 9am–4pm, Sun 8.30am–1.30pm), which provides free maps of the city.

Further west along Calle Sucre (at Coronel Tálbot) lies the **Museo de Arte Moderno** **D** (Modern Art Museum; tel: 07-413 4900; Mon–Fri 9am–4.30pm, Sat–Sun 9am–2pm). This museum

Polychrome religious sculptures and altar in the Catedral Vieja.

Panama hats in all shapes and sizes.

The leafy main square, Parque Calderón, with the Catedral Nueva behind.

has rotating exhibitions of contemporary art as well as art workshops for children.

If you're not tired of churches (Cuenca has 27), go back along Calle Sucre and turn right at Calle Hermano Miguel to the **Museo y Monasterio de las Conceptas** Ⓔ (Museum and Monastery of the Conception; https://647510cd5f31b.site123.me; Mon–Sat 10am–5pm). The entrance to the church contains 17th-century tombstones. The cloister, built 1682–1729, has been restored by the Banco Central. The cloister's museum contains an unusual collection of religious art, including toys presented to the convent by novices entering the order, a silver Nativity scene, and an altarpiece of carved wood and gold by the sculptor Manuel Machina. The museum also houses a great collection of lithographs by Oswaldo Guayasamín. (see page 94).

The **Museo Municipal Remigio Crespo Toral** Ⓕ (https://cultura.cuenca.gob.ec/espacios-culturales/museos-municipales/remigio-crespo/; Tue–Fri 10am–4pm, Sat & Sun 10am–1pm), on Calle Larga 7–25 in front of Plazoleta La Merced, houses the city archives containing historical documents relating to the foundation of Cuenca, as well as treaties, agreements, and letters.

In between visiting museums, you can slake your thirst at **La Compañía Bistro Pub** Ⓖ (Honorato Vasquez and Borrero; www.facebook.com/cervezaartesanal.lacompania?locale=es_LA; Mon noon–late, Tue–Sat from 4pm), where you can try and buy various microbrews (the ruby ale is best) – part of a growing trend in Ecuador.

Next try the **Museo de las Culturas Aborígenes** Ⓗ (tel: 099 040 1207; https://mca-cuenca.com; Mon–Fri 9am–5.30pm, Sat 9.30am–2.30pm) at Calle Large 5–24, close to the banks of the Río Tomebamba. It holds a fascinating collection of ancient pottery and pre-Columbian archeological finds from various cultures throughout Ecuador.

The **Museo y Parque Arqueológico Pumapungo** Ⓘ (Tue–Fri 9am–5pm, Sat–Sun 10am–4pm), the city's pre-eminent museum, is located on

Ⓞ BATHING AT BAÑOS

As in many parts of Ecuador, geothermal activity is present near Cuenca. The water at the thermal water resorts of Baños, 8km (5 miles) southwest of the city (not to be confused with Baños in Tungurahua province, see page 172), emerge from the ground at a superheated 78°C (174°F), the highest temperature of any of the thermal waters in Ecuador. The water is channeled and cooled to a pleasant 38–40°C (100–104°F) before it can enter the pools and steam rooms of resorts at Baños. Its slightly milky appearance is due to the rich cocktail of health-giving minerals it contains. The baths are said to be a cure for anything from rheumatism, psoriasis, kidney stones, and bronchial problems, to anemia, stress, and anxiety.

Two recommended places to take the waters are Hostería Durán (tel: 07-289 2485; www.hosteriaduran.com) and the underground pools at Piedra de Agua Spa (tel: 07-289 2496; www.piedradeagua.com.ec). In addition to the thermal baths, both places offer Turkish-style baths and massage services, as well as on-site gourmet restaurants where guests can indulge themselves further. For a more back-to-nature experience in a spectacular mountain setting, take the local bus towards the village of Soldados (20km west of Cuenca), to the thermal baths at Pumamaqui (www.facebook.com/TermasPumamaqui).

Avenida Huayna Cápac across Calle Larga, above the Pumapungo ruins where Inca and Cañari architecture and artifacts were unearthed. The museum has excellent exhibitions of colonial and republican art and historic photographs of Cuenca. There are interesting numismatic and ethnographic collections, too: the former is fascinating for how it illustrates the freefall of the Ecuadorian currency, the Sucre, before dollarization, and the latter for its amazing shrunken heads. Allow time also to explore the outdoor Inca ruins on the edge of the river.

About 5km (3 miles) northeast, near Km 10 on the Autopista Cuenca–Azogues, lies the **Zoológico Amaru** ➊ (tel: 07-421 3982; www.zoobioparque amaru.com; Mon–Sun 9am–4pm). Cuenca's rescue center-cum-zoo displays more than 120 animal species, most of them native to Ecuador, and well maintained. The zoo puts an emphasis on the conservation of, and research into, fish, reptiles, and amphibians, and is an excellent place to visit, especially for those traveling with kids.

A BLENDING OF CULTURES

Many of the Cuenca Valley people are artisans and farmers. They represent a mixture of Inca, Cañari, and Spanish heritage, although their rich mestizo culture is slowly disappearing as young people adopt modern-style clothing and move to the cities or go to work overseas.

In rural areas and especially at the markets in Sigsig, Gualaceo, Chordeleg, and sometimes in Cuenca, you will still see people in traditional dress, which includes Panama hats for both men and women and colored ponchos, especially burgundy and red, for men.

For fiestas, many of the local menfolk wear beautiful hand-woven *ikat* ponchos. If you're in Cuenca for the weekly Thursday fair or for the smaller Saturday market, check out the plaza between Calle Mariscal Lamar and Sangurima off Calle Hermano Miguel, where *artesanías* including baskets, wool, and *ikat* shawls *(paños)* are sold. On Calle Larga between Aguirre and Santa Teresa is a Panama hat

Selling textiles on Plaza San Francisco, a center for artesanías.

Crumbling colonial buildings in the center of Cuenca.

workshop, where you can see the artisans at work.

Another interesting market to visit is the **Mercado Municipal**  on Calle Mariscal Lamar. Set over three levels, it contains hundreds of colorful stalls and is a veritable cornucopia of tropical fruits, cheeses, seafoods, meat, and baked products. This is a great hub of Cuenca life and commerce and the perfect spot for people-watching, accompanied by a coffee and a fresh bun at one of the stalls.

EXCURSIONS INTO THE COUNTRY

The important agricultural center of Gualaceo is about 36km (22 miles) from Cuenca on paved roads. Buses run regularly between the two places, heading north of Cuenca on the Pan-American Highway, turning east at El Descanso and following the Río Paute. Gualaceo is scenically situated on the banks of the Río Gualaceo and has many *quintas* (summer homes) for people from Cuenca and Guayaquil. The slightly lower elevation makes it ideal for growing peaches, apricots, apples, cherries, guavas, and custard apples. There are several good restaurants along the river, and a pleasant inn, the Santa Bárbara Hostería (tel: 07-225 5010; www.facebook.com/santa barbarahosteria). Six kilometers before the town, on the main road, the excellent ethnographic and craft museum run by the Centro Interamericano de Artesanías y Artes Populares (CIDAP) is well worth a visit. It contains displays of local crafts and a gift shop. The exhibit showing the process of making *ikat* textiles is especially informative.

Chordeleg, built on a pre-Inca Cañari settlement, has artisans of all kinds: *ikat* poncho weavers, Panama hat and basket weavers, potters, embroiderers,

Cañari indígenas at the Sunday market.

Southern Sierra

0   40 km

0   40 miles

and jewelers. The town is just a few kilometers up the mountain south of Gualaceo, a 10-minute trip in the local bus. The road leading into Chordeleg from Gualaceo is lined with stores selling silver and gold jewelry at very reasonable prices, in styles ranging from colonial filigree to modern. A gigantic filigree earring (candonga) is on display in the small municipal museum on the main square. Other local *artesanías* and textiles from Otavalo are sold in shops around the main plaza.

There are pre-Inca ruins in the Chordeleg area, including an enormous snake-shaped stone walkway near the entrance to the town, and sites on nearby hilltops that have been excavated. Chordeleg has a small Sunday market, but most people from the town attend the larger market in Gualaceo. From the plaza in Chordeleg you can catch a bus to **Sigsig**, 20km (12 miles) farther south. Sigsig is a tiny colonial town with an equally tiny Sunday market, but the trip along the river is gorgeous. Two archeological sites, Chobshi and Shabalula, are close by; ask residents for directions.

About 45km (28 miles) south of Cuenca lies the small town of **Girón**. Its historic Casa de los Tratados (House of Treaties; corner of Andrés Córdova and Bolívar; www.facebook.com/casadelostrata dosgiron; daily 9am–5.30pm) where in 1829 a peace treaty with Peru was signed following the Battle of Tarqui. Weapons and banners used in the conflict can be seen on the two floors of this beautiful *casa de hacienda*. In turn, Girón is close to a scenic and dramatic waterfall of the same name.

Outdoor enthusiasts should head for **Parque Nacional Cajas** (www.parque-nacional-cajas.org), 20km (12.5 miles) northwest of Cuenca. This outstandingly beautiful park has hundreds of clear, cold lakes, streams, and rivers at altitudes from 3,500 to 4,200 meters (9,000 to 13,000ft) on the *páramo* beneath jagged mountain cliffs. You can go swimming (if you're brave), or fishing for rainbow trout, and there are miles of good hiking trails, camping grounds, and even a small refuge.

Herds of llamas and alpacas have been brought in as part of a breeding program to reintroduce these animals to the southern highlands. It is also a wonderful spot for bird-watching, especially around the lakes, where numerous exotic species can be found, including hummingbirds and the occasional condor. Buses to Las Cajas (as the park is known) leave in the early morning from the church of San Sebastián, at calles Bolívar and Talbot in Cuenca, and return late in the afternoon. August to January is the best time to visit and it is a good idea to arrive early in the morning, as the afternoon tends to bring fog, mist, clouds, rain, and sometimes snow. Day-trips are offered by Cuenca tour operators, but if you visit independently, be sure to bring a good map and compass: hikers who have come insufficiently prepared have lost their lives here.

⊘ Tip

From Loja it is an easy journey to reach the city of Piura in Peru: buses go direct, stopping at both Ecuadorian and Peruvian immigration for you to get your passport stamped.

Lakes in Parque Nacional Cajas.

Sheep for sale at the Sunday market held in Plaza de las Animales, Cañar.

Farmland in highland Cañar province.

INDEPENDENT TRADITIONS

Cañar province, north of Cuenca, home of the Cañari *indígenas*, has the largest and the most complete accessible Inca ruins in Ecuador. While Cañar is considered a highland province, about one-third of its territory is in the western lowlands, where sugarcane, cocoa, bananas, and other tropical fruits are grown. In both the lowlands and the Sierra, extensive territory is given over to cattle that graze the large tracts of land owned by the big haciendas.

The Cañaris, who were once the principal indigenous group in southern Ecuador have suffered greatly since the arrival of the Incas in the 15th century. At first they resisted the Incas fiercely, at one time defeating them and driving them back to Saraguro. When civil war broke out in 1527 between two claimants to the throne, Atahualpa in Quito and Huascar in Cuzco, the Cañaris sided with Huascar. Atahualpa routed Huascar's army at Ambato and in revenge killed most of the Cañari men and boys, despite their surrender. A year after the Spanish captured and killed Atahualpa in Cajamarca (Peru), a Spanish force under Sebastián de Benalcázar marched north to plunder Quito. When Benalcázar reached Tumipampa he was joined by 3,000 Cañari warriors, eager for revenge against the Quito Inca forces. The Cañaris fought with the Spanish throughout the conquest of Ecuador, but received scant recognition from the Spanish for their help. By 1544 many thousand Cañari men were forced to labor in the gold and silver mines of southern Ecuador, and their numbers were so reduced that in 1547 the Spanish chronicler Pedro de Cieza de León noted that the ratio of women to men was 15 to 1.

Currently there are about 40,000 Quichua-speaking Cañari *indígenas* scattered throughout Cañar province. Most are farmers, but some are sheep- and cattle-herders. They are, on the whole, and perhaps understandably, fairly wary of outsiders.

Cañari men's dress includes the *kushma*, a fine *ikat* poncho for fiesta use, black wool pants, a white cotton shirt with embroidery on the sleeves

and collar and an extremely fine double-faced belt with motifs from local life. Like the men of Saraguro and Otavalo, Cañari men wear their hair in a long braid. The shepherds wear sheepskin chaps and carry a small whip with a wooden handle, which is worn over their shoulder. The typical Cañari hat, worn by both men and women, is handmade of white felt with a small round crown and narrow brim, turned up at the front. Cañari women wear an embroidered blouse, a shoulder wrap held shut with a *tupu* (shawl pin), and a woolen *pollera* skirt in various colors.

EXPLORING CAÑAR

The Pan-American Highway climbs out of Cuenca to **Azogues ❷**, the capital of Cañar province, with over 40,000 inhabitants. Azogues has a quiet colonial air, with wooden balconies and shutters aslant on ancient whitewashed houses. *Azogue* means mercury, and the town was named after the nearby (and long abandoned) mercury mines. The **Convento de San Francisco** (daily 8am– 4.45pm) towers above Azogues on a

hill to the southeast. The colonising Spanish practice of building churches on pre-Hispanic Inca *huacas* (holy places), many of which were located on mountain tops, accounts for the large number of churches that are perched at ridiculous altitudes. If you need the exercise and want the view, it's a half-hour climb to the top.

Azogues has two museums: the **Museo Ignacio Neira** in the Colegio Julio María Matavalle has zoological, archeological, and mineralogical displays, but is open only on request; and the **Museo Arqueológico y Etnográfico** (Museum of Archeology and Ethnography), which houses religious art and artifacts like jewelry, ceramics, and textiles. (tel: 07-224 0077; Mon–Fri 8.30am–12.30pm, 1.30–5pm).

The Pan-American Highway winds past Azogues and into **Cañar ❸**, which is 65km (40 miles) from Cuenca and 36km (22 miles) from Azogues. Cañar is high and chilly at 3,104 meters (10,150ft); this is barley, potato, quinoa, and cattle country. The town has a fascinating market on Sundays, when

Livestock for sale in Plaza de los Animales in Cañar's Sunday market.

Regular-shaped, coursed Inca masonry uses no mortar.

Cañari women wearing traditional felt hats and embroidered pollera skirts.

indígenas, including mounted Cañaris with *ikat* ponchos, whips (*chicotes*), and sheepskin chaps (*zamarro*) come down off the *páramo* to buy, sell, and trade. The Cañari men's belts are beautifully made in a complex intermesh double-faced technique. The best place in town to buy belts is the jail (Centro de Rehabilitación Social), where *indígenas* doing time do not waste time, but spend it weaving. The jailer will unlock the door and let you into the main patio where you will be besieged (in a friendly manner) by prisoners with belts and sometimes ponchos to sell.

ECUADOR'S GREATEST RUINS

Many people visit Cañar for the market and then go on to the UNESCO World Heritage Site of **Ingapirca** (tel: 07-221 7115; daily 9am–5pm). There are several ways to reach the ruins. You can catch a bus from Cañar, take a bus or taxi from Cuenca (2 hours one way), rent your own vehicle, or go on an organized tour. A great alternative is to arrive at Ingapirca on foot. There is a hiking trail to the ruins, following

the route of an Inca road, which takes three days through high-altitude *páramo* from Achupallas, east of Alausí. Ask at the iTur tourist information office in Alausí (opposite the train station), which will be able to put you in touch with Achupallas-based guides. It is possible to do the hike without a guide, but you will need a detailed topographical map that you can only buy at the **Instituto Geográfico Militar** in Quito. Take care with the semi-wild *toros bravos* (fighting bulls) that you may encounter en route. The Ingapirca site is part of the ancient Inca road and defense system stretching from Argentina in the south to Colombia in the north.

Ingapirca means "Inca stone wall"; the name was given to the site by the Cañaris. We know that the Inca Huayna Capac built Ingapirca in the 15th century on the royal highway that ran from Quito to Cuzco and stationed soldiers there to keep the Cañaris under control. Throughout the Inca Empire, outlying Inca settlements had multiple functions and

were intended to be models of Cuzco on a much smaller scale. From what remains of Ingapirca, the site probably had storehouses, baths, a royal *tambo* or inn for the Inca, dwellings for soldiers and others, and a sun temple, the remains of which can be seen in the beautiful ellipse, made of green diorite and modeled after the Koricancha, the main temple in Cuzco. The high-quality stonework indicates that Ingapirca was a very important site.

The Incas often chose hilltops for their settlements, both for defensive reasons and to free up flat valley land for cultivation. Much of Ingapirca was dismantled over the centuries by local people who used the stones for domestic buildings.

Various other remains surround the main buildings. The Ingachungana, or Inca's playground, is a large rock with carved channels that may have been used for offerings or for divination, with water, *chicha* (a fermented drink, usually made out corn), or the blood of sacrificed llamas or guinea pigs poured in the channels. Near the Ingachungana is a chair or throne cut into the rock and called the **Sillón del Inca** (the Inca's Chair). Below in the gorge are several zoomorphic rock carvings – a couple appear to be a monkey and a turtle – and the **Cara del Inca** (the Inca's Face), a large stone outcropping that is probably natural, rather than carved. The site also houses a small, but well laid-out, museum (Mon–Sat) with ethnographic and archeological exhibits. The displays include such artifacts from the Cañari and Inca cultures as ceramics, jewelry, and textile fragments. Less than a mile away is the village of **Ingapirca**, which has a crafts cooperative store next to the church and a couple of basic restaurants. On Fridays the village plays host to a small but attractive indigenous market.

THE FAR SOUTH

Tucked away deep in southern Ecuador between Azuay province and the border with Peru, Loja province is the least visited of the highland provinces, mainly because of its isolation. There

The ruins of Ingapirca, Ecuador's major Inca site.

are flights to the provincial capital, Loja, from Quito and Guayaquil, but not from Cuenca, so travelers heading directly south from Cuenca must go overland along the paved Pan-American Highway. Loja province is primarily rural and agricultural and there are only a few small towns along the road.

The highway south of Cuenca passes through rich, green land until **Cumbe** (14km/9 miles), where it begins to climb to the **Tinajilla Pass** at 3,500 meters (11,445ft). It then traverses the *páramo* of **Gañadel**, which is usually misty and fogged in. In the middle of this wilderness, figures bundled in shawls and ponchos will appear out of the fog to flag down the bus.

The clouds sometimes part to surprise you with extensive views of the Western Cordillera and sunlight streaming through in the distance, a sight that looks like a Renaissance artist's idea of the dawn of creation.

From here the road twists a few miles to **Saraguro ❹**, a high, chilly town, it is the social and commercial center for the Saraguro *indígenas*,

relatively prosperous farmers and cattle traders who live in the small surrounding communities *(barrios)*.

The Saraguros are said to be descendants of the Inca conquerors of Ecuador, who were brought to the region after the Inca Tupac Yupanqui's conquest of the area around 1455 and replaced the indigenous Palta people who were sent to Bolivia by the Incas. Under Inca rule, each ethnic group was required to retain its traditional costume, especially its headdress and hairstyle. The Spanish outlawed certain kinds of Inca headgear and introduced brimmed hats, but each ethnic group insisted on wearing a distinctive style, which accounts for the plethora of hat styles seen in the Andes today.

The *indígenas* of Saraguro were never serfs on the *haciendas* or laborers in textile sweatshops. They have survived as farmers and cattle traders, supplying much of the beef for southern Ecuador. Because of a shortage of pasture in the Saraguro region the Saraguros drive their cattle over the continental divide and down into the

The village of Ingapirca has a small market on Fridays.

tropical lowlands around Yacuambi. The cattle are fattened here and driven back up over the Andes to be sold at the Sunday Saraguro market. The people of Saraguro value formal education and are among the best-educated *indígenas* in Ecuador, with their own high school, and many young adults attending the universities in Cuenca and Quito.

REMEMBERING THE INCA

Saraguro dress is black or dark indigo – blue wool, which many *indígenas* say they wear in mourning for the death of the Inca Atahualpa. Most of the clothes are hand-spun and hand-woven, and everywhere you travel in the Saraguro region you will see women and girls with distaffs and spindles, spinning wool for their family clothing. Most striking, though, is the women's jewelry. Several jewelers in Saraguro specialize in making the large nickel or silver shawl pins *(tupus)* that women use to fasten their shoulder wraps. Fine silver *tupus* are heirlooms, passed down from mother to daughter, as are filigree earrings. Women also wear beaded necklaces. One style has rows of tiny seed beads strung in zigzags, and the colors of the beads and number of rows indicate the woman's community.

The best place to stay among Saraguro's fairly rustic accommodations is the community-run Hostal Achik Wasi (tel 07-220 0331; www.saraurku.com), which can also organise home-stays and cultural tours. Most day-visitors come for the Sunday market. Some crafts, especially the traditional jewelry, are sold in small shops in the main market building and surrounding streets. The town was also an Inca settlement and extensive ruins, which are impossible to find without a guide, are located outside the town in the forests on the slopes of Mount Acacana. These ruins, called **Inca Iglesia** (Inca Church), are large but overgrown,

and contain fine mortarless stonework walls and channels carved in the rock for the water system.

The Cuenca–Loja bus, which makes the round trip several times a day, continues on to Loja after stopping in Saraguro to pick up passengers. Loja is another 61km (38 miles) from Saraguro, a ninety-minute ride along a dizzying corkscrew road.

COLONIAL CENTER

Loja ❺ is the bustling capital of Loja province. It is of most interest to visitors as a base for visiting the surrounding region, particularly the nearby Parque Nacional Podocarpus. Because the Spanish invasion of Ecuador began in Piura on the north coast of Peru, Ecuador was conquered and settled from south to north. Loja was founded in 1548, which makes it one of the oldest cities in the country. The city has been rebuilt twice due to devastating earthquakes, the last being in the 1880s. Cieza de León commented on the prosperity of the region and on the vast herds of llamas, vicuñas, and

Trekking near Vilcabamba.

Native orchid.

The male Andean-cock-of-the-rock has brilliant orange and black plumage.

guanacos when he rode through Loja along the Royal Inca Highway (*Qhapaq Ñan*), but the Spanish conquerors soon hunted them to extinction. Loja has about 203,000 inhabitants and is nestled among the mountains at a pleasant 2,225 meters (7,275ft). Because it is so close to the Oriente it is a major entry point to the southern jungle and the province of Zamora-Chinchipe.

A short tourist circuit runs across the town. Begin at the **Puerta de la Ciudad** (the City Gateway; Mon–Fri 8am–8pm, Sat & Sun 9am–7pm), just north of the center. This castle-like structure was built in 1998 as a replica of a Spanish fortress that was built in Loja in 1571 but later torn down. It houses a contemporary art gallery, a café, and a souvenir shop. Climb the clock tower for splendid views of the town. A path leads from here down to the pleasant Parque Bolívar and from there to Parque Central, the city's main square.

The city has two universities, one of which has a law school, and a music conservatory. It is also home to some modest museums, which include the **Museo de la Cultura Lojana** (UTPL, San Cayetano Alto; Tue–Fri 8am–5pm, Sat & Sun 10am–4pm), situated in a beautiful colonial mansion that was renovated in 2018, and the **Museo de la Música** (Bernardo Valdivieso and Rocafuerte; Mon–Fri 8am–6pm). The **cathedral** and the churches of **San Martín** and **Santo Domingo** are Loja's most interesting religious buildings and have nicely painted interiors. The statue of the Virgin of Cisne is kept in the cathedral from August to November, while the fiesta of the Virgin takes place on September 8. The religious observances and the accompanying agricultural fair attract pilgrims from throughout northern Peru and the southern part of Ecuador. Further south, just past the Plaza de Independencia, is Calle Lourdes, several blocks of which have been restored to highlight their wooden balconies and cobblestone patios. The buildings are home to a wide variety of artisans and galleries. South of the city center, the **Jardín Botánico Reynaldo Espinosa** (Mon–Fri 7.30am–12.30pm, 3–6pm, Sat & Sun 1–6pm) is Ecuador's oldest botanical garden, brimming with native plant species, including orchids, and examples of the area's emblematic podocarpus trees.

VALLEY OF THE ANCIENTS

Loja is the usual jumping off-point for beautiful **Vilcabamba** , 62km (38 miles) due south. Vilcabamba gained a certain reputation in the 1970s as the valley of the ancients, where an unusual percentage of old people were said to live to be 100 to 120 years old. Disappointingly for those looking for the fountain of youth, these tales turned out to be exaggerated. One book on Vilcabamba, for example, contained a document purporting to be a birth certificate proving that one man was 128 years old. The document, on closer scrutiny, turned out to be a land

title in his grandfather's name, which his descendant shared.

Vilcabamba is located at a comfortable, mild 1,500 meters (4,905ft) above sea level and the valley is a visual delight: green, gentle, and pretty. A sprinkling of delightful lodges overlook the valley. The relaxed vibe has attracted a significant ex-pat community and the place is a popular weekend destination for Lojanos who want to slow down the pace of their travels and enjoy the tranquil surroundings. There are also plenty of opportunities for horseback riding, mountain biking and hiking up into the nearby **Parque Nacional Podocarpus** (https://national-parks.org/ecuador/podocarpus), one of the most beautiful cloud-forest areas in Ecuador. The national park has outstandingly diverse ecosystems, and is home to many rare species, including the Andean spectacled bear. It is also a paradise for bird-watching: look out for the flamboyant Andean cock-of-the-rock, toucans, hummingbirds, macaws, and jocotocos, which are endemic to the park. The park is named after a podocarpus conifer (podocarpus montanus) which can grow upward of 40 meters (130ft) and lives for more than 1,000 years.

A couple of tour operators based in Vilcabamba visit the park: just take a stroll around the tranquil main square and you will find their offices.

GOLD-RUSH OUTPOSTS

Although strictly speaking part of the southern Oriente, **Zamora** ⑦ is only 60km (40 miles) from Loja, though with a different frontier-town feel. A colony was founded here by the Spanish in 1549 at about 970 meters (3,180ft) above sea level in the headwaters of the Río Zamora. This colony was wiped out in attacks by the displaced indigenous Shuar population. Undaunted, the Spaniards re-established the settlement in around 1560, to pursue their feverish quest for gold using forced or enslaved labour. Mining, and with it the fortunes of the town, have ebbed and flowed over the centuries: in the 1930s there were fewer than a dozen buildings, but by 1953 it had become the capital of the isolated province of Zamora-Chinchipe, even though the only access was by mule. The first vehicle made it to Zamora in 1962. The town's few visitors generally only pass through to access the lowland sector of the **Parque Nacional Podocarpus**, pausing only to admire the town's enormous hillside floral clock.

In 2019, Ecuador opened its first industrial-scale mine, Proyecto Mirador, to the northeast of Zamora, despite widespread and ongoing protests by indigenous groups and environmental activists. This vast open-cast copper mine also aims to extract silver and gold in smaller quantities. It remains to be seen whether Ecuador's historic public referendums held in 2023, which voted to halt oil extraction and gold mining in other areas of Ecuador, have any impact on mining activity in the south.

Parque Nacional Podocarpus.

The Río Pastaza gorge.

Heliconia flowering in the Ecuadorian rainforest.

THE ORIENTE

Reptiles, anacondas, piranhas, toucans, howler monkeys, and jumping spiders all await you in the Amazon basin. Your transportation can vary from floating hotel to dugout canoe.

You may go to the **Oriente** only once in your life, so it is worth asking yourself what you want from your trip. How important is comfort? Do you need a specialist guide and are you more interested in wildlife, plants, or indigenous culture? Also, what impact is your visit going to have on the rainforest? When you've answered these questions, you can start making plans. Options include a wide range of jungle lodges, an Amazon river-boat, or the burgeoning number of "adventure tourism" groups. Trips can be organized from Quito or arranged in Misahuallí, Baños, Tena, or Coca. If you are looking for an expert guide or a comfortable lodge, it is best to organize the trip in Quito, although they can be cheaper elsewhere.

RIVER TRIPS

For the adventurous, one of the best ways to experience primary tropical rainforest is to take a multi-day canoe trip down one of the rivers of the Oriente. Several qualified guides organize float trips on the **Río Tiputini** or in the **Reserva Cuyabeno**, where you can see wildlife close up. During the day you will see wooly and howler monkeys grazing in the trees, toucans or parrots in flight, or, if you are lucky, an anaconda lazing in the sun. At night you will be serenaded by a symphony of insects and an occasional unidentified animal.

FLOATING HOTEL

At the other end of the scale from canoe trips is the **Manatee Amazon Explorer** (www.manateeamazonexplorer.com). Especially designed for cruises in the Ecuadorian rainforest on the Río Napo, the three-level riverboat allows travelers to dip into the rainforest and return to a certain amount of luxury. Small but comfortable cabins provide the amenities of a modern hotel, while the flotel

Main attractions

Reserva de Producción
Faunística Cuyabeno
Visit to a jungle lodge
Piranha-fishing

Map on page 204

Chorongo monkey.

The rough-skinned green treefrog.

has a bar, observation deck, and dining room where excellent meals are served. The slow but sure flotel visits different parts of the river on itineraries ranging from four to eight days, penetrating deep into the rainforest, and therefore offering more opportunities to see wildlife. Passengers are taken ashore to visit a local community, trek into the rainforest, and marvel at the birdlife from a jungle observation tower.

JUNGLE LODGES

For those who prefer to be based in one location and make daily exploration forays, a jungle lodge is the way to go. These vary from rough-and-ready, shared accommodation that caters for backpackers, to lodges that would pass for five-star resorts. Those more distant from towns or settlements usually have better bird-watching and wildlife-viewing, though their facilities may be more limited. Some lodges have rainforest canopy walkways, which is usually the only way to get a treetop perspective. Whichever you go for, be sure to check that the lodge you choose offers some form of mosquito netting to protect you at night. Excursions offered at most of the lodges are similar: walks and canoe trips for wildlife-viewing, visits to indigenous settlements, and perhaps even some piranha-fishing.

Most people who have arranged river tours or visits to jungle lodges in advance will arrive by air, leaping suddenly from one climate to another. Daily flights dive from Quito to the town of **Coca** deep in the jungle, covering in only 30 minutes the same distance that can take 12 grueling hours by land, as well as providing spectacular aerial views of the changing landscape.

The dazzling white of the snow-capped Andes gives way to an endless mattress of green stretching into the horizon. Dozens of rivers snake beneath huge gray clouds, ready to drop their loads of moisture onto the rainforest.

THE HIGHWAY FROM QUITO

Travelers who want to observe from the ground the subtle shifts in flora

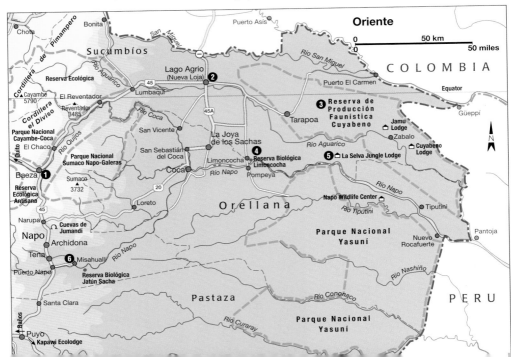

between the Sierra and Oriente gladly sacrifice comfort and speed for a bus window seat along the eastern highway. An hour east of Quito, the bus labors over the sometimes snow-covered **Papallacta Pass** – at 4,100 meters (13,400ft), one of the highest points in Ecuador that can be reached by public transport. The narrow mountain road then plunges down in a series of ear-popping curves to the Oriente and the landscape alters dramatically.

The Oriente (the East), as Ecuador's Amazonian region is called, lies less than 100km (60 miles) from the Papallacta Pass as the condor glides. But the eastern slopes of the **Andes** tumble precipitously, and the road passes lush cloud forests full of giant Andean tree ferns, spiky bromeliads, delicate orchids, and brightly colored birds. This is the very rim of the Amazon basin, and the steepness of the terrain combines with the thick vegetation to make it almost impenetrable.

The heavily forested subtropical slopes of this transitional area are the haunts of a variety of wildlife, including the spectacled bear. Birdlife is more conspicuous and colorful than wildlife in the cloud forest, with iridescent quetzals, glittering hummingbirds, and gaudy tanagers. Each elevation has its own distinct set of bird species, and the same occurs with the plants, resulting in a biological mosaic of unparalleled diversity. The northern Andean cloud forests have a total plant diversity as great as that of the entire Amazon basin, though they cover only a twentieth of the basin area.

Thirty minutes' drive past the Papallacta Pass is the town of **Papallacta** and its nearby hot springs, ideal for anyone in need of a little relaxation. The road drops toward the jungle taking the line of least resistance – a river valley. Amazonian climate patterns ensure heavy rainfall almost year-round, and there are hundreds of minor and major rivers flowing down the eastern Andes toward the Oriente. Although at this point they are only 240km (150 miles) away from the Pacific, these rivers will merge with the waters of the world's greatest river

Male chestnut-breasted coronet hummingbirds having a territorial dispute.

system and finally join the sea at the Atlantic 3,200km (2,000 miles) away.

BAEZA

The road follows the valley of the Río Papallacta, and finally ends up in the first important Oriente town, **Baeza** ❶, near the Río Quijos (named for an indigenous tribe that lived in the region at the time of the conquest). Baeza is a small, ramshackle, subtropical outpost whose tin-roofed appearance belies its long and interesting history. Since before the Spanish conquest, lowland forest natives stopped here on their way to the highlands on trading expeditions. Recognizing the area's strategic importance, the Spaniards founded a missionary and trading outpost here in 1548, just 14 years after conquering Ecuador.

Perched on the edge of the Amazon basin at 1,400 meters (4,600ft) above sea level and 80km (50 miles) east of Quito, Baeza remained Ecuador's last outpost in the northern Oriente for more than four centuries. Today it is its gateway, and can also be reached by a popular road from Baños farther south, via the jungle town of **Puyo**. This is Ecuador's largest jungle town, with a bustling feel, but little to entice visitors other than some pleasant walks beside the Río Puyo, and on clear days, good views of the Sangay and Altar volcanoes. Indigenous community visits and adventurous jungle wildlife tours can usually be arranged from here.

FROM LAGO AGRIO TO TENA

Until the middle of the 20th century, this Andean rim of the Amazon basin was as far as colonists and travelers went. Wildlife and indigenous groups lived relatively undisturbed deeper in the Oriente's interior. This suddenly changed in the late 1960s with the discovery of oil in the jungle. Almost overnight, a good all-weather road was pushed from Quito beyond Baeza and deep into the heart of parts of the Oriente which until then could be reached only by difficult river travel or by light aircraft. The 180km (110-mile) road stretches from Baeza to **Lago Agrio** ❷

Laguna Grande, Cuyabeno.

(literally "Sour Lake"), an oil town built in a trackless region in the middle of the jungle. For much of its length, the road to Lago Agrio parallels the trans-Ecuadorian pipeline, which pumps oil 495km (310 miles) from the oilfields of the Oriente, up across the Andes and down to the Pacific coast for processing and export. At irregular intervals along the pipeline, little communities have been created. Some are next to oil pumping stations, whilst others have been founded by colonists near flat pieces of land that they have cleared.

The famous **San Rafael Falls** are on the Río Quijos, about halfway between Baeza and Lago Agrio. With a height of about 145 meters (475ft), they are the highest falls in the country. They can be glimpsed from the bus as it travels along the road, but for an impressive close-up look you should get off at the NECEL electricity station at **Reventador**. From here, it is a 30-minute walk down an overgrown trail through lush forest to a viewpoint where, if the wind is right (or wrong, depending on your point of view) you can be sprayed by the light mist caused by the crashing water. Sometimes the spray can be so thick that it obliterates the view of the cascading river; at other times the mists clear for a magnificent sight of the falls. Although the construction of dams upstream is likely to reduce the flow of water here, it is also a great place for bird-watching. Nearby Volcán Reventador, the most active volcano in the Cordillera Real, shows its peak above the cloud forest.

In 2002, after 26 years of dormancy, Reventador erupted spectacularly, shooting a column of ash and rock 15km (9 miles) into the sky, which enshrouded Quito and the rest of central Ecuador. Smaller eruptions have occurred since then and heavy rainfall has caused ash deposits in the area to shift, in turn creating major landslides and causing damage to the oil pipeline.

It is currently too dangerous to trek to or explore Reventador.

Lago Agrio itself is one of the fastest-growing places in Ecuador, although not much to look at. It is officially called Nueva Loja (New Loja), named by the first Ecuadorian colonists in the area who mainly came from the province of Loja in the south of the country. It was homesick North American oilmen working for Texaco who nicknamed the town Lago Agrio.

Lago Agrio was part of the huge jungle province of Napo, whose capital is Tena, an all-day drive away over ill-maintained roads. Tena is not an oil town, and the citizens of Lago felt that their very different interests were not represented. But Lago's importance became apparent after an earthquake in 1987 isolated the town, cutting the oil flow and bringing the economy to a grinding halt. A hot and humid climate pervades the town and the unpaved streets are often filled with mud. Yet it is a lively and progressive place; late-model jeeps churn the mud in the streets and the bustling market

⊙ ENVIRONMENTAL LAWSUIT

An environmental battle has long been raging over Ecuador's Oriente, with a multibillion-dollar case against oil company Chevron ongoing since 1993. Brought by a group of US-based trial lawyers led by Ecuadorian environmental lawyer Pablo Fajardo, the case is on behalf of 48 plaintiffs and thousands of indigenous people living in oil-contaminated areas. The suit resulted in the court seeking the biggest ever payout by an oil company for environmental damages: up to $27 billion dollars. In a report compiled by a court-appointed team in 2008, it was concluded that oil spilling and deliberate, uncontained dumping by Chevron had led to 1,401 cancer deaths and countless other long-term health effects. The oil giant allegedly used unlined pits to dump oil sludge in the jungle, which resulted in contaminants entering water sources and the food chain, and was subsequently forced to pay $40 million in a clean-up operation. In 2012 an Ecuadorian court ruled that Chevron should pay $18.2 billion in damages. Chevron challenged the ruling, and in late 2018 the Hague-based Permanent Court of Arbitration overturned the Ecuadorian Court's judgement on the basis of a violation of international law due to purported fraud and corruption underpinning the Ecuadorian case. The ruling has been a disappointment to the indigenous communities who allege oil spills and contamination have destroyed their homes and communities.

Fact

The road makes life a lot easier for travelers, but has had detrimental effects on the environment.

is thronged with shoppers. Sadly, it is also a frontier town that has suffered from the growth of drug-trafficking and armed groups in neighboring Colombia, and travelers are advised to make inquiries about the current safety situation before visiting the region.

Much quieter is the village of **Archidona**, south of Baeza. Archidona was originally a mission, founded in 1560, and still retains a pleasantly hushed air. The village center has a palm-shaded plaza that gets busy only on Sundays, when indigenous people from surrounding communities come in for the market. Just north of Archidona are the Cuevas de Jumandí, which have impressive stalactites and stalagmites, and need a good flashlight and sense of adventure to explore.

Tena lies 75km (47 miles) south of Baeza and is the kayak and rafting capital of Ecuador. The town straddles the Tena and Pano rivers, and you always have the feeling that the water is near. The charming main plaza overlooks the river, on the other side of which is the *malecón* (pier). Operators in town offer

trips varying from wild white-water (and white-knuckle) rides to gentle river floats, and taking one of these is a great way to see some of the beautiful jungle, canyons and cloud forest that surround the town. Visits to waterfalls and indigenous communities can also be arranged from Tena. Situated on an island right across from town is the **Parque Amazónico**, reached by a thatched bridge, where there are great walking trails. You can see a number of species of monkeys in the trees, but sadly most of the animals, including a tapir, an ocelot, and a jaguarundi, are in cages.

About a one-hour bus ride and three-hour hike from the town brings you to the Comunidad Capirona, a network of nine Quichua communities located within the **Grand Sumaco National Park Biosphere Reserve**, an extremely diverse and threatened area. There are opportunities to volunteer with development projects in the community.

INTO THE JUNGLE

If there are no current security problems, it is well worth making the effort to get from Lago Agrio to the **Reserva de Producción Faunística Cuyabeno ❸**, up toward the Colombian border, where some 655,000 hectares (1.6 million acres) of incredibly bio-diverse territory, consisting mostly of flooded forest, have been turned into a national park. It's a full day's travel by bus and motorized canoe along the Río Aguarico to reach the reserve itself.

The best of several lodges in or near the reserve is remote **Jamu Lodge** (www.jamulodge.com), located on the Río Cuyabeno, 15 minutes' motorized canoe ride downriver from Laguna Grande. Jamu has rustic, thatched *cabañas* on stilts, connected by raised walkways through the flooded jungle. The eco-conscious lodge is particularly atmospheric at night, when it's lit with kerosene lamps. Excursions include

The heliconia is also called the false-bird-of-paradise.

canoe trips, swimming in the black waters of nearby lagoons, and the opportunity to wade through flooded forests. There's also an opportunity to visit a Siona community in the reserve, and a very good chance of spotting an elusive pink river dolphin.

CLOSE ENCOUNTERS WITH PIRANHAS AND CAIMANS

On many jungle trips it is possible to try some piranha-fishing. Small pieces of raw red flesh are used as bait on hand-lines, bringing the infamous creatures out in their hundreds. These small fish are surprisingly easy to catch, although watch your fingers as you bring them aboard: their small, triangular teeth are razor sharp.

Contrary to popular belief, it is quite possible to swim in piranha-infested waters. The variety of piranha found in Ecuador will only ever turn nasty on large mammals, such as humans and horses, if there is a large quantity of blood in the water. Even so, such is the reputation of the fish that swimming here is rather unnerving, and many prefer to endure the Amazonian heat rather than test the murky waters.

Another unforgettable Oriente experience is night-time **caiman-watching**. Slip out on a canoe at night and shine a flashlight into the reeds by the lakeside: hundreds of red eyes stare back, the reflections from caimans' retinas (rather like the "red eye" effect in flash photography). The more adventurous guides will take the boat right in among these reptiles; an experience that can feel a little too adventurous if you happen to be in an unstable dugout canoe. Some guides will even grab a small caiman by the tail, to bring it alongside the canoe and give everyone a closer look.

LIMONCOCHA AND POMPEYA

If you have a few days to spare it is possible to visit **Limoncocha** (Lime Lake) downriver from the jungle town of Coca. Oil production has had some impact on the area, but parts of the swamp and surrounding forest remain intact. This unique ecosystem harbors white caiman and over 400 species of bird. Boat trips can be made at the

⊙ Fact

Contact Aves y Conservación (the Ecuadorian Ornithology Foundation; www.aves conservacion.org), for more information on birds and their habitats. See Travel Tips, for details.

A caiman in the wild.

park headquarters of the **Reserva Biológica Limoncocha** ❹ near the town of Limoncocha. Although there is no formal lodge, an extended stay can be arranged at the SEK University research station or in the Limoncocha community.

About 8km (5 miles) from Limoncocha is the Capuchin mission of **Pompeya**. Among the houses built on wooden stilts is an altar with a crucifix above a colored canoe, as well as a curious museum. Here you can handle the various blowpipes used by Amazonian peoples to hunt – many are surprisingly long and heavy – and often used to shoot directly upward into the trees with a dart coated with natural venom that paralyzes the prey. Opposite Pompeya is **Isla de los Monos** (Monkey Island), where you can wander freely and spot wooly monkeys high in the trees above. You will need a little patience, but you should be well rewarded. There have been regrettable changes, however: not long ago the island was literally packed with monkeys, but the Ecuadorian Army chose this location as the site for survival training, and hundreds of these creatures ended up in the soldiers' stews.

AMAZON LODGES ON THE RÍO NAPO

Not every visitor to the Oriente wants to bathe in a jungle river and sleep on the floor of a native hut at the end of a hard day of hiking in the jungle. For those wishing to visit the virgin rainforest, yet return to a comfortable room with a private shower at night, there are several options.

La Selva Jungle Lodge ❺, off the Río Napo, is perhaps the best known of the lodges. The journey there is half the adventure: first by aircraft to Coca, then a motorized dugout canoe for 2.5 hours followed by a rough boardwalk through the rainforest to Laguna Garzacocha and finally a dugout canoe to the lodge. The buildings at La Selva (www.laselvajunglelodge.com), up on stilts and with thatched roofs, have been constructed from secondary rainforest materials to withstand the extremes of jungle climate. Rooms

The Río Napo seen from Misahuallí.

are lit with kerosene lamps, and the lack of a thumping generator outside the cabins ensures that guests are able to hear the myriad sounds of the rainforest. La Selva is a magnet for birdwatchers: parrots, tanagers, toucans, and numerous other species can all be seen. Expert naturalists, many of them English-speaking, can guide visitors on jungle walks and canoe rides, and there is a new observation tower.

Sacha Lodge (www.sachalodge.com) is another excellent option offering plenty of creature comforts (including electricity and hot water) and a great variety of trails and trips. Just north of the Río Napo, it is reached by a 3-hour motorized canoe trip from Coca. The lodge's observation tower enables you to climb 40 meters (130ft) into the canopy for an unobstructed view of miles and miles of intact rainforest, close-up views of plants and birds, and maybe the occasional sloth hanging from a treetop. After a long day exploring the magic of the rainforest, a dip in the Pilchicocha Lagoon in front of the lodge may be a welcome form of relaxation.

Also on the Río Napo is the award-winning **Napo Wildlife Center** (www.napowildlifecenter.com). This luxury lodge with 16 large individual cabañas, located by Lago Anangucocha, within the ancestral territory of the Anangu Quichua Community, and part of the Parque Nacional Yasuní, a UNESCO Biosphere Reserve. In its beginnings in the early 1990s, Napo was one of the pioneering community-built lodges in the Ecuadorian Amazon. Private investment allowed the early rudimentary lodge to develop into the luxurious enclave it is today. Napo is particularly known for the quality of its guiding and for its two freestanding canopy towers.

If you are short of time, on a budget, and just want a taste of the rainforest, there are plenty of trips on offer starting from the small town of **Misahuallí** ➏ in the headwaters of the Río Napo. Here guides can be hired for about $30–40 a day. The area has been colonized and the forest here is secondary growth. The large mammals and birds have mainly been hunted close to extinction, but a short trip will give

Night view of Misahuallí's malecón.

Despite their fearsome appearance, piranhas make a fine meal.

Kapawi Ecolodge and Reserve.

you an experience of the jungle and a look at a variety of plants, insects, and smaller birds.

Near Misahuallí, on the Río Napo, is **Reserva Biológica Jatún Sacha** (www. jatunsacha.org), a center dedicated to conservation, education, and research, where a number of unknown species have been discovered. Tourists can visit the reserve and see fieldwork in progress. For butterfly-lovers this area is paradise: besides hundreds of birds and plants, an astonishing 765 butterfly species have been identified at Jatún Sacha.

One aspect of forest life that can be observed around Misahuallí is colonization: small coffee *fincas* (estates), oil-palm plantations, cattle ranches, and yucca plots are prevalent. As you journey down the nearby river, you may occasionally notice workers washing and sifting material. They are panning for gold – modern descendants of the long line of settlers obsessed with dreams of El Dorado.

A little farther down the Río Napo is **Yachana Lodge** (www.yachana.com),

run by the Yachana Foundation, a not-for-profit organization that funds innovative community projects through profits made by the lodge. The foundation runs a Technical High School, health projects, an organic farming operation, and several other micro-enterprises. Yachana Lodge and the foundation are regarded as one of the best and most effective examples of eco-tourism in Ecuador. Visitors who stay here comment on the meaningful interactions possible with local indigenous people, and this is one of the lodge's highlights.

GOING REMOTE

Kapawi Ecolodge (www.kapawi.com), on the Río Pastaza near the border with Peru, is one of the most highly regarded lodges in the world. Perhaps the best thing about Kapawi is that it is so remote: it's accessible only by a 90-minute flight by small plane from the jungle's-edge hamlet of Shell, some two hours' drive east of Baños, and then by motor canoe to the lodge itself. Kapawi is set deep in some

681,218 hectares (1,683,326 acres) of jungle that is the territory of the Achuar people, where some 6,000 indigenous people live in 64 communities.

Kapawi was set up as a partnership between the Achuar people and an Ecuadorian tourism enterprise with the idea of providing the Achuar with a sustainable income to remain in their ancestral land and defend themselves against oil exploration and exploitation. The project has been a resounding success and the beautiful lodge – built in traditional Achuar style – is highly lauded.

The area also supports abundant wildlife, including pink river dolphins and 570 species of birds, but one of the best things is the close interaction with the Achuar people, who will soon take over and run the lodge completely independently.

FRAGILE BALANCE

It is imperative that anyone thinking of visiting the Oriente region ask themselves whether they are harming the environment and the lifestyles they are so keen to see and to preserve. This is a particularly pertinent question when it comes to visiting indigenous communities. One group that has so far resisted significant contact with outsiders is the Huaorani, who live in relative isolation in an area around the Río Cononaco.

The political organization ONHAE (Organizacion de la Nacionalidad Huaorani de la Amazonia Ecuatoriana) is working to protect the Huaorani from colonization, following the discovery of oil in the region, but it is difficult to predict whether Ecuador will be able to walk the tightrope between economic development and protecting the Huaorani and the rainforest ecosystem.

Most of the Huaorani people, who maintain a hunter-gatherer way of life, do not welcome tourist visits to their communities and it is advisable to respect their wishes, but conversely, some Huaorani are turning to

eco-tourism to protect their culture, and it is possible to spend time with the Huaorani community of the village of Quehueri'ono by prior arrangement.

Living along the Río Aguarico, a small group of Cofan natives work with the help of US-born Randy Borman to encourage tourists to visit their village of **Zabalo** on carefully organized tours. Once there, visitors experience the Cofan lifestyle, traveling in dugout canoes and hiking into the jungle in search of medicinal plants. The idea behind the enterprise is not just to safeguard the jungle, but also to allow the Cofan people to control the rate of change, so that they can retain their language and their sense of themselves as a people.

Some people feel that bringing tourism to a region in need of preservation is self-defeating, but Borman and the village leaders disagree. All the money generated goes to the Cofan, who are able to use and display their traditional knowledge of the Oriente, both for personal survival and as their singular contribution to a changing world.

The large owl butterfly is most active at dusk and takes its name from its wing spots, which resemble owls' eyes.

Leafcutter ant.

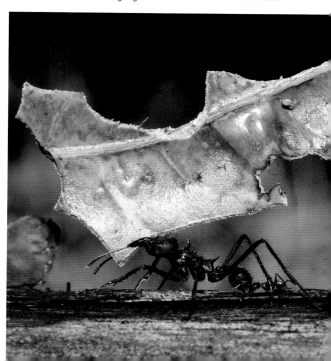

Shining sunbeam hummingbird.

ORIENTE WILDLIFE

Everyone wants to see the armadillos and tapirs, the big cats, and the prolific birdlife. But the armies of insects that most people try to avoid are no less interesting.

The Oriente has such a diverse variety of wildlife that for many people, the chance to see some of it in its natural habitat is reason enough to travel to Ecuador. Whether your interest is in birds, beasts, reptiles, or insects, you will find fascinating species in the Amazonian forest.

FANTASTIC BIRDLIFE

Some 550 species of birds have been recorded in the Napo region alone, and ornithologists and bird-watchers flock to the area to see species with such exotic names as green and gold tanager, greater yellow-headed vulture, purple-throated fruitcrow, puffbird, and toucan.

One of the highlights of a trip to an Amazon lodge is the opportunity to see birdlife gather at patches of soil – often along riverbanks – laden with mineral salts. At dawn, bird-watchers can witness a magnificent display of hundreds of squawking, squabbling parrots feeding at the *saladeros*, as the salt licks are known. Certain bird species need the mineral, which aids digestion of the acidic fruits in their diet. Species such as the blue-headed, orange-cheeked, and yellow-crowned parrot, as well as the dusky-headed parakeet and the scarlet-shouldered parrotlet, are amongst the colorful species one can observe.

MAMMALS OF THE RAINFOREST

The salt licks also attract a variety of jungle mammals. Most of these feed at night and leave only footprints for the curious visitor to observe in the daylight. An adventurous person could spend the night by a salt lick and perhaps be rewarded with moonlit glimpses of a variety of mammals. These may include the nine-banded armadillo, or a rodent called the paca which has spotted fur, weighs up to 9kg (20lb) and is considered excellent

Main attractions
Watching parrots at a salt lick
Spotting a shy tapir
Chancing on an elusive spectacled bear
Going macro on the world of insects

Map on page 204

Scarlet macaw.

food by local hunters. The capybara, the world's largest rodent, weighing around 64kg (140lb), is another animal that you might see.

Some salt licks attract a huge, strange mammal, the South American tapir. The largest land mammals in Amazonia, tapirs can weigh in excess of 270kg (600lb). Their closest relatives are the other odd-toed ungulates, the rhinoceros and the horse. Members of the tapir family are among the most primitive large mammals in the world and are well adapted to life in the jungle. Their short sturdy legs, thick, strong necks, and barrel-like bodies covered with incredibly tough skin enable them to shove through the dense forest undergrowth like a living tank. One of their strangest features is a short trunk, which gives them an excellent sense of smell and is used to pull leaves off bushes and into their mouths.

Locally, tapirs are much sought-after game animals; one is enough to feed an entire village. Apart from the meat, the tapirs' fatty tissues yield an

oil that is much prized for cooking, and the thick skin makes good-quality leather. The South American tapir lives in the Oriente lowlands and the mountain tapir inhabits the upper Amazonian basin and the Andean flanks. Hunting is not as much of a threat to the latter as habitat destruction, and the mountain tapir is regarded as an endangered species.

Apart from humans, the tapir's greatest enemy is the big cat of Amazonia; the jaguar. A fully-grown male can reach 113kg (250lb) in weight and, when hungry, will attack almost any large animal it comes across. Jaguars will leap onto tapirs' backs and attempt to kill them by breaking their necks in their powerful jaws. The tapirs' defense is twofold: the fact that the thick neck is protected by the tough, leathery skin and a bristly mane, and their habit of charging wildly through the dense undergrowth when threatened, thus making it difficult for a predator to hold on long enough to deliver the fatal bite.

Jaguars do not roar, as most other big cats do. Instead, they emit a low, coughing grunt, especially when courting. Generally, jaguars are afraid of humans and only the luckiest of visitors catches a glimpse of them in the wild.

You are also unlikely to see another shy resident, the endangered spectacled bear: fewer than 2,000 individuals are thought to exist in the wild. The only bear found in South America, its habitat ranges from 200 meters (650ft) to 4,200 meters (13,800ft) on the heavily forested subtropical slopes. It is mainly vegetarian, often climbing trees in search of succulent fruits. The bear's habitat is increasingly being encroached upon by colonists, and it is protected by Ecuadorian law.

A MULTITUDE OF MONKEYS

The mammals that visitors most often get to see, however, are the monkeys. The most vocal of these is the very aptly

Spider monkey sitting on a branch.

named howler monkey. Male howler monkeys have a specialized, hollow, and much enlarged hyoid bone in the throat. Air is passed through the hyoid cavity producing an ear-splitting call, which can easily carry for well over a kilometer in the rainforest. This is an astounding feat when one remembers that the forest vegetation has a damping effect on sound. When heard in the distance, the call has been variously described as sounding like the wind moaning through the trees or like a human baby crying. Close up, the call can be quite terrifying to the uninitiated visitor.

The purpose of the call is to advertize a troop's presence in a particular patch of rainforest. This enables troops to space themselves out in the canopy and thus avoid competing as they forage for succulent young leaves. Occasionally, troops do meet in the treetops and the result is often chaotic with howling, chasing, threatening, and even fighting. The energy used in these meetings is better expended in feeding, and thus it pays for a troop

to make its presence known by frequent howling.

Several other species of monkey are frequently seen, including wooly, squirrel, spider, and tamarin monkeys. Often, the best way to observe monkeys is from a dugout canoe floating down a jungle river. A local, trained guide will spot a troop of monkeys early enough to stop the boat in a position that offers a clear view of the animals foraging in trees along the banks. From within the rainforest, on the other hand, animals may be difficult to see in the treetops. In addition, monkeys may display their displeasure at human intrusion by hurling sticks, fruit, and even feces down on the unfortunate visitor's head.

Spiny bush cricket.

WILDLIFE BENEATH YOUR FEET

Many people come to the Oriente hoping to see exotic birds and mammals, while trying to avoid the myriad insects. Yet it is the insects that are the most common and, in many ways, most fascinating creatures of the rainforest.

A pair of red-skirted treefrogs.

⊘ Fact

It is estimated that every second, an area of the planet's rainforests the size of a soccer field is burned. Every year, more than 150,000 sq km (93,750 sq miles) of the world's rainforest are destroyed, and some 50,000 species become extinct; many of them before ever being described by science.

Some are simply beautiful, such as the breathtaking blue morpho butterflies whose huge wings flash a dazzling electric blue. Other species have such complex life cycles that they are still not fully understood by tropical entomologists. Among these are hundreds of ant species, particularly the ubiquitous army and leafcutter ants.

Colonies of leafcutter ants numbering hundreds of thousands live in huge nests dug deep into the ground. Foragers search the vegetation for particular types of leaves, cut out small sections and, holding the leaf segments above their heads like small umbrellas, take them back to the nest. The ants can be quite experimental, bringing back a variety of leaves and even pieces of discarded plastic wrappers. Workers within the nest sort out the kinds of leaves which will mulch down into a type of compost; unsuitable material is ejected from the nest after a few days. The composted leaves form a mulch on which a fungus grows. Ants tend these fungal gardens with care, for they provide the main diet for both the adult ants and for the young that are being raised inside the nest.

The story does not end there. When a particularly good source of leaves has been located, ants lay down a trail of chemical markers, or pheromones, linking the nest with the leaf source, often 100 meters (330ft) or more away in the forest. People frequently come across these trails in the jungle, with hundreds of ants scurrying along carrying leaf sections back to the nest, or returning empty-handed for another load.

Other species, for example army ants, prey on this ready and constant supply of foragers. To combat this the leaf-cutter ants are morphologically separated by size and jaw structure into different castes. Some specialize in tending the fungal gardens; others have jaws designed for cutting; and yet others are soldiers, armed with huge mandibles, that accompany the foragers and protect them from attackers. Close observation of the foragers will sometimes reveal yet another caste, a tiny ant that can ride on the leaf segments without disturbing the foragers and are thought to act as protection against parasitical wasps, which may try to lay their eggs on the ants.

A colony of leafcutter ants may last for a decade or more. New colonies are founded by the emergence of a number of potential queens, who mate and then fly off to found another nest, carrying some of the fungus used for food. This is essential to "seed" the new nest. The rest of the new queen's life is spent laying tens of thousands of eggs, destined to become gardeners, foragers, soldiers, riders, or even queens.

Such complex interactions make the rainforest interesting to biologists and tourists alike. A day with a trained guide will bring to light many such stories about the habits of the forest's vast population of creatures great and small.

A longwing butterfly.

THE VANISHING RAINFOREST

Satellite images show it shrinking: closer up, it is obscured under palls of slash-and-burn smoke. We see it drenched in oil, cut and devastated. And yet still the decimation of the world's rainforests is a daily reality.

The plight of the planet's tropical forests has been well publicized. Huge areas of forest are being logged or burned every day; so much deforestation is occurring that, at the present rate, with more than 25,900 sq km (10,000 sq miles) being destroyed for ranching, farming, and logging each year in Brazil alone, some scientists have predicted that 40 percent of the rainforest will disappear by 2050. Of the almost 2 million known species of plants and animals, about half live only in the rainforest. Estimates of species yet to be discovered are numbered in millions. Most of these unknown species live in the tropical forests, which have by far the greatest biodiversity of any region on the globe. Thus deforestation is causing countless extinctions, before many of the plants and animals as yet have been documented.

THE VALUE OF RAINFORESTS

Numerous medicines have been extracted from forest plants, ranging from malarial prophylactics to anesthetics, from antibiotics to contraceptives. Many more useful drugs will undoubtedly be extracted in the forests, if they are not destroyed first.

The diversity of species growing in the rainforests also comprises a storehouse of new strains of agriculturally important plants that may be destroyed by disease or drought. For example, if banana crops were to be seriously threatened by disease, scientists could search the rainforests for disease-resistant strains to cross with the commercially grown varieties and eradicate the problem.

The forests are also essential for the survival of indigenous peoples. Hundreds of discrete communities living in the jungles of Latin America (and in Africa and Asia) are threatened by rainforest loss.

On a worldwide scale, the moderating effect of the rainforest on global climate patterns is only recently being understood. Deforestation could cause severe global warming, leading to melting ice caps, rising ocean levels, and flooding of coastal regions. Climates would be altered to the extent that some major crops, such as wheat, would no longer grow.

One of the chief reasons the rainforests are being destroyed is the displacement of poor *campesinos* who migrate from other parts of the country looking for free land on which to make a living. Generally, the soils are not well suited for agriculture and are quickly depleted of scarce nutrients. The short-sighted colonization policies causing this damage are now at last being re-evaluated and solutions being sought, but the forest is still being cleared at an alarming rate. Illegal timber-poaching by large forestry companies and clearing of land for large-scale industrial animal farming are other major factors in the disappearance of rainforests.

Debt-for-nature swaps, whereby foreign debts are paid off by the lenders in return for protection of the rainforest, are a move in the right direction, but the developed countries that lend the money must ensure that such incentives reflect the full value of the forests.

Sustainable use, such as rubber-tapping, brazil-nut-harvesting and tourism can also help. Whatever the methods used, protection of the planet's green lung should be regarded as an urgent, global priority.

Tropical forest cleared for cattle ranching.

Traditional weaving, Santo Domingo de los Tsáchilas.

Tsáchila man.

THE WESTERN LOWLANDS

Agriculture has become vitally important in this region. As you travel south from Santo Domingo, you'll find rice on the roads, bananas in bags, and houses on stilts.

The road from Quito to **Santo Domingo** is one of the most dramatic in the country. In a matter of hours the elevation dips a jaw-dropping 3,000 meters (10,000ft) down the western slopes of the Andes. The 2.5-hour drive is one of the most terrifying bus journeys in Ecuador. Truck and bus drivers rely on headlights and horns as they hurtle down the road, paying scant attention to the poor visibility (the roads are often shrouded in fog, especially in the afternoons) or oncoming traffic. Surprisingly, accidents are rare, but it is not without some sense of relief that the traveler finally arrives.

HOME FOR HEALERS

The provincial capital is **Santo Domingo de los Tsáchilas ❶**, after the Tsáchila people (dubbed "*colorados*" by the Spanish), who are indigenous to the area. Their appearance was distinctive: both sexes painted their faces with black stripes and the men plastered down their bowl-shaped haircuts with the brilliant red dye from *achiote*, a local plant. *Achiote* is thought to have been brought from the mountains by a group of shamans many generations ago who said that the dye would help protect the people from yellow fever and other diseases. Some of the men built up a nationwide reputation as *curanderos* (healers). People still come

Achiote, used for hair dye.

from all over Ecuador to be treated for a variety of illnesses, a custom that has seen a resurgence in recent years with the growing trend for alternative and natural medicines.

Many travelers visit Santo Domingo in the hope of seeing the Tsáchilas in their authentic finery or perhaps witnessing or partaking in a healing ceremony. Some are lucky, for the traditions do still exist, but many are disappointed to find that most of the 2,000 or so remaining Tsáchilas now wear Western dress, no longer

⊘ Main attractions

Spectacular Quito–Santo Domingo road journey
Tsáchila culture in Santo Domingo
Giant banana and tropical fruit plantations
Viewing houseboats on the Río Babahoyo

⊙ **Map on page 224**

Tip

It's important not to confuse the two Santo Domingos. Santo Domingo de los Tsáchilas is the name of the western lowland province created in October 2007 from territory previously in the province of Pichincha. The city of Santo Domingo de los Tsáchilas is the provincial capital, but the name for the city and the province are sometimes used interchangeably.

paint their faces, and have largely abandoned their traditional appearance and customs. The Tsáchilas are spread out over eight areas between Santo Domingo and Quevedo, inhabiting a reserve of around 8,000 hectares (19,800 acres). The **Museo Etnográfico Tsáchila**, a living museum and cultural center in the Tsáchila community of Chigüilpe (tel: 099 109 5289) is well worth a visit. It is located about 10km (6 miles) from Santo Domingo, just off the road to Quevedo. A brief tour gives an introduction to the people's music, dance, cooking, use of medicinal plants and shamanism. All activities happen in and around traditional cane-and-thatch buildings.

Santo Domingo de los Tsáchilas has a tropical climate and is the nearest place for Quiteños to come and enjoy the lowland heat. There are several small resort hotels nearby where visitors can relax next to a swimming pool in a tropical garden or try their luck in the casino. It is also the hub of a network of paved roads radiating out into the western lowlands.

INTO BANANA LANDS

The road south of Santo Domingo leads through vast plantations of bananas and African oil palms. Until the discovery of petroleum in the Oriente in the late 1960s, Ecuador was the archetypal banana republic, with bananas being by far the most important export. Even today, Ecuador remains the largest exporter of bananas in the world, with annual exports averaging about 24 percent of the world's supply.

Bananas were not always such an important party of Ecuador's economy. For a long time, the main export was cacao. This crop was grown along the rivers of the western lowlands, and floated down to Guayaquil for export. In the 1930s, cacao remained the principal export, followed by coffee, which was also grown in the western lowlands. After World War II, banana production became increasingly important, and by the 1970s, cacao had dropped to second place.

Heavy floods during the El Niño phenomenon of the past two decades severely disrupted the cacao

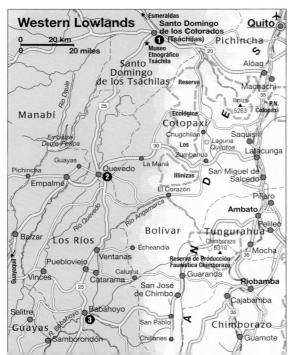
Cutting sugarcane.

industry. It has since recovered so that cacao and coffee accounted for 3 percent of exports in 2023 and bananas accounted for 10 percent; canned fish and shrimps have taken over, however, now accounting for around a quarter of all exports.

The banana trees in the plantations are arranged in regular rows for ease of harvesting, and travelers driving past are soon mesmerized by the endless lines of plants. The monotony is broken occasionally by the sight of workers collecting the ripe fruit with long-handled shears. Often bunches of bananas are sleeved in large blue plastic bags before harvesting; the polythene in the bags releases a chemical signal which hastens the fruits' ripening.

MARKET CENTER

An hour and a half's drive south of Santo Domingo lies the largest market town of the western lowlands, **Quevedo** ❷. Not only bananas, but cacao, coffee, rice, sugar, African palm oil, and citrus and tropical fruits pass through this important center. Quevedo was founded in the mid-1800s and is thus a relatively modern town. You may sometimes hear the town referred to as "the Chinatown of Ecuador" because many Chinese immigrants, some of whom came to work on the railway construction around the turn of the 20th century, eventually settled here. Most of the better restaurants along Quevedo's main streets are chifas, as Chinese restaurants are called locally.

In the past, produce from the area was able to reach the coast at Guayaquil along the narrow and convoluted Río Quevedo, which runs a few blocks north of the city's downtown area. The journey was a difficult and hazardous one, with frequent sandbanks, log jams, and shallows to obstruct the unwary. Today, with the construction of a good paved road to Guayaquil, the river is used

as a playground by the local children seeking relief from the tropical sun. Although the river port is no longer used, the accompanying street market is still found along the banks of the river.

South of Quevedo, a number of rivers dissect the land, which becomes increasingly subject to flooding during the rainy season, which lasts from January to April. It is after these rivers that the province **Los Ríos** is named. This kind of low-lying terrain is admirably suited to the cultivation of rice, and paddy fields proliferate. The occasional trees between the fields serve as roosts for flocks of wading birds. White American egrets look especially pretty at sunset, when they gather like hundreds of huge white flowers, virtually blanketing the treetops.

During the dry months, rice is set out to dry on huge open-air platforms of concrete in the many commercial piladoras found along the road. Piladora is a local word meaning a drying and husking factory. Some of the poorer farmers are unable to afford the cost

Tsáchila girl dancing.

of using the *piladora* and so spread out their modest crops on the nearest available flat and dry surface. This may be the tarmac top of the highway, and drivers do their best to avoid running over the crops.

HOUSEBOATS AND STILTS

Rice and other agricultural products frequently make their way through **Babahoyo** ❸, the provincial capital of Los Ríos. The city is a modern one, but it has a long history. A settlement existed here before the arrival of the *conquistadores*, and Spanish records indicate the presence of a town here as early as 1576.

The present city dates from 1867, after a catastrophic fire destroyed the previous town. Before the building of the road, Babahoyo was an important port known as Bodegas, meaning storehouses. There were frequent steamships linking the coast at Guayaquil with the inland river port of Bodegas, where goods were stored to await transport to the highlands and Quito by mule.

The city is a mere 7 meters (23ft) above sea level and flooding always seems to have been part of the way of life. For many years the houses in Babahoyo were built on stilts to raise the sleeping rooms above the annual floodwaters. Today, some of the inhabitants live in a picturesque floating village of houseboats on the Río Babahoyo, while the Vinces district, nicknamed Little Paris, has a number of well-preserved colonial mansions once owned by wealthy cocoa merchants.

The western lowlands are an important part of Ecuador's agricultural and tropical life. The exotic crops, equatorial climate, gorgeous birds, and interesting people make this a fascinating area to visit. Yet it is very much off the beaten track. Most travelers pass through Babahoyo on their way to somewhere else.

ANCIENT FORESTS

This region was not always rich in agriculture. At one time much of it was covered by dense tropical rainforest. The renowned British mountaineer, Edward Whymper, arrived in Guayaquil in December, 1879, with the aim of climbing Ecuador's major peaks. In his *Travels Amongst the Great Andes of the Equator* he describes his journey through the western lowlands, where he saw "forest-trees rising 150ft [46 meters] high, mastlike, without a branch, laden with a parasitic growth."

This terrain was very different from the Amazonian forests to the east of the Andean chain. The pronounced rainy and dry seasons produced a distinctive array of plants and animals that contributed to Ecuador's great variety of species. Ecuador holds the record for the highest biological diversity per unit of land of any Latin American country, but sadly much of the natural vegetation in this part of Ecuador was cleared long ago to make way for agriculture.

Women and children washing clothes near Santo Domingo.

BIRD-WATCHING

One of the most remarkable things about Ecuador is its incredible biodiversity. Bird-spotters will be thrilled by the avian riches here.

Ecuador is a bird-watcher's paradise. The wide variety of habitats, from tropical rainforests to wind-swept highlands, from mangrove swamps to hilly forests, provide a wider range of species than any other country in the Americas. More than 1,600 bird species have been recorded here, twice as many as in the US and Canada combined.

In the páramo (high-altitude plateau) habitat of the Parque Nacional Cotopaxi, one of the most surprising sights is a tiny hummingbird, the Andean hillstar, which survives the freezing nights by lowering its body temperature from about 40°C (104°F) in the daytime to about 15°C (59°F) at night, a remarkable feat for a warm-blooded creature. At the other end of the size scale is the Andean condor, which, with its 3-meter (10ft) wing span, is one of the largest flying birds in the world.

Other páramo species include the carunculated caracara, Andean lapwing, Andean gull, páramo pipit, great thrush, and bar-winged cinclodes. If you camp out, you may hear the loud hoot of the great horned owl as it searches for prey, or the eerie drumming of the Andean snipe's outer wing feathers as it careens by in the dark.

HUMMINGBIRDS APLENTY

The Andes of Ecuador are split into two ranges between which lies the temperate central valley. The less extreme elevation of 2,800 meters (9,200ft) ensures a pleasant climate and attracts a variety of fascinating birds. More than one-fifth of Ecuador's 132 or so species of hummingbird are found in the central valley, and one of the best places to see them is the Refugio de Vida Silvestre Pasochoa, run by Fundación Natura. It is one of the last original stands of temperate forest in the central valley; 14 hummingbird species, plus a variety of doves, furnarids, tapaculos, tyrant flycatchers, honeycreepers, and tanagers can all be seen, just one hour's drive from the capital. Spend a couple of days driving to Mindo down the Chiriboga and Nono roads, toward the western lowlands, looking for the cock-of-the-rock, plate-billed mountain toucans, and mountain tanagers.

On the eastern Andean slopes the road to Coca takes you over the Papallacta Pass through the páramo, dropping down through cloud forest, with its barred fruit eaters and gray-breasted mountain toucans, into the Amazon basin. Once there, bird-watching can get a little tricky as the lush vegetation hides a huge diversity of birds. You will need considerable patience and experience if you are to see them. Here it really pays to take an organized tour or have a guide to point out some of the 550 bird species found in the area. Parrots, toucans, macaws, vultures, kingfishers, puffbirds, antbirds, herons, and hummingbirds are all there, waiting for the patient bird-watcher. Serious enthusiasts should consider the Magic Birding Circuit (www.magicbirdingcircuit.com), a set of lovely lodges situated in eight private reserves covering 15 ecosystems promising an unparalleled number of bird sightings (see page 212), Sacha Lodge (see page 211), and Napo Wildlife Center (see page 211)

The Galápagos, on the other hand, is a great place for bird-watching beginners to cut their teeth. Here, the 25 endemic species are relatively easy to spot, and there are many other fascinating species to interest even the most inexperienced twitcher.

One of Ecuador's 132 species of hummingbirds.

Frigate birds and pelicans circle the fishing fleet at Puerto López.

Surfing the waves at Puerto López.

THE PACIFIC COAST

Palm-fringed beaches are the main draw. But there's much more to a trip to the coast: marimba rhythms, mangrove swamps, the bustling port of Manta, and an echo of Africa all add to the fun.

The north Pacific coast of Ecuador is one of the best places on the continent to take a break from the sometimes demanding rigors of travel. Much of this varied coastline consists of largely empty, palm-fringed beaches, which present the ideal opportunity to practice one of the foremost customs of ancient Ecuador: sun worship.

This area bore the brunt of the devastating floods of 1982–3 and 1998–9, brought about by the El Niño current, when roads, beaches, trees, crops, and a significant number of dwellings were washed away, although things had largely recovered before an earthquake measuring 7.8 on the Richter scale hit 27km (17 miles) inland from the northern coastal town of Muisne. Damage occurred hundreds of kilometers from the epicenter, and the worst hit areas may take years to fully recover.

Nevertheless, new resorts are being built along the coast. This development testifies to Ecuador's growing stature as a tourist destination, due partly to its own charms, and partly to its neighbors' ill fortunes. For example, large sections of the Peruvian coastline are washed by the Humboldt Current that brings damp, misty weather and ice-cold waters. Because of this, Ecuador has cornered the market in tropical beaches along South America's west coast. However, Ecuador's northern Pacific coast has been known to see some of the armed violence that was once more prevalent across the Colombian border. When Colombia signed a ceasefire with FARC rebels in 2016, militants who refused to adhere to it are believed to have crossed the border into Ecuador. Be sure to check your country's travel advice and local news before traveling to this region. Wherever you go on Ecuador's coast, it is still not a good idea to walk alone along beaches during the day, or stroll along the beaches at night.

⊙ Main attractions

La Tola–Esmeraldas road trip
Pacific beaches
Panama hat-making in Montecristi
Parque Nacional Machalilla
Whale-watching in Puerto López

Map on page 232

Juice stall.

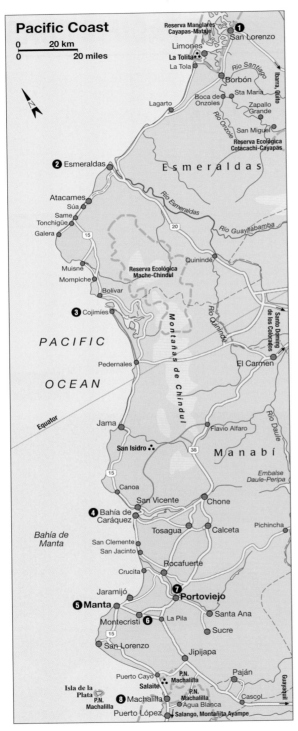

Pacific Coast

0   20 km

0   20 miles

Reserva Manglares
Cayapas-Mataje   **1**
San Lorenzo
Limones
La Tolita
La Tola
Río Santiago
Ibarra, Quito
Borbón
Sta María
Boca de
Onzoles
Lagarto
Zapallo
Grande
Río Onzole
San Miguel
Reserva Ecológica
Cotacachi-Cayapas
2 Esmeraldas
E s m e r a l d a s
Atacames
Súa
Same
Tonchigüe
Galera
15
Río Esmeraldas
20
Río Guayllabamba
Muisne
Reserva Ecológica
Mache-Chindul
Quinindé
Mompiche
Bolívar
3 Cojimíes
Santo Domingo
de los Colorados
PACIFIC
Montañas de Chindul
Río Quinindé
OCEAN
Pedernales
El Carmen
Equator
Jama
Flavio Alfaro
M a n a b í
San Isidro
38
Río Daule
15
Embalse
Daule-Peripa
Canoa
San Vicente
Chone
4 Bahía de
Caráquez
Tosagua
Calceta
Pichincha
Bahía de
Manta
San Clemente
San Jacinto
Rocafuerte
Crucita
Jaramijó
7 Portoviejo
5 Manta
6
La Pila
Santa Ana
Montecristi
Sucre
15
San Lorenzo
Jipijapa
Puerto Cayo
P.N.
Machalilla
Paján
Isla de la
Plata
Salaite
P.N.
Machalilla
Guayaquil
P.N.
Machalilla
8 Machalilla
Agua Blanca
Cascol
Puerto López
Salango, Montañita Ayampe

LAND OF TWO SEASONS

The wet season on the Ecuadorian coast runs from December to June, the remainder of the year being dry – or perhaps, more accurately, not so wet. During the wet season, when flooding is commonplace and high levels of humidity make life uncomfortably sticky, the beaches – despite being below par – are well patronized. All things considered, August to October is the best time to visit this relaxed region.

The coastal topography consists of a thin lowland strip, which turns from forbidding mangroves in the north to dry scrubland on the Santa Elena Peninsula, west of Guayaquil. A short distance inland runs a range of low, rounded, crystalline hills. The region is cut by numerous rivers meandering down from the Andes, which regularly flood the alluvial plain that lies to the east of the hills. Huge alluvial fans, often consisting of porous volcanic ash eroded from highland basins, spread out from the major river mouths, providing very fertile soil.

The province of Esmeraldas is one of dense, luxuriant rainforest characterized by two main botanical strata: a high canopy of towering evergreen broadleaf species sprinkled with palms; and at eye level, clusters of giant ferns, shrubs, and vines. Among these are spectacular smaller plants such as orchids and bromeliads, which proliferate in the Amazonian forest.

South of Esmeraldas is a zone of deciduous scrub woodland that drops its leaves during the dry season. A narrow strip of tropical, semi-deciduous forest lies just north of Manta; and from here down to Guayaquil, most of the mangrove forest that used to line the coast has been replaced with infertile scrubland down to Santa Elena. Among the commercially used plants of the coastal forests are the balsa tree, source of the world's lightest timber; the ivory-nut palm (tagua), used to make buttons; and the toquilla reed, from which the renowned Panama hat is manufactured.

The coastal region, which contains almost half of Ecuador's nearly 18 million people, is populated by a veritable melting pot of ethnic groups. Here, more than in the Sierra and the jungle, the trails of history incorporate all the colors of the rainbow. At the time of the Spaniards' arrival, the centers of coastal indigenous habitation were Esmeraldas, Manta, Huancavilca, and Puná; these peoples were either exterminated outright, or else they mixed to the point where the distinctness between groups was completely extinguished.

A century or so later, the Spanish-indigenous mixture (called mestizo) was infused with African blood as slaves were brought from West Africa, creating the mulatto (Afro-Hispanic mix) and montubio (indigenous-African mix) ethnic identities. Indigenous Caribs were also shipped to Ecuador to work the plantations, adding a fourth element to this ethnic conglomeration. Most coastal people identify as mestizos, but the Afro-Ecuadorian culture is one of the region's most interesting features, pervading all aspects of life.

FROM THE COLOMBIAN BORDER

A journey that begins in **San Lorenzo** ❶, in Ecuador's northwestern corner, can only get drier. The sea is the town's *raison d'être*, and fresh, salty breezes fill the potholed streets. The land around San Lorenzo is mostly mangrove swamp, navigated by motorized dugout canoes, while the town itself is frequently sodden with rainwater that has nowhere to run off. A road links San Lorenzo to Ibarra and Quito, and there is a bus service. However, the rare travelers who find themselves here may have come up the coast by boat.

Despite its isolation, San Lorenzo can generate a certain amount of bustle. It possesses the best natural harbor on the Ecuadorian coast, and a hinterland still largely untouched due to its inaccessibility. The population has grown from 2,000 in 1960 – when, in the days prior to the discovery of oil

Enjoying the beach at Galera.

Fishing huts at Santa Rosa.

in the Oriente, this was Ecuador's El Dorado, the alluring, untapped frontier – to 28,000 today. Timber traders have made profitable incursions into forests rich in mahogany, balsa, and rubber, creating industries and bringing itinerant laborers to this long-neglected outpost. However, illegal logging has put the forests under threat.

It should be noted that San Lorenzo has no immigration office, nor any official currency exchange, so crossing the Colombian border to Tumaco is near to impossible and, given the security risks in this part of Colombia, certainly not advisable.

AFRICAN LEGACY

San Lorenzo has the feel of a town invented by Gabriel García Márquez. The descendants of people from distant continents have been washed up by history on this forbidding shore, and made the most of their displacement. Enslaved Africans transported in the 17th and 18th centuries were unloaded in Cartagena (Colombia) and marched southward to labor on the coffee,

banana, and cacao plantations; less than half of this human cargo survived the privations of passage to reach their destinations.

The legacy of Africa lives on here today in the form of ancestor worship and the voodoo rituals of *macumba*, whereby spirits are summoned to cure and curse. Beneath the Latinized veneer of regular Sunday Mass lies an ancient belief in macabre spirits or *visiones* such as *La Tunda*, who frightens bad children to death and then steals their bodies, or *El Rivel*, who feasts on corpses.

African rhythms anchor the up-tempo beat of marimba music, which can be heard in San Lorenzo. Esmeraldeña marimba retains purer links with its origins than does the Colombian style, which has borrowed heavily from the Caribbean jingles of salsa and often resembles Western pop music. Both types of music, alongside the accompanying chants and dances made it onto the UNESCO Intangible Heritage list in 2015. Talented musicians and dancers of both marimba styles can be seen rehearsing on Wednesday nights, and when they hit the downtown bars, San Lorenzo starts jumping. Men are said to come of age when they begin to *andar y conocer*; literally, "to walk and to know," or "to travel and learn." In local idiom, this commonly used phrase means "to strut," and is heavily loaded with sexual innuendo.

To get to the coast road you have to go by boat from San Lorenzo to **La Tola**. Services are cheap and regular and take about 2.5 hours. En route to La Tola lies the island of **La Tolita**, an important ceremonial center from 500 to 100 BC. Tribal chiefs were buried here, their tombs filled with artifacts of gold, silver, platinum, and copper. In recognition of its historical significance, La Tolita has been declared an Archeological National Park. However, like many such sites in South America, La Tolita has been savagely plundered

A street in Montañita.

by thieves, its treasures sold on the international black market. Fortunately, however, the government's attention was attracted in time to salvage a substantial portion of the relics, and another gap in the jigsaw puzzle of ancient Ecuador is slowly being filled. An archeological museum has been erected on the site, showcasing finds from the digs and recovered artifacts.

LIMONES AND AROUND

Opposite La Tolita at the mouth of the Río Santiago is **Limones** (which must also be reached by boat). It is a small town of some importance as the center of the local timber industry, but without a lot to offer tourists. Wood is floated downriver to the sawmill here, and processed for further distribution.

The timber camps, isolated in the dense, upriver jungle, were quite notorious in their early days during the 1960s for a form of outpost exploitation worthy of the author Joseph Conrad. The mestizo owners forbade their workers – mostly *morenos* (a generic term for dark-skinned people in Latin America) – to leave camp. Instead, sex workers and alcohol were shipped into the camps each pay day; a kind of slavery with overpriced and monopolistic fringe benefits.

This delta region is the home of the Chachi, who – along with the Tsáchilas of Santo Domingo – were the only indigenous coastal people to evade extermination by the Spaniards. In both cases, survival was due to the inaccessibility of their homelands. Today, the Chachi number approximately 4,000. They are sometimes seen selling their finely woven hammocks and basketwork in the markets of Limones and La Tola – and occasionally Esmeraldas – but they prefer the privacy of Borbón and the inhospitable upper reaches of the Río Cayapas. A turnoff on the La Tola–Esmeraldas road runs to **Borbón**, but this country is decidedly off the beaten track, and travel can be numbingly difficult, especially in the wet season.

A better option is to take a motorized dugout from Limones upriver to Borbón. From there continue another couple of hours up the Río Cayapas to the community of **San Miguel** (www.sanmiguelcayapas.com), which has been offering community-based tourism for years. This far-flung Afro-Ecuadorian village offers board and lodging, in a rustic hotel with a hammock-strewn veranda overlooking the river. They can also arrange boat trips to the **Reserva Ecológica Cotacachi-Cayapas**.

The reserve covers some 204,400 hectares (505,000 acres) and its habitat varies from lowland tropical forest, in this region, to cloud forest, to windswept plain, and accordingly has an enormous range of flora and fauna. It is also the home of the Chachi, who continue to live in their traditional way, trying to avoid the encroachment of Western values and influences. The reserve receives protection from the Ecuadorian government and from international conservation organizations.

Eat

The Hotel Súa has rooms with balconies and sea views. The restaurant is recommended both for fish and a wide variety of other meals.

San Lorenzo fishermen.

A refreshing tropical fruit juice.

Fishermen in Canoa.

Guided tours in dugout canoes can be arranged with the park rangers.

Travel in other parts of Ecuador is rarely as adventurous as in these alluring backwaters, which few visitors make the effort to explore. The Chachi people's counterparts in the Oriente –ancient peoples such as the Jivaro and the Huaorani – have received far greater international exposure, which in turn has attracted more tourists. This exposure may, however, prove beneficial as the search for oil in the Amazon basin is a much greater threat to indigenous lifestyles than anything the Chachi are up against.

THE ROAD TO ESMERALDAS

The road from La Tola to **Esmeraldas** ❷ is rough and never ready: *rancheros*, which are open-sided trucks fitted with far too many wooden benches, take 5 hours to cover the 100km (62 miles); regular buses do the journey in 3 hours. The northern half of this road may suffer severe flooding during the wet season, but otherwise it is a carefree, breezy ride past cattle farms and swamps teeming with birdlife. A few small towns are strung out along the way, but offer little reason to pause.

It was near Esmeraldas that the *conquistador* Bartolomé Ruiz and company landed, the first Spaniards to set foot on Ecuadorian soil. Esmeraldas is named after the precious stone found in bountiful quantities in the like-named river, at whose mouth the city lies. The indigenous Cara, who inhabited this area before migrating to the mountain basins around Otavalo during the 10th century, worshiped a huge emerald known as Umina. Today, the treasures are more industrial than geological: Esmeraldas is the major port of the north coast, whence timber, bananas, and cacao are shipped abroad. The 500km (300-mile) trans-Andean oil pipeline ends here, and the construction of an oil refinery has brought new jobs and money to the city.

The treatment of previously fatal tropical diseases has contributed significantly to the growth of Ecuadorian ports, notably Guayaquil, Manta, and Esmeraldas. The eradication of yellow

fever from these towns early in the 20th century was the first step, followed by the discovery and availability of quinine as an antidote for malaria, which as recently as 1942 accounted for a quarter of all deaths in Ecuador. The treatment of tuberculosis, cause of almost one-fifth of deaths in Ecuador just a generation ago, completed the region's health improvements, providing the basis for the international maritime trade, although the area is one of the poorest in the country.

BLACK CAPITAL

Esmeraldas' population of 640,000 consists of mostly mestizos and Afro-Ecuadorians, with a surprising minority of mountain *indígenas* looking forlorn and far from at home. Esmeraldas is the center of black culture in Ecuador. It is here that the visitor is most likely to encounter a full marimba band, complete with huge conga drums, led by the *bomero*, who plays a deep-pitched bass drum suspended from the ceiling. Esmeraldas is, like its music, a vibrant city that embodies the distinctive elements of coastal urban life. The people are gregarious and no-nonsense, playing with far greater enthusiasm than they work. The energy level on the streets soars as the sun dips into the Pacific, and bars and restaurants – serving dishes of delicious *cocado*, fried fish in a spicy coconut sauce – fill to overflowing.

For the more cerebrally inclined, the **Museo Arqueológico** (Tue–Sun 8.30am–4.30pm; free) has exhibits on many of the region's pre-Inca cultures: Bahía, Valdivia, Chorrera, and Tuncahuan, as well as some small golden masks from La Tolita. There is also the **Casa de la Cultura Ecuatoriana** (tel: 06-271 0393; Mon–Fri 8am–12.30pm, 2.30–5pm; free) with a collection of colonial and contemporary art, but do not be surprised if you are the only visitor. Discotheques far outnumber museums in Esmeraldas, which is a fair reflection of the hedonistic spirit of the ancient peoples whose suggestive figures are on display here.

GOLDEN SANDS AND PALM TREES

To the immediate southwest of Esmeraldas begins a stretch of coastline containing the finest beaches in Ecuador. The beach suburb of **Las Palmas** is a more pleasant alternative to staying in the rather unattractive downtown area of Esmeraldas, but the beach is polluted and reported to be a dangerous place for tourists and single women. The road to the other, less visited beaches passes the Petro Ecuador oil refinery before reaching the coast. Much of this region was badly damaged by the 2016 earthquake, although the rebuilding was fairly swift.

The road from Esmeraldas is reasonable and there is a bus service down the coast to Muisne. Mompiche, about 100km (62 miles) south of Esmeraldas was once a sleepy fishing backwater. Now it has become one of the most talked-about surf destinations

> **Fact**
>
> Ecuador's shrimp breeding industry is burgeoning, but to the detriment of the coastal mangroves, which were cleared to build shrimp farms. You can see the last of the healthy mangroves around Same and Muisne; and once you've observed the destruction the farms cause, you may think twice before you eat shrimps.

At a barber's in Puerto López.

Súa beach shack for refreshing fruit juice.

Sunset over Ayampe beach.

in Ecuador. Around Mompiche are wonderful gray-sand beaches, but boat tours out to the nearby Isla Portete cost around $5 and it's here, on this small island, that you will find the region's best surfing. There's also good bird-watching here.

The resort town of **Atacames**, 30km (18 miles) from Esmeraldas, is popular with *serranos* wanting to let their hair down at the beach, though foreign visitors rarely visit. It has gained a reputation as a noisy party town, where the music blasts out 24 hours a day, particularly during the June–September high season. Beach bars are so tightly jammed together that they block the view of the sea and their vast speakers thump out beats in competition. The town has blossomed into the largest resort on the north coast, with countless hotels, resorts, cabins, and lodges. Atacames has a cooperative of artisans, presided over by *El Tío Tigre* (Uncle Tiger), which manufactures and sells bracelets and necklaces of black coral, found just offshore to the south. Buying such artifacts cannot be encouraged, however, since in many areas the coral has been pillaged to the point of virtual extinction. Bringing black coral home without a permit is illegal in many countries.

While the beach at Atacames looks harmless, there is a powerful undertow. There are no lifeguards, and the current sweeps some swimmers to their deaths every year. Sea snakes washed up on the beach pose another risk: they are venomous and should be avoided. A less avoidable problem is theft, which has been steadily increasing in Atacames in recent years. There have also been several reports of assault on the beach late at night, so solitary midnight strolls are not recommended, and if you hit the dance floor at night, make sure you are in a group.

Some 6km (4 miles) farther south lies **Súa**, a small, beautifully situated fishing village, and friendlier than Atacames. The fishermen haul their catch right up onto the small beach, which immediately becomes an impromptu local market. The sky fills with seabirds such as frigates and pelicans, who do a fine job gobbling up fish heads and guts. While a stay in Atacames is chiefly a matter of relishing the elements, Súa offers glimpses of life in a small seaside town with its eye less on tourists than on the next catch.

LUXURY AND ADVENTURE

A further 8km (5 miles) along the ocean road lies an unpaved side track to the beach of **Same** (pronounced "Sa-may"), perhaps the finest along this stretch. There is little here other than a collection of mostly expensive and tasteful hotels. Same does have the air of a place on the verge of overdevelopment, as it has become a resort for wealthy Quiteños who have erected an endless line of high-rise condos, but it remains the quintessential "away-from-it-all-in-comfort" destination.

The villages of **Tonchigüe** and **Galera**, both with lovely beaches

nearby, lie a short distance west of Same. At this point, the road leaves the coast and cuts southward through undulating banana plantations before re-emerging at the shoreline opposite the island of **Muisne**, 83km (51 miles) from Esmeraldas. Motorized dugouts ply the short distance from the mainland to Muisne and, since few visitors bother to come this far from Esmeraldas for just another beach, Muisne exudes the alluring, timeless languor characteristic of any remote tropical island. The beaches here are enormous and empty; there is a handful of cheap, basic hotels and good seafood restaurants, and nothing more. The ghost of Robinson Crusoe may well haunt Muisne's beaches; if you see another set of footprints in the sand, it must be Friday. Inland from Muisne there is an isolated community of indigenous Chachi, some of whom may be seen around town at the Sunday market.

From Muisne to **Cojimíes** ❸, 50km (31 miles) to the south, there is no road. One or two motorized dugouts make

the 2-hour journey each day, some continuing as far as Manta; the boats hug the coastline all the way, making it a safe and picturesque trip. An adventurous alternative is to head off under your own steam: the town of **Bolívar**, from where boats depart for Cojimíes, is about 23km (14 miles) from Muisne, making a feasible, if challenging, day's walk. There are several rivers to be forded en route, but locating a ferry is usually easy, and an early start should bring you to Bolívar, where there are no established hotels, in time to catch a boat to Cojimíes before dark. The wildlife along this pristine, largely uninhabited coastline is unsurpassed on Ecuador's mainland shore: jellyfish and crabs proliferate, as does the full gamut of pelagic birds. Again, check the security situation before making this journey.

Cojimíes lies at the northern end of the road that follows the coast down to Manta. It is a quiet and welcoming town, the site of a pre-Columbian settlement that still awaits comprehensive excavation. Transport connections

Condos overlooking Same.

⊙ RELAXING RETREATS

Everything about Esmeraldas province says "laidback." For many visitors, the languid climate and the pleasant slowness of the pace of life is conducive to spending a quiet few days at a beach retreat or secluded backcountry lodge. Here are a few recommended destinations for your get-away-from-it-all holiday-within-a-holiday in Esmeraldas:

Playa Escondida (tel: 09-9650 6812; www.playaescondidaec.com) is a shady, quiet retreat right on the seashore, and set in 40 hectares (100 acres) of ecological reserve, 3km (2 miles) west of Tonchigüe. This is not luxury, but being so close to nature makes up for that.

The **Playa de Oro** community, up the Río Santiago near the border of Reserva Ecológica Cotachachi-Cayapas, runs a rustic jungle lodge with private bathrooms and mosquito nets. Jungle tours and meals are included.

Seaside Garden Lodge (tel: 0995560077; www.seasidegardenlodge.com) at Mompiche has comfortable rooms in this spacious, breezy bamboo-and-thatch structure, bang on the beach.

El Acantilado (www.elacantilado.net), located on the edge of the beach, 1km (0.6 miles) south of Same, is a quiet oceanfront retreat with simple cabañas or suites set in a lush garden with a big swimming pool.

Pre-Columbian Manabí ceramic figurine, Museo Bahía de Caráquez.

are delightfully whimsical: the unpaved road is impassable in the wet season, and the daily *rancheros* usually run along the beach in a race against the rising tide. Just south of Pedernales, the road crosses the equator – marked by a small monument – and then forks. The left-hand turn runs through more farms and plantations to **Santo Domingo de los Colorados** (see page 223), while the coastal road continues on to the small market town of **Jama**. Another 50km (31 miles) south lies **Canoa**. This peaceful village is the center of a fast-developing deep-sea fishing industry and is a backpacker favorite thanks to its location alongside one of the widest, loveliest beaches in the country. There are some interesting caves and rock formations nearby.

SCENIC ROADWAY

The inland loop through Santo Domingo returns to the coast at Bahía de Caráquez, and is a refreshing change for anyone suffering from an overdose of empty, sun-drenched beaches. This route through the heartland of Manabí province is among the most scenic in the coastal region, and passes several interesting stop-offs. Past more banana plantations and cattle farms, the road runs to **El Carmen**, whereafter green hills rise from the plain. Much of Manabí, particularly the southern area, suffers a dearth of rainfall, due primarily to the lifeless winds of the Humboldt Current. Nevertheless, the province is the agricultural core of Ecuador, with coffee, cacao, rice, cotton, and tropical fruits cultivated widely. The Poza Honda Dam, built mostly with German finance, is fed by the Río Portoviejo and irrigates large areas of previously uncultivatable lowlands.

Chone (population over 52,000) prospers on the strength of these industries, as well as the manufacture of leather saddles and a type of straw hat called a *mocora*. The banks of the Río Chone, twisting through the undulating **Cerros de Bálsamo** (Bálsamo Hills), sustain increasing numbers of shrimp farms, an indication of Ecuador's modern industrial diversification, although they have also led to the destruction of

Colorful sun shelters on Canoa beach.

mangrove forests. The road climbs to a vantage point offering splendid views of Bahía de Caráquez and the mangrove islands dotting the bay, and then slides down to the coast.

The resort village of **San Vicente** stands at the mouth of the Río Chone, opposite Bahía de Caráquez. The church of **Santa Rosa** has an ornate, eye-catching facade and mosaic and glasswork by the Ecuadorian artist Pelí, but otherwise there are few diversions except for the beach. About 70km (43 miles) inland along a makeshift road is the important archeological site of **San Isidro**. The ancient inhabitants of San Isidro excelled in the art of ceramics, and imitations of their beautifully crafted figurines are today sold throughout Ecuador.

BANANA CENTERS

Bahía de Caráquez ❹ is named after the indigenous Cara who, legend has it, came "by way of the sea" and settled in this bay. Formerly an important export center for bananas and cacao, Bahía entered semi-retirement when the focus of banana exporting – in which Ecuador continues to be a world player – shifted south to Guayaquil and Machala. The cacao industry, in turn, has been steadily declining since it was struck down by a crippling blight in 1922–3, at which time Ecuador was the world's foremost producer. In 1999 Bahía became an eco-city in recognition of its strong green movement and the efforts made by the local community to rebuild the city in an ecologically sound way after the disastrous El Niño floods and earthquakes of 1997–8. A stroll along the palm-fringed riverside *malecón* (pier), past rows of stately old mansions, some of them in Victorian "gingerbread" style, reveals remnants of former prosperity. Nevertheless, Bahía's strategic river-mouth location ensures its continued existence as a minor port, and it remains the largest coastal town – with around 20,000 inhabitants – between Esmeraldas and Manta.

Much of Bahía's energy today is devoted to tourism: unlike many of Ecuador's north-coast towns, it is

Fishermen on the beach at San Vincente.

Tip

Parque Nacional Machalilla is the only coastal park in Ecuador, and it protects varied habitats including tropical beaches and coastline, cloud forests, and rare tropical dry forests, as well as over 350 species of bird together with monkeys, anteaters, lizards, iguanas, and deer.

easily accessible on good roads from Quito, and is one of the most popular resorts in the country. While there are few noteworthy sights in the town, it does offer some simple pleasures. An ascent of **La Cruz** hill is rewarded by sweeping views of the river and coastline, and a sojourn to a riverside café affords relief from the burning sun. There is also a fine collection of pre-Columbian Manabí pottery in the Museo y Centro Cultural de Bahía de Caráquez (Mon–Fri 8.30am–5pm, Sat & Sun 10am–4.30pm).

From Bahía, tours can be arranged to the **Río Muchacho Organic Farm** (tel: 05-302 0487; www.riomuchacho.com). While many farms in the area have destroyed the ecosystem and rendered the land desert-like, Río Muchacho is covered with vegetation. You can go horseback riding around the farm or try shrimp-fishing. Multiple-day tours can include Spanish lessons and the opportunity to interact with the Montubios, the local indigenous people. Beach tours are also available on open-sided *chiva* buses, which tour

the bay, stopping at a number of sites of interest.

Venturing slightly further afield, launches can be hired to visit **Isla de los Pájaros** and **Isla Corazón** in the bay. These two islands, as the former's name indicates, have raucous seabird colonies. A boardwalk has been constructed on Isla Corazón, which leads right over the mangroves.

Some 20km (13 miles) south of Bahía de Caráquez are the friendly, peaceful fishing villages of **San Clemente** and **San Jacinto**; driving along the beach at low tide may look tempting, but is inadvisable as many cars have died a watery death here. Instead, follow the Portoviejo road and turn off just before **Rocafuerte**; this route leads to San Jacinto, and on to San Clemente 5km (3 miles) away to the north. Along this road, which is notable for the giant ceiba trees lining the way, lies **Crucita**, a beach resort and a perfect spot for paragliding. Shortly thereafter, and just 15km (9 miles) east of Manta, is the fishing village of **Jaramijó**. This is the site of an extensive pre-Columbian

Worker at Río Muchacho organic farm, near Bahía de Caráquez.

settlement and where Eloy Alfaro, one of Ecuador's best-remembered presidents, lost an important naval battle against conservative forces in December 1884: the wreck of his ship, the *Alajuela*, can still be seen. Also near San Clemente is the archeological site of **Chirije** which dates back to the Bahía culture (500 BC–AD 500). A small museum on the site has finds from the ongoing excavations of the area.

PRE-COLUMBIAN HEDONISTS

For 1,000 years prior to the arrival of the Spaniards, **Manta ❺** was the center of one of Ecuador's pre-eminent indigenous cultures. It was known as Jocay – literally, "fish house" – by the local inhabitants, whose exquisite pottery was decorated with scenes of daily life. And what a life it was. The exuberant hedonism of contemporary coastal Ecuadorians can be traced back directly to the ancient Manteños with their pervasive fertility cult and enjoyment of coca. Their concept of physical beauty was expressed by the practice of strapping young children's heads to a board in order to increase the backward slope of their chins and foreheads. The desired effect was an exaggeration of the rounded, hooked nose.

The Manteños sacrificed their prisoners of war by ripping out their still-beating hearts. Their culture was part-settler, part-wanderer, as they cultivated fruit and vegetables while also trading with highland tribes – their source of precious metals – and navigated the ocean in rafts and dugouts as far as Panama and Peru, and possibly the Galápagos Islands. Their skill extended to the arts of stone-masonry, weaving, and metalwork; in short, a cultural sophistication of great breadth and depth.

The Spaniard Francisco Pacheco founded the modern settlement of Manta just 10 days before Portoviejo in 1535. Nine years earlier, however, his fellow countryman Bartolomé Ruiz

had encountered a balsa sailing raft with 20 Manteños aboard: 11 of them had leapt into the sea in terror, while the remaining nine served as translators before being set free. Perhaps this rare instance of Spanish tolerance has contributed to the unique character of modern Manta, for it is the most relaxed and habitable city of the entire coastal region.

In its previous incarnation as Jocay, the main thoroughfare of Manta was lined with statues of the chieftains and head priests. The Catholic Church ordered its place to be taken by inoffensive jacaranda and royal poinciana trees. Today, with a population of approximately 300,000, Manta has an international airport and is a major seaport, with coffee, bananas, cotton textiles, and fish comprising the bulk of the exports. For all this, the city feels much smaller than similarly sized Esmeraldas, the pace of life being much slower. Large numbers of Ecuadorian tourists vacation here.

Manta is divided by an inlet into a downtown and a resort district, the

Monument to fishermen, Manta.

Stall in Manta's fish market.

PANAMA HATS

US soldiers wore them, prohibition gangsters loved them, but do these coveted accessories have a future?

Montecristi is the capital of Panama hat-making. For 150 years the best *superfinos* have been woven in this peaceful, nondescript town, and it is here that tourists come to buy the genuine article directly from the weavers' hands. Why are these world-famous *sombreros* called Panama hats if they come from Montecristi? A mistake, apparently, attributed to some 19th-century gold-miners who forgot where they bought their innovative headgear.

The Panama hat production trail begins in the low hills west of Guayaquil, a region cooled by the sea breezes of the Humboldt Current, and where rainfall is plentiful but not excessive. In these conditions, the *Carludovica palmata* – named after King Carlos IV and his wife Luisa by two Spanish botanists in the late 18th century – thrives.

Today the plant is cultivated in fields divided according to the families' seniority in the trade. The stalks of the plant can grow as high as 6 meters (20ft), but it is the material inside the stalks, the new shoots containing dozens of very fine fronds, each about a meter long and a few millimeters wide, that is used. These fronds are boiled in water for an hour

Panama hat shop, Montecristi.

and sun-dried for a day. The procedure is repeated to ensure maximum strength when woven.

WORKS OF ART

The finest weaving is done at night or on dull days, as direct sunlight makes the fronds too brittle, and hot sweaty hands don't produce tight weaves. Women and children make the best hats, because their fingers, being smaller, are more agile. A *superfino* – as the best hats are called, those most tightly woven with the thinnest, lightest straw – takes up to three months to complete. The test of a true *superfino* is that it should, when turned upside down, hold water without any leakage. It should also fold up to fit neatly in a top pocket without creasing.

No one knows exactly how long straw hats have been woven in Ecuador, but the craft certainly preceded the Spanish conquest. The *conquistadores* were impressed by the headgear worn by the indigenous inhabitants of Manabí province, and adapted it for their own use. A few of the Panamas were sent to the United States in the late 18th century. During the Spanish-American War of 1898, the hats were considered ideal headgear for soldiers and the export market to the US really took off. They first hit Europe at the 1855 World Exposition in Paris, and, as illustrated by many of Renoir's paintings, soon became a debonair fashion item.

CHICAGO CHIC

America fell in love with the Panama, and for the next 50 years kept the industry going. The gangsters of the Prohibition period took such a shine to them that the Manabí manufacturers still call the wide-brimmed variety *El Capone*. The industry peaked in 1946, when 5 million hats were exported, constituting 20 percent of Ecuador's annual export earnings. In those days every household in Montecristi produced top-quality Panamas, but numbers have now dwindled to a handful. The international demand has fallen steadily since the early 1950s. Within Ecuador, the center of hat production has moved to Cuenca. China and Taiwan now produce cheaper imitations that are sufficiently like the genuine item to satisfy all but the most discerning, and many of the weavers of Manabí now earn their living by making mats and wickerwork furniture.

latter called Tarqui. Along the expansive **Tarqui Beach**, local fishermen unload and clean their catch – tuna, shark, dorado, eel, and tortoise – whipping the attendant gulls and vultures into aerial frenzy. A towering statue of a Manabí fisherman overlooks the proceedings, noticing few material changes from earlier times.

The **Museo Centro Cultural Manta** (www.culturaypatrimonio.gob.ec/museo-centro-cultural-manta-provincia-de-manabi; Tue–Fri 8.30am–5pm, Sat–Sun 10am–4pm) houses the finest collection of Manteño artifacts in Ecuador and is well worth a visit. Manta's outdoor theater is the venue for occasional performances, especially during the agriculture and tourism exposition held each October. **Playa Murciélago** is an unprotected surfing beach a few kilometers west of town, site of the comfortable Hotel Oro Verde (www.oroverdemanta.com).

ECUADOR'S "PANAMA" HAT

Straddling the highway between Manta and Portoviejo is the deceptively non-descript town of **Montecristi** ❻, for more than a century the home of the renowned Panama hat. In the past, the majority of Montecristi's 9,000-odd inhabitants were engaged in the weaving of these remarkable headpieces, made from the straw fronds of the *Carludovica palmata*. A few still are, but Montecristi has had to move with the times, and some have switched to making fine wickerwork furniture and decorations. It is the quintessential cottage industry and many houses contain a rudimentary factory and showroom. The lack of any signs of wealth in Montecristi is sad testimony to the inequitable distribution of the industry's hefty profits. Like Portoviejo, which we will come to next, Montecristi owes its existence to pillaging pirates: in 1628, a group of Manteños left the coast in search of an inland refuge following pirate raids. Their colonial-style houses, now in a state of chronic disrepair, line the quiet, dusty streets and, in combination with the non-mechanized weaving, this physical neglect creates the air of a town stuck in another time.

Weaving a good-quality Panama hat can take two months or more.

The cathedral at Montecristi.

⊙ Tip

To learn more about eco-projects in and around Bahía de Caráquez, visit www.planetdrum.org.

Montecristi's religious atmosphere is similarly dated: the beautiful church contains a famous statue of the Virgin to which several miracles were once attributed. And Montecristi's favorite son is now long dead: Eloy Alfaro, president of Ecuador at the turn of the 20th century and a committed liberal reformist, was born here. His statue overlooks the main plaza, and his house is now a mausoleum, with his library and many personal effects on display. Almost alone among towns in coastal Ecuador, Montecristi survives as a relic, an impression heightened by the sight of modern-day tourists and Panama hat dealers roaring into town in search of a bargain.

PORTOVIEJO'S MEMORIES

From Montecristi it is only 24km (15 miles) to **Portoviejo 7**, a town with a long history. In fact, it was one of the earliest Spanish settlements in Ecuador, founded on March 12, 1535, just three months after Benalcázar re-founded Quito atop abandoned Inca ruins. Guayaquil, founded in January 1535, was the first Spanish coastal community, but the local people, based on the nearby island of Puná, repeatedly launched marauding raids of such ferocity that alternative sites were sought.

The original settlement, founded by Francisco Pacheco on the orders of Francisco Pizarro and Diego de Almagro, was, as its name ("Old Port") suggests, located on the coast. The omens, however, were far from auspicious: in 1541, a fire destroyed the town, and 50 years later the local indigenous population staged a fearsome uprising. Finally, when English pirates ravaged the port in 1628, it was decided that a spot further inland would be out of harm's way. Since then, Portoviejo has existed in the shadow of Manta, though as capital of Manabí province it remains an important administrative and educational center. Its population is close to passing the 300,000 mark, most of which is engaged in commerce, industry, and the rich agricultural pickings of the hinterland. Portoviejo's bustling streets are prettily bordered with rows of trees and flowering shrubs, and a stroll through the **Parque Eloy Alfaro** is perhaps the most pleasing pastime. Opposite the park is one of Ecuador's starkest modern cathedrals, Jesús el Buen Pastor; beside it stands a statue of Pacheco, the city's founder.

There are two museums: the **Casa de la Cultura Ecuatoriana** (Mon–Fri 8am–5pm), with a collection of traditional musical instruments, and the **Museo y Archivo Histórico de Portoviejo** (Mon–Fri 9am–4.30pm), which houses archeological and ethnographic collections and historic documents, as well as works by local artists. Portoviejo has a few old colonial buildings still standing, but otherwise little testimony to its long and tumultuous history.

Leaving Portoviejo, go back the way you came for 14km (8 miles), then turn off the Guayaquil road to the village of **La Pila**, which is an interesting

⊙ WHALE-WATCHING

Dusty, sleepy Puerto López is at first glance perhaps not a typical visitors' paradise. That all changes between June and September, however, when the waters offshore fill with frolicking whales, and Puerto López becomes the whale-watching capital of Ecuador. During these months, humpback whales *(Megaptera novaeangliae)* migrate with the Humboldt Current from the Antarctic to mate and give birth to their calves in the warm, shallow waters around Parque Nacional Machalilla. Humpback whales, which can reach 16 meters (53ft) in length and weigh 30–40 tonnes, are the most acrobatic of the bigger whales, often breaching out of the water and slapping the water's surface dramatically with their large pectoral fins and tail flukes. The excitement becomes palpable in town during whale-watching season when many professional – and some fly-by-night – operators open up shop and loudly tout their tours to make the best of the short, but lucrative, season. Most operators offer whale-watching tours with snorkeling or diving and park excursions. Book well ahead. Recommended operators include: Exploramar, with 8–12-person boats and PADI divemasters (tel: 099-9500 0910; www.exploradiving.com), and Mantaraya, which also has an excellent lodge (tel: 02-336 0887; www.mantarayalodge.com). Puerto Cayo is also becoming another center for whale-watching along this part of the coast and has a handful of operators that offer good boat tours.

stop-off. In the wake of the discovery of exquisite pre-Columbian ceramics in the area, the resourceful inhabitants of La Pila began producing indistinguishable imitations to cash in on their forebears' artistry. Nowadays they have embraced originality and appear to have inherited not only the enterprise but also the considerable artistic skill of their ancestors.

In contrast, **Jipijapa** – a town of 45,000 inhabitants situated another 40km (25 miles) along the highway to Guayaquil – appears to have been swallowed up by Ecuador's flourishing agricultural industries, particularly coffee and cotton. At Jipijapa, a side road climbs into the damp, luxuriant hills of southern Manabí before descending to the coast near **Puerto Cayo**, a fishing village with pristine beaches.

A large tract of the surrounding area was designated the **Parque Nacional Machalilla** in 1979. It protects a 55,000-hectare (135,910-acre) expanse of tropical dry forest, which is home to a wide variety of bird and animal life, as well as a stretch of coast and two islands. Some 15km (9 miles) offshore is **Isla de la Plata**, an ancient Manteño ceremonial center currently undergoing excavation. The island is named for an incident in the late 16th century, when Sir Francis Drake captured a silver-laden galleon and made camp on the island to tally his spoils. There have been a number of archeological finds from pre-Columbian times. Today it is inhabited only by sea turtles, blue-footed boobies, and a number of magnificent frigate birds and even some Galápagos albatross, and can be reached by hired motorboat from Puerto Cayo; a trip of two hours. Look out for shells of the spondylus oyster, which in pre-Columbian times served as a unit of currency, and as such was regularly interred in the tombs of chieftains. There is good diving and snorkeling here as well, and a number of agencies in Puerto López can provide gear and transportation.

You can enter the park from the coast road, or from the Manta to Guayaquil highway south of Jipijapa. Park admission costs $20 for the

Tourist trinkets and souvenirs for sale in Puerto López.

Playing pool in Puerto López.

⊙ **Fact**

The ancient city of Manta had a population of 20,000 and traded with the coastal peoples of Mexico and Peru.

mainland parks and Isla de la Plata (ticket valid for five days), and tickets can be purchased at the park office in Puerto López (Alvaro and Moreno; daily 7am–6pm) or at the park.

Continuing south, the well-worn coast road passes through **Machalilla** ❽, the center of the culture of the same name that flourished between 1800 and 1500 BC. It is rich in archeological remains, especially in the vicinity of **Salaite** and **Agua Blanca**, where there is a small archeological museum. Another attraction is the therapeutic mud bath at the nearby lagoon. A pleasant 45-minute walk from Machalilla brings you to the deserted horseshoe beach called **Los Frailes** (the Friars). About 10km (6 miles) further south, fleets of heavily laden fishing boats dock in the village of **Puerto López** each afternoon at about 4pm, and the skippers sell their catch there and then.

FROM SALANGO TO MONTAÑITA

About 5km (3 miles) south of Puerto López is **Salango**, a small fishing

Mouth-watering ceviche.

village close to a site where dozens of people took part in the largest archeological dig in the country, providing insights into the fragmentary history of pre-Columbian Ecuador. The relics of a host of successive cultures – Valdivia, Machalilla, Chorrera, Engoroy, Bahía, Guangala, and Manteño – that inhabited this fertile stretch of coastline as early as 2000 BC were painstakingly recovered. A museum here is filled with artifacts found in the area.

Ask most Ecuadorians to name their favorite beach getaway and they will mostly likely tell you about **Ayampe**, about half way along the road from Salango to Montañita. It's a relaxed, undeveloped fishing village, but at the rustic Finca Punta Ayampe (tel: 09-189 0892; www.fincapuntaaayampe.com) you can nevertheless stay overnight and take surfing lessons.

Around 23km (14 miles) south from here, **Montañita**, which for many years was simply a locally known surf spot, has blossomed into the largest surf resort in the country, one of Ecuador's biggest backpacker hangouts, and very much part of the hip traveler "scene." Many cheap hotels, jewelry stands, restaurants, and bars and clubs line the cluster of streets. The town is a good base for arranging tours into Machalilla National Park, Isla de la Plata, and for whale-watching, paragliding, or kite-surfing.

The beach is crowded during the summer months and filled with umbrellas, beer vendors, surfers, and carts selling *ceviche de ostra* (oyster ceviche). More upmarket accommodations can be found at the north end of the beach, known as Baja Montañita, and in the town of Olón a few kilometers north.

Some 3km (2 miles) south of Montañita is **Manglaralto**, which is a small, cozy town with several small yet decent hotels offering great value for money, such as Hotel Manglaralto just off the beach beside the central park.

Surfer in Montañita.

Cerro Santa Ana.

Guayaquil cityscape.

GUAYAQUIL AND THE SOUTH COAST

The vibrant port city of Guayaquil and the beach resorts of the Santa Elena peninsula show a different side of Ecuadorian life.

Many visitors to Ecuador are surprised to learn that the seaport of **Guayaquil** ❶ is the country's largest city, with an unofficial population of 3.5 million, which is much larger than Quito. This bustling commercial city offers a stunning waterfront, some fascinating museums and stately plazas along with plenty of mosquitoes. Guayaquil is not for the meek. Situated on the west bank of the busy Río Guayas, navigable for the biggest of ocean vessels heading in from the Pacific via the Golfo de Guayaquil, this city handles 90 percent of Ecuador's imports and 50 percent of its exports. Having previously lacked tourist attractions, the city has redefined itself amid a flurry of building projects and investments in several districts in the early 21st century. The regenerated Malecón 2000, formerly Malecón Simón Bolívar, has parks, malls, restaurants, museums, and markets. The faded Las Peñas district – the city's oldest neighborhood – was completely restored, and has become a much friendlier place.

During the rainy season, January to April, the heat and humidity are oppressive, but from May to December the climate is pleasant, with little or no rain and cool nights. And Guayaquil, with its fresh image, is dotted with wide concrete boulevards, spacious parks, and colorful gardens, as well as impressive monuments, museums

with rich archeological and art collections, and excellent restaurants. Its most obvious attraction is the **Guayas** itself. The chocolate-colored river teems with ships, small boats, dugout canoes, and rafts loaded with produce from the inland villages and plantations. Considered one of the cleanest deepwater ports in this part of the world, it has since the early 2020s come under increasing scrutiny as Ecuador has become an important transhipment route in the drug trade, with cartels from various countries

Main attractions
Iguana-viewing in Parque Bolívar
Malecón 2000
Buque Guayas
Cerro Santa Ana and Las Peñas
Salinas

Maps on pages 254, 260

Parque del Centenario.

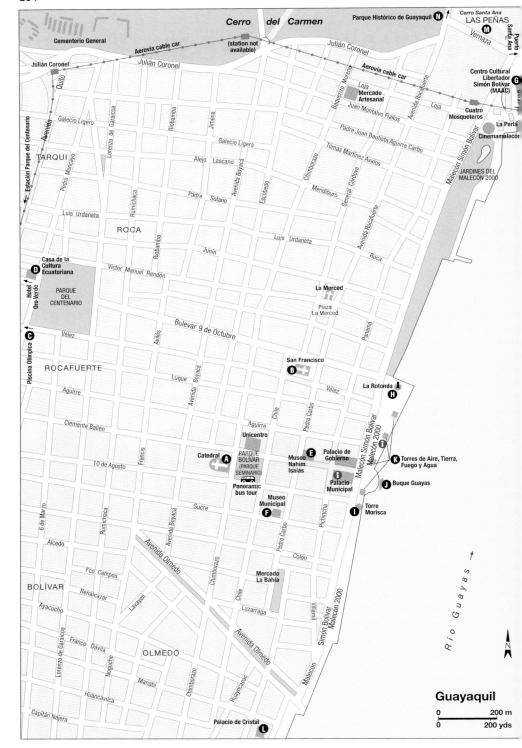

Guayaquil

fighting for control. As a result, the security situation in the city has deteriorated somewhat. But by taking sensible precautions, there's still much that can be enjoyed safely in Guayaquil. In addition to the sights and museums, a number of travel agencies offer river tours, taking visitors past small settlements, farms, and cattle ranches along this lush tropical river and through locks into the Salado estuary where the city's seaport area is located.

A NAME INSPIRED BY TRAGEDY

Although Spanish explorer Francisco de Orellana – credited with "discovering" the Amazon River – claimed to have founded Guayaquil, it was inhabited long before the Spanish arrived. The Valdivia people flourished in the area around 2000 BC, followed by the Huancavilcas. Legend has it that the Huancavilca chieftain, Guayas, killed his beautiful wife Quil then drowned himself so that the Spaniards would not capture them. The tragedy of this doomed couple is allegedly what inspired the city's name.

While fairly calm and conventional Quito was worrying only about infrequent earthquakes, Guayaquil spent its first 400 years fending fires. The last major blaze, in 1896, destroyed a large number of Guayaquil's charming wooden houses. The different natures of Quito and Guayaquil – one a sophisticated center for art and culture, the other a center of commerce occupied by tattooed sailors and hard-working, hard-drinking laborers – bred a rivalry between the cities. It is common for competing presidential candidates to be from one or the other, and while Quiteños think the Guayaquil residents rough and unrefined, Guayaquil dwellers think the residents of the capital are dull and backward, not to mention foolish for living in a city with no nightlife and no beaches. Guayaquileños claim that they make the country's money and the Quiteños spend it.

BRASSY WEALTH

Despite its development problems Guayaquil is a growth area, a center of industry with oil and sugar refineries, cement mills, breweries, and all types of manufacturing. Few visitors see Guayaquil as a tourist destination, but with a little effort and dedication, you can find some luxurious hotels, fine restaurants, clubs for tennis, golf, yachting, and swimming, exciting nightclubs and upscale shopping, including a bevy of duty-free stores. While the once high crime rate has been drastically reduced in many areas of the city, Guayaquil still has a well-deserved reputation for being dangerous. The Malecón and Las Peñas district are heavily policed and generally quite safe during the day, but Guayaquileños warn that care should be taken anywhere else around town, and to be particularly circumspect at night: muggings and armed robbery are common. Taxi-hijackings have become rife in the city, so it is advisable to order your taxi by phone from a hotel or through a reputable taxi

Eat

Guayaquil has traditionally been the means by which the world gets Ecuador's renowned chocolate. To sample great chocolate within the city, try Hotel Oro Verde's Le Gourmet restaurant (for the much-sought-after chocodinners) or the Pepa de Oro café at the Grand Hotel Guayaquil, which serves divine hot chocolate.

Guayaquil's Las Peñas district has plenty of pretty colonial buildings.

service, rather than hailing one in the street. Leave valuables and your hotel room key behind when you go out.

There is no straightforward way to see the sights of Guayaquil, but a suggested route is to visit the scattered downtown places of interest first, then follow the extensively refurbished *malecón* along the water's edge, past the docks to Las Peñas and Cerro Santa Ana. Start with a visit to the neo-Gothic **Catedral Metropolitana**  on the west side of Parque Bolívar, on Calle Chile between 10 de Agosto and Clemente Ballén. The cathedral was built in 1948, with lovely stained-glass windows and a Cuenca marble altar. Its side altars are overwhelmed by innumerable votive candles lit by the devout; some people even hold candles in their hands while walking around the church praying. The original wooden cathedral, built in 1547, burned down in one of the city's many fires.

Parque Bolívar o Seminario (popularly known as Parque de las Iguanas) is perhaps the most interesting park in the city. The old, well-maintained

An iguana strikes a pose in Parque Bolívar.

botanical garden earned its nickname from its equestrian statue of Bolívar; around the statue's base are bas-relief depictions of that mysterious Guayaquil meeting between Bolívar and San Martín (see page 257). The pavilion and gates in this century-old park came from France. The park is best known, however, for the hundreds of green iguanas – some of them a meter in length – that roam freely. A small pond is home to several species of turtles and tortoises.

On the other side of the park is the glitzy **Unicentro Shopping Center** (www.unicentroguayaquil.com). From here, walk two blocks along Calle Chile to the plaza and church of **San Francisco** ❸. The church was built in 1603 and beautifully restored in 1968. You will also see that many streets in the central district preserve porticoes protecting pedestrians from the elements. Going west along Bulevar 9 de Octubre you will come to the **Parque del Centenario**, the city's largest plaza, covering four city blocks. It is filled with monuments, the most important being

⊘ PARTY TOWN

Guayaquileños like to party. They will take any opportunity the year's calendar presents and turn it into a city-wide celebration that can go on for days. The biggest events in Guayaquil's calendar are the anniversaries of Símon Bolívar's birthday and the day of the founding of the city: July 24 and 25. The city goes crazy with parades and pageants, exuberant dancing, and fireworks, much of it fueled by liberal amounts of drinking. People dress up, take to the streets, book out restaurants, and party hard day and night. Hotel rooms are hard to come by on these (and surrounding) dates.

The other main holidays are celebrated in October: Independence Day on October 9 and Día de la Plurinacionalidad e Interculturalidad on October 12. Formerly known as Día de la Raza, and a celebration of the Hispanic heritage of Latin America, the name was changed to reflect Ecuador's multi-ethnic heritage and celebrations are equally diverse. The holiday usually stretches into the 10th and 11th as well, with colorful parades on the malecón. Carnival is held on the days before Ash Wednesday in the run-up to Easter, and is another excuse for dressing up and parading. Watch out on the streets, however, as townspeople enthusiastically defend the tradition of throwing water, and other less innocuous liquids. You might fall victim to water bombs, eggs, or flour, and inevitably you need to be alert to pickpockets and less well-meaning folk.

the patriotic liberty monument with the likenesses of Ecuador's heroes, and smaller statues representing history, justice, patriotism, and heroism. Five blocks further west on Bulevar 9 de Octubre is the **Hotel Oro Verde**, the best spot in town for a full-works American-style breakfast. Go south from here down Calle García Moreno, and you will find the **Piscina Olímpica** Ⓒ (Olympic Swimming Pool).

PRE-COLUMBIAN ARTIFACTS

Just outside Parque del Centenario on 9 de Octubre and Moncayo is the **Casa de la Cultura Ecuatoriana** Ⓓ (Mon–Fri 9am–6pm; www.guayas.casadelacultura. gob.ec) with a museum displaying pre-Columbian artifacts found in archeological digs on the country's coast. This museum once had an impressive collection of gold items – reported to be Ecuador's most valuable pre-colonial gold collection – but many of them mysteriously disappeared; those that remain at the museum are not publicly displayed. Current exhibits range from clay whistles known as *ocarines* to molds for casting gold masks and colonial art. More impressive are the greater number of pre-Columbian exhibits (actually 8,000 of them) of the Valdivia culture on display at the Presley Norton Museum (Av. 9 de Octubre and Carchi, Mon–Fri 9am–5pm). The best of colonial art can be seen at the **Museo Nahim Isaías** Ⓔ (Pichincha and Clemente Ballén; tel: 04-232 4182; Mon–Fri 9am–5pm). The collection consists of more than 2,000 16–18th-century paintings and sculptures. Perhaps the most intriguing museum in town is the nearby **Museo Municipal** Ⓕ (Tue–Sat 9am–5pm; www.museoarteyciudad.com; free on presentation of ID) on Calle Sucre. There are pre-Hispanic artifacts from the Huancavilca and Valdivia peoples, colonial art, and a gallery of paintings of the presidents of Ecuador here. The museum also contains the Act of Independence document,

but its real treasures are a collection of shrunken heads – *tzantzas* – prepared by some groups of people living in the rainforest using secret processes that shrink them with their features still perfectly intact, to the size of a fist. The heads are only on display in February, however, when the museum celebrates the culture of the peoples of the Ecuadorian Oriente.

ON THE WATERFRONT

Running along the Río Guayas from Las Peñas at the north end to the building that until 2022 housed the very exclusive Club de la Unión is the tourist-friendly promenade Malecón 2000, formerly Malecón Simón Bolívar. The well guarded tree-lined boardwalk is filled with restaurants, roaming vendors, parks, monuments, and activities for families. At the Las Peñas end is the **Centro Cultural Simón Bolívar** Ⓖ housing the excellent **Museo Antropológico y de Arte Contemporáneo** (MAAC; Tue–Sun 9am–5pm; www. facebook.com/maacec), which combines the ancient and the new with more

Green iguana at home in Parque Bolívar.

View of the waterfront with Cerro Santa Ana in the background.

than 50,000 archeological pieces and 3,000 works of modern art. There is an independent movie and IMAX theater next door. Take a short walk east on Dr. Julián Coronel Oyarvide to reach the **Mercado Artesanal** (Mon–Sat 9am–5pm, Sun 10am–3pm) with around 250 shops and workshops offering jewelry as well as products made of leather, wood, textiles, toquilla straw, steel, copper, and silver.

Heading south down the *malecón*, at the foot of Bulevar 9 de Octobre, you will see the semicircle of **La Rotonda** ⊕. This statue commemorates the historical but mysterious meeting between the continent's two great liberators, Venezuelan Simón Bolívar and Argentine General José de San Martín. Bolívar had freed the countries to the north and San Martín was responsible for the independence of Argentina and Chile but their final plans differed; Bolívar wanted the countries united under a democracy with an elected president, while San Martín envisioned a monarchy. The meeting resulted in the Acuerdo de Guayaquil (Guayaquil Accord), which established

the short-lived Gran Colombia, uniting Venezuela, Colombia, and Ecuador. There was no witness to the exchange between the two men and the only thing that is known for sure is that when the meeting ended, Bolívar remained and San Martín went into exile in France. La Rotonda is built so that people can stand on either side of the statue, whisper, and hear one another, though these days that may be difficult above the noise of the traffic. From here you can enjoy impressive views to the north of the hill known as Cerro del Carmen and, far beyond, the Guayaquil–Durán bridge, the country's longest at 4km (2½ miles) long.

Continuing south from La Rotonda, one comes to the **Torre Morisca** ⓘ, a Moorish clock tower dating from 1770. The clock tower's gardens are a favorite meeting spot for young couples in the early evening. Across the street is the stately colonial **Palacio Municipal**, which is separated from the severe **Palacio de Gobierno** by a plaza with a statue dedicated to General Sucre, hero of Ecuador's war of independence.

La Rotonda.

Just south of here, moored at the end of a riverside pier is the **Buque Guayas** ❶ (Mon–Fri noon–6pm, Sat–Sun 10am–6pm) a glorious three-masted tall ship belonging to the Ecuadorian Navy, on which it trains its cadets. The vessel is open for inspection, but it does disappear periodically on training voyages.

Close by are the four postmodern monuments known as the **Torres de Aire**, **Agua**, **Tierra y Fuego** ❿ (Air, Water, Earth, and Fire), built as part of the refurbishment of the *malecón*, and a landmark waterfront meeting place.

A great way to get a different perspective on the city is to take a boat trip on the Guayas. Kacique Tours boats leave from a dock close to the MAAC. (Tue–Fri 3–6pm, Sat & Sun 11am–7pm; tel: 096442143). Alternatively, for a land-side view, catch the Van Service panoramic bus tour (daily hourly departures from Parque Centenario 10am–7pm; www.vanservice.com.ec/bus-2pisos/guayaquil). This hop-on-hop-off bus allows you to do the whole two-hour tour at one go. However, since a ticket is valid for 24 hours, you can get off at any site of particular interest and resume the tour on a later bus. The route passes many places of interest, including the attractive park and waterways development at the **Malecón del Salado** in the west of the city. A bilingual guide is included. For an aerial view of Guayaquil, head for La Perla, the giant ferris wheel close to the MAAC.

At the very far southern end of the *malecón* at Plaza de la Integración, you will find the Eiffel-designed Antiguo Mercado Sur de 1907, known as the **Palacio de Cristal** ❶, or Crystal Palace. This serves as an exhibition hall and gallery displaying temporary exhibits, but is worth a visit for its graceful architecture alone.

RIVERSIDE HEIGHTS

Back at the northern end of the *malecón*, past restaurant boats, working docks, and the Durán ferry exit, Calle Numa Pompilio Lloma mounts the side of **Cerro Santa Ana** and enters the picturesque bohemian district of **Las Peñas** ❿. The area's romantic 19th-century neoclassical houses are today inhabited by many artistically minded Guayaquileños, and many are filled with craft shops, cafés, bars, and galleries. The city's most upmarket nightlife is here; for the more thumping clubs your best bet is to head to the Zona Rosa, towards the southern end of Malecón 2000 around Calle Aguirre – although always go in a group, or in the company of locals.

On the small **Plaza Colón**, two cannons commemorate the defense of the city against pirate invasions. Continued investment in the area has paid off, and Las Peñas is now filled with tourists who climb the scenic 444 steps from the *malécon* up through the district to the *mirador* above for spectacular views. At the top there is a small fortress with cannons and naval artifacts, as well as a church. For refreshments, there's the very touristy Pirate Bar, or

Torre Morisca, an 18th-century clock tower.

The district of Las Peñas on Cerro Santa Ana.

⊙ Fact

The Malecón del Salado on the west side of Guayaquil's Downtown has also undergone urban renewal. The large, manicured Parque Baquerizo Moreno, and the long waterfront walkways on the Estero Salado, make a pleasant refuge from the buzz of the city. The illuminated fountains show with music is also popular.

you could walk back down to Las Peñas and choose from the many, much more authentic, bars and restaurants. The security situation is much improved on Cerro Santa Ana these days, but climbing the hill late at night is not recommended.

The Las Peñas area also has an open-air theater – Teatro Bogotá – and, just behind it, the oldest church in Guayaquil, **Santo Domingo**, founded in 1548, with beautiful Baroque altars crafted in Carrara marble in the lateral naves. A patio at the left-hand side of the church's nave contains a spring credited with miraculous healing powers. From here, stairs to the right of the church and the steep Buitron Street lead to **Cerro del Carmen**, topped by the Cristo del Consuelo monument. At the foot of the hill is the dazzling white cemetery, the **Cementerio General**, with its avenue of royal palms leading to the grave of 19th-century President Vicente Rocafuerte, elaborate marble sculptures, and imposing neo-Greco-Roman mausoleums. Because of problems with crime, it is

Cerro Santa Ana.

not recommended that tourists visit Cerro del Carmen independently. Go with a local or join a tour.

HISTORY RECONSTRUCTED

If you are craving a glimpse of what Guayaquil looked like in the days before fire destroyed much of the old town, you can take a trip to the **Parque Histórico de Guayaquil** Ⓝ (Wed–Sun 9am–5pm; tel: 04-2832958) on a long snaking peninsula in the Río Guayas, half way across below the road bridge to Durán and the south. You can see here recreations of early 20th-century Guayaquil (mixed with other buildings more typical of a rural community, such as haciendas). Several of these buildings are in fact originals: moved by developers with foresight when they were threatened with demolition in their former central locations. This is all just part of a rather gorgeous riverside park that includes a small zoo and restaurants, some with suitably historic decor. It sounds far tackier than it actually is, and makes for a tranquil break from the city's hubbub. The park regularly

hosts festivals, concerts, workshops, and cultural events.

A block away lies the **Teatro Sánchez Aguilar** (www.teatrosanchezaguilar. org) Ecuador's best modern theater, which opened in 2012 and attracts world-class theatre, dance, and music performances.

BEACHES OF THE SOUTH

Guayaquil is an important meeting city for business executives but rarely the sole destination of tourists. Rather, it is the jumping-off point for the Galápagos Islands and the beaches of Ecuador's southern coast. There has been a surge of development on the coast from Guayaquil to Manta and resorts have appeared where once there was only dirt road. Endless stretches of sandy beaches are lapped by warm water and toasted by the tropical sun. People with fair skin should take precautions under these burning rays; sometimes less than half an hour of sun can cause severe sunburn on unprotected skin. Although weekends and the December to April vacation season see much beach activity, the area is all but deserted during the week. The road southwest from Guayaquil passes through dry scrubland, with the scenery undergoing an astonishing change from wet fields of rice and bananas to an arid – but attractive – landscape with strange bottle-shaped kapok trees and scattered bright flowers. Coastal developments are modern, to appeal to holidaying Guayaquile-ños; those seeking a more rustic feel should head further north to the likes of Canoa and Ayampe.

Traffic on the coastal road, which passes the busy villages of **Cerecita** and **Progreso** about 70km (42 miles) outside of Guayaquil, is heavy from January to April during local vacation months, and on weekends. In Progreso (officially called Gómez Rendón), the road forks off to the right to Salinas and Santa Elena. A left-hand fork leads to the popular beach resort of **Playas** ❷ (officially known as General Villamil), also an important fishing village. Old balsa rafts, similar to craft used in pre-Inca times, line the beaches and are still used by some of the fishermen who bring in their catch every afternoon. However, the main focus of this little town is tourism, and the sandy beaches are the lure for weekend crowds. An alternative to the main beach with its hotels, including the popular Playas and Rey David, and the villas used as escape destinations for Guayaquil residents, is the beautiful beach to the north, called the Pelado. It is a long and lonely stretch set against the backdrop of a cliff. For overnight stays in Playas, the best lodgings are to be found at Playa Paraíso (tel: 04-370 2806; http:// playaparaiso.com.ec) just outside the village on the main road to Data.

About 14km (8 miles) south along the coast from Playas is **Data de Villamil**, notable for its traditional wooden ship-building industry. An inland road from here passes the old village of El Morro with its huge wooden church. Further

The design of the balsa rafts still used by fishermen off the south coast has not changed much since before the time of the Incas.

Traditional balsa raft on the beach at Playas.

⊘ Eat

Machala has a wide range of inexpensive Chinese restaurants, known in Ecuador, and other Andean countries, as *chifas*.

Gaily painted fishermen's boats on a south coast beach.

south is the popular **Playa Varadero** near Data de Posorja with an attractive 2.5km (1.5-mile) long beach and a food court with over 20 restaurants, mainly serving seafood and freshly caught fish. Farther along the coast is Posorja, with commercial boats and hundreds of seabirds wheeling around the **Canal de Morro**, that is used by overseas vessels bound for Guayaquil. Shrimp farming produced an economic boom in the village, which has grown rapidly over the past few years. This is a pleasant stop on a day trip, even though the beaches are not really good for swimming.

Opposite Posorja is the large island of **Puná**, which was already inhabited in pre-Inca times as evidenced by the traces of two settlements from the Valdivia culture that archeologists have found there. The island is quite difficult to reach as there is no public transport, but fishermen at Posorja will take you over to the island for a fee, where you can camp and stroll around the various trails, deserted beaches and mangroves.

CACTUS AND TUNA

To get to Salinas, Ecuador's most fashionable resort town, you must go back to Progreso, and take the left-hand road through an increasingly dry, cactus-covered landscape. At Km 35.6 outside Progreso is the road to the fishing village of **Chanduy**, a haven for archeologists who have made important discoveries while excavating the remains of Valdivia, Machalilla, and Chorrera indigenous settlements. This is considered to be the oldest agricultural settlement on the continent where ceramics were made, and may have been a ceremonial center. Nowadays, as at all the fishing villages along this route, the biggest fish, such as tuna and marlin, are brought close to the shore with the cold Antarctic-born Humboldt Current to feed on smaller, warm-current fish.

Just before reaching Chanduy is the **Complejo Cultural Real Alto** (Tue–Sun 9am–4pm; www.complejoculturalrealalto. org), which takes the form of two giant huts covered with straw roofs. The center primarily exhibits finds from the archeological site, though the exhibition makes links with the present-day cultural practices of the local communities.

Back to the main roadway, at Km 49.5, a right-hand deviation in the road leads to the **Baños de San Vicente**, a large complex in which water is channeled into swimming pools and mud baths that are said to have curative powers. Farther down the main road is **Santa Elena**, interesting only for its church and usually bypassed in favor of La Libertad and Salinas. However, on the outskirts of the town near a Mormon temple with a small tower is the **Museo Los Amantes de Sumpa** (The Lovers of Sumpa; Tue–Sun 9am–5pm; tel: 04-294 1020) archeological site. Two human skeletons estimated to be 3,500 years old are entwined in an after-life embrace in the grave, and make a poignant sight. **La Libertad**

the largest town on the peninsula, with over 110,000 inhabitants, is a busy port with a market and serves as the hub for bus services farther north.

To travel north along the coast toward Manglaralto, take the right-hand fork in the road from La Libertad. There are several fishing villages along this stretch of coast, where Guayaquileños have vacation homes, but there are no restaurants or hotels. **Punta Blanca** has an exquisite, isolated beach that attracts shell collectors. **Ayangue**, 45km (28 miles) farther north, has white, gently sloping beaches, and no big waves, making it ideal for children. **Valdivia ❸**, 5km (3 miles) up the coast, is the center of Ecuador's oldest culture, established around 3000 BC, and has a modest museum of local finds (although its best pieces are in museums in Quito and Guayaquil).

SUMMER BEACH MECCA

Salinas ❹ lies on a half-moon bay at the tip of the **Santa Elena peninsula**, a total of 150km (90 miles) from Guayaquil. It has pleasant beaches, high-rise hotels, good restaurants, a casino, and a yacht club, all of which lure throngs of swimmers and sun-worshippers. It is also the site of a naval base, and in the season (June–Sept) whale-watching trips are offered.

Lined with new hotels and resorts, and countless seafood restaurants, the stretch of road heading north from Salinas to Manta is known as the Ruta del Sol (the Sun Route). About 9km (5 miles) from Salinas is **Punta Carnero** with a beach several kilometers long.

THE DEEP SOUTH

To get to the next destination you must return to Guayaquil and take the road to Azogues, turning off after about 20km (12 miles) onto the Pan-American Highway toward Machala in **El Oro**, the southernmost of Ecuador's provinces, which owes its name to the rich gold deposits mined here during the 16th century. It is now Ecuador's leading shrimp- and banana-producing region, its fields blanketed by massive banana plantations, and the ripening fruit protected by plastic bags. **Machala ❺**, the main city, is known as the "Capital Bananera del Mundo (World Banana Capital). The International Banana and Agricultural Festival is held here every year in late September and draws large crowds. With over 288,000 inhabitants, Machala is Ecuador's sixth-largest city. Although not particularly attractive, it is a thriving city with some comfortable hotels and an international port, **Puerto Bolívar** (near the popular **El Coco** beach), from where around 1 million tonnes of banana and shrimp are exported annually. From its boat pier, motorized dugouts can be taken to the archipelago of **Jambelí**, an extraordinarily beautiful area that is little explored by visitors to the region, although it's popular with locals for weekend or day trips to the beach.

Other side trips are available from Machala, including a journey to the pleasant farming center of **Santa Rosa**,

La Libertad malecón.

Machala is the self-proclaimed "Capital Bananera del Mundo".

Shellfish and limes are two key ingredients for making ceviche.

on the Loja road, and then on to the beautiful old coffee-growing town of **Piñas** (take a left-hand turn about 20km/12 miles from Santa Rosa). The road is flanked by banana, coffee, and cacao plantations.

TOWARDS THE PERUVIAN BORDER

The road from Piñas continues to **Portovelo**, from where you can see the town of **Zaruma** ❻ stuck to the mountainside like a swallow's nest. This mining town of 9,000 inhabitants was founded during the colonial-era gold boom and has attracted renewed interest with the discovery of pre-Columbian ruins at Chepel, Trencillas, Payama, and Pocto. Although the ruins have not yet been fully excavated, they have led archeologists to conclude that the area was densely populated in pre-Inca times.

The town conserves some of its colonial past: a smattering of wooden houses, elaborately decorated balconies and church are well worth seeing. From the main plaza, there is a fantastic view of the surrounding valley. Nearby is the **Museo Municipal** (daily 8am–6pm), with an eclectic display of archeological artifacts, colonial art, and Zaruma's history. Interesting visits to abandoned gold and silver mines can be arranged through the tourist office, just off the main square, or with the local travel agent.

Heading southwest off the Loja road down some minor byways takes you to the little visited but fascinating Bosque Petrificado de Puyango (petrified forest; daily 8am–5pm). This tropical dry forest is full of fossilized tree trunks up to 120 million years old and hosts prolific birdlife too.

Southeast of Machala, 50km (31 miles) farther on, the route ends at **Huaquillas** ❼, right on the border with Peru. Most maps have been reprinted to show the new border along the Cordillera del Condor, which was agreed on in 1998. Since the signing of the peace treaty, relations between the two countries have been cordial. This border not only marks the beginning of Peruvian coastal desert, but is one of the continent's main cross-border commercial centers – although much of what is bought and sold is contraband.

Huaquillas is a busy, dusty, and unattractive town with stagnant water lying on its rutted roads and a reputation for pickpockets – who generally seek out tourists, sometimes returning stolen passports if a reward is proffered and no charges are pressed.

The main street of Huaquillas leads to the **International Bridge** into Peru and is lined with street vendors, money-changers, police and border officers, and people offering to carry luggage. Travelers must cross the bridge on foot unless they are driving their own car or on a direct bus to Tumbes, Peru. Note that this is one of the most notoriously dangerous border crossings in Peru, so be careful (more unfortunately, it is one of the principal crossings too).

⊘ MANGROVE RESERVE

Just off the Pan-American Highway, between Guayaquil and Machala, is the Reserva Ecológica Manglares Churute, which protects the largest remaining area of mangroves in the country. As well as safeguarding other endangered native vegetation – many species of trees and shrubs can adapt to saline conditions and be found in mangrove swamps – 70 percent of the reserve is occupied by ancient mangrove forests, growing up to 30 meters (99ft) high, and with spectacular tangles of roots. The mangrove ecosystem is important in protecting against erosion and offers a safe environment for young marine organisms. The reserve is also home to 270 species of bird, various species of monkey, three-toed sloths, ocelot, armadillo, and otters, plus vicious mosquitoes, so you'll need to come prepared. Off the coast dolphins, pelicans, flamingos, and fish eagles can often be seen, and the highly endangered coastal crocodile is also found here. The reserve's information center is located close to the highway 46km (28 miles) south of Guayaquil, and here park rangers can arrange boat trips that allow you to see the mangroves close-up, though advance booking is preferred with the Ministry of the Environment (tel: 04-2320391). There are also various good hiking trails in the park. Buses plying the highway between Guayaquil and Machala will usually drop off and pick up visitors at the park entrance.

Galápagos land iguana.

A blue-footed booby flying over Bartolomé Island.

Recently formed lava fields at Espinoza Point on Fernandina Island.

Bartolomé Island.

THE GALAPAGOS ISLANDS

For ever associated with Charles Darwin and giant tortoises, the Galápagos archipelago is without doubt one of Ecuador's greatest attractions.

Sea lion colony at Gardner Bay on the island of Española.

The Galápagos Islands had their fame guaranteed in 1835 when the 26-year-old naturalist Charles Darwin landed on one of their black volcanic coasts. No other place would prove to be quite as fertile for his work as the Galápagos. In 1859, Darwin published *On the Origin of Species*, making the creatures of the Galápagos a cornerstone of his theory of evolution by natural selection, and in one stroke overturning the whole train of Western scientific thought. Wildlife is still the main reason why visitors fly the 960km (570 miles) from mainland Ecuador to the Galápagos archipelago, which was designated a World Heritage Site in 1979 and subsequently a World Biosphere Reserve by UNESCO in 1985.

The islands are the ultimate nature reserve, where bizarre fauna exist totally free and fearless of people. Giant lumbering tortoises, blue-footed boobies, and equatorial penguins carry on their daily routine, indifferent to their audience of human visitors only feet away. Baby sea lions play with swimmers in the water and perform somersaults. Come as close as you like, and the marine iguanas sunning themselves on black rocks will just sit and stare blankly back.

Until recently, permanent human settlement had been kept to a minimum. In 1959, the Ecuadorian government declared the islands a national park and restricted human settlement to the small outposts already established. However, enforcement has been poor. Today the Charles Darwin Research Station on Santa Cruz, founded in 1964, and the Marine Research Reserve, cre-ated in 1986, have their hands full trying to restore the Galápagos

Colorful Sally Lightfoot crab.

ecosystem to that of the days before humans began to upset the delicate ecological balance. In December 2001, UNESCO also declared the Marine Reserve around the islands a World Natural Heritage Site in an attempt to stop illegal fishing and in recognition of the conservation issues it faces. But the sad fact is that however hard the conservationists, scientists, and author-ities work together, it seems the only way the islands and their inhabitants will be preserved unharmed is by severely reducing the numbers of tourist visits. Yet, numbers continue to rise at alarming rates – over 270,000 in 2022. It is therefore worth asking, before deciding whether to include these unique islands on your itinerary (which will probably add an extra $2000 or more onto your budget), whether you want to add to those tourist numbers.

Wooden boardwalk on Bartolomé Island.

THE GALÁPAGOS ISLANDS: DARWIN'S LABORATORY

The volcanic archipelago teems with rare bird and marine life that can be seen nowhere else in the world.

The "living laboratory" of the Galápagos archipelago is set in the Pacific Ocean some 960km (570 miles) west of the Ecuadorian coast. It consists of 13 major islands, six small ones, and 42 islets that are barely more than large rocks. All are of volcanic origin and spread over roughly 80,000 sq km (30,000 sq miles) of ocean. Their highest point is Volcán Wolf, at 1,707 meters (5,600ft) on Isabela, which, at 4,600 sq km (1,800 sq miles), is by far the largest island.

Visited at different times by explorers from around the world, most of the islands have two or even three different names. British pirates gave them solid, English names like Jervis and Chatham; the Spanish dubbed them from their standard stock of religious names, such as Santa Cruz and Santa Fé; while the Ecuadorian government in 1892 tried to clear up the confusion by giving the islands official titles, so now each usually has at least two names still in use.

AN ECCENTRIC CLIMATE

The Galápagos year can be divided into two seasons: the "hot" or "wet" season lasts from January to early May with an average temperature of 28°C (82°F), while the "cool" or "dry" season from May to December has an average of 18°C (64°F). The cooler period is also referred to as the *garua* season, named after the bank of clouds that generally settles over the islands at this time.

Altitude also has an effect on the climate: it can be hot and dry in the low-lying parts of the islands, and almost cold and humid in the highlands (above 22 meters/72ft). The winds, the marine currents, and the geological formation of the soil can alter the climatic conditions considerably generally speaking, the beaches with white sands are cooler on the feet, while stretches of black lava can reach temperatures of up to 50°C (120°F).

 Main attractions

Volcanic landscapes
Arid zone vegetation
Blue-footed boobies
Galápagos penguins
Galápagos flightless
 cormorants
Marine iguanas
Giant tortoises
Sea lions

Map on page 292

Charles Darwin.

Two masked boobies.

Two marine currents pass along the archipelago. The cold Humboldt Current originates in the south of Chile and brings the *garúa* with it in May. It has a moderating effect on the whole climate of the Galápagos, which should be more punishing than it actually is, given the islands' position directly on the equator.

The other current is the warm northern stream called El Niño, "the boy child," because it arrives around Christmas time, although its effects are rarely welcome: it brings heavy rains and – on occasion – floods and tidal waves to the Ecuadorian mainland, and also affects global weather patterns. With climate change, El Niño is occurring more frequently.

GEOLOGY OF THE ISLANDS

What we see of the Galápagos Islands is the tips of various gigantic "shield volcanoes" poking up some 10,000 meters (30,000ft) from the ocean floor and composed entirely of basalt. It is widely accepted that the archipelago was formed mainly by the accumulation of lava from successive underwater volcanic eruptions.

It appears that the earliest of the islands were formed roughly 4 to 5 million years ago, and that some of the western islands, such as Fernandina and Isabela, are only 1 million years old. The process of island formation is still going on as the Galápagos lie on the northern edge of the Nazca tectonic plate.

Over time, its gradual continental drift heads toward the southeast – precisely over one of the world's so-called "hotspots." These volatile, unmoving points beneath the tectonic plates build up heat over time to create a volcanic eruption that will rise above the ocean's surface.

The southeastern islands of the Galápagos were the first formed in this way, and the more recent, western islands still have active volcanoes; the highest of which, Volcán Wolf, erupted as recently as in January 2022 and Sierra Negra volcano on the island of Isabela began erupting again in 2018, triggering an evacuation. Fernandina's

La Cumbre, an active shield volcano, also erupted in 2020.

Relatively fresh basalt lava flows can still be seen around Isabela, often making fascinating patterns. They include pahoehoe or "ropy" lava – where the skin of the lava flow has been wrinkled by the heat of the still-flowing lava beneath. Another type is aa – pronounced "aah aah" – that looks like twisted black toffee.

ANIMAL COLONIZATION

The volcanic lumps that first burst forth from the Pacific 4 million years ago were utterly devoid of life. Yet now the islands are teeming with plants and animals. Somehow, they must have made their way from South America, and, since the islands were never connected to the continent, this fauna and flora must have crossed the 1,000km (620-mile) stretch of water.

Only certain types of creatures could survive the journey: this explains the present-day predominance of sea-birds (that could fly), sea mammals (that could swim) and reptiles (that apparently floated across from the American coast on accidentally formed vegetation rafts and, unlike amphibians and land mammals, could survive for long periods without food or water). Meanwhile, plant seeds and insects could have come across stuck to birds' wings or in animals' stomach contents. Once they had landed on the bleak islands, only certain animals could survive. Those that did found that their traditional predators had been left behind on the South American coast. The animals' lack of timidity probably stems from this general absence of predators; a fact that also explains why recently introduced domestic goats and pigs are able to wreak havoc so easily.

Charles Darwin was the first to observe how each arriving species had adapted over time in order to thrive and survive. The most famous case is "Darwin's finches," the 13 similar species of finches that probably descended from one original species. Each modern species has differences that suit its particular environment: some have short, thick beaks so that they can split

Prickly pear cacti, Rábida. Island.

Sullivan Bay and Pinnacle Rock, Bartolomé Island.

seeds; others have long, thin bills to catch insects.

Many years after his visit to the Galápagos, Darwin attributed the process to natural selection. After their arrival on the Galápagos, each finch produced offspring that were imperceptibly different from the parent. In this strange new environment, some chicks were better able to survive. They were the ones that reached maturity and produced young, passing on new genetic traits to their offspring. Over thousands of generations, some traits were thus "selected" as fitting the finches' new home, until the differences between the new creature and the original qualified it to be renamed as a new species.

Darwin propounded this theory in his classic work *On the Origin of Species*. It became particularly controversial when applied to humans, not only suggesting that the animal kingdom did not spring ready-made from the hand of God, but that humans are, in many respects, no different from other forms of animal life.

Blue-footed boobies.

HUMAN HISTORY

While it is possible that there was settlement by Manteño people and that the Inca Tupac Yupanqui organized an expedition to the Galápagos during his rule in the 1400s, most historians accept that the islands were first discovered by accident in 1535 by the Spanish cleric Fray Tomás de Berlanga, Bishop of Panama. On the way to Peru, his boat was becalmed and drifted to the Galápagos. The cleric landed in search of water but "found nothing but seals and tortoises that each could carry a man on top of itself" and birds "so silly that they do not know to flee." He dubbed the islands "Las Encantadas," the Enchanted Isles, because they tricked his navigator's eyes and seemed to appear and disappear in clouds of mist.

For the next two centuries, the islands, far from the Spanish trade routes, were a hideaway for Dutch and English buccaneers. They began the practice of killing large numbers of giant tortoises for their meat, having found that the creatures could be stacked upside down in their ships' holds without food and water for over a year and still be turned into fine soup. This practice was taken up most devastatingly by 19th-century whalers. Between 1811 and 1844 there were said to be more than 700 whaling ships in the Pacific, and many of them called in on the Galápagos Islands to stock up on tortoise meat.

The first permanent colonist on the Galápagos was an Irishman named Patrick Watkins, who arrived at Floreana in 1812. His story is included in a series of sketches called *The Encantadas* by Herman Melville. Melville's portrait of the islands was not a flattering one: "Take five and twenty heaps of cinders dumped here and there in an outside lot; imagine some of them magnified into mountains, and the vacant lot the sea; and you will have a fit idea of the general aspect of the Encantadas."

When the Ecuadorian government claimed the islands in 1832, Floreana was given as a reward for bravery to a local Creole officer. He brought 80 people from the mainland and kept them enslaved using giant dogs. But the so-called "Dog King of Charles Island" was forced to flee when the enslaved population rebelled. A brutal penal colony was set up on San Cristóbal in the 1880s, with the prisoners worked hard, flogged mercilessly, and marooned on desert islands to die slowly of thirst as punishment for misdemeanors.

When the United States entered World War II, it chose the Galápagos as a defense base against attacks on the Panama Canal. An airstrip was built on Baltra Island that is still in use today. In 1958, the last convict colony was closed, and in the 1960s regular passenger flights began to operate. Since then, tourism has been ever-increasing. In September 1995, the islands' tourist trade was brought to a halt when locals, led by a Galápagos

legislator, Eduardo Véliz, seized San Cristóbal airport, the National Park office and the Charles Darwin Center, demanding more control of and benefits from tourism. Some kind of peace was secured, but only after two weeks of fierce protesting, complete suspension of all visits, and intense negotiations in Quito.

In 2012 the world's first ecological airport was built on the island of Baltra using recycled steel oil pipes, and metal and wood from the old Seymour Airport building. The Galápagos Ecological Airport is powered by renewable energies (35 percent solar and 65 percent wind).

CONCERN FOR CONSERVATION

Scientists have been observing the Galápagos periodically ever since Darwin's work in the mid-19th century. In the 20th century, it became obvious that many of the animals introduced by humans had turned feral and were devastating the natural ecology of the islands. Everything from goats to pigs,

Fact

Charles Darwin (1809–82) visited the Galápagos Islands from September 15 to October 20, 1835 as a young naturalist on board The Beagle. Although he never set foot on the Ecuadorian mainland, on his visits to Chatham, Charles, Albermarle, and James Islands he noted the similarity of the finches to those he had seen earlier in Chile. His interest lay mainly in researching the birds, plants, and geology of the island, while the tortoises provided fresh meat for the onward journey to Tahiti.

Sierra Negra, Isabela Island.

Lava cactus is unique
to the Galápagos
Islands.

Snapping sea lions.

rats, dogs, and cats were breeding furiously. They were taking other animals' food, devouring turtle eggs and baby land iguanas, eroding the soil, and destroying the plants.

In 1930 an expedition led by Gifford Pinchot from the USA suggested creating a wildlife sanctuary in the archipelago. Five years later, laws were passed to protect the fauna of the islands, but it was not until 1959 that the Galápagos were declared a national park, with the aim of protecting the islands and encouraging scientific research.

Also created in 1959 was the Charles Darwin Foundation for the Galápagos Islands, an international organization under the auspices of UNESCO and the International Union for the Conservation of Nature. In 1964 the foundation established the Charles Darwin Research Station, with scientific, educational, and protective objectives. The scientific program provides assistance for experts and biology students who visit the islands. The educational program is aimed at improving environmental awareness, particularly among students. And the protective program attempts to overcome the negative effects of introduced animals, and prevent other disasters caused by humans.

Various protective programs have been undertaken in cooperation with the national park administration. So far, they have been successful in eliminating black rats on Bartolomé and wild goats on Santa Fé, Española (Hood), and Rábida. Measures have been taken to control dogs, which attack young tortoises and land iguanas, as well as to limit the spread of the invasive hill raspberry (Rubus niveus), whose berries are poisonous.

A law has been passed restricting human colonization. Only residents and their children are allowed to live permanently in the Galápagos Islands. This has slowed the tide, but illegal migration continues as impoverished fisherfolk seek richer tourist pickings in Galápagos. The islands' resident population has grown from around 15,000 in the 1980s to an estimated 30,000 in 2023. In 2011, restrictions

⊘ ECONOMIC BOOM

Booming tourism, the dominant industry on the islands, has helped the Galápagos become one of the world's fastest-growing economies. Increasing numbers of visitors has drawn in settlers from mainland Ecuador and neighboring Colombia and Peru. The impact of the influx has devastating and imperils the islands' status as a UNESCO World Heritage Site. New residents have taken up agriculture and fishing, pressuring the islands' flora and fauna along with imported goats, cats, dogs, and rats.

Many Galapagueños have little or no interest in the islands' unique environment, preferring to make a profit and hoping the islands will one day become mostly a beach resort destination, with all the money-making opportunities that would offer.

were also placed on cruise ship visitors, with stays limited to four nights per passenger per ship. Critics of this scheme, however, say that this is just a way of balancing numbers and that big-money cruise tourism will not be reduced but merely distributed over more islands, with ports at Tagus Grove and Santa Fé now equipped to receive larger boats, and the islands of Española, Genovesa, and Fernandina now permitting smaller vessels.

TOURISM TAKES OFF

Before the 1960s, a visit to the Galápagos involved a long and uncomfortable sea voyage on the old ship *Cristóbal Carrier*, which ran once a month from Guayaquil to the archipelago. Travel between the islands was often nearly impossible. Not surprisingly, most visitors were wealthy and could afford their own yachts and cruise the islands at leisure. All this changed when regularly scheduled air transportation was made available to the public, and passenger ships run by Ecuadorian tourist agencies started to make the journey.

In 1970, an estimated 4,500 tourists arrived; in 1978 the figure was 12,000; in 1990, it was 66,000; and today, more than 170,000 visitors are estimated to come to the islands annually. Although tourism is tightly controlled (all visitors must pre-register via www.gobiernogalapagos.gob.ec or at the airport, see page 291), the numbers are too high, and more must be done to preserve the islands. There are some 56 visitor sites and 62 marine sites where tourists are allowed outside of towns, and then only in the company of trained guides. Trails are marked with small stakes painted in white to stop you crushing plants and animals underfoot, and also to keep crowds away from crater borders, where serious erosion can occur. (See page 294 for guidelines on responsible tourism in the islands).

A RANGE OF PLANT LIFE

Every island in the Galápagos is unique. Many are virtual deserts. Others, more mountainous, are relatively lush. Thanks to the icy Humboldt Current, the islands are not as hot as you

⊘ Fact

About 20 percent of locals work in agriculture, ranging from ranching to growing of bananas, sugar-cane, and coffee. Along with fishing, most of this activity is highly problematic due to the uneven terrain and a ban on using fertilizers and pesticides. In spite of the challenging conditions, Hacienda El Cafetal on San Cristóbal produces 100 percent organic coffee and a nearby wind farm produces clean electricity, reducing demand for diesel fuel.

Visitors traveling in a Zodiac boat view Darwin's Arch.

*Six species of opuntia
(prickly pear) cacti are
endemic to the
Galápagos.*

would expect, but the sun can still be punishing, and few can stand more than a few hours hiking steep trails. Micro-climates abound. There are six different vegetation zones on the Galápagos, beginning with the shoreline and ending with the highlands. The low islands are the driest, as clouds pass by here without discharging. Meanwhile, the mountainous islands often block clouds, which turn into fog, drizzle, or rain showers and help flora to thrive.

The shoreline is populated by plants that can tolerate high levels of salt, such as mangrove, saltbush, myrtle, and other minor aquatic plants. Next comes the arid zone, characterized by thorny plants with small flowers: different types of cactus (particularly *opuntia* and *cereus*), brushwood *(matorrales)*, the ghostly-looking *palos santos*, carob trees *(algarrobos)*, and lichens *(líquenes)*. In the transition zone, perennial herbs and smaller shrubs are dominant, among them the *matazarnos* and the pega pega *(Pisonia floribunda)*.

The high humid area – called scalesia after the zone's dominant tree,

typically covered with bromeliads, ferns, and orchids – extends between 200 and 500 meters (650 and 1,650ft) above sea level. Several typical plants are found in this zone: locust and guava trees, *passiflora*, and fungus. Above 500 meters (1,650ft) is the miconia zone, which is also the main area used for cultivation and pasture on the inhabited islands, where coffee, vegetables, oranges, and pineapples are planted. In the highest zone, called fern-sedge, grow mainly ferns and grasses, including the giant Galápagos fern tree, which can sometimes reach 3 meters (10ft) in height. Of around 1,400 plant species so far recorded on the islands, around 30 percent are endemic.

FASCINATING WILDLIFE

Fifty-eight resident bird species have been recorded here, of which 28 are endemic. The remainder are either found in other parts of the world or are migratory, spending some part of the year living or breeding away from the islands. They can be classified into seabirds and land birds: among the latter are the famous Darwin's finches, mockingbirds (distinguished by their gray and brown streaks), the Galápagos dove, and the endemic Galápagos hawk.

Seabirds tend to be more impressive for non-naturalist visitors. The world's entire population of yellow-billed, waved albatrosses (15,000 pairs) nest on the single island of Española (Hood). These magnificent creatures are famous for their extraordinary courtship displays, dancing about and "fencing" with their beaks – literally, standing face to face and clicking their beaks together at a great rate.

One of the most common birds is the blue-footed booby, which is not endemic. They are an unforgettable sight, as their feet really are a bold striking blue. They were named "boobies" after the Spanish word *bobo* (dunce) by early sailors, who were amazed that the birds would not fly

away when men approached. The boobies have a somewhat comical courtship ritual: they "dance" toward one another, plodding about with blue feet working up and down, "skypoint" (pushing their wings up to the heavens) and give one another twigs as presents. They are often seen diving into the water from heights of 20 meters (65ft) to catch fish.

Another common seabird is the magnificent frigate bird. They can look quite sinister when hovering overhead, and are not above preying on other birds' young. The males' puffed scarlet chest sack (gular sac) makes an impressive sight when they are mating. With only 300–400 pairs still alive, the Galápagos lava gull is said to be the rarest bird species on earth. The Galápagos also have the world's only two flightless seabirds: the Galápagos penguin and the flightless cormorant.

The penguin is a big favorite on the islands, clumsily waddling about on land but speeding like a bullet under the waves. They are the most northerly penguin species, probably first coming up from the south with the icy Humboldt Current. They are mostly found on Isabela and Fernandina, although they can also easily be seen on Bartolomé. Like the penguin, the endemic flightless cormorant makes an entertaining sight – if you are lucky enough to spot one, since there are only around 1000 breeding pairs in existence – on the remote, far coasts of Isabela and Fernandina. The flightless cormorant has no enemies to fear, so does not suffer from its inability to fly – it scampers along flapping what look like the shreds of lost wings. It is, however, a good diver and can easily catch the fish it needs for its food.

PREHISTORIC CREATURES

It was Darwin who called the Galápagos "a paradise for reptiles." Most common are the endemic black marine iguanas, often found sunning themselves on cliffs and shorelines. Darwin himself found their dragon-like appearance rather horrifying: he called them "imps of darkness... of a dirty black color, stupid and sluggish in [their] movements." They are probably relatives of a land-going reptile species that died out 100 million years ago. But these creatures have adapted themselves to the ocean to feed on seaweed, often diving to 12-meter (40ft) depths. They have developed unusual glands connected to their breathing systems that accumulate the excess of salt in their bodies. Every so often the salt is snorted out through the nose; not an attractive sight. While they are usually black, the males change color during mating to orange, red, and blue.

The rarer-to-spot land iguanas are yellow in color and often larger than their seagoing relatives. They are one of the species that was hardest hit by the animals introduced by humans. Tiny lava lizards can be found on all the Galápagos Islands, frequently seen doing somewhat absurd "push-ups" on pathways, which is a sign that they

Endemic Galápagos penguins.

are marking out their territory against intruders.

SLOW-MOVING GIANTS

The most famous of the Galápagos reptiles is the giant tortoise. Countless thousands were killed for their flesh by whalers during the 18th and 19th centuries, and now only an estimated 20,000 remain. There were 14 subspecies of giant tortoise here – distinguished most easily by the different shell shapes – but three are now extinct (the last example of one species was found at the turn of the 20th century by an expedition from a San Francisco museum: the scientists promptly dispatched the creature in order to study its shell).

The giant tortoise is one of the most ancient of reptiles, but also among the rarest – it exists only here, on the island of Aldabra in the Indian Ocean, and on Fregate Island in the Seychelles. Weighing up to 250kg (550lb), it has two types of shell: the dome-shaped type is found in humid environments such as Santa Cruz, where vegetation is low and abundant; this type of tortoise has a short neck and short legs. The second type has a shell that resembles a horse's harness and lives on islands with uneven soil and no low grass, such as Española (Hood). These tortoises are more agile (relatively speaking) and have long legs and necks in order to feed themselves. The shell indentation allows them to protrude their necks further.

Legend has it that these tortoises can live for centuries. One, given to the Queen of Tonga by Captain Cook in the 1770s, is said to have survived until 1966, but there is no certain evidence for them living for more than 100 years.

Saving these magnificent creatures has been a major task of the Charles Darwin Research Station: a program of breeding seems to be successful. On Española, only 10 males and two females of a subspecies were still alive until, after years of breeding in captivity, some 100 healthy specimens were returned to the island. But the tortoise population is still at risk: on Santa Cruz a mysterious disease killed several of them in 1996, and so visitors were banned for a while.

The last survivor of the subspecies from the island of Pinta, who went by the name of Lonesome George, sadly died in 2012, thus ending the species. He was discovered on the island of Pinta in 1971, during a period of goat removal, and was transferred to the captive breeding program at the Charles Darwin Research Station soon after. He was estimated to be over 100 years old. Despite a $10,000 reward for a female of the species, no mate was found for him. Attempts were made to interbreed George with similar species, but to no avail. Lonesome George now stands as a symbol of the importance of conservation on the Galápagos Islands and the rest of the world. Easier to spot in the wild is the Pacific green sea turtle, which snorkelers can often observe underwater.

A mess of Galápagos marine iguanas on Santiago Island.

PLAYFUL SEA LIONS AND DOLPHINS

There are fewer land mammals than there are birds or reptiles in the Galápagos because they were much less likely to survive the journey across from coastal South America. Storms may have blown the hoary bat to the Galápagos, while the rice rat may have made it across on a vegetation raft. Sea mammals, however, simply followed the currents to the islands, and these days they make up some of the Galápagos' most popular creatures with visitors.

Topping the list is the sea lion. The young are incredibly cute and playful; they will swim about snorkelers and tease them, even staring into your goggles and pretending to charge you before turning away. The *machos*, or older males, do, however, stake out their territory very jealously. They can turn aggressive and have been known to bite swimmers, so a degree of caution should be used in their presence (guides will know which areas are the preserve of the bull lions).

Fur seals have more hair than sea lions, and are smaller and very shy: they prefer to live in colonies, on distant cliffs. Bottle-nosed dolphins are often seen surfing the bow spray of boats, while no fewer than seven whale species have been sighted at or near the Galápagos archipelago, although getting a close look at them is a fairly unlikely prospect.

AN UNDERWATER WORLD

Under the waves, snorkelers will be constantly surrounded by many of the 550 species of fish recorded in the Galápagos, and more are being documented every year. In 2012, the previously-unknown bottom-dwelling catshark was discovered off the islands: more evidence science still has so much to learn about the fauna here.

Schools of brightly colored tropical fish pass over the sea floor and around rocks, making a spellbinding sight. Hammerhead and white-tipped Galápagos sharks can also be seen in the waters around the islands, but they are not dangerous. The grace of these creatures is particularly impressive. Since records began in 1854, there have only been eight shark attacks, and none fatal.

Keep an eye out for the different types of rays that glide majestically along the ocean floor. The giant manta ray can sometimes be spotted leaping out of the sea and landing with a loud slap on the waves. None of the rays are dangerous except for the stingray – on some beaches they lie in shallow water beneath a layer of sand, and can give quite a sting if trodden on. When you enter the water, it's worth giving the sand a shuffle with your feet to scare off any basking rays.

Invertebrates such as jellyfish, sponges, mollusks, and crabs, proliferate. The most commonly seen of these is the bright yellow-and-orange Sally Lightfoot crab, which can be found on almost every rock in the Galápagos.

> ### ⊘ Quote
>
> "The really surprising fact in this case of the Galápagos Archipelago… is that the new species formed in the separate islands have not quickly spread to the other islands. But the islands, though in sight of each other, are separated by deep arms of the sea, in most cases wider than the British Channel, and there is no reason to suppose that they have at any former period been continuously united.
>
> On the Origin of Species, Charles Darwin"

The thirteen species of Galápagos giant tortoise are the world's largest living tortoises.

📷 BIRDS OF THE GALÁPAGOS

From the marbled godwit to the black-necked stilt, the birdlife on the Galápagos Islands, which taught us about evolution, is still rich, rare, and rewarding.

Where else in the world will birds practically come out to greet you? Life without predators has made the birds of the Galápagos fearless, which means that many of them are easy to spot. There are 56 native resident species, of which 28 are endemic, as well as many migratory birds. The seabirds are the most frequently seen: in the dry coastal areas you are likely to spot three species of the booby family, the waved albatross – found nowhere in the world except on the Galápagos island of Española (plus a few on Isla de la Plata), which supports a nesting colony of 17,000 pairs – and the world's only flightless seabirds, the Galápagos penguin and the flightless cormorant. The best time for bird-watching is in winter (October to February) when most migrants are visiting, and birds are reproducing. Then, a serious ornithologist might see 50 species in a week, and even a dilettante should be able to spot two dozen.

There are dangers in paradise, however: the introduction of mainland animals brought over by economic migrants to the islands has been disastrous. Cats and rats prey on the birds, while goats destroy the birds' habitats. Farming on the inhabited islands also destroys habitats (agriculture supports 20 percent of the locals), and a natural phenomenon, the El Niño current, brings mosquito-carried disease and disrupts the food chain.

The magnificent frigate bird (Fregata magnificens) and close relation the great frigate bird, can be seen near the coasts of many islands. The male is remarkable for the red gular pouch which puffs out in the mating season.

The female Galápagos hawk (Buteo galapagoensis) is larger than the male. Males are monogamous but females will mate with up to seven males per season to ensure that breeding will be successful.

Unlike much of the other local birdlife, the greater flamingo – mostly found on Floreana, Isabela, and Rábida islands – is quite shy.

One of Darwin's finches.

The secret of Darwin's finches

The finches of the Galápagos were vitally important in the development of Charles Darwin's ideas about evolution and the formation of species. When he set off on his voyage around the world on HMS *Beagle* (1831–6), he believed, like most people of his time, in the fixity of species. But on the Galápagos he observed that 13 different species of the finch had evolved from a single ancestral group, and it was this (together with his observations of the islands' tortoises) which led to his contention that species could evolve over time, with those most suited to their natural environment surviving and passing on their characteristics to the next generation.

The main differences he noted between the finches was the size and shape of their beaks, leading him to conclude that the birds which survived were those whose beaks enabled them to eat the available food.

The 13 species of finch are divided into two groups: ground finches and tree finches, of which the mangrove finch, found only in the swamps of Isabela Island, is the rarest. You are unlikely to see all of them on a short visit, but it's a challenge to see how many you can spot.

e vermillion flycatcher (Pyrocephalus rubinus) has a h-pitched, musical song and builds a distinctive cup-ped nest.

blue-footed booby lays two or three eggs and both of parents share the task of incubating them. Once they re become independent, the young birds leave the islands do not return to breed until some three years later.

Galápagos brown pelicans are found around the harbors of most islands.

A pair of blue-footed boobies.

A typical coastal Galápagos scene with marine iguana, black volcanic rocks, prickly pear cactus, and turquoise sea.

VISITING THE ISLANDS

Uncontrolled, tourism could destroy this Pacific paradise. The hundreds of thousands of visitors who follow in Darwin's footsteps must follow strict rules if the wildlife of the archipelago is to survive.

There are no direct international flights to Galápagos; most foreign travelers arrive by air via Quito or Guayaquil. LATAM, Avianca and Equair operate daily flights from Quito and Guayaquil. Equair also operates flights from Manta. Most flights land at Baltra, from where a bus and ferry will take you across to Puerto Ayora on Santa Cruz. The other commercial airport is on San Cristóbal while Isabela only receives light aircraft. On arrival, you must have your passport ready, and sufficient cash to pay the entrance tax ($100 for adults, $50 for children) and purchase a Transit Control Card ($20); without these essentials, you will not be able to enter the islands.

Many travelers will have pre-arranged their cruise around the islands on one of the larger luxury ships. Two of the best on offer are the *Silver Origin*, a liner operated by Silversea (www.silversea.com), which leaves from Baltra; and the *Santa Cruz II*, run by Metropolitan Touring (www.metropolitan-touring.com), which leaves from San Cristóbal. Both offer all the comforts of a five-star hotel, with excellent food, swimming pools, evening slide shows, and the like. They also have English-speaking guides who are all qualified naturalists. Although the capacity of these ships is 90 people, they operate with groups of no more than around 12 per guide, landing

A scuba diver approaches a whale shark.

them by small dinghies called *pangas* for twice-daily excursions. The large boats have the advantage of covering a lot of territory by night, easily reaching the more remote islands without unduly rough passages. Smaller luxury boats carrying 16–20 passengers, such as the *Beluga* run by Enchanted Expeditions (www.enchantedexpeditions.com), offer a more intimate experience.

Independent and budget travelers may organize their own cruise on one of the dozens of smaller boats on the islands. This can be arranged in Quito

Main attractions
Charles Darwin Research Station
Tortoise Reserve
Plaza Sur
Isla Seymour
Puerto Egas
Cerro Bartolomé
Tagus Cove

Map on page 292

or Guayaquil, but is cheapest when done in Puerto Ayora on Santa Cruz, though a few small boats also operate from San Cristóbal. Take your time, meet up with other like-minded travelers, find a captain, and agree a price. This usually takes two or three days, but if you have more time than money it's worth doing. The main advantage of organizing your own trip is flexibility: you can choose which islands you want to visit, for how long, and when. However, the guides often do not speak English, may be of variable quality, and rough weather conditions can make night journeys on these boats difficult for those with delicate stomachs. It is also possible to travel between the three airports by light place (www.galapagosinterislandflights).

A GUIDE TO THE VISITOR SITES

The only places where boats may land on the islands are at the 60+ designated terrestrial visitor sites, and even then, visitors must be accompanied by a guide. Some of the more fragile sites are further restricted so that only small groups are allowed to visit, or limits are imposed on the numbers each month. The landing by *panga* is either wet or dry; your guide will tell you which to expect. Wet landings simply mean that you leap into the water up to your ankles (sometimes up to your knees), so keep your shoes aside; dry landings are at natural or constructed jetties, where you should keep your shoes on.

The most densely populated island in the Galápagos, as well as its second-largest (at 986 sq km/380 sq miles), is **Santa Cruz ①**. Most tours start here at the township of **Puerto Ayora**, and even those that begin at San Cristóbal call here to visit the **Charles Darwin Research Station ②**.

Puerto Ayora has grown in size and population in recent years. The wide, turquoise **Academy Bay** is full of small boats and makes a picturesque sight, while the town docks are usually crowded with small children running, swimming, and playing with sea lions. At night, especially at weekends and holiday periods, the music will

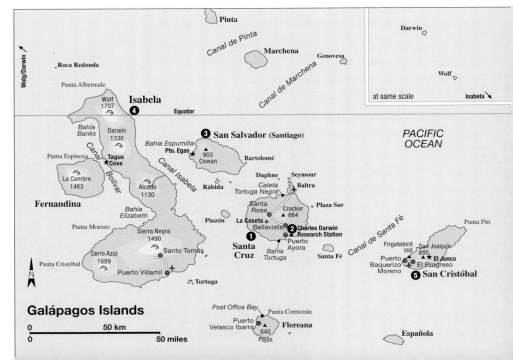

Galápagos Islands

be pounding in the bars on the main strip, which is something to bear in mind when choosing where to stay. Across the bay, on a secluded cove, the award-winning, ecologically-minded Finch Bay (www.finchbayhotel.com) is a top luxury choice.

The town's main attraction is the research station. This is the classic place to have your photo taken with one of the giant tortoises: mature specimens of several subspecies are kept in pens here. Your compulsory guide, who will be allocated at the entrance, will allow you to approach to up to the permitted two meters from these amazing creatures. The station has a tortoise breeding house, where the young can be seen, and a small museum and information center.

There are several trails from Puerto Ayora that are worth exploring. Some 7km (4 miles) westward is **Bahía Tortuga** (Turtle Bay), with fine white sand and waters rich in lobsters. You can go there to swim and relax without a guide, although the fish and animals are still protected. The highland interior of Santa Cruz, in the national park, offers several attractions: the lava tubes are long underground tunnels made when lava solidified on the surface of a flow but kept going underneath. Climbing **Cerro Crocker**, an 860-meter (2,800ft) high hill, shows the range of vegetation zones on the island. And a day excursion can be made to the Chato **Tortoise Reserve**, which is one of the few places to see giant tortoises in the wild; organize your trip beforehand, either with a tour guide from town, or independently: you can rent a bike, or take a taxi or bus then tackle the trails (with a guide) to see these creatures wallowing in the mud.

THE CENTRAL ISLANDS

The islands close to Santa Cruz are the most visited, although not necessarily the most interesting for naturalists. Day trips are run by various agencies from Puerto Ayora: this means a lot of traveling time on the water if you want to visit more than one. It is more fun and – if properly organized – only slightly more expensive to visit several on your own cruise.

The trail to Punta Pitt at the eastern end of San Cristóbal.

PRESERVING THE ISLANDS

Tourism is a mixed blessing for the Galápagos: follow these guidelines to ensure that you minimise your impact.

No natural object – plant, animal, shell, bone, stone, or scrap of wood – should be removed or disturbed. It is illegal and alters the islands' ecological conditions.

Be careful not to transport any live material to the islands, or from island to island. Before leaving the boat, check your shoe soles for dried mud, as it may contain plant seeds and animal spores. Inadvertent transport of these materials represents a special danger to the Galápagos: each island has its own unique fauna and flora, and introduced plants and animals can quickly destroy them. Obviously no other animals or plants should be brought to the islands.

For the same reason, do not take any food to the uninhabited islands. Along with the food may come insects or other organisms that might threaten the fragile island ecosystems. Fresh fruits and vegetables are especially dangerous: a dropped orange pip, for example, may become a tree.

Animals may not be touched or handled. Young animals that have been handled may be rejected by their mothers because of their smell. They soon die as a result.

Passion flower in bloom, Santa Cruz Island.

Animals may not be fed. Not only can it be dangerous but in the long run it can destroy the animals' social structure and affect their reproduction.

Do not startle or chase any animal from its resting or nesting spot. Exercise extreme caution among the breeding colonies of seabirds. These birds will fly from their nests if they are startled, often knocking the egg or chick to the ground or leaving it exposed to the sun. (A recently hatched booby chick will die in 20 to 30 minutes if it is exposed to the sun; frigate birds will also eat any unguarded chick.)

Do not leave the designated visiting sites. Where trails to points of interest are marked with wooden stakes, you should remain within the stakes.

Litter of all types must be kept off the islands. Disposal at sea must be limited to certain types of garbage which can be thrown overboard in selected areas. Keep all rubbish in a bag or pocket, to be disposed of on your boat. The crew of your vessel is responsible to the national park for proper trash disposal. Never throw anything overboard.

Do not buy souvenirs or objects made from plants or animals. Black coral is now endangered by islanders' carvings. If anyone offers you any of these souvenirs, please advise the national park. Camping anywhere within the Galápagos without a permit is against the law. Camping is permitted only in certain sites designated by the national park. Contact any of the national park offices to get a camping permit.

All groups visiting the national park must be accompanied by an approved, qualified guide. The visitor must follow the guide's instructions, while the guide must ensure compliance with the national park regulations.

Notify the national park service if you see any serious damage being done. You may be a decisive factor in the preservation of the islands. The head office is a 10-minute walk east of the main town of Puerto Ayora (tel: 05-252 6189; Mon–Fri 7am–12.15pm and 1.45–4.30pm), but there are also offices on San Cristóbal (Puerto Baquerizo Moreno; tel: 05-252 0497), Floreana (Puerto Velasco Ibarra; tel: 05-252 4869), and Isabela (Puerto Villamil; tel: 05-252 9178). Also use the very good Galápagos Conservancy website (www.galapagos.org) for planning an environmentally-conscious trip.

Only 24km (15 miles) from Puerto Ayora is **Isla Santa Fé** (also known as Barrington). A compulsory wet landing is the start of a short trail into a dry landscape crowded with opuntia cacti. Santa Fé is one of the best places to see the shy land iguana, but the steep path is one of the more difficult on the Galápagos, so a swim from the beach near the landing site comes as a welcome relief.

On the northeastern coast of Santa Cruz is the tiny island of **Plaza Sur**. Only 13 hectares (32 acres) in area, its coast is so crowded with sea lions that everyone on the *panga* needs to clap and shout to clear a landing space. Swimming is not encouraged here, since the *macho* or bull sea lions are particularly aggressive. Plaza Sur is unusually crowded with animal life; there are plenty of land iguanas and the impressive black cliffs are populated with seabirds, as well as the rare Galápagos hawk. Nearby is a "convalescent home" for bachelor *macho* sea lions: after losing a brawl over territory, they come here to recuperate before returning to the fray.

Isla Seymour is separated from the larger island of **Baltra** by a channel. Baltra has little to interest a visitor, whereas Seymour is one of the Galápagos' best breeding grounds for seabirds: blue-footed boobies are so common that visitors have to be careful not to step on any of the nests that may have been built on the trails.

The strange, block-shaped island of **Daphne** is 10km (6 miles) away. Access is restricted to only a few boats a month. Landing here is difficult, with a leap onto nearly sheer rocks that becomes somewhat hair-raising in rough weather. But it is worth the effort: at the end of a trail, a large crater is dotted with hundreds of blue-footed booby nests, making a decidedly surreal sight.

VOLCANIC ROCK AND IGUANAS

One of the larger islands, relatively close to Santa Cruz, is known as either **Santiago** or **James**, although its official title is **San Salvador ❸**. It has a number of landing sites, by far the most popular being **Puerto Egas** on the west coast.

Dried lava patterns.

Sea lions provide an underwater photo opportunity.

This is one of the best places to see hundreds of marine iguanas sunning themselves on black volcanic rocks, while fur seals can be spotted swimming nearby. The **Sugarloaf Volcano** dominates the horizon here. Swimming is good at Espumilla Beach and Buccaneer Cove. If you are in a small group, try snorkeling at the **fur seals' grotto**. You can swim with these characters for hours through the pools that have formed under natural stone archways.

Sitting off the east coast of San Salvador, the small 120-hectare (300-acre) island of **Bartolomé** is one of the most photographed in the Galápagos. The centerpiece of a visit is the steep climb up **Cerro Bartolomé**: the view is spectacular, looking over lunar fields of dried lava, craters, and out over the jutting, honeycombed **Pinnacle Rock**. The heat is also quite intense, so after working up a sweat, transfer to the second landing site, one of the most pleasant beaches on the islands. The snorkeling is excellent, especially around Pinnacle Rock itself: apart from the tropical fish moving in formation, you have a chance of spotting teams of penguins hunting underwater. A path leads over to the other side of the island, where dozens of reef sharks patrol only meters from the edge of the water.

Charles Darwin called marine iguanas "imps of darkness."

South of San Salvador is the island of **Rábida** (Jervis), which has a dark-red sand beach (due to its high iron-oxide content) along which lounge hundreds of bloated sea lions. Indolent and clumsy on land, they are surprisingly energetic in the water: this is a great place to observe the baby sea lions.

A path into the interior of the island passes a marshy lake full of bright pink flamingos (the pinker the flamingo, the healthier it is; the feather color comes from the diet of shrimps they sieve through their beaks). In the trees by the beach are a large number of brown pelicans.

Another unusual point on Rábida that is well worth visiting is **Caleta Tortuga Negra** (Black Turtle Cove). This tidal lagoon leads into a maze of mangroves: it can be visited only by *panga*, cutting the motor and paddling quietly through the natural tunnels made by trees. The brackish waters of the area are full of white-tipped sharks and mustard rays. But it is most famous as a mating spot for the green Pacific turtles. With luck, you can spot the two heads coming up for air during copulation, which lasts for many hours.

When cruising the south coast of San Salvador, keep an eye out for **Sombrero Chino**, literally "Chinese Hat," named for the island's sweeping conical shape. One of the more recent islands, it has a 400-meter (1,300ft) long path around its circumference, along which sea lions relax in abandonment.

THE WESTERN ISLANDS

Some 120km (75 miles) in length and shaped like a seahorse, **Isabela ❹** is the largest of the Galápagos Islands. It is still recovering from fires that blazed across the island in 1994. The fires were eventually extinguished, but not

without a severe impact on vegetation. One of the island's main attractions, the giant tortoises, were rescued by helicopter and taken to the other side of the island to the safety of a breeding center. Isabela is one of the islands that still has volcanic activity, and there are five cones still visible: **Wolf** at 1,707 meters (5,395ft) – which most recently erupted in 2022; **Alcedo** at 1,130 meters (3,600ft); **Sierra Negra** (also called Santo Tomás) at 1,490 meters (4,885ft); **Cerro Azul** at 1,689 meters (5,540ft), and **Darwin** at 1,330 meters (4,200ft).

Some 3,000 people live on Isabela, mostly in and around **Puerto Villamil** on the south coast. Cruise ships rarely visit since it is difficult to enter the bay, especially when the sea is rough. It does, however, have a fine sandy beach and several basic hotels and restaurants. About 18km (11 miles) away is the village of **Santo Tomás** and the Muro de las Lágrimas (Wall of Tears) built of lava stone in the convict colony that was closed in 1959. The crater Santo Tomás has a diameter of 10km (6 miles), making it the second-largest in the world, while Alcedo has a still-steaming fumarole and scores of giant tortoises living at its rim. The slopes of Wolf Volcano are the only place to spot the endemic and critically endangered pink land iguana.

Most of Isabela's visitor sites are on the west side of the island. Probably the most popular is **Tagus Cove**. Here you can climb up a path to see the lava fields. A *panga* ride along the cliffs reveals colonies of penguins and other seabirds. It is probably also the best place to see the unique, but difficult to sight, flightless cormorant. Other landings can be made at **Urbina Bay**, **Elizabeth Bay**, and **Punta Moreno**.

Across the water is **Fernandina**, one of the least visited islands because it is so remote; the island is the most westerly in the Galápagos. It has one visitor site at **Punta Espinosa**, with some impressive lava flows (this was probably the most recently formed major island, and still has some volcanic activity). Along its shores are more penguins and hordes of marine iguanas.

The Floreana "post office".

⊘ DIVING

Not to be outdone by the unique life above ground, the Galápagos Islands are one of the world's premier diving areas. At 133,000 sq km (51,350 sq miles), it's the biggest marine reserve in Latin America. Some 450 species of fish have been catalogued. Diving tours on yachts are the best way to reach remote diving spots such as Darwin and Wolf islands at the northwest end of the archipelago; both are excellent locations to see schools of endemic Galápagos, white-tipped, or black-tipped sharks, hammerheads, and even gigantic whale sharks. These, the largest species of fish in the world, can be seen June through November. Giant manta rays are common off Cabo Marshall on Isabela. High quantities of nutrients in the water, however, can limit under-water visibility.

*Nazca booby on
Española.*

ISLA FLOREANA

Of historical interest on **Isla Floreana**, to the south of the archipelago, is the post box at **Post Office Bay**, where whalers used to leave mail in the late 18th century. Having been replaced several times, the box is still in use. It is the custom to look through the mail and take anything addressed to your home country, putting a local stamp on it when you arrive there and sending it on its way.

Of the visitor sites on Isla Floreana, **Punta Cormorán** is a sandy beach with a greenish tinge from the tiny crystals of olivine, a mineral silicate. From here a trail leads to a lagoon, where occasionally pink flamingos nest. Nearby is a second beach called Stingray, which has glistening white sands. The **Devil's Crown** is a sunken crater that forms a semicircle of rocks: this is perhaps the best site for diving in the whole archipelago. Apart from the schools of brilliant tropical fish, you will probably be joined by some baby sea lions that will race snorkelers through a natural underwater archway.

THE OUTLYING ISLANDS

The most southerly island in the Galápagos is **Española** (Hood). Española is famous for its seabirds, particularly the waved albatross. An estimated 17,000 pairs nest here, the world's entire population. During the mating season, they begin "fencing" by knocking their beaks together and waddling about "like drunken sailors," as one observer put it.

The whole astonishing range of seabirds can be seen on this island, as well as the beautiful beach of Gardner's Bay. Keep an eye out for the blowhole, which spouts water 50 meters (165ft) into the air whenever waves hit. At the eastern point of the archipelago lies **San Cristóbal ❺** (Chatham), the second-largest human population center after Santa Cruz: some 5,500 people live in **Puerto Baquerizo Moreno**, the Galápagos' provincial capital. The introduction of flights here caused a development boom, and several hotels and restaurants service the town. There is a monument to Darwin, and, at the entrance of the port, a rock called **León Dormido** (Sleeping Lion), which can be climbed for a good view of the island.

A road leads to the village of **El Progreso** and the 895-meter (2,935ft) high **Volcán San Joaquín** and **El Junco**, a freshwater crater lake. **Cerro de las Tijeratas (Frigatebird Hill)** is, as the name suggests, a good place to see frigate birds and only a short walk from the town. The nearby Galápagos National Park Visitor Center (tel: 05-252 1538; daily 7am–noon and 1.30–5pm), has a number of exhibits about the island's natural history and ecosystems. **La Lobería** is a beach crowded with sea lions and **Puerto Grande** a small cove particularly popular for swimming.

Other far-flung islands include **Marchena**, **Pinta**, and **Genovesa** (Tower), which is home to the main colony of red-footed boobies, three types of Darwin's finch, and everything from red-billed tropic-birds to storm petrels

Sea lions sun themselves on the beach at Gardner Bay, Española Island.

Riding to Quilotoa, Avenue of the Volcanoes.

ECUADOR & GÁLAPAGOS

TRAVEL TIPS

TRANSPORTATION

By air

Ecuador has several international airports but the largest two are the Mariscal Sucre airport outside Quito and Guayaquil (José Joaquín de Olmedo). Mariscal Sucre airport is the main point of air arrivals into the country. If Guayaquil is your entrance point into Ecuador, but you plan to head for the capital, make sure that your international ticket includes the onward connection, otherwise you will need to buy another ticket in Guayaquil airport. The flight time between Quito and Guayaquil is approximately 30 minutes.

Flights from the US and Canada

Travelers heading to Ecuador from the US can fly to Quito or Guayaquil with **American Airlines, United or Delta** from various US cities, often via their US hubs. **LATAM** flies direct from Miami, and JetBlue from Fort Lauderdale. You can also fly to Quito with **Avianca** from various US cities via Bogotá; LATAM via Lima; and **Copa** to several American destinations via Panama City.

Travelers from Canada will generally need to go via the US with **Air**

International airlines

Airlines operating flights to Quito and Guayaquil include:
Aeroregional www.aeroregional.com
American Airlines www.aa.com
Avianca www.avianca.com
Copa www.copaair.com
Delta Airlines www.delta.com
Iberia www.iberia.com
JetBlue www.jetblue.com
KLM www.klm.com
LATAM www.latam.com

Canada, American Airlines, Delta or United although Avianca flies to Quito from Toronto via Bogotá.

American Airlines

Quito Av. de los Shyris N35-174 y Suecia, Edif. Renazzo Plaza, Piso 4, Oficina 403-404; tel: 02-299 5000.
Guayaquil Mall Policentro, Av. del Periodista Juan Arzube and Calle 10; tel: 04-259 8800.

Avianca

Quito Av. Coruña 143 and Bello Horizonte; tel: 02-255 3248.
Guayaquil Av. Francisco de Orellana, Manzana 111; tel: 04-216 9417.
Cuenca Av. Circunvalación and Flavio Reyes. Manta Shopping, local 25; tel: 05-262 8899.

United

Quito Av. 12 de Octubre 1830 and Cordero; tel: 02-245 3810.

Copa

Quito Av. República del Salvador 361 and Moscú; tel: 02-227 3082.
Guayaquil Av. 9 de Octubre and Malecón; tel: 04-230 3000.
Cuenca Miguel Cordero and Av Paucarbamba, Work Center, Ground floor, Oficina N09; tel: 07-288 4410.

Delta

Quito Av. Los Shyris and Suecia N35-174, Edificio Renazzo Plaza; tel: 02-281 8262.

LATAM

Quito Av. Amazonas and Pasaje Guayas E3-131; tel: 1-800-101 075.
Guayaquil Mall del Sol, ground floor; tel: 04-216 9240.

Flights from Europe

Iberia flies daily direct from Madrid whereas **KLM** flies less frequently to Quito from Amsterdam. Alternatively, you can take any flight that goes via the US or South America.

Iberia

Quito Av. Eloy Alfaro 939 and Amazonas, Edif. Finandes, 5th floor; tel: 02-281 8072.
Guayaquil Av. 9 de Octubre 101 and Malecón; tel: 04-292 4656.

KLM

Quito Av. 12 de Octubre N26-97 and A. Lincoln; tel: 02-395 4200.
Guayaquil José Joaquín de Olmedo Airport; tel: 04-216 9070.

Flights from Australia, New Zealand, and Asia

Travelers can take **LATAM** flight from Sydney via Auckland to Santiago de Chile, with connecting flights to Guayaquil or Quito; or fly to Los Angeles and take one of several connecting flights from there.

Alternatively, **United** and **Delta** fly from Sydney to Los Angeles, from where you can fly to Quito via Houston, Mexico, or Miami; or via San Salvador, Panama City, or Miami to Guayaquil.

Getting to and from airports

Mariscal Sucre International Airport (UIO; tel: 02-395 4200), is located 18km (11 miles) east of Quito. **Aeroservicios** (www.aeroservicios.com.ec/horarios) operates an hourly shuttle service between the UIO and the company's bus terminal at the old city airport. The non-stop journey takes about an hour, depending on traffic, and costs $8. Shuttle buses are modern, and equipped with Wi-Fi, GPS, and individual screens. Tickets can be bought online or at the Aeroservicios stand next to the arrivals' hall.

Less expensive ($2 per ticket) public buses run between Quito and the airport – one operates from the terminal on Av. Río Coca in the north of the city (5.30am–10pm), while the other goes from the Quitumbe terminal in the south (5.30am–7pm).

✪ Air travel taxes

As of 2012, entry and departure taxes are included in the price of air tickets. However, before boarding a flight to the Galápagos from Quito or Guayaquil, tourists have to purchase a Tarjeta de Control de Tránsito (Transit Control Card), which can be done online (www.gob.ec/cgreg/tramites/emision-tarjeta-control-transito-turistas-transeuntes).

The journey takes longer, however, due to stops en route.

A taxi into Quito will cost between $25–30. Two official taxi companies operating at the airport are **La Cooperativa de Taxis Aeropuerto Mariscal Sucre No. 34** and the **Asociación de Cooperativas del Valle (Univalle)**. Tel: 02-252 1112 for reservations. In addition, most large hotels offer a shuttle service.

José Joaquín de Olmedo International Airport (GYE; www.tagsa.aero) is located 5km (3 miles) north of Guayaquil city center. If you already have a reservation, make arrangements with your hotel to pick you up. Otherwise, take one of the official taxis run by **Cooperativa de Taxis Aeropuerto Guayaquil** and marked "airport taxi," that can be found upon exiting the arrivals hall. The journey to the city center should not cost more than $5.

Alternatively, take the blue **Metrovía** public bus (route T2; www.metrovia.atm.gob.ec/metrovia/fundacion-metrovia) which crosses the city from the south (Terminal 25 de Julio) to the north (Terminal Río Daule). It operates every 10–15 minutes between 5am and 11.45pm and stops in front of the airport's terminal.

Cuenca's airport (www.aeropuertocuenca.ec) is a five-minute walk beyond the bus terminal and is easily accessible by city bus or taxi.

By bus

It is common for backpackers to travel overland into Ecuador, crossing at either Huaquillas or Macará on the Peruvian border or Tulcán/Rumichaca on the Colombian side, although currently there are serious safety issues in this region due to increased drug-trafficking and the activities of illegal armed groups. At both borders, minibuses and trucks

run between bus centers on both sides for a small fee. The borders are usually open from around 8am to 6pm. Be sure to get an entry stamp and tourist card.

Several companies run comfortable buses on the longer routes, including **Panamericana Internacional** (www.panamericana.ec) and **Latin Bus** (http://latinbus.com), which run domestic and international services from Quito and Guayaquil. These two cities are also served by Peruvian company **Cruz del Sur** (www.cruzdelsur.com.pe, see page 304).

By road

To drive a private car across a border into Ecuador, you are required to have a Carnet de Passage en Douane (CDP), an international customs document. These are normally obtained through the automobile club of the country where the car is registered. Motorbike and bicycle riders just need to show relevant registration papers.

GETTING AROUND

Until the 20th century, transport and communications in Ecuador were

✪ Car rental agencies

In addition to the locations listed below, all of the following agencies have branches at the international airports in Quito and Guayaquil.
Avis
Av. De Los Granados E11-26 and Av. Seis de Diciembre, Quito, tel: 601 6000. Av. de las Américas, Centro Comercial Aeroplaza, Guayaquil, tel: 396 3800; www.avis.com.ec
Budget
Av. Elo Alfaro S40-153, Quito, tel: 02-224 4095; Av. de las Américas 900 and Alejandro Andrade, Guayaquil, tel: 04-228 4559; www.budget.com
Hertz
Mariscal Sucre Int. Airport, Quito, tel: 02-281 4410; J.S de Olmedo Int. Airport, Guayaquil, tel: 04-216 9035; www.hertz.com
Localiza
Av. Shyris, Suecia 36-106, Quito, tel: 02-600 2975/2977; J.J. de Olmedo Int. Airport, Guayaquil, tel: 04-602 5611; www.localiza.com

poorly developed. Most people got around by mule or donkey until the railway network was developed. The road network has expanded considerably since World War II, and the main roads are generally quite good, although many have been badly affected by landslides and flooding and have dangerous potholes. Of the 43,000km (26,718 miles) of highways, about 18,000km (11,160 miles) are open all year and about 10,000km (6,213 miles) are paved.

By car

Traveling by private car is generally more convenient in Ecuador than in other Andean countries, because the main roads are in a comparatively better state due to massive investments in recent years, the running costs are economical, and the country is safer than in neighboring republics.

Nevertheless, beware of bus drivers, who often go very fast, and make sure that your car has good ground clearance. As insurance and rental costs become more prohibitive and incidents of ambushes at night increase in certain regions, more travelers tend to opt for buses rather than driving themselves.

Car rental

To rent a car in Ecuador you need to be at least 25 years of age, carry a valid driving license and a widely accepted credit card. Car rental is as expensive as in Europe or in the United States. Charges start at about $70 a day, with unlimited mileage. Always make sure quoted rates include tax and comprehensive insurance.

It is often more economical and less stressful to hire a taxi for several hours, which will take you to remote areas or to another town: be sure to agree the costs beforehand.

Automobile club

The Automovil Club del Ecuador (**ANETA**) (Avenida Eloy Alfaro N28-16 and Berlín; tel: 02-250 4961/1800 556677 (free); www.aneta.org.ec) offers an emergency breakdown towing and repair service to members and offers discounts to members of the AAA from Canada or the US.

By bus

Local buses

Local buses run frequently and are inexpensive. Destinations are shown

☉ Domestic airlines

Aeroregional Martín de Utreras 31–234 y Av. Mariana de Jesús, tel: **02-393 0360**; www.aeroregional.net
Avianca Ecuador Carrión 710 and Av. Amazonas, Quito, tel: 02-255 3248; Mall del Sol, Guayaquil, tel: 04-208 2316; www.avianca.com
LATAM Av. La Coruna 2208, Quito, tel: 1-800-000 527; Blvd. 9 de Octubre 100, Guayaquil, tel: 1-800-000 527; www.latam.com

on the front of the vehicle. All the main towns and cities are served by urban bus lines. The buses are mostly small and usually extremely overcrowded, especially at peak hours. The large *selectivo* buses running in Quito's New Town are a pleasant exception. Beware of pickpockets.

There is a trolleybus system (**Trolébus**) operating between the north and south of Quito which forms part of the integrated system of metropolitan transport (SITM-Q) which currently consists of five trolley/bus traffic-free lines called *corredores*. Unfortunately, buses and trolleys get very crowded at peak hours. Pickpockets also work this network. The **Metrobús** and **EcoVía** also form part of the public system. A single journey costs $0.35. Quito's sole **Metro** line should be running by 2024.

Since taxis are very cheap in Guayaquil, buses and *colectivos* are mostly avoided by foreign visitors, but *busetas* or minibuses are safe to ride. *Servicio especial* buses, marked with blue-and-white diagonal stripes, are slightly more expensive but relatively efficient. Take great care with taxis in Guayaquil, due to a spate of taxi-kidnappings. It is better to order one by phone from a company recommended by your hotel than to flag one down in the street.

If you want to get off a local bus, shout *¡baja!* (down!), *¡parada!* (stop!) or *¡esquina!* (corner!), when the driver will stop at the next corner.

Long-distance buses

Bus travel is not always comfortable, but the numerous companies connect all the main towns at frequent intervals, serve smaller localities, and the fares are incredibly low.

In general, buses leave from central bus terminals. The new,

comfortable, luxury buses leave on time; regular buses may or may not. One can usually buy tickets one or two days in advance and choose the seat number; note that the front seats tend to have slightly more leg room than the back seats. During long holiday weekends or special fiestas, buses are generally booked up for several days in advance, so early booking is recommended.

Try to travel by daylight, as there are fewer road accidents and also less likelihood of being held up by bandits or armed gangs.

Four types of buses are used:
1) small buses (*busetas*) for 22 passengers, which have cramped leg room and are not very comfortable;
2) larger buses (*buses*), which have more space;
3) luxury buses (*autobuses de lujo*), serving routes between major cities;
4) trucks with roofs, open sides, and wooden plank seats, called *chivas* or *rancheros*, which are found mainly around the coast.

Buses from Quito

Long-distance buses leave mainly either from Quitumbe (Southern terminal) or Carcelén (in the North) where most bus companies operate.

There are many buses a day to major destinations, including Ambato (2.5hours), Bahía de Caráquez (9 hours), Baños (3.5 hours), Coca (8 hours), Cuenca (9 hours), Guaranda (5 hours), Guayaquil (8 hours), Ibarra (2.5 hours), Lago Agrio (5 hours), Latacunga (2 hours), Loja (12 hours), Machala (10 hours), Manta (9 hours), Otavalo (2 hours), Portoviejo (8 hours), Puyo (5 hours), Riobamba (3.5 hours), Santo Domingo (3 hours), Tena (5 hours), Esmeraldas (6 hours), Otavalo (2.5 hours), Ibarra (2.5 hours), and Tulcán (5 hours).

La Ofélia terminal, also in the north, has buses travelling to Mindo (2 hours) and Mitad del Mundo (30 min).

A private **Ormeño** terminal at Los Shyris N34-432 and Portugal, opposite Parque la Carolina is a hub for buses leaving for Bogota and Cali (Colombia), Lima, Cusco, Piura (Peru), Buenos Aires (Argentina, a five-day journey), Caracas (Venezuela), Santiago (Chile), and São Paolo (Brasil). **Panamericana Internacional** (Av. Colón and Reina Victoria; tel: 02-255 7133) operates a direct service from Quitumbe terminal to Caracas in Venezuela, several

destinations in Peru, including Lima, as well as to many cities in Ecuador. Check http://latinbus.com for routes, timetables, and other details.

Long-distance buses in Ecuador are not expensive; fares cost approximately $2 per hour.

Buses from Esmeraldas

The Terminal Terrestre is located at Av. Universitaria and Manabí (tel: 06-270 2198). **Trans Esmeraldas** (www.transportesesmeraldas.com) operates services to and from many cities in Ecuador. There are frequent daily buses to Quito and Guayaquil. Other companies operating to and from Esmeraldas include **Aerotaxi** (http://coop_transporte_aerotaxi.amawebs.com) and **Transportes Occidentales** (http://transportesoccidentales.com).

Provincial buses operated by **La Costeñita** run to Atacames and Súa (1 hour), Muisne (3.5 hours), La Tola (3 hours), and San Lorenzo (5 hours) between 4am and 10pm.

Buses from Cuenca

All long-distance buses leave from the Terminal Terrestre on Avenida España, northwest of the city center. Destinations include Riobamba (6 hours; Express Sucre, Patria, Santa), Ambato (7 hours; Patria, Santa), Quito (10 hours; Express Sucre, Patria, Turismo Oriental), Loja (5 hours; Loja, Pullman Viajeros), Guayaquil (5 hours; Alianza), Macas (9 hours; Turismo Oriental), and Gualaquiza (6 hours; Express Sigsig).

☉ Taxis

Taxis are very cheap compared to many European and North American countries. In 2014, taximeters were made obligatory in all taxis across the country, but in practice meters are most often used by drivers in Quito, and sometimes a nudge is needed. Where taxi meters aren't happening, tell the driver your destination and agree on a charge beforehand. In Guayaquil, in particular, you'll be unlikely to persuade a driver to use the meter: be sure to ascertain the fare beforehand, or you could be overcharged. In smaller towns, meters do not exist; at weekends and at night fares are 25–50 percent higher. Avoid unlicensed taxis at all times.

Buses from Guayaquil

The Terminal Terrestre is 2km (1.2 miles) north of the airport and the bridge over the Río Guayas, and most long-distance buses leave from here. The terminal includes shops and a food court. There are ticket booths at the terminal, but it is advisable to book ahead if traveling on Fridays, weekends, or public holidays as buses tend to fill up quickly. Destinations are: Quito (8 hours; Transporte Ecuador, Aerotaxi, Panamericana, or Flota Imbabura), Cuenca (4 hours; Alianza), Riobamba (4.5 hours; Patria), Santo Domingo de los Colorados (5 hours; Zaracay), Manta (4 hours; Reyna Camino, Coactur), Esmeraldas (7.5 hours; Aerotaxi, Occidentales, Trans Esmeralda), Portoviejo (3.5 hours; Rutas Portovejenses, Reina Camino), Bahía de Caráquez (6 hours; Coactur, Reina Camino), Machala (3 hours; Ecuatoriana Pullman, Rutas Orenses), Huaquillas (4 hours; Ecuatoriana Pullman, Rutas Orenses), Ambato (6.5 hours; CITA Express, Transandina), and Alausí (4 hours; Cooperativa Alausí). There are also frequent buses to Salinas (2.5 hours; CICAS) and Playas/General Villamil (2 hours). There is a shared-taxi service to Machala (2.5 hours) leaving from next door to the Hotel Rizzo, Downtown.

By rail

An expensive and extensive restoration programme which began in 2008 briefly breathed new life into the nearly defunct Ecuadorian railway system. Parts of the famous line between Quito and Guayaquil reopened in 2013 with many local sections in the Sierra also being revamped and turned into tourist attractions for day-trippers. But after struggling financially for a number of years, and being forced to close during the pandemic, the national rail company was liquidated in 2021 by former President Moreno.

The Nariz del Diablo (Devil's Nose) section of the Alausí–Sibambe route is one of the most spectacular train rides in the world, famous for its dramatic switchback as it plunges off the Andes. It is understandably the most popular ride to take, so should be up and running first. The train leaves Alausí for Sibambe and this journey takes 2.5 hours. Other lines that may, or may not, be resuscitated include Ibarra–Salinas, Ibarra–Otavalo (Tren de la Libertad), Quito–Alausí (Ruta del Chagro), Quito–Latacunga; Riobamba–Urbina and Ambato–Urbina (Tren del Hielo), Riobamba–Colta (Sendero de los Ancestros), and Durán–Bucay (Tren de la Dulzura). Check the tourist office for details on which services are running.

Quito's train station is 2km (1 mile) south of the center, on Sincholagua s/n and Maldonado (Mon–Fri 8am–4.30pm; tel: 02-399 2100).

Tourist information offices in Quito, Ibarra, and other cities can also help with purchasing tickets.

By air

Air transport is well developed, although since the dissolution of the national airline, TAME, in 2021, fewer cities are served. The Oriente is the one area where airlines have virtually no competition from other forms of transport. There are many villages whose only contact with the rest of the country is by air; besides numerous small strips, 34 airports can handle bigger planes, some of them modern jet aircraft.

There are scheduled domestic flights between the main cities. **LATAM**, **Avianca**, and Aeroregional all connect Quito with Cuenca and Manta, with at least one return flight a day. LATAM additionally operates flights from Quito to Coca and Guayaquil. Avianca also flies to Guayaquil while Aeroregional offers connections to Machala and Loja. Flying time between Guayaquil and Quito is about 30 minutes, while journey times for other domestic flights is usually less than one hour.

Air taxis (Cessnas or Bonanzas) can be rented. Small airlines' offices are found at the Guayaquil and Quito airports. For routes and timetables check the airport websites (Quito: www.aeropuertoquito.aero; Guayaquil: www.tagsa.aero; Cuenca: www.aeropuertocuenca.ec). Tickets for domestic flights are relatively cheap and rarely cost more than $140, and often a lot less with the exception of the Galápagos Islands.

Flights to the Galápagos

Flights to the Galápagos Islands are heavily booked, so you should confirm and reconfirm your seat and check in early at the airport, unless you have booked your cruise through an agency, in which case they will reconfirm for you.

☺ Foreign exchange

If you are flying to Quito or Guayaquil and straight on to the Galápagos Islands, and taking a tour on one of the large cruise ships, exchange facilities are available. Independent travelers can change foreign currency in Puerto Ayora, but at a poor rate, so bring whatever you need in dollars from the mainland.

Avianca, and **LATAM** operate regular services to both Baltra and San Cristóbal. After landing at Baltra, a quick ferry and connecting buses make the short trip to Puerto Ayora. Many cruises pick up their passengers directly at the airport and return them there. All non-Ecuadorian travelers to the islands must pay a $100 park entrance fee (plus $20 at the mainland airport for a Transit Control Card) on arrival at the airport. Payment must be made in dollars and not by credit card. Keep the receipt: you may have to show it again.

There are also regular flights between some of the islands with **Emetebe** (www.emetebe.com.ec; tel: 04-230 1277), a local airline, subject to demand. You will be restricted to luggage of 13kg (30lb) or less (non-negotiable). There are several flights a week between Baltra and Isabela, as well as between Baltra and San Cristóbal.

With the exception of flying to the Galápagos Islands (which can cost $400–600 Quito-Galápagos return, less from Guayaquil), domestic flights are fairly inexpensive (a return flight Quito-Guayaquil is about $100–150). Passengers are required to show up one hour before the departure of domestic flights, for baggage handling and check-in procedures. Many flights give marvelous views of the snow-capped Andes, so it is worth getting a window seat. Seats are given on a first-come, first-served basis.

By boat

It is sometimes possible to travel some of the Pacific coast by boat. Check at the local *capitanía del puerto* (harbormaster's office) about boat departures (most often to Guayaquil and Manta).

Traveling by boat is the principal means of transport in the Amazon,

⊙ Passport checks

On buses, always carry your passport (or a copy) with you. There are regular police checks on all the roads leading out of main towns, and you can get into serious trouble if you are unable to present your documents when requested since it is a legal requirement.

and many lodges are only accessible by motorboat or canoe. The *Manatee Amazon Explorer* and The Anakonda Amazon Cruise (www.anakondaamazoncruises.com) floating hotels (see page 203) offer a more luxurious way of visiting the area.

Cruises in the Galápagos

The Galápagos archipelago is almost entirely a national park, and no visitor is allowed to enter it without a qualified guide on an organized tour. There are a couple of ways that this can be done. Some travelers choose to take a series of different day trips from Puerto Ayora on Santa Cruz to the islands nearest that island, but, while this is cheap, it is not very satisfying especially as the quality of guiding can be variable. Tour operators on the island will offer day trips for anything between $80–250 a day depending on the season, type of activity, length of trip, luxury of boat, quality of guiding, and what's included. The great majority of visitors go on cruises around the islands, taking at least three nights; the more, the better. If you are going to spend the cash to come all this way, it is a pity to miss out or cut corners on one of the world's great travel experiences. If you can book at the last minute, there are often some real bargain cruises to be had.

Large cruises

For many, a trip on one of the largest cruisers is the most comfortable and convenient way to visit the islands. The *Silver Origin*, operated by **Silversea**, is one of the most luxurious of the boats touring the islands. Contact any travel agency that specializes in Latin America, or visit www.silversea.com. The *Santa Cruz II*, run by **Metropolitan Touring** (see page 313), has all the comforts of a luxury liner, including excellent food. By traveling overnight, these cruisers can easily reach outer

islands that smaller yachts sometimes struggle to get to. The going is smoother on a large ship as well.

Both boats are based in the Galápagos, taking around 90 passengers on three- to seven-day cruises. Passengers visit the islands in groups of 10 on motorboats (pangas) accompanied by English-speaking naturalist guides who all have university degrees in their fields.

The cost is over $1500 per person per night on a twin-share basis (all inclusive, except for bar and air fare), depending on cabin and length of cruise.

Smaller yachts

Dozens of yachts carrying from eight to 20 people operate cruises around the islands. Most work out of Puerto Ayora, although a growing number are now based in Puerto Baquerizo Moreno. The boats are categorized into five classes: luxury, first class, superior tourist, standard tourist, and economy class. Tours on them can be booked on the mainland from a number of agencies, or beforehand through a travel agency specializing in Latin America. Rates here range between $400–700 per night. **Quasar Expeditions** (see page 313), for example, offers a selection of luxury yachts, including *Grace* and *Evolution*. These trips are more costly than on the larger cruises, but are also more intimate and allow more time on the islands. One of the most reliable companies offering both luxury small yachts and tourist-class yachts is **Enchanted Expeditions** (see page). They offer the Passion luxury yacht, *Beluga*, a superior first-class yacht, both accommodating 16 people, and one slightly cheaper option, the first-class *Cachalote*.

Cheaper tours on small boats can also be arranged at places such as **Galasam Galápagos Tours** on 9 de Octubre 424 and Chile, Guayaquil (tel: 04-381 0920; www.galasam. com.ec). When booking in Quito or Guayaquil, expect to pay around $300 a day including food for a reasonable boat. (see page 106)

Ecoventura operates a variety of cruises from three to seven nights, and can be booked in the US through **Galápagos Network** (5805 Blue Lagoon Drive, Suite 160, Miami, FL 33126; tel: 305-262 6264; www.ecoventura.com). Aggressor III (tel: 1 706-993-2531; www.aggressor.com/destination/Galapagos) is arguably the archipelago's top liveaboard dive vessel.

Organizing your own tour

There are many economy-class boats that can be booked in Quito quite cheaply or at the last minute. Dozens of backpackers turn up at Puerto Ayora and begin getting people together to charter a boat – if you look like a candidate, they are likely to stop you in the street and ask about your plans. The only drawback is that you need a few days to get the required number of people together and arrange a boat, so it's not a good idea to try to set it up in a hurry.

Boats take 8 or 12 people, and the cheapest cost from $300 a day with all meals but excluding tips for the crew. However, if your budget allows, it is worth paying for a more expensive boat, as the cabins are likely to be bigger, the food better, and the guides more informed. A few points to bear in mind: Boat owners like to fill their boats to capacity. The group is usually expected to share the cost of any unsold passenger space.

When dealing directly with the boat owner, bargaining is expected.

Bottled drinks are not included in the cost of the cruise. Bring as much mineral water as you think you will need; it is sold at the Puerto Ayora supermarket (at the docks).

Boat travel to outer islands such as Española and Genovesa can be quite rough, especially from September to November.

Make sure the boats have enough sets of snorkeling gear. The water is cold from July to December and wetsuits are recommended.

Traveling between the islands

INGALA (Instituto Nacional de Galápagos) has official inter-island passenger services between Santa Cruz, San Cristóbal, Isabela, and Floreana. There are daily transfers from Puerto Ayora on Santa Cruz to Puerto Baquerizo Moreno on San Cristóbal and from Santa Cruz to Isabela, both for around $30. The transfer between Santa Cruz and Floreana is only twice a week. For more information call 05-252 6189. The INGALA office in Puerto Ayora is next to the hospital. In Puerto Baquerizo Moreno, it is on the road leading inland at the edge of the town.

There are also numerous private companies in Puerto Ayora and Puerto Baquerizo Moreno operating speedboats between the islands. Try to negotiate a price, especially if there are several of you.

A – Z

A

Accessible travel

In large cities and major tourist areas, most large hotels and attractions are equipped with ramps and/or elevators. Several high-end hotels in Galápagos are also now wheelchair accessible and geared to mobility-impaired travelers. Special accessibility-focused tour operators, such as Latin America For All (www.latinamericaforall.com), provide vacations for a range of travelers with specific needs.

Accommodation

Hotels

The country has no shortage of hotels, but luxury options are limited to Quito, Guayaquil, Cuenca and Manta, plus first-class jungle lodges in the Oriente and a couple of the haciendas in the Sierra. The local Oro Verde chain (www.hotelesoroverde.com) offers business-style luxury hotels in several cities. Most other areas rely on more basic country inns (*hosterías*), *pensiones*, or *residenciales*. In high season (June to September in the Sierra, December to January on the coast), during fiestas, and the night before market days (in Otavalo particularly), finding accommodations can be difficult, so it is worth making a reservation; at other times just turn up.

A room in a luxury hotel might cost $150–250 a night; in a first-class hotel, $75–150, while a double room with private bath in a comfortable residencial can be had for $40–60. Decent backpacker hostels with shared bathrooms are generally $40–50 for shared room. In most places, apart from budget hotels and hostels, service (10 percent) and tax charges (12 percent, but 8 per cent for registered lodgings on public holidays) will be added to the bill.

Guesthouses

Officially a tier below hotels for comfort, many guesthouses (known in Spanish as *hospedajes*, *hosterías* or *hostales*, the last of which should not be confused with international backpacker-friendly hostels) actually equal some mid-range hotels in quality. However, they occupy a huge segment of the accommodation market and standards vary wildly, from top-end boutique-style rooms ($80 or more) to drab options inferior in facilities to dorm rooms in backpacker hostels ($15 or less).

Camping

Camping is a cheap and popular option in many coastal areas, and most campsites provide access to bathrooms and running water. In the Galápagos, there are only three official sites: on the islands of Santa Cruz, San Cristóbal and Isabela. Permission needs to be sought via the national park office at least 48 hours in advance. You can also camp in most national parks, though facilities may be rudimentary.

Eco-lodges and haciendas

Ecotourism is the big "E" in Ecuador these days and a stay at an eco-lodge or hacienda offers top-end accommodation with the added karma of "giving something back" to the country. These two options are similar in the fact that both are located in remote areas (eco-lodges generally in the Oriente, or in the cloud-forests of the Chocó-Andino region, haciendas generally in the Sierra), have great wildlife-watching opportunities in close proximity and are often involved in eco-projects of their own.

You do not have to be part of a tour to stay at the majority of eco-lodges or haciendas although, due to their locations, but it may be necessary, or desirable, to spend several days there (in which case prices will be given not per night but per for a multi-day package). Prices range from $80, in the cheapest, more rustic lodges, to $250 or more, usually inclusive of room, all meals and guided activities, and English is invariably spoken. Alternatively, it may easier to arrange these accommodations through a tour operator.

Addresses

Quito street addresses can be confusing. In 1998 a street numbering system was introduced in Quito based on N (norte), S (sud), E (este), and O (oeste), followed by a street and building number.

Admission charges

Charges for museums are usually no more than a few dollars; children often pay less. National park entrance fees are costlier, around $10–20 (or even $100 in the case of Galápagos) for several of the popular national parks and reserves like Cotopaxi.

B

Budgeting for your trip

Ecuador falls into the middle when comparing prices to other Latin American countries. Since dollarization in 2000, prices have climbed. Cities such as Quito and Guayaquil remain more expensive than other places. The difference is mainly noticeable in accommodation and food prices, as well as taxi fares.

In the large cities and major tourist destinations budget

accommodation will run from as little as $12 per night, but a top hotel will charge several hundred dollars for a room. Getting around by bus is fairly cheap, and journeys are never more than a few hours due to the size of the country.

Transportation by long distance buses averages about $2 per hour, depending on the level of comfort. Within cities, taxis are cheap and ubiquitous, and rarely will a ride within a city – even Quito or Guayaquil – cost more than a few dollars. Some locations in the Oriente, as well as the Galápagos, can only be reached by airplane, which can be expensive. A round-trip plane ticket to the Galápagos will cost about $550.

The cost of food varies heavily. In large cities, and especially the Galápagos, rarely will you be able to eat out for less than $5, and meals can cost as much as $40 per person for a top restaurant. In rural areas, small local restaurants will serve set menus, usually including several hearty courses, for a few dollars. Drinks tend to be relatively cheap, as a beer will generally cost just over a dollar in most bars and pubs, although in a large club in a place such as Quito, you will likely have to triple that price. Cover charges at clubs tend to be anywhere between $3–15.

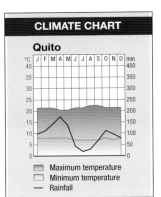

CLIMATE CHART

Quito

- Maximum temperature
- Minimum temperature
- Rainfall

changes little between seasons. However, mornings are generally sunny and fresh, becoming warmer toward midday; in the afternoon it often rains, and toward the evenings it gets chilly, and the nights are cold. This means that in Quito the daily range of temperature is generally around 8° to 21°C (46° to 70°F). Above 3,800 meters (11,400ft) temperatures reach freezing during the night. Occasional snowstorms also occur. There is one rainy season in the Sierra, from November to May, when there is frequent rainfall during the afternoon and evening. However, it rains quite often during the dry season too, and the sun shines in the rainy season for at least a couple of hours every day.

The coastal lowlands and Amazon basin are very hot year-round, with temperatures ranging from 22°C (73°F) at night to 33°C (100°F) during the day. Humidity is extremely high. The rainy season in both areas is from May to December, although tropical downpours are regular in the dry season also. In the Galápagos Islands, there are also two seasons, produced by the ocean currents: the rainy (warm) and dry (cool) seasons. During the rainy season, from January through June, the weather is warm and sunny, while the water temperature is a comfortable 23°C (75°F); heavy tropical showers occur occasionally. This is the best time to visit. For the rest of the year, a mist called the *garua* settles over the islands and makes the day cloudy, and the water begins to cool. It rarely rains, but it can be windy.

What to wear

Ecuador has three very different climatic zones, so what you wear

depends completely on where you are headed.

The Sierra is where most travelers begin. Quito is called the "City of Eternal Spring," although "eternal fall" (autumn) might be more accurate. When the sun is shining, Sierran days are warm and pleasant, but when the clouds roll in and winds begin to blow, you need a sweater. Nights can be quite cold, so a warm overcoat or fleece is recommended.

Ecuadorians, like most Latin Americans, like to dress up and look their best when they go out, even at more casual restaurants and nightspots. Note that Quito tends to have more conservative dress standards than the rest of the country.

Of course, this doesn't apply to many backpacker hangouts, and even in the ritzier establishments, backpackers are forgiven for a more laidback appearance than Ecuadorians. But remember that a night out in a restaurant is more of a big deal for an Ecuadorian, and dressing too unkemptly can seem like an insult to the other clients. If in doubt, err on the side of smartness.

The coast and Galápagos Islands are tropical regions, so dress for the heat. Guayaquil and the coast are very casual, so shorts for men are widely accepted for many social situations, though not in restaurants outside the beach resorts. Away from the beach itself, women are more likely to wear a light dress. Remember to use sun protection, and sunglasses with UV protection are advisable, even in the Sierra.

Dress in the Oriente is even more functional. All clothes should be light, because of the stifling heat, but loose-fitting long trousers and long-sleeved shirts are recommended to guard against insects. Bring some sneakers for walking. Lodges will provide rubber boots if you need to wade through any mud; the same is true of haciendas in the Andes.

Rain can strike in any part of Ecuador, whether it is the rainy season or not, so bring protection.

What to bring

What you bring depends on where you are going to go and what you are going to do. A few recommended items: antibacterial handsoap or gel, hand wipes, a personal stereo, basic first aid kit, sunscreen, sunglasses, a Swiss Army knife, and

C

Children

Ecuador is a great place to travel with children. Ecuadorians are very child-focused, and traveling with your children is a great way to break the ice. Most tourist attractions and transport offer children's entrance fees and fares. Take a good medical kit when traveling with a child and know how to use its contents. Anti-diarrhea drugs are a must, as are electrolytic salts to combat dehydration, which can be rapid in children.

Climate

Because it is on the equator, Ecuador has only two seasons: wet and dry. Weather patterns vary greatly between the different geographical regions, however.

In the inhabited inter-mountain basin of the Sierra, the temperature a Latin-American Spanish phrase book. Bringing water purifying tablets (available at any outdoor store) is a good idea so that you can refill your water bottle rather than be reliant on bottled water.

If you intend to partake in any adventure activities, check with your tour operator ahead of time to see what exactly you will need. Often for more technical activities such as climbing it is best to bring your own equipment. You can buy or rent climbing or hiking equipment in Quito and many towns such as Baños. However, prices tend to be much higher than they would be in the US or Europe.

Crime and safety

Most of Ecuador is relatively safe, although petty theft does occur in large cities and there's no denying that crime is on the rise as a result of widening social inequalities and economic difficulties following the Covid-19 pandemic. Armed robberies can occur on isolated mountain trails, but this is somewhat rare – always seek local advice and avoid hiking alone. In major cities it is best only to travel in marked taxis. It is best to order a taxi by phone from a reputable company in Quito or Guayaquil, rather than stop one in the street. Don't walk alone at night in big cities and avoid poorly lit streets. Going to a nightclub is unadvisable in many cities unless accompanied by a local. In hostels, particularly dorms, secure your belongings in a locker (travelers are not just at risk from crime by Ecuadorians, but also by other travelers). Avoid traveling within 20km (12 miles) of the border with Colombia, if possible. Although drugs such as marijuana and cocaine may seem common in areas where many travelers visit, use or purchase is punishable by up to 16 years in prison, where a number of foreigners now reside.

⏻ Electricity

110V/60Hz is the standard current throughout the country. Ecuador uses the North American flat-pronged plug. Travelers from other countries will need to bring an adapter with them.

Customs regulations

Each traveler may bring 5 liters of alcohol, 500ml of perfume, 400 cigarettes, one unused smart phone and up to US$10,000 into Ecuador duty-free.

E

Eating out

Quito has a very good selection of restaurants, serving everything from local dishes to international cuisine. Surprisingly, there are fewer good restaurants in Guayaquil, often in the bigger hotels. In the provinces it is possible to eat well at reasonable prices. A restaurant need not be fancy to serve delicious and healthy food. Quito's best restaurants are sprinkled between the New Town and the Centro Histórico.

In Quito and Guayaquil, expect to pay around $20–25 for a main course in a fine-dining establishment, whereas in a good mid-priced restaurant a main course will cost around $15. If you order a bottle of wine, however, the bill will be much higher, because wine is often imported. These days the 20 percent tax (and service charge) is usually included in the menu prices, but check before you order. It is customary to leave an additional tip of 5–10 percent for the waiter if you have had especially good service.

Restaurants are open for lunch from noon until about 3pm. They often offer inexpensive menú ejecutivo "executive lunches." Many local comedores serve good, set two- or three-course lunches, with a drink included (menu del día) for as little as $4. Dinner is from 7pm until midnight. In the evening, ordering is à la carte. Most restaurants are closed on Sunday or Monday, but hotel restaurants are open every day.

Embassies and consulates

Quito
British Embassy
Av. Naciones Unidas and República de El Salvador, Edificio Citiplaza, 14th Floor; tel: 02-397 2200; www.gov.uk/government/world/organisations/british-embassy-in-ecuador
Canadian Embassy

☎ Emergency numbers

Emergency number for all services: 911
Policía de Turismo, Quito tel: 02-254 3983
This is where to make a declaration (denuncia) if you are robbed in Quito. An official police report will be required by your travel insurer. There is also tourist police presence at the airport, in the main bus station, in Quitumbe, and at Mitad del Mundo.

Av. Amazonas 4153 and Unión Nacional de Periodistas, Eurocenter Building, 3rd Floor; tel: 02-245 5499; www.canadainternational.gc.ca/ecuador-equateur
The Canadian Embassy also provides limited assistance to Australian nationals.
US Embassy
Avigiras E12-170 and Eloy Alfaro; tel: 02-398 5000; https://ec.usembassy.gov

Guayaquil
Australian Honorary Consulate
Pinturas Unidas S.A., Km 16.5, on the road to Daule; tel: 95981 1614.
British Honorary Consulate
Córdova 623 and Padre Solano; tel: 04-256 0400
Canadian Honorary Consulate
Av. Francisco de Orellana No.234; tel: 04-263 1109
Honorary Consul of Ireland
Samborondón Business Center, Torre B, 3rd Floor, Office 301 Km 1.5 on the road to Samborondón,; tel: 99569 7020.
US Consulate
Calle Santa Ana and Av. José Rodríguez Bonin; tel: 04-371 7000; https://ec.usembassy.gov

Etiquette

Ecuadorians are polite to each other and respectful of authority and age. People shake hands when meeting for the first time. Men may embrace each other if they are good friends, and both men and women kiss once when they meet friends. It is impolite to point at someone, instead point by puckering or pursing the lips in the direction you want to indicate. There's no great value placed on punctuality in Ecuador. Arriving 15 to 20 minutes late is considered "on time" for social engagements, though business meetings do often run more to schedule. Before you start eating, you may say *buen provecho* to your fellow diners. Remember also to greet people before asking for information or making a request, with buenas días, buenas tardes or buenas noches.

Health and medical care

It is a good idea to consult a tropical medicine clinic before traveling. Vaccinations against diphtheria, polio, tetanus, typhoid, and hepatitis A are strongly recommended. A yellow fever certificate is compulsory if arriving from a tropical South American or African region. If traveling into the Amazon or the tropical lowlands, take precautions to avoid insect bites. Remember, too, to cover exposed areas of skin with loose-fitting clothing around and after dusk, and use an insect repellent. Since incidence of malaria is low, prophylactics are rarely advised, but consult a travel clinic several weeks before departure.

If you are hiking or cycling in rural areas, a rabies vaccination will mean more time to get to medical help and fewer post-bite shots if you get bitten by a rabid dog (rabies is not common).

The most common illness for tourists is, of course, mild diarrhea, which hits most visitors at some stage. Sufferers should have plenty of liquids (hot tea without milk is ideal, but definitely no coffee), avoid eggs and dairy products, and rest as much as they can. Rehydration products, such as Dioralyte and Rehidrat, taken regularly, help prevent dehydration. Boiled water with a little sugar and salt added has a similar effect.

The symptoms of diarrhea can be stopped with medication like Imodium. This does not cure the ailment, and is really only useful if you have a long bus journey or flight and don't want a sudden attack. If the complaint continues for several days, consult a doctor. Also, if you suffer severe abdominal cramps, fever, or nausea, or if blood or pus is evident in your stool, you need a test to see if you've caught amoebic dysentery. But in almost all cases, diarrhea is simply a matter of becoming accustomed to different bacteria and unfamiliar food, and the gut returns to normal after a couple of days.

To avoid diarrhea, do not drink the tap water in Ecuador. Ask instead for mineral water con or sin gas (sparkling or still). *Güitig* (pronounced "gwee-tig") is the best brand. Bringing water purification tablets (available at most outdoor adventure stores) to add to tap water and reusing the same plastic bottle helps guarantee clean water as well as avoiding contributing to plastic waste. Stay clear of ice, uncooked vegetables, salads that haven't been properly treated, and unpeeled fruits.

Most food in the larger cities, or in the restaurants where most travelers eat, is perfectly safe. Hepatitis is a danger if you eat food prepared in dirty conditions, and it is advisable to have a gamma globulin shot to protect against this. There is also the drug Havirix, which gives 10-year protection, although you need a booster after the first year.

A more everyday health risk is the fierce equatorial sun, a danger even in the cold Sierra. Newcomers to Ecuador should not expose their skin to the sun for long periods, especially during the middle of the day. Bring strong sunscreen lotion. Wearing a hat is a good idea.

Altitude sickness (*soroche*) can sometimes affect travelers arriving in Quito by air. Most people will need a couple of days to get used to the thin Andean air, so take it easy at first: eat light meals, steer clear of excessive alcohol, and don't go on strenuous walks; a chocolate bar can sometimes help. Drink tea, relax, and let your body become accustomed to the height.

Mountain sickness is a more serious problem for climbers, who may be exerting themselves at altitudes over 5,000 meters (15,000ft). Symptoms can include headache, vomiting, rapid pulse, and failing blood pressure. The only real cure is to descend to a lower level. Before starting out, most climbers drink *mate de coca* (coca-leaf tea), which is the local preventative remedy.

There are several good private hospitals in Quito and Guayaquil, but they are expensive. Visitors are advised to take out travel insurance.

Drugstores

Regular medicine can be bought without a prescription in most pharmacies (*farmacias*). In major cities pharmacies carry a wide range of drugs, antibiotics, and treatments. The government sanitation website (www.controlsanitario.gob.ec/turnos-de-farmacias/#) lists the country's *farmacias de turno*, which are open on Sunday or at night. In Quito a number are open 24 hours a day; look out for an illuminated "Turno" sign. Most drugstores will give injections as well as disposable serum needles (beware of non-disposable needles).

Medical services, Quito
Ambulance
Tel: 02-911/131 for emergencies
Clínica de la Mujer
Av. Amazonas N39-216 and Gaspar de Villaroel; tel: 02-245 8000; www.clinicadelamujer.com.ec
Women's and childrens' clinic with neonatal unit. Laboratory analysis for parasites.
Hospital de Clínicas Pichincha
Veintimilla E3-30 and Paez; tel: 02-299 8700
Hospital Metropolitano
Av. Mariana de Jesús and Occidental; tel: 02-399 8000; http://hospitalmetropolitano.org
Best and most expensive hospital in Quito. English-speaking doctors available.
Hospital Voz Andes
Juan Villalengua 0E2-37 and Av. 10 de Agosto; tel: 02-397 1000; www.hospitalvozandes.org
Run by HCJB, an American Christian organization. Has an emergency room. Most of the doctors speak some English.

Medical services, Guayaquil
Clínica Guayaquil
Padre Aguirre 401 and Córdoba; tel: 04-256 3555; www.clinicaguayaquil.com
Private clinic. Dr Roberto Gilbert speaks English.
Clínica Kennedy
Av. del Periodista, Av. 11 NO; tel: 04-228 9666/228 6963; www.hospikennedy.med.ec
The best hospital in the city. English-speaking doctors, consulting rooms for external patients.

Medical services, Galápagos
There is a basic hospital in Puerto Ayora. Consultations cost $15.

Medical services, Cuenca
Clínica Los Andes
Mariano Cueva 14-68 and Pio Bravo; tel: 07-284 2942

Clínica Santa Ana
Av. Manuel J. Calle 1-104; tel: 07-281 7564
Good medical center, 24-hour emergency service.

Internet

Free wi-fi has become so ubiquitous in hotels, cafés and public spaces that most internet cafés have closed down. Most places have a good connection, though the free wi-fi on some buses and in the local park can be slow. That said, you will come across the occasional internet café, often combined with a call center.

LGBTQ+ travelers

Although same-sex marriage was legalized in Ecuador in 2019, homosexuality is often shunned in Ecuador, as with most Catholic Latin American countries. However, in large cities, particularly Quito, gay communities have developed, and sexual diversity is slowly becoming more accepted. The Mariscal Sucre district of Quito tends to be the center of Ecuador's gay scene, replete with saunas and nightclubs. For more information for LGBTQ+ travelers in Ecuador, check the Ecuador entries on the IGLTA website (www.iglta.org).

Lost property

Considering that many people in Ecuador live below the poverty line, the chances are that if you lose a bag or an item, you are unlikely to see it again. That said, if you leave an item on a bus, it is worth checking at the bus company's office.

Maps

The best selection of maps of Ecuador is produced by the Instituto Geográfico Militar (tel: 02-397 5100; www.geograficomilitar.gob.ec) on top of the hill on Avenida T. Paz and Mino, off Avenida Colombia in Quito. Large-scale maps of the whole country, ranging from 1:1,000,000 one-sheet maps to 1:50,000 topographical maps, are available here. The Sierra has been covered in detail, but the Oriente and parts of the Western Lowlands are not well served. Decent road maps of Ecuador have been produced by National Geographic, Reise Know-How and ITMB, which can be ordered online in advance of your trip.

Media

In Quito, there are several good newspapers: El Comercio, Diario Hoy, La Hora, and Ultimas Noticias are the most established. In Guayaquil, you can choose from Expreso, El Telégrafo, and El Universo. There are also a few English-language publications, including the Ecuador Times (www.ecuadortimes.net).

TV and radio

Cable TV in Ecuador carries many of the same channels and shows as the United States. News channels, such as the BBC and CNN, and sports channels, such as ESPN and Fox Sports, are common in most cities, although rural areas may be limited to a few basic channels.

There is a plethora of local radio stations in nearly every part of the country, that you will no doubt hear blasting away on any rural bus. Most play a combination of popular and regional music.

Money

Ecuador's official currency is the US dollar. Major credit cards (particularly Visa and MasterCard) are accepted in the larger hotels, restaurants, and tourist-oriented shops. Most ATMs will give cash withdrawals against Visa or Mastercard; a few will accept debit cards too. Most ATMs charge withdrawal fees, but fees vary, and the lesser-known Banco Internacional does not. ATMs are ubiquitous, even in small Ecuadorian towns although they may not always be working or have money to dispense. It is always good to be circumspect when withdrawing a wad of cash, especially in the cities. Try to find an ATM that is not on the street. Getting change can be a problem, and in rural areas it is best to travel with small-denomination notes.

US dollars are by far the best currency to take to Ecuador, but other foreign currencies can be exchanged in banks and casas de cambio (currency exchange offices) in the business districts of Quito (Avenida Amazonas), Guayaquil, and Cuenca. Outside major city centers, however, it becomes difficult to exchange other currencies. On Sundays and holidays, when banks and casas de cambio are shut, you can always exchange money in the major hotels, though usually at a higher rate.

It is easy to have money transferred to Ecuador, through organizations such as Western Union.

Major Ecuadorian banks
Banco Guayaquil; www.bancoguayaquil.com
Banco del Pacífico; www.bancodelpacifico.com
Banco de Pichincha; www.pichincha.com

Money transfer
Western Union; www.westernunion.com

Tipping

In many restaurants 22 percent service and tax is added to the bill, and increasingly is included in the advertised prices, but some cheaper establishments will leave it to your discretion. It is customary to leave a 10 percent tip for the waiter if you have received good service. Airport porters should be paid 50 US cents per bag. Taxi drivers do not expect a tip. Tour guides are usually tipped, but ask your tour operator in advance about the norm.

Opening hours

Government offices in Quito are open to the public Mon–Fri 8.30am–4.30 or 5pm.

Bank opening hours vary depending on the bank and the location of the branch. Generally, they are open Mon–Fri 8.30–10am to 4.30 or 5pm with some also open 9am–2pm on Sat, and even Sunday, if in a shopping mall. They are closed on public holidays. Private companies generally work weekdays 8am–5pm with an hour for lunch.

☺ Public holidays

Ecuador has numerous public holidays and it is worth bearing in mind that shops, banks, and services may be closed around these dates.

When an official public holiday falls at a weekend, offices may be closed on the Friday or Monday. When a public holiday falls midweek, it may be moved to the nearest Friday or Monday to create a long weekend. Major holidays are often celebrated for several days around the actual date.

Banks and businesses are closed on official public holidays.

If you plan to travel on a major holiday, book ahead if possible as transport can get very crowded, and if you're going to a small place, make sure you carry cash as the ATM may well run out.

Stores are generally open Mon–Fri 8.30am–6 or 7pm, then Sat 9am–2pm, with many now staying open during lunchtime. Shopping centers and small grocery stores stay open until 8 or 9pm. Drug stores (farmacias) are open long hours and some are listed "on duty" 24 hours a day. Check out the times for the Fybeca chain of pharmacies (www.fybeca.com).

P

Photography

Digital camera accessories are widely available, although big cities are better if you are going to make a purchase. In Quito, Abfotovideo (www.abfotovideo.com) in the Multicentro mall in the New Town has a good range of cameras and accessories while in Guayaquil, try Foto Access (www.fotoaccess.com) in the Dicentro mall.

Equatorial shadows are very strong and come out almost black on photographs, so the best results are often achieved on overcast days.

Not surprisingly, Ecuadorian indígenas may resent having a camera thrust in their faces and often turn their backs on pushy photographers. Ask permission beforehand. Many will ask for a small fee or "tip", which you should comply with, rather than trying to shoot people without being noticed. Better still, establish a relationship first by talking to people.

Postal services

The national postal service (Correos de Ecuador) was dissolved in 2021, and has been replaced by the new state Servicios Postales del Ecuador. However, this entity has been suffering from teething problems, so if you want to send something home a courier service is advisable. DHL, FedEx, or one of the other international courier services can be found across the country.

R

Religious services

Roman Catholic services are held regularly in Quito's churches. Other services are held at:
Carolina Adventist Church
Av. 10 de Agosto 3929; tel: 02-223 9995.
Meetings on Saturdays at 9am.
Central Baptist Church
Los Ríos at the corner with Briceño
Sunday services 8am and 11am.
Church of Jesus Christ of the Latter Day Saints
Francisco Robles E4-151 Av Amazonas
Sunday service 9.30am.
Lutheran Church
Isabel la Católica 26-31; tel: 02-250 7494.
Sunday services: 9am in English.
Synagogue
580 Roberto Andrade; tel: 02-248 3800
Services Friday 7pm.
Khaled ibn al-Walid Mosque
Avenida Los Shyris and Avenida Eloy Alfaro; tel: 096 292 0586

S

Shopping

Dedicated shoppers will love Ecuador for its huge range of well-priced, hand-crafted souvenirs. Embroidered cotton clothing, richly colored textiles, uniquely patterned carpets, art – both folk and fine – and a great range of ceramics and jewelry are to be had from both street markets and retail outlets. Bargaining is standard at markets, not shops – but don't be merciless: think of what an item is worth to you considering all the hours of work that have gone into it. Books – particularly the glossy, photographic kind – are also a good buy as souvenirs. Libri Mundi in Quicentro Mall, Quito is the best bookshop. Quito and Guayaquil both have shiny malls where you can buy the latest fashions, at international prices.

Student travelers

ISIC (International Student Identity Card) discounts are few and far between. At times you may be able to get airline and bus tickets for a reduced fare, and the occasional museum entry. Check at the local ITur offices for details of discounts.

T

Telephones

The countrywide adoption of What's App has made most of the call centers – previously in every city, town, and village – largely redundant. That said, you can still find the odd centro de llamadas to make local or long-distance, and international telephone calls, as well as calls to cell phones, can be made at a Centro de Llamadas (call centers, sometimes simply called cabinas). Charges are cheap: even international calls rarely exceed $0.60 per minute.

Cellular phone SIM cards for Claro, Movistar and CNT can be readily bought. Claro offers the best coverage. It is also possible to hire a mobile phone for the duration of your stay in Ecuador. Some people prefer to make collect (reverse-charge) calls from their hotel, or organize international roaming on their cell phone before leaving home. If using a hotel line, check tariffs carefully for hefty surcharges.

Telephoning Ecuador

The country code for Ecuador is 593. To call a number in Ecuador from abroad, dial the international access code (011 from the US, 00 from Britain), the country code (593) the area code without the 0 (2, 3, 4,

5, 6, or 7, depending on the area) and the seven-digit local phone number. Area codes are divided by province. Examples of codes for popular destinations are:
Quito **02**; Cuenca **07**; Ambato **03**; Baños **03**; Riobamba **03**; Guayaquil **04**; Manta **05**; Galápagos Islands **05**; Esmeraldas **06**; Otavalo **06**.
Mobile phone numbers begin with **09**, followed by eight digits.

Toilets

Most of the toilets in Ecuador are Western-style flush toilets, although in some rural areas you may encounter a few that are little more than holes that use pails of water to flush. Regardless, you should never flush paper down the toilet. It should be disposed in the small wastebasket provided beside the toilet. Public toilets usually have an attendant selling toilet paper at the entrance.

Tour operators and travel agents

Tours can be arranged through tour operators and travel agents in Europe or the US, but it is simple to organize an itinerary on arrival in Ecuador.

Quito

There are many reliable travel agencies all along Avenida Amazonas and in the major hotels. Some of the best include:
Anaconda Amazon Cruises Gaspar de Villarroel N40-143 and 6 de Diciembre; tel: 02-336 0887; www.anakondaamazoncruises.com
Luxury cruises in the Ecuadorian Amazon aboard the Manatee Explorer or Anakonda.
Enchanted Expeditions
Tel: +1-800-560-5894 Toll Free US/Canada
Tel: 02-334 0525 Ecuador; www.enchantedexpeditions.com
Quality excursions throughout Ecuador at reasonable prices: Galápagos trips on the boats *Beluga*, *Cachalote*, and Passion.
Gala Cruises
N22-118 9 de Octubre and Veintimilla, Quito; tel: 02-255 6036; www.islasgalapagos.travel

⊙ Time zones

Mainland Ecuador is 5 hours behind GMT. The Galápagos are 6 hours behind.

Cruise agency for Galápagos boats and a number of other mainland tours.
Metropolitan Touring
De las Palmeras Av. N45-74 and de las Orquideas; see website for numerous toll-free numbers and WhatsApp links; www.metropolitan-touring.com
Oldest, largest, and most efficient travel agency network in Ecuador, which owns and operates several hotels/lodges and Galápagos boats.
Quasar Expeditions
Ponce Carrasco E8-06 and Av. Diego de Almagro; tel: 02-382 5681; www.quasarex.com.
Excellent upmarket bespoke tours in the Galápagos on the company's own luxury yachts.
Sierra Nevada
Joaquin Pinto E4-150 y Cordero; tel: 02-255 3658; www.sierranevada.ec.
Outdoor adventures specialists: initially, hiking and climbing, now expanded to biking and rafting.

Baños
Geo Tours
Calles Ambato and Haflants; tel: 03-274 1344; www.geotoursbanios.com
Rainforestur
Calles Ambato 800 and Maldonado; tel: 03-274 0743; www.rainforestur.com

Cuenca
Expediciones Río Arriba
Cnr. Hermano Miguel and Córdova; tel: 07-283 0116; email: negro@az.pro.ec

⊙ Tourist information

Tourist information
The Ministry of Tourism has an excellent website (www.ecuador.travel), and its iTur tourist offices can be found throughout the country. Many tourist towns also have a municipal tourist office and website to match.

Quito
The main tourist office is in the Centro Histórico, in the Palacio Municipal, on the corner of Calle Venezuela and Espejo; tel: 02-257 2445. These are also iTur desks at the airport and the Quitumbe bus terminal.

Otavalo
Corner of Modesto Jaramillo and Manuel Quiroga on the Plaza de Ponchos; tel: 06-292 7230.

Baños
Plaza Central; tel: 03-289 3566.

Cuenca
Avenida Mariscal Sucre, opposite Parque Calderón; tel: 07-282 1035.

Loja
Olmedo and Bolívar; tel: 07-258-1251.

Manta
Avenida Malecón, Playa Murcielago; tel: 05-261 0171.

Guayaquil
The municipal tourist office is at 10 de Agosto and the Malecón; tel: 04-259 4800.

Metropolitan Touring
Mariscal Sucre 662; tel: 07-283 7340; www.metropolitan-touring.com
Terra Diversa
Calle Larga 8-41 and Cordero; tel: 07-282 3782; www.terradiversa.com
Southland Touring
Calle Larga 5-24 and Mariano Cueva; tel: 07-283 3126; www.southlandtouring.com

Guayaquil
To avoid disappointment, plan ahead for your Galápagos trip; flights, cruises and day trips get very heavily booked up.
Ecuador Expeditions
Victor E. Estrada 1305 y Costanera, tel: 04-288 8335; www.ecuadorexpeditions.com.ec
Metropolitan Touring,
Av Fco de Orellana, Edif WTC Millenium Galery Planta Baja Local 7; tel: 04-263 0900; www.metropolitan-touring.com
San Playa
Bellavista mz. 25 villa 18, tel: 04-222 0722; http://sanplaya.com
Spring Travel
Edif. Torres de la Merced 12th Floor, of. 2, tel: 04-230 6776; www.springtravelecuador.com

UK
For a useful list of some of the many excellent companies offering trips in Ecuador, check out www.lata.org, the website of the **Latin American Travel Association** in the United Kingdom. They can also give

impartial advice on how to plan a trip to Ecuador.

Inspiring Travel Company, tel: 01244 435091. www.inspiringtravelcompany.co.uk

Intrepid Travel, tel: 0203 308 9753. www.intrepidtravel.com Specialising in small-group tours offering in Galapagos and the Amazon

Journey Latin America, tel: 020-3393 7184. www.journeylatinamerica.co.uk

Select Latin America, tel: 020-7407 1478. www.selectlatinamerica.co.uk The director is a former naturalist guide in the Galápagos.

The Ultimate Travel Company, tel: 0203 553 2024. www.theultimatetravelcompany.co.uk

Quasar Expeditions, which operates bespoke tours in Ecuador and the Galápagos is represented in the UK by Penelope Kellie Worldwide Yacht Charters & Tours, tel: 01962-779317. www.kellieworldwide.com

US, Canada and Australia

Bookings for tours operated by Metropolitan Touring can be made in the US through

Exito Travel, tel: 1-800-655 4053. www.exitotravel.com

Travel Inti, tel: 1-403-760 3565. www.travelinti.com

Wilderness Travel, tel: 1-800-368 2794; www.wildernesstravel.com.

Visas and passports

To visit Ecuador as a tourist, you need a valid passport (valid for at least six months before arrival) and a return ticket. Visas are required by citizens of a few countries including China, Nepal, and Pakistan. Check with the local Consulate of Ecuador before traveling. Ecuadorian Immigration Police will give you a free T-3 Tourist Card; keep this safe as you need it to leave the country. It is valid for up to 90 days. An extension (prórroga) costs $150. You need to apply, and make the payment, before the 90 days expire, otherwise you will have to pay a substantial fine in addition to the fee. The form can be downloaded from the immigration directorate's website (www.migracion.gob.ec/serv-emision-de-prorrogas-de-permanencia-en-el-pais). Once completed, it can be taken to the nearest immigration office (migración). There you will be given the department's bank details, and after depositing the requisite sum, you can return to collect your visa extension In Quito, you need to go to the Dirección Nacional de Migración in Quito (Av. Amazonas 32-171 and República).

Carry your passport, or a photocopy of it, at all times, as the police have the power to arrest anyone without ID should a check be made. Foreigners are unlikely to be bothered in this way in Quito, but it is important to have your passport handy on bus trips in the countryside, where checks may be more common.

Weights and measures

The metric system is used to calculate distances and weights.

⊘ Websites

www.quito.com.ec
Quito's municipal tourism site has restaurant and hotel listings, and a comprehensive list of things to do.
www.guayaquilesmidestino.com
Guayaquil's tourism site has gastronomic, shopping and events information, along with a good overview of the city's main sights.
www.ecuador.travel
Ministry of Tourism website with resources and articles.
www.turismoguayas.com
A Guayaquil-based site focusing on things to do in Guayas province.
http://manabiturismo.com
The regional tourism site for the Manabí region.
www.rutadelsol.com.ec
Information about surfing and travel on the Ruta del Sol and around the Pacific coast.
www.galapagos.org
Source of information about travel to the Galapagos Islands.
www.cuencaecuador.com.ec
Cuenca's municipal tourism website, with plenty of attractive visuals.

Women travelers

Machismo is far less prominent in Ecuador than in some other Latin American countries, though not altogether absent. Ecuador is relatively safe for solo women travelers, though they can be as exposed to safety risks as male travelers (see Crime and Safety): late at night, avoid flagging down taxis or walking alone.

LANGUAGE

PRONUNCIATION

Anyone with a working knowledge of Spanish will have no trouble making themselves understood in Ecuador, but there are a few interesting local variations. In order to emphasize an adjective, the ending *aso* is added: for example, something that is very good would be *buenaso*. An expression you will hear everywhere, and which is difficult to translate, is *no más*. *Siga no más*, for example, can mean "Hurry up (and get on the bus/move down the line, etc)," or "Just carry on". *Come no más* means "Just eat it/It'll get cold/it's nicer than it looks, etc." You will soon get the hang of it.

Indígenas almost all speak Spanish, but you will hear Quichua words which have crept into the language: *wambras* translates as "guys," and *cheveré* means "cool."

Vowels

a slightly longer than in cat
e as in bed
i as in police
o as in hot
u as in rude

Consonants

These are approximately like those in English, the main exceptions being:
c is hard before **a, o,** or **u** (as in English), and is soft before **e** or **i**, when it sounds like **s** (as opposed to the Castilian pronunciation of **th** as in think). Thus, censo (census) sounds like senso.
g is hard before **a, o,** or **u** (as in English), but where English g sounds like **j** – before **e** or **i** – Spanish **g** sounds like a guttural **h**. G before **ua** is often soft or silent, so that agua sounds more like awa, and Guadalajara like Wadalajara.

h is silent.
j sounds like a guttural English **h**.
ll sounds like **y**.
ñ sounds like **ny**, as in the familiar Spanish word señor.
q is followed by **u** as in English, but the combination sounds like **k** instead of like **kw**. *¿Qué quiere usted?* is pronounced: Keh kee-ehr-eh oostehd?
r is rolled, and more so for double **r**.
x between vowels sounds like a guttural **h**, e.g. in México or Oaxaca.
y alone, as the word meaning 'and', is pronounced **ee**.
Note that **ch** and **ll** are separate letters of the Spanish alphabet; if looking in a phone book or dictionary for a word beginning with **ch**, you will find it after the final **c** entry. A name or word beginning with **ll** will be listed after the **l** entries.

BASICS

Yes *Sí*
No *No*
Thank you *Gracias*
You're welcome *De nada*
Please *Por favor*
Excuse me (to get attention) *¡Perdón!*
Excuse me (to get through a crowd) *¡Permiso!*

◎ Numbers

1 *uno*	**101** *ciento uno*
2 *dos*	**200** *doscientos*
3 *tres*	**300** *trescientos*
4 *cuatro*	**400** *cuatrocientos*
5 *cinco*	**500** *quinientos*
6 *seis*	**600** *seiscientos*
7 *siete*	**700** *setecientos*
8 *ocho*	**800** *ochocientos*
9 *nueve*	**900** *novecientos*
10 *diez*	**1,000** *mil*
11 *once*	**2,000** *dos mil*
12 *doce*	**10,000** *diez mil*
13 *trece*	**100,000** *cien mil*
14 *catorce*	**1,000,000** *un millón*
15 *quince*	**2,000,000** *dos millones*
16 *dieciséis*	**first** *primer(o)/a*
17 *diecisiete*	**second** *segund(o)/a*
18 *dieciocho*	**third** *tercer(o)/a*
19 *diecinueve*	**fourth** *cuart(o)/a*
20 *veinte*	
21 *veintiuno*	**Note**
25 *veinticinco*	In Spanish, in numbers, commas are used where decimal points are
30 *treinta*	used in English and vice versa. For
40 *cuarenta*	example:
50 *cincuenta*	

English Spanish
$19.30 $19,30
1,000m 1.000m
9.5 % 9,5 %

60 *sesenta*	
70 *setenta*	
80 *ochenta*	
90 *noventa*	
100 *cien*	

Excuse me (sorry) *Perdóneme*
I'm sorry *Lo siento/Perdone*
Wait a minute! *¡Un momento!*
Can you help me? *¿Me puede ayudar?*
Do you speak English? (formal) *¿Habla inglés?*
Please speak more slowly *Hable más despacio, por favor*
Could you repeat that please *¿Podría repetírmelo, por favor?*
I (don't) understand *(No) entiendo*
I don't know *No lo sé*
No problem *No hay problema*
Where is...? *¿Dónde está...?*
I am looking for... *Estoy buscando*
Here it is *Aquí está*
There it is *Allí está*
Let's go *Vámonos*
At what time? *¿A qué hora?*
Late *tarde*
Early *temprano*
Yesterday *ayer*
Today *hoy*
Tomorrow *mañana*

FINDING YOUR WAY

Where is the (men's/women's) lavatory? *¿Dónde está el baño (de caballeros/de damas)?*
Where is (the tourist office)? *¿Dónde está (la oficina de turismo)?*
town hall *ayuntamiento*
bank *banco*
currency exhange bureau *casa de cambio*
library *biblioteca*
post office *correos*
hotel *hotel*
youth hostel *albergue*
camping *camping*
parking *aparcamiento*
straight *derecho*
to the left *a la izquierda*
to the right *a la derecha*
street *calle*
square *plaza*
corner *esquina*
a block *un cuadra*

AT THE HOTEL

Do you have a vacant room? *¿Tiene una habitación disponible?*
I have a reservation *Tengo una reserva*
I'd like... *Quisiera...*
a single/double (with double bed)/a room with twin beds *una habitación individual (sencilla)/una habitación matrimonial/una habitación doble*
for one night/two nights *por una noche/dos noches*
with a sea view *con vista al mar*

Does the room have a private bathroom or shared bathroom? *¿Tiene la habitación baño privado o baño compartido?*
Does it have hot water? *¿Tiene agua caliente?*
Could you show me another room, please? *¿Puede mostrarme otra habitación, por favor?*
What time do you close (lock) the doors? *¿A qué hora se cierran las puertas?*
I would like to change rooms *Quisiera cambiar la habitación*
How much is it? *¿Cuánto cuesta?/¿Cuánto sale?*
Do you accept credit cards/travelers' checks/dollars? *¿Se aceptan tarjetas de crédito/cheques de viajeros/dólares?*
What time is breakfast/lunch/dinner? *¿A qué hora es el desayuno/el almuerzo/la cena?*
Please wake me at... *Por favor despertarme a...*
Come in! *¡Pase!/¡Adelante!*
I'd like to pay the bill now, please *Quisiera cancelar la cuenta ahora, por favor*

IN THE RESTAURANT

I'd like to book a table *Quisiera reservar una mesa, por favor*
Do you have a table for...? *¿Tiene una mesa para...?*
breakfast/lunch/dinner *desayuno/almuerzo/cena*
I'm a vegetarian *Soy vegetariano(a)*
May we have the menu? *¿Puede traernos la carta?*
wine list *la carta de vinos*
What would you recommend? *¿Qué recomienda?*
fixed-price menu *el menú fijo/la merienda*
special of the day *plato del día/sugerencia del chef*
waiter *mozo*
What would you like to drink? *¿Qué quiere tomar?*
Is service included? *¿Incluye el servicio?*
The bill, please *La cuenta, por favor*

MENU DECODER

Entremeses/Primer Plato (First Course)

ensalada mixta **mixed salad**
pan con ajo **garlic bread**

sopa/crema **soup/cream soup**
sopa de cebolla **onion soup**

La Carne (Meat)

a la brasa/a la parrilla **charcoal-grilled**
a la plancha **grilled**
a punto **medium**
ahumado(a) **smoked**
al horno **baked**
alas **wings**
albóndigas **meat balls**
aves **poultry**
bien hecho **well done**
cerdo/chancho/puerco **pork**
chivito **goat**
chuleta **chop**
conejo **rabbit**
cordero **lamb**
costillas **ribs**
crudo **raw**
empanizado(a)/apanado(a) **breaded**
frito(a) **fried**
guisado(a) **stewed**
hamburguesa **hamburger**
hígado de res **beef liver**
jamón **ham**
jugoso(a) **rare**
lengua **tongue**
lomito **tenderloin**
milanesa **breaded and fried thin cut of meat**
morcilla **blood sausage**
pato **duck**
pavo **turkey**
pechuga **breast**
pernil **leg of pork**
piernas **legs**
pollo **chicken**
rebozado(a) **batter-fried**
riñones **kidneys**
salchichas/panchos **sausages or hot dogs**
término medio **medium rare**
ternera **veal**

Pescado/Mariscos (Fish/Seafood)

almejas **clams**
anchoa **anchovy**
atún **tuna**
bacalao **cod**
calamares **squid**
camarones **shrimp**
cangrejo **crab**
corvina **sea bass**
dorado **dolphinfish**
langosta **lobster**
langostinos **prawns**
lenguado **sole or flounder**
mariscos **shellfish**
mejillones **mussels**
ostiones/ostras **oysters**

pargo **snapper**
picudo **marlin**
pulpo **octopus**
sierra **mackerel**
trucha **trout**

Vegetales (Vegetables)

ajo **garlic**
alcaucil **artichoke**
arvejas **peas**
batata/camote **sweet potato**
berenjena **eggplant/aubergine**
brócoli **broccoli**
calabaza **pumpkin or yellow squash**
cebolla **onion**
chauchas **green beans**
choclo **corn (on the cob)**
coliflor **cauliflower**
espárrago **asparagus**
espinaca **spinach**
habas **broad beans**
hongos, champiñones **mushrooms**
lechuga **lettuce**
papa **potato**
pepino **cucumber**
pimentón **green (bell) pepper**
porotos **Lima beans**
puerro **leeks**
remolacha **beets/beetroot**
repollo **cabbage**
zanahorias **carrots**
zapallo **yellow squash**
zapallito **green squash**
zapallito largo **zucchini/courgette**

Frutas (Fruit)

aguacate **avocado**
banana/guineo **banana**
cereza **cherry**
ciruela **plum**
durazno **peach**
frambuesa **raspberry**
fresa **strawberry**
guayaba **guava**
higo **fig**

☺ Emergencies

Help! *¡Socorro! ¡Auxilio!*
Stop! *¡Pare!*
Call a doctor *Llame a un médico*
Call an ambulance *Llame una ambulancia*
Call the police *Llame a la policía*
Call the fire brigade *Llame a los bomberos*
Where is the nearest hospital? *¿Dónde queda el hospital más cercano?*
I want to report an assault/a robbery *Quisiera reportar un asalto/un robo*

lima **lime**
limón **lemon**
maracuyá **passion fruit**
mandarina **tangerine**
manzana **apple**
mora **blackberry**
naranja **orange**
pera **pear**
piña **pineapple**
plátano **plantain**
pomelo **grapefruit**
sandía **watermelon**
uvas **grapes**

Drinks

agua mineral con/sin gas **carbonated/non-carbonated mineral water**
cerveza **beer**
chocolate caliente **hot chocolate**
coca **cola**
jugo de fruta **fruit juice**
mate de coca **coca-leaf tea**
té (con leche) **tea (with milk)**
té manzanilla **camomile tea**
vino blanco/tinto **white/red wine**

Miscellaneous

arroz **rice**
azúcar **sugar**
canguil **popcorn**
empanada **savory turnover**
fideos **spaghetti**
huevos (revueltos/fritos/hervidos) **eggs (scrambled/fried/boiled)**
ice cream **helado**
mantequilla **butter**
mermelada **jam**
mostaza **mustard**
pan **bread**
pan integral **wholewheat bread**
pan tostado/tostadas **toast**
panceta **bacon**
pimienta negra **black pepper**
queso **cheese**
sal **salt**
salsa picante **spicy sauce**
sandwich **sandwich**
tortilla **omelet**

SHOPPING

I'd like... *Quisiera...*
I'm just looking *Sólo estoy mirando, gracias*
How much is this? *¿Cuanto cuesta/sale?*
Do you have it in another color? *¿Tiene en otro color?*
Do you have it in another size? *¿Tiene en otro talle/número?*
smaller/larger *más pequeño/más grande*

trousers *pantalones*
skirt *falda*
dress *vestido*
shirt *camisa*
jacket *chaqueta*
suit *traje*
coat *abrigo*
underpants *calzoncillos*
socks *calcetines*
shoes *zapatos*
hat *sombrero*
swimsuit *traje de baño*
I would like some of that... *Quisiera un poco de eso...*
I would like a kilo of... *Quisiera un kilo de...*
I would like half a kilo of... *Quisiera un medio kilo de...*
A little more/less *Un poco más/menos*
That's enough/no more *Está bien/nada más*
Would you like anything else? *¿Quiere algo más?*
expensive *caro*
cheap *barato*
clothes store *tienda de ropa*
bookstore *librería*
hairdressers *peluquería*
bakery *panadería*
cake shop *pastelería*
butcher's *carnicería*
fishmonger's *pescadería*
green grocery *verdulería*
market *mercado*
grocery store *tienda de abarrotes*
newsstand *kiosco*
shopping center *centro comercial*

TOURIST ATTRACTIONS

tourist office *oficina de turismo*
postcard *postal*
handicrafts *artesanía*
market *mercado*
art gallery *sala de exposiciones*
indigenous community *comunidad indígena*
Old Town *ciudad vieja*
ruins *ruinas*
bridge *puente*
tower *torre*
monument *monumento*
statue *estatua*
fort *castillo/fuerte*
palace *palacio*
chapel *capilla*
church *iglesia*
cathedral *catedral*
convent *convento*
park *parque*
playground *parque infantil*
botanical garden *jardín botánico*
zoo *zoológico*

cable car *teleférico*
viewpoint *mirador*
hill *cerro*
mountain *montaña*
stream *quebrada*
river *río*
lagoon *laguna*
lake *lago*
sea *mar*
Pacific Ocean *Océano Pacífico*
island *isla*
glacier *glaciar*
beach *playa*
hot springs *aguas termales*
swimming pool *piscina*
discotheque *discoteca*

AIRPORT/TRAVEL AGENCY

flight *vuelo*
arrivals *llegadas*
departures *salidas*
connection *conexión*
customs and immigration *aduana y migraciones*
travel/tour agency *agencia de viajes/ de turismo*
ticket *boleto pasaje*
I would like to purchase a ticket for... *Quisiera comprar un boleto (pasaje) para...*
When is the next/last flight/departure for...? *¿Cuándo es el próximo/ último vuelo/para...?*
How long is the flight? *¿Cuánto tiempo dura el vuelo?*
What time do I have to be at the airport? *¿A qué hora tengo que estar en el aeropuerto?*
Is the tax included? *¿Se incluye el impuesto?*
What is included in the price? *¿Qué está incluido en el precio?*
departure tax *el impuesto de salida*
I would like a seat in first class/ business class/tourist class *Quisiera un asiento en primera clase/ ejecutivo/clase de turista*
I need to change my ticket *Necesito cambiar mi boleto*
lost-luggage office *oficina de reclamos*
on time *a tiempo*
late *atrasado*

TRANSPORTATION

luggage *equipaje* bag(s) *valija(s)*
bus *colectivo* (urban), *autobús* (long distance)
bus stop *parada*

bus terminal *terminal de pasajeros*
first class *primera clase*
second class *segunda clase*
tourist class *clase de turista*
one-way ticket *boleto de ida*
round-trip, return ticket *boleto de ida y vuelta*
What time does the bus/boat/ferry (leave/return)? *¿A qué hora (sale/ regresa) el autobús/la lancha/el ferry?*
Which is the stop closest to...? *¿Cuál es la parada más cerca de...?*
Is this seat taken? *¿Está ocupado este asiento?*
Could you please advise me when we reach/the stop for...? *¿Por favor, puede avisarme cuando llegamos a/a la parada para...?*
Is this the stop for...? *¿Es ésta la parada para...?*
Next stop please *La próxima parada, por favor*
train station *estación de tren*
platform *el andén*
sleeping car *coche cama*
car *coche/automóvil*
car rental *alquiler de coche*
dock for small boats/large boats *embarcadero/muelle*
ferry *ferry*
sailboat *velero*
yacht *yate*
ship *barco*

HEALTH

(shift duty) pharmacy *farmacia (de turno)*
hospital/clinic *hospital/clínica*
I need a doctor/dentist *Necesito un médico/dentista (odontólogo)*
I don't feel well *Me siento mal*
I am sick *Estoy enfermo(a)*
It hurts here *Duele aquí*
I have a headache/stomach ache/ cramps *Tengo dolor de cabeza/de estómago/de vientre*
I feel dizzy *Me siento mareado(a)*
Do you have (something for)...? *¿Tiene (algo para)...?*
cold *resfrío*
flu *gripe*
cough *tos*
sore throat *dolor de garganta*
diarrhea *diarrea*
constipation *estreñimiento*
fever *fiebre*
heartburn *acidez*
aspirin *aspirina*
antiseptic cream *crema antiséptica*
insect/mosquito bites *picaduras de insectos/mosquitos*

☉ Greetings

Hello *¡Hola!*
Good morning *Buenos días*
Good afternoon *Buenas tardes*
Goodnight *Buenas noches*
See you later *Hasta luego*
Goodbye *Adiós*
Welcome *Bienvenido*
How are you? (formal/informal) *¿Cómo está?/¿Qué tal?*
Fine, thanks *Bien, gracias*
And you? (formal/informal) *¿Y usted?/¿Y tú?*
What is your name? (formal) *¿Cómo se llama usted?*
My name is... *Me llamo...*
Mr/Miss/Mrs *Señor/Señorita/ Señora*
Pleased to meet you *¡Encantado(a)!/Mucho gusto*
I am English/American/ Canadian/Irish/Scottish/ Australian *Soy inglés(a)/ norteamericano(a)/canadiense/ irlandés(a)/escocés(a)/ australiano(a)*

insect repellent *repelente contra insectos*
sun block *bloqueador solar*
toothpaste *pasta de dientes*
toilet paper *papel higiénico*
tampons *tampones*
condoms *condones*

DAYS OF THE WEEK

Monday *lunes*
Tuesday *martes*
Wednesday *miércoles*
Thursday *jueves*
Friday *viernes*
Saturday *sábado*
Sunday *domingo*

MONTHS OF THE YEAR

January *enero*
February *febrero*
March *marzo*
April *abril*
May *mayo*
June *junio*
July *julio*
August *agosto*
September *septiembre*
October *octubre*
November *noviembre*
December *diciembre*

FURTHER READING

BIRDS AND WILDLIFE

The Birds of Ecuador by R. Ridgeley and P. Greenfield.
A Guide to the Birds of Colombia by Steven Hilty and William Brown.
A Guide to the Birds of the Galápagos Islands by Isabel Castro and Antonia Phillips.
Wildlife of Ecuador: A Photographic Field Guide to Birds, Reptiles, Mammals and Amphibians by Andrés Vásquez Noboa and Pablo Cervantes Daza. Well organised, compact guide on mainland species with fabulous photos and plenty of interesting info.

CRAFTS AND CULTURE

Otavalo: Weaving, Costume, and the Market by Lynn Meisch. A good overview of the textile crafts of Otavalo.

HISTORY AND SOCIETY

The Conquest of the Incas by John Hemming. The classic account of the Spanish conquest.
Indians, Oil, and Politics: A Recent History of Ecuador by Allen Gerlach. A study of Ecuadorian politics since the 1970s.
Savages by Joe Kane. First-hand account of the Huaorani people's struggle to preserve their way of life.
Life in Oil: Cofán Survival in the Petroleum Fields of Amazonia by Michael Cepek and Bear Guerra. Informative and nuanced accounts from the Cofan about their struggles to protect their lands and way of life by someone who has spent 20 years living among them.

THE GALÁPAGOS

A Field Guide to the Fishes of the Galápagos by Godfrey Merlen.
Galápagos by Kurt Vonnegut. An apocalyptic satire of human evolution set in the Galápagos.
The Galápagos Affair by John Treherne. An entertaining account of the scandals and murder occurring on Floreana in the 1930s.
Galápagos: A Natural History by M.H. Jackson. The 2020 edition is without doubt the best guide to the islands.
Galápagos, Islands Born of Fire by Tui de Roy. This tenth-anniversary edition of the Galápagos classic is a beautiful hard-cover photographic tour de force

celebrating the landscapes, wildlife, and habitats of the Galápagos.
Galápagos Wildlife by David Horwell and Pete Oxford.
Galápagos, World's End by William Beebe. A wry, wonderfully evocative account of a 1924 scientific expedition. All the romance of science and adventure in this far-flung corner of the world.
On the Origin of Species by Charles Darwin. The seminal work for evolutionary theory.
The Voyage of the Beagle by Charles Darwin. Shortened journal of Darwin's five-year voyage around the world. A classic.

☉ Send us your thoughts

We do our best to ensure the information in our books is as accurate and up-to-date as possible. The books are updated on a regular basis using destination experts, who painstakingly add, amend and correct as required. However, some details (such as opening times or travel pass costs) are particularly liable to change, and we are ultimately reliant on our readers to put us in the picture.

We welcome your feed back, especially your experience of using the book "on the road", and if you came across a great new attraction we missed.

We will acknowledge all contributions and offer an Insight Guide to the best messages received.

Please write to us at:
Insight Guides
PO Box 7910
London SE1 1WE

Or email us at:
hello@insightguides.com

TRAVEL LITERATURE

Living Poor by Thomsen Moritz. Life as a Peace Corps worker in 1960s Ecuador.
The Lost Lady of the Amazon by Anthony Smith. The story of Isabel Godin's harrowing journey through the Amazon in search of her husband.
Maíz y Coca-Cola by Diane Terezakis. One woman's journey through Ecuador, from the Andes to the Amazon.
The Panama Hat Trail by Tom Miller. The story behind the famous hats.
Sweat of the Sun, Tears of the Moon by Peter Lawrie. A student's quest to find the legendary hoards of gold paid by the Inca for the freedom of their king, Atahualpa, who had been captured by conquistadors.
Personal Narrative of a Journey by Alexander von Humbolt, abridged and translated by Jason Wilson. The 19th-century scientist's account of his expedition to Ecuador.
Travels amongst the Great Andes of the Equator by Edward Whymper. Memoirs of the famous 19th-century British mountaineer.

FICTION

Cumandá by Juan León Mera. Considered one of the seminal works of Ecuadorian literature: focussing on the racial divisions of Ecuador following independence.
Huasipungo by Jorge Icaza Coronel. Another landmark piece of literature: the first to bring to light the plight of Ecuador's indigenous people.
Fire from the Andes: Short Fiction by Women from Bolivia, Ecuador, and Peru edited by Susan E. Benner and Kathy S. Leonard. This short story collection finally gives a long-unheard voice to Andean women writers with some eye-opening prose.

CREDITS

PHOTO CREDITS

Corrie Wingate/Apa Publications
8MR, 10BR, 10M, 10BL, 11BL, 11TL, 18, 19T, 19B, 21, 26, 28, 29, 30, 33, 36, 40, 49, 53, 54, 56L, 56R, 59L, 59R, 60, 63, 64/65T, 64BR, 64BL, 65BR, 65ML, 65TR, 67, 68, 70L, 73, 74, 87, 89, 90, 96, 97, 109, 110, 111, 112, 113, 114, 115, 116/117, 121B, 121T, 126, 129, 130T, 130B, 132, 133, 134B, 135T, 135B, 136, 137T, 137B, 138B, 138T, 140, 141, 143, 144BR, 144/145T, 144MR, 144BL, 145ML, 145BR, 146, 147, 150/151, 152, 153, 154B, 154T, 155, 156, 157T, 157B, 158T, 158B, 160, 161T, 161B, 162, 163, 164, 165, 168T, 168B, 169, 170T, 170B, 171B, 171T, 172, 173, 174T, 174B, 175, 176/177B, 177T, 177B, 178T, 178B, 179, 180, 181, 182BR, 182BL, 183ML, 183BR, 183TR, 184, 185, 187, 188T, 188B, 189T, 189B, 190, 192T, 192B, 193, 194T, 194B, 195, 196, 197, 198T, 220/221, 222, 223, 224, 225, 226, 231, 233T, 234, 236T, 237, 238T, 240T, 240B, 241, 242, 243T, 243B, 244, 245T, 245B, 247T, 247B, 248, 249, 253, 255, 256, 257T, 259T, 259B, 261T, 261B, 262, 264T, 278, 287BL, 288/289, 300, 302, 306/307, 314/315

Dreamstime 61, 103, 149, 203, 209, 273T, 283, 287BR, 290, 291

iStock 9TL, 9BR, 11BR, 22, 27, 57R, 58, 98, 99, 106, 198B, 202, 204, 205, 208, 211, 212T, 212B, 213T, 214, 215, 216, 217B, 217T, 218, 219, 227, 252, 268/269, 270/271, 273B, 276, 277B, 280T, 281, 282, 284, 285, 286/287, 286BR, 286BL, 287ML, 295B, 295T, 296, 299

Library of Congress 275

Mary Evans Picture Library 34, 37, 41, 43, 44, 45, 46, 47

Presidencia de la República del

Ecuador/Flickr/public domain 48
Public domain 39
Quito Visitors Bureau 71, 134T, 145MR, 167
Richard Nowitz/Apa publications 11TR
Shutterstock 1, 4, 8BL, 8BR, 8ML, 9BL, 9ML, 9TR, 12, 13, 14/15, 16/17, 20, 23, 24/25, 31, 32, 35, 38/39, 42, 50, 51, 55, 57L, 62, 65BL, 66, 69, 70R, 72, 75, 76, 77, 78, 79, 80, 81, 82, 83, 84, 85, 86, 88, 91, 92, 93, 95, 100/101, 102, 104, 105, 107, 108, 118/119, 120, 127, 131, 139, 142, 148, 176T, 182/183T, 183BL, 191, 199, 200/201, 206, 210, 213B, 228/229, 230, 233B, 235, 236B, 238B, 239, 250/251, 257B, 258, 260, 263, 265, 266/267, 272, 274, 277T, 279, 280, 287TR, 293, 294, 297, 298
The Picture Desk 94
Tips Images 52

COVER CREDITS

Front cover: Tortoise *in* the Galapagos Islands *Shutterstock*
Back cover: Wild horses and Cotopaxi *Shutterstock*;
Front flap: (from top) Quito *Shutterstock*; Grande Cuyabeno

National Park *Shutterstock*; Otavalo market *Shutterstock*; White water rafting in Zamora *Shutterstock*
Back flap: Corpus Christi paradein Pujili *Shutterstock*

INSIGHT GUIDE CREDITS

Distribution
UK, Ireland and Europe
Apa Publications (UK) Ltd;
sales@insightguides.com
United States and Canada
Ingram Publisher Services;
ips@ingramcontent.com
Australia and New Zealand
Booktopia;
retailer@booktopia.com.au
Worldwide
Apa Publications (UK) Ltd;
sales@insightguides.com
Special Sales, Content Licensing and CoPublishing
Insight Guides can be purchased in bulk quantities at discounted prices. We can create special editions, personalised jackets and corporate imprints tailored to your needs. sales@insightguides.com
www.insightguides.biz

Printed in Czech Republic

This book was produced using **Typefi** automated publishing software.

All Rights Reserved
© 2024 Apa Digital AG
License edition © Apa Publications Ltd UK

First Edition 2007
Eighth Edition 2024

Every effort has been made to provide accurate information in this publication, but changes are inevitable. The publisher cannot be responsible for any resulting loss, inconvenience or injury. We would appreciate it if readers would call our attention to any errors or outdated information. We also welcome your suggestions; please contact us at:
hello@insightguides.com

www.insightguides.com

Editor: Rachel Lawrence
Author: Sara Humphreys
Picture Editors: Tom Smyth and Piotr Kala
Cartography: original cartography Polyglott Kartographie, Berndtson & Berndtson, updated by Carte
Layout: Grzegorz Madejak
Head of DTP and Pre-Press: Rebeka Davies
Head of Publishing: Sarah Clark

CONTRIBUTORS

This new edition was commissioned by Rachel Lawrence. It was thoroughly updated by Sara Humphreys. It builds on earlier editions produced by Sally Burch, Mary Dempsey, Sean Doyle, Andrew Eames, Nicholas Gill, Dominic Hamilton, Stephan Kueffner, Jane Letman, Gabi Mocatta, Rob Rachowiecki, Paul Stafford, Mark Thurber, and Betsy Wagenhauser.

The principal photographer for the book was Corrie Wingate; other talented photographers who contributed their work, include Eduardo Gil and Peter Frost. The index was compiled by Helen Peters.

ABOUT INSIGHT GUIDES

Insight Guides has more than 50 years of experience in publishing high-quality, visual travel guides. We produce hundreds of full-colour titles, in both print and digital form, covering more than 200 destinations across the globe, in a variety of formats to meet your different needs.

Insight Guides are written and updated by local authors, whose expertise is evident in the extensive historical and cultural background features. Each destination is carefully researched by regional experts to ensure our guides provide the very latest information. All the coverage in **Insight Guides** is independent; we strive to maintain an impartial view. Our inclusions are carefully selected to guide you to the best places in a destination, so you can be confident that when we say a place is special, we really mean it.

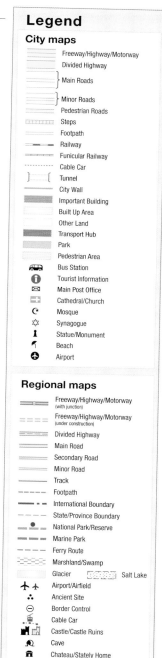

INDEX

324 | INDEX